THE SERBS

THE SERBS

*History, Myth and the
Destruction of Yugoslavia*

TIM JUDAH

YALE UNIVERSITY PRESS
NEW HAVEN AND LONDON

For Rosie

Copyright 1997 by © Tim Judah

Set in Photina by SX Composing DTP, Rayleigh, Essex
Printed and bound in the United States of America

Library of Congress Cataloging-in-Publication Data

Judah, Tim, 1962–
    The Serbs: history, myth, and the destruction of Yugoslavia/Tim
Judah.
    Includes bibliographical references and index.
    ISBN 0-300-07113-2 (cloth: alk. paper)
        0-300-07656-8 (pbk.: alk. paper)
    1. Serbs—Yugoslavia—History.   2. Yugoslavia—History.
3. Yugoslav War, 1991– —Causes.   I. Title.
DR1230.S45J83   1997
949.6'00491822—dc21   96–52212
                                                          CIP

A catalogue record is available from the British Library.

2 4 6 8 10 9 7 5 3

CONTENTS

Contents

Contents

ILLUSTRATIONS

Between pages 110 and 111

1 Paja Jovanović, *Migration of the Serbs*, 1896 (Pančevo Museum); **2** St Sava and Stefan (Simeon) Nemanja, line drawings by Branislav Živković (from a booklet on Studenica monastery published by the Institute for the Protection of Cultural Monuments of the Socialist Republic of Serbia); **3** Tsar Dušan and King Uroš from the fresco of the Nemanjić family tree in the monastery of Visoki Dečani (from Rade Mihaljčič, *The Battle of Kosovo*, Belgrade, 1989); **4** Slobodan Milošević, 28 June 1989, photograph: Draško Gagović (Vreme); **5** Stefan Lazarević, from a fifteenth-century fresco in Resava monastery (National Museum, Belgrade); **6** Lazar from a label on a bottle of Tsar Lazar wine; **7** print of Obilić killing the Sultan, 1871 (National Museum, Belgrade); **8** Serb in peasant costume, in 1989, kissing the open coffin of Lazar in Gračanica monastery, photograph: Draško Gagović (Vreme); **9** Serbian peasant house with man playing the gusla, line drawing (from Spiridon Gopcevic, *Serbien und die Serben*, Leipzig, 1888); **10** the church of Peć patriarchate (author's photograph); **11** portrait of Karadjordje (Museum of the 1804 Revolution in Topčider, Belgrade); **12** portrait of Miloš Obrenović (National Museum, Belgrade); **13** portrait of Ilija Garašanin (National Museum, Belgrade); **14** Njegoš, Prince-Bishop of Montenegro (National Museum, Belgrade); **15** a Montenegrin soldier wearing traditional cap, 1991 (author's photograph); **16** Uros Predić, *The Kosovo Girl*, 1919 (National Museum, Belgrade); **17** the Serbian Army retreating across the battlefield of Kosovo Polje, 1915 (Imperial War Museum, London); **18** Nena Mejra sitting next to the body of her dead, seven-year-old great granddaughter killed by a Bosnian Serb militia (author's photograph); **19** 'Montenegrins stone a Turk', Shköder, 1913 (Imperial War Museum, London); **20** herding pigs, print (from Spiridon Gopcevic, *Serbien und die Serben*, Leipzig, 1888) **21** Serbian infantry enter Skopje, Macedonia, just liberated from the Turks, 1912 (Imperial War Museum, London); **22** Vizir's Bridge, Albania, the Serbian Army in retreat, 1915 (Imperial War Museum, London); **23** Serbian cavalry cross the Black Drin river during their retreat across Albania, 1915 (Imperial War Museum, London); **24** portrait of the Serbian premier Nikola Pašić (National Museum, Belgrade); **25** portrait of King Alexander Karadjordjević (National Museum, Belgrade).

Between pages 238 and 239

26 General Draža Mihailović and Colonel Bill Hudson, 1942 (Imperial War Museum, London); **27** partisans in Belgrade, 1945 (Imperial War Museum, London); **28** Tito, 1954, photograph: Jovan Ritopečki (Tanjug/Vreme); **29** Serbian police beating an Albanian, Kosovo, 1989, photograph: Srdjan Ilić (Vreme); **30** Kosovo Serbs marching on Belgrade in protest, 1988, photograph: Tomislav Peternek; **31** Mihalj Kertes greets Dobrica Ćosić as he arrives for his inauguration as President of Yugoslavia, 1992, photograph: Draško Gagović (Vreme); **32** Serbs gathered for the Kosovo anniversary celebrations, 28 June 1989, photograph: Draško Gagović (Vreme); **33** Radovan Karadžić, Alija Izetbegović and Stjepan Kljuić meeting in 1990, photograph: Miloš Cvetković (Vreme); **34** civilians and soldiers during fighting in eastern Slavonia, 1991, photograph: Tomislav Peternek; **35** the Yugoslav Army positioned above Dubrovnik, 1991, photograph: Zoran Sinco (Vreme); **36** a JNA unit deserting the front in eastern Slavonia, 1991, photograph: Tomislav Peternek; **37** Fikret Abdić and Milan Martić (Tanjug/Vreme); **38** Serbian soldier looking down on Sarajevo from Mount Trebević, summer 1993, photograph: Srdjan Ilić; **39** Radovan Karadžić and General Ratko Mladić, January 1993, photograph: Zoran Jovanović (Vreme); **40** Aleksandar Knežević ('Knele'), photograph: Vican Vicanović (Vreme); **41** the wedding of Arkan (Željko Ražnatović) and Ceca, February, 1995, photograph: Petar Kujundžić (Vreme); **42** Dafina Milanović during the financial crisis of 1993, photograph: Emil Vas (Vreme); **43** detail from the Niš skull tower (author's photograph); **44** Serbian heads (Vreme); **45** Slobodan Milošević and Franjo Tudjman, 1991, photograph: Imre Sabo (Vreme); **46** Serbs leaving Sarajevo for Pale and other parts of Bosnia, March 1996, photograph: R. LeMoyne (UNHCR); **47** Serbian refugee from the Krajina in the Čačak collective centre, Serbia, October 1995, photograph: A. Kazinierakis (UNHCR); **48** Croatian refugees arriving in Croatia after crossing the Sava river, photograph: R. LeMoyne (UNHCR).

Maps

PREFACE

In the south, in Kosovo, the medieval churches of the Serbian kings are like rafts on the sea of history. They are like rafts because Kosovo, once a land inhabited by Serbs, is now a land overwhelmingly populated by Albanians. In the 1690s, following an uprising against the Turks, thousands of Serbs migrated northwards and settled in the fertile lands beyond the Danube. When they left they took with them the remains of Lazar, their greatest medieval prince, who had died in 1389.

On 12 June 1941 a group of Serbs, including women and children, came to beg the newly established Italian authorities in Knin, an overwhelmingly Serbian town in Croatia, for protection.[1] Rampaging gangs of Ustashas, Croatian fascists, had begun a reign of terror. Fifty years later Serbs in Knin instituted their own reign of terror and Croats fled. Some of those who did not later found themselves begging United Nations troops in Knin for protection. In 1995 the Croatian Army returned. Those Serbs who did not flee immediately also begged the UN troops for help.

From the middle ages to today all these events are connected. Obviously the history of any people explains why they are where they are today, but in the Serbian case a new look at their history goes far towards explaining how and why they went to war in 1991. When Serbian peasants from villages surrounding Sarajevo began to bombard the city they did so confusing in their minds their former Muslim friends, neighbours and even brothers-in-law with the old Ottoman Turkish viziers and pashas who had ruled them until 1878.

It is unfashionable to link the past and present when writing about the wars in the former Yugoslavia. One stands the risk of being accused of implying that somehow the people of the former Yugoslavia are more predisposed to war than anyone else in Europe or that they went to war *because* of their history. This is not true. The Serbs went to war because they were led into it by their leaders. But these leaders drew on the malign threads of their people's history to bind them and pull them into war. If Serbian history had been different, today's generations could not have been manipulated in the same way. In the most obvious case there might have been no Serbs in Croatia or Bosnia.

The aim of this book is to trace the history of the Serbs and to explain how they came to be where they are, and in the case of Croatia were until 1995. It is to trace the way that the centre of Serbian life migrated with its people from south to north and to explain how the idea of 'Serbdom', as the Serbs call it, was kept alive during the centuries of Ottoman rule. It is also to explore why, with the fall of communism, they enthusiastically acclaimed Slobodan Milošević, an opportunistic and cynical leader who was interested only in power.

This is neither a straight history book nor a simple analysis of the immediate problems that led to war. Although the contemporary parts draw on my own experience, equally this is not intended as a book of journalistic reportage. The idea is to draw together history, modern politics and the war. That is why the book is part thematic, part chronological and part descriptive.

For four years, from the outbreak of war in 1991, I lived with my family in Belgrade. As a journalist I covered the conflict for *The Economist* and *The Times*. I travelled constantly, reporting from all sides. Other journalists and academics have already written books, either about the conflict in general or about particular corners of it, for example Sarajevo. I decided to write this book because it seemed that amid all that was being written there was an obvious gap. Although the Serbs were most often cast as the villains of the piece, no one had actually written anything of substance about *them* nor about some of the extraordinary events which took place in Serbia and among the Serbs during these years, for example hyperinflation of 313,500,000 per cent per month or the weird world of Pale, the Bosnian Serb headquarters town. Here the director of a local TV soap opera borrowed tanks being used in the siege of Sarajevo to use as props.

I also wanted to write about the extraordinary cynicism of the war. Leaving aside political cynicism, few realise just how much money was made by gangsters, politicians and army officers trading across the frontlines. Whole communities became pawns to be pushed across the board like so many chess pieces, but the kings grew rich in the process.

Above all, though, this is a book about the Serbs. In discussing the Balkans it is very common, when citing an example relating to one side or another, for the person to whom you are talking to interject angrily, 'But what about . . .' This is *not* an exhaustive study of the history of the South Slavs, or a book covering the whole war in Yugoslavia, or one describing the international diplomacy that surrounded it. It simply follows the history of the Serbs and their experience in the war that accompanied the break-up of Yugoslavia. Given that these are vast topics, this is also a subjective survey. The book traces the things that I think are interesting and relevant, and even here there are gaps because of the pressure of space. I have provided a selective bibliography for further reading which is aimed mainly at English speakers.

For this paperback edition, I have made only a couple of very minor adjustments. These signal the emergence of a more moderate Bosnian Serb leadership and the worrying signs of what may yet prove to be the first shots of a new war, this time in Kosovo.

The war in Yugoslavia was a disaster for all concerned, it was unnecessary and the cynicism of Serbian and other leaders was breathtaking. Most Europeans, and westerners in general, have rightly been horrified by the cruelty of the war, but no one has the right to be complacent. It is true that between 1941 and 1945 hundreds of thousands of Yugoslavs died at the hands of other Yugoslavs; like the rest of Europe, however, they lived at peace with one another for the next forty-five years. It was the conjunction of historical circumstances, personalities, arrogance and misjudgements which led to the war, and it is important to keep in mind that the Serbs, as a people, are no different from anyone else in Europe. How otherwise, to cite one obvious example, could one explain why the cultured and civilised Germans did what they did under Hitler? The Serbs too were misled but they were not sheep. Supremely confident of victory, too many were happy to be misled.

ACKNOWLEDGEMENTS

My thanks are due first to Robert Baldock of Yale who turned up at the right time.

When I got into trouble with the writing my wife Rosie was there to point the way out. Quite correctly she applied 'slash and burn' techniques to the text in order to find the right path.

In Belgrade, Dejan Anastasijević and Žarko Korać pointed me towards the missing links. Bojan Radić's comments on my historical sections were invaluable. I am also indebted to Professor Stevan Pavlowitch of Southampton University for his suggestions and help.

My thanks to Marcus Tanner, who read the manuscript, raised many sceptical points and directed me towards many important sources. Thanks to Adrian Brown and Ines Sabalić for their valuable remarks on the manuscript, and Jim Pavilidis for his painstaking attention to detail in drawing the maps. I am also indebted to the National Museum in Belgrade for supplying me with historical pictures.

Author's Note

Spellings

Serbs or Serbians?

According to the Oxford University Press style manual: 'If you take hyphens seriously, you will surely go mad.' I think this is a useful dictum to apply with Serbo-Croatian words and names used in an English context. The reason for this is that there is no generally accepted standardisation. For example one could debate for several hours whether *Krajina* or *the Krajina* is the correct form. Quite simply both have equal validity and one often sounds better in one context than another.

By contrast I have tried to stick to writing about *Serbs* as people rather than *Serbians* but to talk of *Serbian* leaders or actions. There are cases however where I have not applied this rule, as one form may sound jarring in a particular context.

I have rejected an old rule by which Serbs from Serbia used to be described as *Serbians* but Serbs from Bosnia or the old Austro-Hungarian territories were distinguished by calling them *Serbs*. Today I believe that such a distinction is confusing, especially since few people know that it ever existed. Another premise which I reject: some believe that citizens of Serbia, be they ethnic Serbs or not, should all be described as *Serbians*. I do not think that this adds to clarity because it would clearly be absurd to describe a Kosovo Albanian as a *Serbian*. Likewise some insist that when writing about Albanians in Kosovo one should always write about *ethnic Albanians* to distinguish them from *Albanians* from *Albania*. I think that *Kosovo Albanian* is often a perfectly suitable alternative and there seems to be no reason for dogmatism over which term to use.

Aleksandar or Alexander?

The question of whether to Anglicise names can often lead to inconsistencies. My rule has been not to Anglicise any names. A few exceptions include the Karadjordjevićs of this century, that is King *Peter*, Prince Regent, later King *Alexander*, Prince *Paul* and, after 1941, King *Peter*. The reason for this is that they were always known in the English-speaking world by their Anglicised names and to switch to Prince *Pavle* for example would be to invite confusion.

Likewise *Belgrade* not *Beograd*. I also prefer *Ustasha* and *Ustashas* to *Ustaša* and *Ustaše*, *Chetniks* rather than *Četniks*, but *Hercegovina* rather than *Herzegovina*.

One name from outside the former Yugoslavia: I have used *Salonika* for the Greek port rather than *Thessalonika*.

If someone whom I have quoted has used different rules I have not changed their text.

My apologies to any Montenegrin offended where, after 1991, I have used the name Serbia as a shorthand for the Yugoslavia of both Serbia and Montenegro.

Sources

If quotations from the years 1991–5 are not referenced this means they come from my own interviews or from the local media, written down at the time in my notebook. Certain (unreferenced) quotations relating to particular topics, for example epic poetry, or about the Second World War, are also from my own interviews.

ABBREVIATIONS

AVNOJ	Anti-Fascist Council for the National Liberation of Yugoslavia
DM	Deutschemark
FRY	Federal Republic of Yugoslavia
HDZ	Croatian Democratic Union
HVO	Croatian Council of Defence
IFOR	Implementation Force
JNA	Yugoslav People's Army
KOS	Yugoslav military counter-intelligence
LDK	Democratic League of Kosova
NDH	Independent State of Croatia
RAM	plan of the Military Line
RS	Republika Srpska
RSK	Republic of Serbian Krajina
SAO	Serbian Autonomous Region
SDA	Party of Democratic Action
SDB	secret police
SDS	Serbian Democratic Party
SPS	Socialist Party of Serbia
TO	Territorial Defence
UNHCR	UN High Commissioner for Refugees

1

DEATH DOES NOT EXIST

There were and there always will be, eternally, migrations as there will always be births for life to continue.
Migrations exist.
Death does not exist!

From *Seobe* (Migrations) by Miloš Crnjanski[1]

Deep in the bowels of the patriarchate building of the Serbian Orthodox church in Belgrade is a great canvas depicting one of the most traumatic events in Serbian history. It shows Patriarch Arsenije Čarnojević leading tens of thousands of his people into exile. In 1689, Arsenije encouraged the Serbs living in the Ottoman Empire to rise in rebellion and aid the Austrian Army, which had penetrated deep into Turkish-held lands. On New Year's Day 1690 the Austrians and Serbs were crushed in battle. Fearing the wrath of the vengeful Turks, Arsenije led great columns of refugees away from their ancestral homes, mostly from Kosovo, the heart of old Serbia. He was truly a Serbian Moses – but leading his people away from the promised land.

The original painting was commissioned in 1896 by Patriarch Georgije Branković. The artist was Paja Jovanović. He was one of the most illustrious Serbian painters of his generation and his depictions of the greatest moments of Serbian history placed him firmly at the centre of the national artistic renaissance of the time. In the foreground of his painting is a moustachioed fighter. He has swords stuffed into his belt, a rifle slung over his shoulder, and he is striding purposefully into the future. His arm is carried in a blood-stained sling. Just behind him are a mother and child atop a horse laden down with their possessions. The lances of a thousand Serbian soldiers bristle in the background and in the centre is Patriarch Arsenije flanked by a Serbian flag. On the other side an old man with a switch whips his sheep into line and behind him lumber wagons with families and their belongings. It was these scenes that Patriarch Georgije could not stomach. It lowered the tone, especially the inclusion of the sheep. It made the exodus look like a rabble on the run, he said. Paja Jovanović was made to paint the picture all over again. Almost everything was exactly the same, except that the sheep and carts had disappeared from the second version – which is the one now hanging in the patriarchate building.

Perhaps one day a future patriarch will commission a picture of the great exodus of 1995. After four years of war and isolation, the Serb will to resist finally gave way. For all this time the Serbs had defied the world and carved out mini-states for themselves in Croatia and Bosnia. When Krajina, the Serb-held part of Croatia, collapsed that August along with defence lines in western Bosnia, the resulting exodus looked remarkably like Paja Jovanović's epic pictures – but with more cars and tractors than horses and carts. And, whether old Patriarch Georgije would have liked it or not, there were sheep this time around too.

By the time the Croats launched their offensive on Knin, the capital of what had for four years been the rebel Republic of Serbian Krajina, few put up much resistance. Worn down by poverty, hopelessness and the very public war-profiteering of the few, morale was at rock bottom. The offensive began at 5.00am on Friday, 4 August 1995. Artillery opened up along every front. It continued all day, dying down only at about 11pm. The radio was off the air and most people huddled in their shelters and basements uncertain of what was going on. When the shelling stopped, the shocked and traumatised people grabbed what they could carry and fled for their lives. In some places the move was spontaneous. People began to run once they saw the army in retreat. In other areas the army or police gave orders for people to be ready to leave within the hour. Two days later, more than 170,000 people were on the roads. That was all the time it took for the Serbian Orthodox population of these lands, which had lived there for several centuries, to vanish.

'Everything was normal on Thursday,' said Radovan Borović, aged twenty-seven, from Knin. 'Cafés and kindergartens were open but then at 5.00am the next morning the shelling began.' Whole families were squeezed into their cars, crushed beneath all the belongings they could carry. Old people stared vacantly between the slats of cattle lorries that had brought them from Krajina and pregnant women lay flopped in the back of their cars, in which they had been travelling for two days. Exhausted and dirty refugees piled out of the lorries into which they had squeezed in their bid to flee and began to plead for lifts to Belgrade. Marica, aged thirty, clutching her eight-year-old daughter, was one of them. She had come from the riverside town of Dvor na Uni where, on the day the Croatian offensive began, she had buried her husband. 'He had been on the frontline,' she said. 'I lost no property, only my love.'

Her story was one of those stupid, horrible twists of fate that were so common in this war. Her husband had been a Croat. He had fought in the Krajina Serb Army 'because he chose to stay with me and our child. He said it was his destiny. But now he has stayed there for ever.'

The first to cross the border came in cars. Soon though, backed up along the road, came tens of thousands on tractors, and lastly those in horse-drawn carts. In the final humiliation for the people who had followed the call to rebel in the name of Serbdom, a massive tailback began to build up as the refugees, who had just lost their homes, were forced to root around in their pockets for the few coins they needed to pay the motorway toll on the road to Belgrade. In a desperate scene along the road a Krajina soldier went berserk at a stop where people were waiting for petrol. He killed his children, his wife and finally himself. A policeman reported that 'an old woman who was asleep on a truck just fell down dead'. Beside the road two men committed suicide by hanging themselves from trees.

It was perhaps cruel justice that the most nightmarish scenes for the gathering refugees should be in Banja Luka, a hellish place of fear for the remaining Croats and Muslims in Serb-held northern Bosnia. The police stopped most of the refugees entering the town centre, so that it took two hours to get through the clogged roads to cover the last ten minutes into town. At night tens of thousands slept on the pavements, under their tractors or crammed into the old Yugoslav People's Army (JNA) Kozara barracks. On the outskirts of town a harassed policeman asked for help. An old woman, totally alone, had been found sleeping on the road. It was late and it was raining. She was bent double with age. 'My son is somewhere on the front,' she said. 'Please take her to the hospital,' said the policeman. 'But there is nothing wrong with me,' she protested. At the Kozara barracks almost every inch was taken up, but eventually, exhausted, she sank down in a space she found between the pairs of feet of a sleeping family.

Within days of this new Serbian migration came reports that the Croats were putting much of the former Krajina to the torch. Whole towns began to burn as the cycle of revenge began again. Barely 8,000, mainly elderly Serbs remained behind. The United Nations began to protest that gangs of Croat looters were killing and terrorising at random and that they believed that hundreds had been murdered.

These were the lands that were supposed to have become the new Serbian marches. Playing on their old spirit of rebellion Serbia's politicians had gambled with its people and the people had lost. In the small town of Srb, celebrated among Second World War Partisans for its 1941 uprising, a new Croatian police unit seemed to be the only inhabitants. Along the road burned-out cars and scattered clothes bore witness to the refugees that never made it down the hills, through the town and over the border into Bosnia. In Kistanje only a handful of people remained behind. It was said that Croats from nearby villages had torched Kistanje in revenge for the razing of their villages by the Serbs in 1991. But the Croats had managed to preserve the nearby Krka monastery, a fourteenth-century foundation which had police guards posted at the gates. Inside everything was eerily untouched. On the walls the portraits of Serbian saints and heroes looked down upon the monastery's new occupants. Here a returned Serbian émigré priest had once preached the most virulent Serbian nationalism, and Krka itself had over the last four years played an important role in bolstering Krajina's martial spirit. Now it appeared helpless, washed up hundreds of miles away from the nearest inhabited Serbian settlements. It was here that the historic tides of Serbian migrations had reached their furthest extent, but in the last few days they had turned eastwards again. In the eighteenth century the Dalmatian bishop Simeon Končarević wrote a history of the local Serbs from about 1350; he said of Krka, 'God's blessing was on this home; and since that time it has always been, until the present day, the shelter for the suffering and the fortification of our holy religion.'[2]

By preserving Krka the Croat message was that 'unlike the Serbs' they did not desecrate holy monuments. As the water spilled from a lazy fountain in the middle of the cloister, the sun began to set, bathing the surrounding hills and rocky landscape in a strange pink twilight. 'I was almost taken in myself,' said a UN human rights monitor, 'and then you realise what a con it is. Krka may be fine but Kistanje has been completely destroyed and there are almost no people left there.'

In the late 1980s, at the height of Serbia's nationalist euphoria, hundreds of thousands could be relied upon to demonstrate for 'Serbian Unity' and 'All Serbs in One State'. Now the Serbs faced defeat. Vilified throughout the world as the people who had driven out hundreds of thousands of Croats and Muslims in their drive to make their own new Serb state, hundreds of thousands of Serbs were now refugees and Serbia was bankrupt. Ashamed, barely a couple of thousand Belgraders came out to demonstrate against their government, which had turned the Serbs into international pariahs and then nonetheless failed to hold on to what most of them believed was rightfully theirs.

In 1986 a small group of intellectuals at the Serbian Academy of Arts and Sciences had written the so-called *Memorandum* which stated that 'In the general process of disintegration which has encompassed Yugoslavia, the Serbs have been hit hardest. . . . This process is directed towards the total breaking up of the national unity among the Serbian people.'[3] This, added to the emigration (or 'genocide', as they put it) of tens of thousands of the remaining Serbs in ethnic Albanian-dominated Kosovo, led them to conclude, 'one cannot imagine a worse historical defeat in peacetime'.[4] It was a phrase that was to capture the spirit of the times. It was an idea which aroused in Serbs a sense of anger and a feeling that something should be done. And the up-and-coming politician Slobodan Milošević understood this. Later he was to roar, 'If we don't know how to work well . . . at least we know how to fight well.' This too was something that many Serbs could identify with. And, as the war began, what they were fighting for was defined by Mihailo Marković, a dissident Marxist under communism who became the ideologue of Milošević's Serbian Socialist Party: 'The primary Serbian national interest is that the Republic of Serbia should conduct the strategy of defence of the Serbian population in Croatia.'[5]

Exactly four years later all this was long forgotten. It may have been in Serbia's national interest in 1990 to arm the Serbs in Croatia and Bosnia, but things were different now, said Professor Marković:

> Those Krajina people did not want to fight. They said: 'You fight for us.' Look at the Second World War. They went to the woods and defended themselves. If they had wanted to stay they could have made sacrifices and stayed. If not, well good, at least they have returned home. They left in the fifteenth and sixteenth centuries and it was a migration too far. They are mostly young people who are coming now, so that's a benefit for us. Now the Serbs are concentrated in a smaller ethnic space but it's more homogeneous.

It was cynicism of a depth which beggared belief. Professor Marković had been part of the team that had composed the *Memorandum*, the first blow struck for the Serbs. It was clear then that he and his colleagues saw no need for remorse or guilt for the process they had helped to set in motion. Indeed, with Olympian detachment all they needed to do now was to put things in context. The Serbs had always been a people on the move and some moves were better than others.

Migrations

The great exodus of the Krajina Serbs in 1995 was not unique in either Serbian or Balkan history. The 1991–5 war in former Yugoslavia displaced at least three and a half million people out of a pre-war population of twenty-three million. Europe had seen nothing like it since the end of the Second World War. But what sets the history of the Balkans apart from much of the rest of Europe, and particularly the history of the Serbs, is that their story has always been one of migrations. The Serbs, as part of the Slav tribes, migrated to the Balkans in the sixth century AD. The conquests of the Turks in the fourteenth century provoked vast upheavals. The Serbian rebellions against them in the seventeenth and eighteenth centuries and at the beginning of the nineteenth also prompted large movements of peoples, Serbs and non-Serbs. During the Balkan Wars of 1912 and 1913 hundreds of thousands of people across the southern Balkans fled as a consequence of the fighting.

It would be wrong, however, to think of all Balkan migrations as resulting from war and from what has now become known as ethnic cleansing. Throughout Balkan history peoples have also been on the move for economic reasons. In the middle ages nomadic herdsmen and their clans ranged far and wide in search of pastures for their flocks. In the eighteenth and nineteenth centuries hundreds of thousands of Serbs migrated from the rocky wastelands of Hercegovina and Montenegro to rich and fertile Serbia, and in this century too people have moved in search of better jobs, houses and farmland.

There is no better place to feel this historical ebb and flow than Ras, the walled fortress high atop a hill in the Sandžak area of Serbia. To get there you have to follow a narrow track through a forest and then climb over the tumbling walls of the medieval castle. Ras is the stronghold from which the first Serbian princes or *župans* built their state, and it is easy to see why they picked this windswept spot. From the castle walls you can see far into the valleys below and so have ample warning of any approaching enemy. Novo Brdo, in neighbouring Kosovo, is another fortress built before the Ottoman conquest. Likewise perched high on a hill, it is so impregnable that even today it is impossible to get to when snow lies deep on the mountain tracks.

While the Serbs built their first forts and settlements high up, the Turks who had conquered all of Serbia by 1459 had a different philosophy. Not fearing attack from the *rayah* or subjugated peasantry they wanted to encourage trade, so they built their towns in the valleys along which great merchants' caravans were to flow. So, close to Ras, which was abandoned, they built Novi Pazar, which means 'New Market'. Founded in 1455, it lay along the main road between Constantinople and Ragusa, the great trading city now called Dubrovnik. The area was also a vital link between Turkey and Bosnia and, as in Bosnia, a part of the population was to convert to Islam. Before the Yugoslav wars broke out in 1991, about half of Sandžak's population was Muslim.

Close to the old fort of Ras an old Serb and his wife struggle to keep their hilltop farm going. Happy to sell some *kajmak* or soft cheese to his visitors, the man talked about his Muslim neighbours: 'Thank God for Slobo,* the police and the army', he said. 'If it wasn't for them they would have cut off our ears.' But, feeling physically secure for the

---

* The most common nickname of President Slobodan Milošević.

moment, the old man said that life was getting tougher by the year because all his children had moved away and there was no one left to work on the farm. Like most people in modern Europe, they had not wanted to work on a farm on the top of a hill and preferred a comfy flat in town with a job. The farmer said that all his children had gone to the big cities of Serbia because in Novi Pazar 'The Muslims take all the jobs for themselves.' In fact Muslims too have been leaving. Like the Serbs who wanted nice flats and jobs in the big cities, Sandžak Muslims had been emigrating for years to Sarajevo and the cities of Bosnia. When the Bosnian war broke out the Yugoslav Army cleared the Serbian side of the border of Muslim villages and many began to emigrate for good to Turkey and Scandinavia in search of a new future for themselves and their families. So, in peacetime and in war, people were moving. Just as they had always done.

The Arrival of the Slavs

Most of the Balkans had been part of the Roman Empire since the first century AD. When, in the fourth century, the decision was taken to divide the empire between Rome and Constantinople, the area was home to a mix of peoples such as Greeks, Thracians, Illyrians, Romans, Dacians and many others. There were no Slavs though. The Slavonic-speaking peoples began to migrate to the Balkans only in the early sixth century. At first they came as raiders, but by the seventh century they began to settle.

Some contend that the Slavs came from the land between the Danube and the Carpathian mountains. Others believe that they came from the Caucasus and that they were ruled by an Iranian-derived elite. What can be said with certainty is that, unlike the earlier raiding Goths and Huns who left no lasting traces in the Balkans, the Slavs came to stay. By the 580s they were a powerful force, although they appear often to have fought as subordinates to the more powerful Avars, who lived roughly in the area of modern Hungary.

The constant warfare of this period led to the depopulation of large areas into which the Slavs were to move. These first Slavs cannot be identified as Serbs, Croats or Bulgarians – they were 'undifferentiated' Slavs. These three named tribes were now to arrive by diverse routes. The Croats migrated from the kingdom they had established during their migrations in southern Poland. The Serbs moved to the Balkans after briefly settling in areas that now fall within the Czech lands. It is also possible that there is a connection with those areas of north-eastern Germany, around Bautzen, where the Sorbs, a Slavonic-speaking community, still live.

Before these migrations, in the second century AD, Greek geographers wrote of an Iranian tribe called the Serbi or Serboi living on the River Don. Professor John Fine, one of the foremost historians of the region, writes that if the first Serbs and Croats, like the Turkic Bulgars, were not Slavs but Iranian, this is 'not important in the long run since the Iranians were a small minority in a population of Slavs. They quickly became assimilated by the Slavs and the resulting society was clearly Slavic (despite the non-Slavic origin of its ruling class).'[6] Constantine VII Porphyrogenitus, the Byzantine emperor and historian, writing in the mid-tenth century notes that some of the Serbs or *Servloi* were originally given land around Salonika at Serblia by the Emperor Heraclius (610–41) but that they had not stayed there, had migrated north of the Danube and had then turned southwards again.[7]

While the origins of the Serbs and Croats are still shrouded in mystery it is clear that from the very beginning these two distinct but close tribes moved one beside the other. Their histories have always been entwined. How close the tribes were is attested by the fact that they spoke, and still speak, virtually the same language. The Slav spread through the Balkans carried on until about 800 when it not only stopped but, in certain areas such as Greece and Albania, appears to have been reversed.

The arrival of the Slavs overwhelmingly changed the ethnic and linguistic composition of the peoples of the southern Balkans. But it seems that at least one pre-Slav group, who came to be known most commonly as Vlachs, survived the onslaught. With the arrival of the Slavs, they took to the uplands or migrated. Their most important distinguishing feature was their language, which was derived from Latin and, as is evident from the small groups that still survive today, is closely related to Romanian. It seems that, living in many areas cheek by jowl with the Serbs, a good part of the Vlachs were to assimilate with them, so contributing to the later creation of Orthodox and thus eventually Serb populations in parts of Bosnia, Hercegovina and Croatia.

The First Kingdoms

While the Croatian tribes moved down the Adriatic coast and settled in areas roughly coterminous with today's Croatia, the Serbs settled first in the area called Raška, in the region where the fortress of Ras was later built. They also settled on lands which are today in Montenegro, Hercegovina and southern Dalmatia. Raška gave the Serbs another name, the 'Rascians', by which they were commonly known for many centuries. Today Raška is more likely to be known by its Turkish name of Sandžak (literally the 'district' of Novi Pazar), which despite the best efforts of Serbian nationalists continues to be its most popular name.

Following the arrival of the Serbs in the Balkans they lived in tribes and clans dominated by *župans*. While the Serbs increasingly became subject to missionaries from Orthodox Constantinople, the church in Rome sought to reassert its influence in Dalmatia and among the Croats. The first Serbian grand *župans* believed to have accepted Christianity did so in the late ninth century and the conversion of the rest of the pagan Serbs would have taken place after that.[8] For another 300 years the Serbian tribes and the lands they lived in tended to be dominated by either the Byzantines or the Bulgarians. These were centuries scarred by war and tussles for power both between local princes and between the Bulgarians and the Byzantines.

It was in the eleventh century that the first Serbian kingdom began to emerge in the area of present-day Montenegro. Around 1036 Stefan Vojislav renounced his allegiance to the emperor in Constantinople, pronounced himself for Rome and began to bring the neighbouring Serbian tribes under his control. In 1077 Zeta, as the land was then called, became a kingdom under Constantine Bodin, who ruled as a Catholic.

With Bodin's death, however, his state began to dissolve into civil war and power started to shift towards Raška. Here in the 1160s Stefan Nemanja was to found a dynasty that was to rule for 200 years and create an expanding Serbian state which was to become a major military power in the Balkans. With the death in 1355 of Tsar Dušan, however, the Nemanjić Empire began to disintegrate. And by this time a new force had entered the region. In 1371 the Turks inflicted their first major defeat on the Serbs at a battle on the Maritsa river in modern-day Bulgaria. In 1389 they met them in battle again at Kosovo, after which Serbia's rulers were forced to their knees and made to pay tribute to the sultans until their lands were finally overrun in 1459.

The Arrival of the Turks

Following the turmoil caused by the arrival of the Slavs there were no more really massive movements of people until the irruption of the Turks into Europe. With the steady advance of the Ottomans through the Balkans, many Serbs fled northwards towards Hungary and also towards the Adriatic. While these migrations began after the defeat at the Battle on the Maritsa and continued as Serbs, and other Christians, moved into the semi-free vassal Serbia, far larger migrations began after its fall in 1459. The Turks themselves took tens of thousands into slavery and many were settled around Constantinople. Before the

Ottoman conquest of Bosnia, groups also fled westwards, some even reaching Italy. It was not only flight from the Turks that prompted these movements but also famine and plague, which wrought periodic devastation and left whole areas depopulated and deserted. The Serbian rebellions of 1689 and in the 1730s led to mass exoduses as the Serbian patriarchs, after twice encouraging their people to rise, were forced to lead them into exile in Hungary. None of these movements, however, explains how large numbers of Serbs came to live in Bosnia and in the Krajina region of Croatia.

Several different historical movements were to create these populations. It is important to note that, other than in the border regions such as eastern Bosnia, there were no large Orthodox populations in Bosnia proper before the Ottoman conquest in 1463. This contrasted with Hercegovina, which was mainly Orthodox. In neighbouring Dalmatia there were also long-established Orthodox communities. In the 1350s, for example, Jelena, the sister of Tsar Dušan and widow of the local ruler, founded the monastery of Krka. There is no dispute about the longevity of the Orthodox presence in the region, but it is less easy to establish the ethnic origin of these people. While many of those who came from Hercegovina or Montenegro could be considered Serb by virtue of their Orthodoxy, another group cannot. These were the Vlachs, who were moving before the Turkish conquest and who were encouraged by the Turks to continue to do so afterwards. The Vlachs were mostly but not all Orthodox. The two main areas towards which they moved were Dalmatia and north and north-west Bosnia: regions which were later to have substantial Serbian populations.

Today it is believed that the ancestors of the Vlachs were nomadic clansmen who crisscrossed the Balkans following the rise of cities in classical antiquity. The cities needed food and so a class of nomads or semi-nomads arose to take care of large flocks of sheep, goats and other cattle which they drove over long distances to take advantage of seasonal grazing lands. In Roman times cheese from the flocks of Dalmatia and areas now in modern Albania and Serbia was exported to other parts of the empire. Many of the people who subsequently came to be called Vlachs began to speak Latin during the centuries of Roman rule and preserved this tongue as they moved higher into mountainous regions with the arrival of the Slavs. But in the middle ages a new dynamic was at work. Vlachs, and others, continued to cover large distances across the Balkans, often with huge flocks of thousands of animals. They were encouraged in this by the Byzantine taxation system, which was easier to evade if one was constantly on the move rather than if one was attached to the estate of a feudal baron. In the late eleventh century Vlach cheese and woollen garments were recorded as being found in the markets of Constantinople.[9]

The Turks encouraged the Vlachs in their activities because of the demand in Ottoman cities for milk, cheese, wool and leather. What becomes far less clear is to what extent nomads in areas also inhabited by Serbs were in fact Serbs, because many of these Vlachs would have become Orthodox, like their more settled neighbours, and, over time, adopt their language too. They also started to settle permanently in areas of Dalmatia and Bosnia and may well have mixed with other Latin-speakers who had fled to the hills to escape the Slav invasions of the Adriatic coastal cities. While we know that there were Serbs and Orthodox populations in early medieval Dalmatia, it subsequently becomes harder to disentangle later Vlach and Serb migrations. Many Serbian historians claim that by the early middle ages all Vlachs were so Slavonicised as really to be Serbs, but the issue is far from being so clear-cut. Alberto Fortis, who toured Dalmatia in the late eighteenth century, wrote in some detail of the Morlacchi, or Vlassi as they called themselves. Fortis placed them in inland Dalmatia, in areas around the River Krka, which runs by Jelena's monastery and through Knin. He added that they also lived along the border with Bosnia, through Hercegovina and down to the Bay of Kotar in modern-day Montenegro. Their language, he wrote, resembled 'Rascian and Bulgarian'.

In his account Fortis outlined the divisions and tensions among the people of the region called 'Morlacchia'. The Vlassi despised the people of the coastal towns, who heartily detested them in return. However, between themselves, 'A most perfect discord reigns . . . as it generally does in other parts, between Latin [that is, Catholic] and Greek [that is, Orthodox] communion, which their respective priests fail not to foment, and tell a thousand little scandalous stories of each other. The churches of the Latins are poor, but not very dirty: those of the Greeks are equally poor, and shamefully ill kept.'[10] In other words, whatever their origins, these Vlassi, Vlachs or Morlachs were the progenitors not only of a good part of the Serbian population of Dalmatia but of the Catholic Croats as well. As late as May 1941 briefing notes prepared for Mussolini, whose troops had just moved into Dalmatia, talked of Orthodox Serbs from the mountains as being 'for the most part ex-Morlachs'. Likewise reference was made to 'Catholic Morlachs, peasants, today self-styled Croats'.[11]

In many parts of Dalmatia and Bosnia Croatian or Serbian identity was not so deeply entrenched, even well into this century, as people would describe themselves as Catholic or Orthodox or Dalmatian before they would as Serb or Croat. National identity was to develop late in these mixed regions.

Some of Fortis' other observations are also worth recording here. Describing the Hajduks or bandits of the region, he wrote:

The greatest part of the Haiduks look upon it as a meritorious action, to shed the blood of the Turks; a mistaken zeal for religion, joined to their natural and acquired ferocity, easily lead them to commit such acts of violence; and the ignorance, and national prejudices of their priests are too apt to inflame their barbarous fanaticism.[12]

Despite these details, at no time does Fortis talk of the Orthodox population as anything else but Morlach or Vlach. The word Serb is never employed and nor is the word Croat for the Catholics. He does record, though, that as far as he could discern there was no mention of these people in the records of Dalmatia before the thirteenth century. It does not help us either that in Bosnia especially the term Vlassi or Vlach has always been a pejorative term for Serb and that in Trieste the term Morlach is still used contemptuously to describe the neighbouring Slavs in general. But it is clear that these Vlachs/Vlassi/Morlachs were securely enough established in the region for the records to speak definitely of their presence by 1345. One source from 1376 names a Petar Martić as a 'Duke of Knin and the Vlachs'.[13]

In Bosnia similar complicated demographic shifts during the middle ages were to contribute to the complex patterns of settlement which characterised the republic before the 1992–5 war. Although many Serbs fled the initial Turkish onslaughts, the creation of a large Orthodox population came later, after the conquest of Bosnia. Hercegovina by contrast was predominantly Orthodox, although the Catholic church made major inroads there in the century before the arrival of the Turks. The legacy of this was that on the eve of war in 1992 eastern Hercegovina was predominantly Serbian, while western Hercegovina was mainly Croat.

In northern Bosnia the years after the Ottoman conquest were to see an influx of Orthodox populations brought to the area by the Turks, who needed to repopulate it after the devastations wrought by war and plague. Vlachs were encouraged to move by reductions in the tax on their flocks if they lived or roamed in a certain area.[14] Serbs too were to arrive or be brought by the Turks to the same regions, where as in Dalmatia they were eventually to absorb the Vlach part of the Orthodox population. In this the Serbian Orthodox, that is, national, church was to provide Serbian identity with a major boost and so give the Serbian part of the population the dominating edge over the Vlachs, who had no national institutions of their own.

After taking Serbia and Bosnia, the Turks were not to take Slavonia, the land north of the Sava river, until 1537. Between 1459 and that date many Serbs and Vlachs living along the Danube border were given privileges in exchange for military duties. In this way they frequently found themselves fighting Serbs and Vlachs who were also being granted privileges for military services by the Hungarians. But with the Ottoman advance into Slavonia the Turks needed people to repopulate the land from which many of the Catholic inhabitants had fled. Serbs and Vlachs were thus resettled here, either voluntarily or forcibly. This movement was simultaneous with the Ottoman shifts of population in northern Bosnia and other border regions.

The Military Frontier

The granting of privileges to soldiers and their families on the Habsburg side of the border was the precursor of the Military Frontier, the Vojna Krajina. At its zenith this great defensive line was to stretch 1,000 miles, varying in width from 30 to 100 kilometres. It was to begin at the Adriatic, skirt around the western and northern borders of Ottoman Bosnia, along the Danube and then along Transylvania's borders with the Ottoman Danubian principalities. These military marches were a prodigious feat of organisation and many of the frontier's great fortresses still survive. Only with the defeat of the Krajina Serbs in 1995 was their final living vestige erased from the map of Europe.

If there is a Croatian national myth it is that of the *Antemurale Christianitatis*, that is to say the 'outer wall' or bulwark of Christianity. During the centuries of the Ottoman presence in Bosnia this had a literal meaning, but it has resurfaced in subsequent conflicts with the Serbs in a different guise. With the break-up of Yugoslavia, Croatian leaders presented themselves to the world as the defenders of western civilisation against the last gasp of Serbian 'Bolshevism' and sought to represent Croatia as a Central European country as opposed to a 'Byzantine' Balkan one.

The creation of the Military Frontier was the physical *Antemurale*. Following the conquest of Bosnia in 1463, the Ottoman threat to Croatia and Slavonia was very real. By 1471 Turkish cavalry had even reached Ljubljana on a campaign of pillage across the Croatian and Slovenian countryside. In 1493 the Croats suffered their historic defeat at Krbavsko Polje. After this, much of Croatia and Dalmatia fell to the Ottomans and it was lamented that what was left outside Turkish control was but the 'remains of the remains'. It was into these newly acquired lands that the Ottomans brought Vlachs and Serbs to serve as their frontiersmen. In time many of these people were to cross over to what had become Habsburg as opposed to simply Hungarian lands after 1527. There they swore loyalty to the imperial crown while pledging to defend the imperial frontiers. In 1538 for example Emperor Ferdinand I granted privileges to a group of Serbs who were settling around Žumberak on the border between Croatia and Slovenia. In return for their military services they were exempted from taxes for the next twenty years. The charter also stated that 'everything they take from the Turks . . . and pillage, it all belongs to the Rascians themselves'.[15]

In this way Serbs and Vlachs, to the extent that they remained distinguishable, were encouraged to keep crossing into the Military Frontier from Bosnia and the Ottoman-held lands. They were further encouraged as comparable 'Vlach' privileges were eroded within the Ottoman Empire.[16] Catholics who had fled or emigrated from parts of Bosnia, Hercegovina and Slavonia also settled there.

A major act in the development of the Military Frontier was the building of the garrison town of Karlovac in the late sixteenth century. Around Karlovac, a region was set up in which the peasant soldiery was not only granted privileges but exempted from Croatian authority. Later, under Ferdinand II, the areas that were to become the Military Frontier were subjected directly to imperial rule and were divided into two parts, the Croatian Krajina ('Frontier') governed from Karlovac and the Slavonian Krajina from Varaždin. At that time Karlovac was on the border of the Ottoman Empire. In 1991 it was to become a border town again, with Krajina Serbs bombarding it heavily from its southern suburbs, which were again the frontlines. This was no accident of history: there was a high concentration of Serbs there as a direct legacy of the wars with the Ottomans.

In 1630 Ferdinand II issued the *Statuta Valachorum*, which defined the status of the Serbs, or Vlachs as they are called in the decree. Again the key principles were military service in exchange for exemption from feudal taxation and Croatian authority and a large measure of local self-government. After 1691, as a result of a deal struck between Patriarch Arsenije, the leader of the Serbian exodus from Kosovo, and the imperial authorities, Emperor Leopold I granted the Serbs the equivalent rights they had possessed under the Ottoman dispensation. This meant that the patriarch could rule not just in spiritual matters but in secular ones as well. In 1712 Sremski Karlovci became the patriarchate for the Serbs of the Habsburg Empire, and so a powerful hub of religious, intellectual and political authority too. Naturally these privileges were vigorously opposed by the Catholic church, the Croatian nobility and the Hungarians and had to be no less vigorously defended.

During the war of 1683–99, in which the Turks were pushed back from Croatia and Slavonia, the boundaries of the Military Frontier as they were to last until 1881 began to take shape. The expulsion of the Turks from these newly liberated lands was helped in areas such as Lika by the fact that the Serbs there who had been Ottoman frontiersmen simply switched sides. In the summer of 1688 as the imperial army took eastern Slavonia, Ilok and the fortress of Petrovaradin and began its march on Belgrade, thousands more Serbian men deserted the Turks *en masse*. Large numbers also crossed the River Sava out of Bosnia and into the Habsburg lands. At the same time tens of thousands of Turks and Muslim converts fled from the reconquered regions, including Hungary. Angry and dispossessed as they were, it is easy to imagine the logic of village burning, massacres, expulsion and flight taking hold. During the 1991–5 war this came to be known as ethnic cleansing, but of course only the name was new.

Although the Military Frontier was a key part of the Habsburg defence system, the imperial authorities did not always act in such a manner as to keep its peasant soldiery happy. The Habsburgs were constantly caught between the conflicting demands of the Croatian and Hungarian nobility, who wanted to impose their authority in the area, and the privileges they had granted to their Grenzer or border guards. There were also periodic attempts to convert the Orthodox settlers to Catholicism or at least to have them join the Uniate church, by which they could maintain their rituals but would accept the pope as their ultimate spiritual leader. Forms of pressure included the occasional expulsion of Orthodox priests from various areas and the imposition of a quota of one-third on the number of Orthodox as opposed to Catholic or Uniate Grenzer officers.

Living conditions varied in the frontier regions, corruption was rife and much of the area remained poor. Mutinies and uprisings were common, especially before the introduction of reforms in the middle of the eighteenth century. The border came to be organised in such a way that land was owned not by those who farmed it but by the authorities, who granted it to *zadrugas* or extended family units who in turn were obliged to provide the army with a fixed number of soldiers. This made the average peasant soldier inordinately proud of his status as a free man rather than a serf on a feudal estate. In 1627 the Duke of Sachsen-Hildburghausen reported that soldiers around Varaždin had said that they 'would rather be hacked to pieces than separated from their officers and become subjects of the Croatian nobility'.[17] In 1741 the Croats succeeded in having Orthodox jurisdiction abrogated, but it was reinstated following a revolt of Serbian soldiers stationed in Bavaria. Another mutiny broke out in 1744 after a rumour went around that Orthodox families were to be forcibly converted to Catholicism while their menfolk were fighting abroad. Further pressures prompted many to emigrate to Russia.

It was not only the frontiersmen who had problems. As the Turkish threat declined, the soldiers of the Military Frontier came to be used increasingly in Habsburg wars throughout Europe. But, as Gunther Rothenberg an historian of the frontier has written, this:

created serious command problems. . . . Officers were unable to restrain the Grenzer, whose passion for drink and plunder was ungovernable and who, even in friendly territory, were a terror to the inhabitants. In enemy territory they were given to every species of rapine. Indeed, their brutality became proverbial and the term 'Croat' an epithet.'[18]

Of course the term Croat used in this connection meant Serb as well, because both peoples were part of the frontier regiments. A survey of 1802 found soldiers in the regiments from the regions around Glina and Petrina to be two to one Orthodox to Catholic. The Lika regiment was almost completely Orthodox, while Catholics predominated in regiments from Varaždin, Slavonski Brod and Gradiška. By contrast the soldiery from Petrovaradin (on the opposite bank of the Danube from the modern city of Novi Sad) was almost totally Orthodox.[19] The survey foreshadowed modern population censuses, which until 1991 showed a similar mix of Serbs and Croats in the same places. Not all areas with Orthodox and hence Serb populations within this part of the Habsburg Empire were part of the Military Frontier. This was the case with Knin and southern Dalmatia for example.

The legacy of the Austro-Turkish wars and of the Military Frontier was the creation of a belt of land either inhabited solely by Serbs or mixed with Croats. It was to last until the 1991–5 conflict when first the Croats were expelled and then the Krajina Serbs in turn. The mutinous history of the frontiersmen also helps explain the roots of the conflict in Croatia. While it is easy to see how the Krajina Serbs could be whipped up into a state of terror by the prospect of a newly independent Croatia, owing to the memory of the attempted genocide of the Second World War, it is also clear that the notion of protecting Serbian or Orthodox rights against Croatian authority and Catholicism was deeply rooted.

2

AN EMPIRE ON EARTH

Although it was migrations which determined where Serbs lived, it was the kingdom of the Nemanjas which transformed these hitherto disparate tribes into a people and gave them an identity which would survive hundreds of years of Ottoman domination. It is for this reason that the period is one of such fascination for Serbs today and indeed such a crucial historical reference point.

Before the Nemanjić era, the Serbs were a collection of loosely organised tribes. After the Nemanjas, within two decades of the demise of Tsar Dušan in 1355, the Serbs were again divided. And it was this inglorious bickering of feudal barons which was to seal Serbia's fate and ease the way for the Ottoman conquest. After falling under Turkish rule the Serbs were to have no more independent existence until 1804. Thus the 200 years of Nemanjić rule were the only extended period of greatness to which Serbs could later look back and from which they could draw inspiration.

Above all the Nemanjić heritage was preserved by the church, which as a national institution was essentially that dynasty's creation. Under the Turks it was also the *only* Serbian institution and so, along with popular epic poetry, it came to celebrate and cherish the Nemanjas' memory. With the birth of modern nationalism in the nineteenth century historians and artists also provided the public with drama and pictures with which they could mentally and emotionally recreate the lost golden age of those kings. These images in turn were to help inspire the nation with a determination to recreate Dušan's empire in fact and not just in fantasy. In this way hundreds of years after their line had died out the Nemanjas were unwittingly to give the Serbs the political vision they needed to liberate the lands which still lay under Turkish or Austro-Hungarian rule.

Such a heritage, and the experience of the wars in 1912, 1913, 1914, 1941 and 1991, has also eroded for Serbs the sense that history is something you read about in books. The wartime press centre of the

Bosnian Serb leadership after 1992 was infamous for the lack of help it gave to journalists and for its reluctance to divulge information. However, Marko Gašić, one of its English-born Serbian volunteers, delighted in reminding visitors that 'We are living history right now, it's not just something that happened in the past.'

Birth of a Dynasty

Stefan Nemanja, the father of the dynasty, was born into an old noble family in Ribnica near Podgorica, the capital of present-day Montenegro. As Zeta, as it was then called, came under the ecclesiastical jurisdiction of coastal Bar he was baptised a Catholic. In the period 1172–3 he was a prisoner of Emperor Manuel in Constantinople, an experience which filled him with wonder for the splendours of Byzantine civilisation. So impressed was he that on his return to Zeta he determined that the Serbs should opt definitively for Byzantium and Orthodox culture. Consequently he was rebaptised into the faith of Constantinople by the bishop of Raška, the area from which Nemanja now began to build his power.

In 1185 a Bulgarian uprising against the Byzantines led to the foundation of a new Bulgarian empire covering wide swathes of the Balkans. One area that the Bulgarians did not capture was Nemanja's Raška. The rise of this new Bulgaria coincided with the cataclysmic sack of Constantinople by the Catholic Crusaders and their temporary destruction and division of the Byzantine Empire. Not only did this mean that Bulgaria could prosper, but, sheltering behind it, the Serbia of the Nemanjas also had the opportunity to expand.

The importance of Stefan Nemanja did not lie simply in his foundation of a strong dynasty. He also began the Serbian tradition of royal church- and monastery-building, a practice which was of course common in the Europe of his time. What was unforeseen, however, was just how great a role these institutions were to play in the future. As we have noted, it was thanks to these churches and their clergy that the memory of the Serbian state and the Nemanjas was preserved during the centuries of Turkish rule. By the time of his abdication in 1196, Nemanja ruled not just Zeta and Hum (modern Hercegovina), but also much of Kosovo and what is today central Serbia. North of Raška he founded the monastery of Studenica. Supported by later Nemanjas, Studenica was to become a powerhouse of the Serbian church, a tradition that was to continue even under the Turks. However, the link between the Nemanjas and the church was to be even more fundamental than the monastic legacy.

Influenced by his third son Rastko, more commonly known by his monastic name of Sava, Stefan Nemanja gave up the throne. In Studenica he took holy orders and then in 1197 he retired to a monastic life on Mount Athos. In a ceremony in the church of St Peter, which still stands on a hillside outside Novi Pazar, Stefan Nemanja conferred the succession on his second son Stefan. Teodisije, a thirteenth-century monk, has left this description of the event:

> After having heard the mass and prayed, the sovereign and the holy bishop made a blessing with the cross and both putting their hands on the head of Stefan proclaimed him grand *župan* and sovereign of all Serbian land. And all the well-born lords bowed down, asking God to grant him long life. . . . And when they came out of the church they found long tables which had been set. And in the middle of the feast and joy rich gifts were brought to each of the well-born lords according to their age, faithfulness and merits. They were gifts of the sovereigns, one of whom was giving up power and the other who was acceding to it. And everyone rejoiced, made merry and revelled. Thus it was done.[1]

Despite the festivities, the abdication of Stefan Nemanja was to herald the beginning of another Serbian tradition, that of paralysing political infighting. A bitter feud now ensued between Stefan, the new sovereign, and his elder brother Vukan, who was not content with being palmed off with a mere duchy. He sought out papal support and in 1202 the Catholic King Imre of Hungary invaded Serbia, banished Stefan and brought Vukan to the throne. The next year a Hungarian Catholic bishop was ordered to depart for Serbia to replace the Orthodox bishops and thus deliver the country to Catholicism. But the plan collapsed because in 1204 King Imre died, and Stefan soon regained his throne. The feud was then ended because the two brothers were reconciled by their younger brother Sava, who returned from Mount Athos bringing with him the remains of their father. He was soon to be venerated as Simeon, the first Serbian saint. After he was buried at Studenica, a holy oil was said to seep from his tomb. Today visitors to the monastery can still see the receptacles that were hollowed out of the marble below his sarcophagus to catch the oil, but the miracle is said not to have occurred for 300 years.

Effecting the reconciliation of the two brothers was the least of Sava's achievements. Taking advantage of the situation abroad he now moved to solidify the Nemanjić position. After 1204, Byzantium had been divided into feudal Latin crusader states, although in Nicaea in Asia Minor Theodore I Lascaris kept the Byzantine tradition alive. The fact that the once mighty Byzantines were now in no position to exert their influence over the Serbs meant that Sava, a wily diplomat, was able to extract the maximum advantage. In 1217 he sent an emissary to Pope

Honorius III asking for his blessing for Serbia and 'the royal wreath for his brother Stefan'.[2] The pope acceded and thus Grand Župan Stefan was crowned king. From now on he became known to history as Stefan Prvovenčani or the 'First Crowned'. The act of securing this papal blessing, even for an Orthodox state, was the equivalent of international recognition today.

The Holy Roots

Sava's job was only half finished. Having dealt with the temporal side of Serbian statehood he left for Nicaea to visit Theodore I Lascaris. From the enfeebled and exiled Byzantine emperor and the Orthodox patriarch Manuel Saranten Hariopoulos he secured, in 1219, autocephaly (or autonomy) for the Serbian national church, the single most important event in forging the idea of the church, and became its first head. In this way Sava founded the Serbian statehood and national identity. Without such a church the history of the Serbs, especially during the centuries of Ottoman domination, would have been very different.

Returning to Serbia, Sava drew up a code of canon and civil laws called the *Nomocanon*. The code, which had its roots in Byzantine legal texts, sought to harmonise the relationship between church and state. Thus Sava laid the foundations for the binding together of church and medieval state which was to outlive the family connection. He centred the church at Žiča, but it was later moved to Peć in Kosovo. Following his death in 1236 Sava, like his father, was canonised. Today Serbian churchmen still lament his passing and that of the Nemanjas, because church power was never again so strong.

It is impossible to overstate Sava's contribution to the shaping of Serbian history. Not only did his acts underpin the foundations of the Nemanjić state but he was to bequeath the Serbian people something far more intangible and durable. As the historian Miloš Blagojević has argued, the canonisation of Sava and his father 'gave to the Serbian people saints who had come from among their ranks and would in heaven be tireless protectors of the Serbian state, Serbian rulers, Serbian people and the entire patrimony. Their contemporaries confidently looked up to them for protection.' Blagojević suggests that the canonisations were a vital step in entrenching Nemanjić power by conferring upon the dynasty 'sacred properties', especially since future Nemanjić kings would be made saints. Stefan Nemanja came to be described as the 'holy root' and 'his successors were "saplings" or "offsprings" of this holy root'.[3] As saints the Serbian royal family immediately entered church liturgy and, if that was not enough to impress the illiterate peasantry, the Nemanjas were immortalised in the frescoes that adorn the churches and monasteries into which they poured their treasure. The central idea of the 'holy root' was conveyed by painting family trees. A classic example can be seen today in the patriarchate church in Peć. Here, aligned in four rows, are the Nemanjas, over whom presides Christ himself blessing the royal family. He is flanked by two angels swooping down towards them, crowns in hand. In the family-tree fresco in the church of Visoki Dečani, twenty-two members of the dynasty are depicted, with Stefan Nemanja at the base holding up the construction.

The sanctification of the Nemanjas was taken even further by Sava and later medieval writers when he began to describe his father with reference to the biblical patriarch Abraham. 'He was also a "New Israel", so that his descendants – the Serbs – became the "elected people".' The theory of divine right was also employed, as Stefan Nemanja himself had recorded that God 'in his great and infinite mercy and love of man bestowed upon our great-grandfathers and our grandfathers the rule of the Serbian lands'. As Blagojević notes:

> Thus, God had ordained that Nemanja's ancestors, he himself and sub-sequently his heirs should sovereignly rule 'the Serbian land'. They should take care of the 'flock' entrusted to them, i.e., of the Serbian people, defend it and keep all evils away from it, as well as keep it together. All these [ideas] largely influenced the feeling of belonging to a common ethnic group – the Serbian nation.[4]

High Noon of Empire

The thirteenth century was a period of steady expansion and consolidation for Serbia and the Nemanjas. The tribal *župans* became lords and nobles, while peasants were increasingly reduced to serfdom on the feudal estates. Apart from agriculture the mainstay of the medieval economy was mining. During the reign of Stefan Uroš I (1243–76) several new lead, copper and silver mines were opened. Saxon Germans were brought from Transylvania as miners and commercial links with Italy were strengthened. Throughout the middle ages Ragusa (Dubrovnik) played a key role in the economy of the region as its main commercial and entrepôt port city.

Abroad, in 1261, the Byzantine Empire was restored in Constantinople. Emperor Manuel VIII Palaeologus won back some of the old imperial lands, but his state was to remain weak.

The Serbian kings continued to seek immortality in their monastical bequests. Uroš I was the founder of Sopoćani, and Milutin (1282–1321) of Gračanica, which is close to modern Priština. Under

Milutin, the gold mines of Novo Brdo started work, and lead is still mined there. Milutin's fourth wife was Simonida, the daughter of the Byzantine emperor. She had originally come to him as a child bride despatched from Constantinople at the age of six. In Gračanica's church her frescoed portrait shows her perfect oval face topped by a magnificent crown. Her body is wrapped in sumptuous bejewelled robes. Under Milutin, Byzantine tradition, court customs and institutions came ever more to be emulated and Simonida's mother, the Empress Irene, in Constantinople would shower her son-in-law and daughter with precious gifts. Milutin's claim to the throne, which he in fact wrested from his brother Dragutin, who had in turn seized it from his father Uroš I in war, is emphasized by means of another frescoed Nemanjić family tree. It shows him at the top with angels bringing him the crown and other symbols of his power and majesty. Milutin was clearly no longer content with being just the king of a peripheral Balkan backwater, even if St Sava had buttressed the Serbian kings' claim by invoking divine right. He had begun to hunger for something more. Desanka Milošević, who has written about Gračanica, notes that Milutin's portrait atop the family tree contained in it an important political message for those who could decode such symbolism:

> With this act, with this painting, the king had all the prerogatives of power of the Byzantine Emperor, except for the title. The crown, the garments, the loros and the sceptre were all identical to the Byzantine Emperor's. Before Milutin, something like this would have been absolutely unthinkable, for only the Byzantine Emperor was Christ's regent on earth and only he ruled by God's grace.[5]

Today Gračanica, like the other Serbian monasteries of Kosovo, stands like a small Serbian island in an Albanian sea. In the middle ages Kosovo and Metohija, to give the region its full Serbian name, was inhabited almost entirely by Serbs. This began to change after the Ottoman conquest and especially after the great Serbian migrations of the seventeenth and eighteenth centuries. During this period the movement of mostly Muslim Albanians into Kosovo began to change the province's ethnic make-up. Today barely 10 per cent of its population is still Serb.

There is something pathetic, then, in the small clusters of people who gather for mass in Gračanica's vaulted gloom on an icy-cold winter's evening. They are a kind of living remnant of Serbian history, a poignant reminder of past glories and of the terrible menace of the unresolved problem that now hangs over the region. But when the English writer Rebecca West visited Gračanica in 1937, twenty-five years after the Serbs had recaptured Kosovo from the Turks and in an era when the Serbs still bathed in the reflected glory of their First World War heroism, she saw the church in an entirely different light:

> From the immense height of the cupolas light descends on three naves, divided by three gigantesquely sturdy columns, and arrives there multi-coloured, dyed by the frescoes which cover every inch of the wall. There is here a sense of colossal strength, of animal vigour, of lust so lusty that it can sup off high pleasures as well as low, and likes crimson on its eye as well as wine on its tongue and a godhead as well as a mistress.[6]

Although the Nemanjić monasteries were all of course Orthodox there was still not the total alienation between the two branches of Christendom that in this region was to develop later. The Nemanjas married Catholic princesses and, during the several conflicts between brothers or between sons and fathers that plagued the Nemanjas, one side often allied with a Catholic party such as Hungary and would pledge to bring Serbia into the Roman fold.

Born in 1307 Dušan was to be the greatest of the Nemanjić monarchs. He seized power from his father Stefan Dečanski and had him locked up in the fortified town of Zvečan. In 1331 Dušan was crowned king of Serbia and two months later Stefan Dečanski was strangled.

Dušan had his father buried in Visoki Dečani – High Dečani, the monastery Stefan Dečanski himself had begun to build and which his son was to continue. It is one of the most striking of all the Serbian monastery churches. While indubitably Byzantine and Orthodox inside, its outer walls are lined with strips of polished marble recalling the western, Dalmatian and Italianate styles of the time. Indeed its main architect was a Catholic, Fra Vita from the coastal town of Kotor. Stefan Dečanski is celebrated as a saint, and his sarcophagus is opened on important feast days. Although Dušan was to be the greatest Serbian leader to date, he was not canonised because of his presumed part in the murder of his father.

With Byzantium at the time plunged into civil war, Dušan now seized the opportunity to expand the old Serbian state based around Raška and Kosovo. Soon he had taken all of Macedonia save Salonika and also much of Albania. After that Epirus and Thessaly, deep in modern Greece, were to fall to him. In 1343 Dušan supported John Cantacuzenus as a claimant to the throne of Byzantium. Cantacuzenus' daughter had already been married to Orhan, the leader of the increasingly menacing Ottoman Turks. After his alliance with the Serbs broke down, Cantacuzenus called on the Turks to help fight the Serbs. It was a turning point not just for the Balkans but for the whole of Europe too, for in this way the Turks made their first major incursions on to the

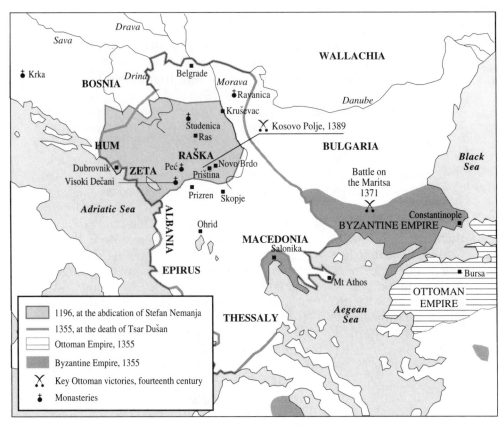

1196–1355: Medieval Serbia

continent. Cantacuzenus had appealed to the Turks because Dušan's ambition now embraced the throne in Constantinople itself. Such divisions within the Christian ranks were of course characteristic of the times and could only profit the Turks. Within just over one hundred years they had not only overwhelmed what remained of the Serbian state but had taken Constantinople as well.

In the meantime Dušan had himself crowned the 'Emperor of the Serbs and Greeks'. The coronation took place in Skopje, in Macedonia, on Easter Sunday in 1346. Later he added the Albanians and Bulgars to his title. Only a patriarch could crown an emperor, but as Dušan was in conflict with Constantinople the patriarch there clearly could not approve such a move. Dušan therefore had to create his own patriarch. He convoked a council of Serbian and Bulgarian churchmen and had them promote the most senior Serbian archbishop, Joanikije, to the status of patriarch. This led to a schism with the church in Constantinople. Dušan did not fulfil his ambition to take the city as he died suddenly in 1355.

Dušan has come down through history with two suffixes to his name. One is 'the mighty' in recognition of his short-lived empire. The other is 'the lawgiver' because of the new legal code he introduced in 1349 and which was expanded in 1354. The code, like Sava's *Nomocanon*, was based on Byzantine models but adapted and expanded. Its first part deals with church matters and the 'Latin heresy'. However, a large section is devoted to the medieval fight against crime, including bribery, theft and the forging of coins. Other portions deal with issues ranging from taxation to border lords, who are to be punished if they fail to prevent enemy incursions. Punishments were severe but no more so than elsewhere in Europe. Juries were selected from the defendant's peers, but there was no question of equality before the law. Slaves, serfs, nobles and others were punished according to a sliding scale, with the lowest classes bearing the heavier punishments. Article 51 is a good example:

> If any lord take a noblewoman by force, let both his hands be cut off and his nose be split. But if a commoner take a noblewoman by force, let him be hanged; if he take his own equal, let both his hands be cut off and his nose split.[7]

Retreat from Empire

By 1355 Serbia was an empire which stretched from the Danube to the Peloponnese. It had a strong ambitious leader, an established dynasty and a national church, and it was by far the most powerful state in the Balkans. After Dušan's death everything began to unravel. He was succeeded by his son Stefan Uroš V, who had neither the authority of his father nor his military abilities. He is often dubbed Uroš the Weak. John Cantacuzenus wrote at the time that Uroš' first challenger for power was his uncle Simeon, who sought:

> to rule over all the lands of Serbia, thinking that his claims were stronger, and many of the Serbian landed aristocracy supported him. And Uroš, the king's son, gathered an army to protect his fatherland from his uncle. But his mother, Jelena, did not join either him or her brother in law, Simeon. Instead she took many cities for herself. . . . The most powerful members of the aristocracy drove out the humbler and the weaker members, seized any of the surrounding towns they could grab; some then joined the king and some Simeon, his uncle, not as vassals and subjects to their master, but rather as allies and friends offering support. . . . And thus broken and divided into a thousand parts, they started quarrelling.[8]

While the general picture painted by Cantacuzenus is accurate, his time scale is blurred. He does not say for example that the first attacks on the empire came, not from within the Serbian camp, but from outside. With support from the Venetians a local ruler managed to wrest areas now in modern Albania from Serbian control. Those parts of Greece which had been part of the empire soon fell away too, with Simeon declaring himself emperor there. In the north Serbia was attacked by the Hungarians. In Zeta the Balšić family managed to take power, which they held until 1421.

By 1361 two brothers, Vukašin and Jovan Uglješa, known to literature as the Mrnjavčevićs, had emerged as leading actors on the political stage. These great feudal landowners from Macedonia were later to be condemned for usurping power from Uroš. In fact, according to Rade Mihaljčić, a leading expert on the period, they at first worked with him, unlike his treacherous uncle Simeon. However, the Mrnjavčevićs did have ambitions and, to the fury of the nobility of Raška, Vukašin was declared king under the nominal sovereignty of Emperor Uroš. As Uroš had no children this placed the Nemanjić succession in jeopardy. After 1365 Uroš faded from the political scene, remaining emperor in name only. Slated for succession then was the son of Vukašin. He is known to history and in the legends that were to be woven around him as young King Marko or Kraljević Marko.[9]

In the end there was to be no final power struggle. As Dušan's empire crumbled away, it soon became clear that the balance of power in the Balkans was shifting. The main threat to the Serbs was no longer the Bulgarians or the Byzantines but the military might of the Ottoman Turks, who were rapidly advancing from out of Asia Minor. In 1371 Vukašin and Jovan Uglješa died at the Battle on the Maritsa, where the Serbs met the Turks in battle. Soon afterwards Uroš died and with him ended the rule of the Nemanjić dynasty. The Battle on the Maritsa was a crushing victory for the Turks, and as a consequence Bulgaria, Macedonia and parts of southern Serbia fell under their sway. In strategic terms its consequences were far greater than those of the Battle of Kosovo in 1389, but because of the myths and legends that have grown up around the latter the first has tended to be forgotten.

As there was obviously no native Turkish or Muslim population upon which to base the Ottomans' Balkan rule at this time, the first stage of conquest was generally to leave a defeated territory under the control of its native rulers. Some did not even wait to be conquered, bowing before the overwhelming force of the Turks and submitting to the sultan's authority. The price of power though was that these rulers became vassals. This meant that not only did they have to pay tribute to the sultan but they had to fight alongside him when called upon to do so. Kraljević Marko became the first Serbian leader to fight with his men in the army of Sultan Murad I (1360–89). His career as a Turkish vassal did not preclude him from becoming one of the central figures of Serbian folklore, in which his character often defies his master, the sultan. One legend about him has him saying on the eve of battle: 'I . . . pray God to help the Christians, even if I am the first to be killed in this war.'[10]

After the Battle on the Maritsa, what remained of Serbian land was divided between several feudal lords. The Balšić family had already taken control of Zeta. The feudal lord Vuk Branković held parts of Raška, Kosovo and northern Macedonia, while one Lazar Hrebeljanović rose to prominence in the region covering today's central Serbia and parts of Kosovo including the citadel and mines of Novo Brdo. Lazar also greatly expanded his territory on the border of Bosnia when, in alliance with the Bosnian leader Ban Tvrtko Kotromanić, he fell upon the *župan* Nikola Altomanović, partitioning his lands between them in the autumn of 1373.

As the hero of the Battle of Kosovo and the figure that above all others bestrides Serbian history from the downfall of the Serbian state to modern times, it is striking that so little is known of Prince or Knez Lazar until 1371. Later eulogies and chronicles sought to magnify his origins, but apart from the fact that he was born around 1329 near Novo Brdo little is known for sure. He appears to have served at Dušan's court in a noble capacity, and he clearly distinguished himself, acquiring the title of *knez* and marrying Milica, who came from a junior branch of the Nemanjić family.

With his successful conquest of Nikola Altomanović's lands Lazar was now emerging as the most powerful of the lords ruling the territory of the former Serbian kingdom. He made alliances through marriage, Vuk Branković was his son-in-law, and he came to be supported by the church 'as the most suitable person for uniting the traditional lands of the Nemanjićs and for restoring their state'.[11] Lazar welcomed many churchmen to his territory who had fled the lands now under Turkish rule. Clearly seeing the coming danger, they encouraged him to seek a reconciliation between the Serbian church and the patriarchate in Constantinople. Relations had been broken after Stefan Dušan's coronation in 1346. Lazar mended the breach, and formal renunciation of Dušan's excommunication was read over his tomb in Prizren in Kosovo.[12] Lazar was generous in giving to the church. Among the most important of his foundations was the delicate Ravanica monastery church which stands in the Morava valley in central Serbia.

As his power grew, Lazar started to describe himself as the 'ruler of all Serbs', though this was an ambition rather than a reality. At the same time Ban Tvrtko had had himself crowned 'King of the Serbs and of Bosnia' at the monastery of Mileševa in 1377. Despite this apparent clash of aims the two remained on good terms. Possibly Lazar deferred to Tvrtko here because the latter had Nemanjić blood in his veins while Lazar did not. At the time it was widely believed that Vukašin had died at the Battle on the Maritsa because he had taken the title 'king' without springing either directly or indirectly from the Nemanjić 'holy root'.

The Turkish advance through south-eastern Europe was greatly aided by the divisions among the Christian leaders. By the time of the fateful Battle of Kosovo, Lazar may have been the biggest lord on the Balkan block but that was not enough, despite the support he was to receive from Vuk Branković and King Tvrtko. Lazar's Serbia had been strengthened by the arrival of refugees from the lands which had already fallen under the Turks, but still this did not mean his principality had power enough to resist for any length of time. Moreover, the system of Christian vassal princes ensured that Serbs, among others, made up a part of the force which faced Lazar's army at Kosovo Polje, the Field of Blackbirds, on 28 June 1389.[13]

3

IT IS BETTER TO DIE IN BATTLE
THAN TO LIVE IN SHAME

The rise of Slobodan Milošević, the man who was to become Serbian president, was sealed by an apparently impromptu speech he gave in Kosovo Polje on 24 April 1987. The leader of the League of Communists of Serbia emerged from a meeting of angry Kosovo Serbs who were complaining of harassment at the hands of the local ethnic Albanian-dominated authorities:

> First I want to tell you, comrades, that you should stay here. This is your country, these are your houses, your fields and gardens, your memories. You are not going to abandon your lands because life is hard, because you are oppressed by injustice and humiliation. It has never been a characteristic of the Serbian and Montenegrin people to retreat in the face of obstacles, to demobilise when they should fight, to become demoralised when things are difficult. You should stay here, both for your ancestors and your descendants. Otherwise you would shame your ancestors and disappoint your descendants. But I do not suggest you stay here suffering and enduring a situation with which you are not satisfied. On the contrary! It should be changed, together with all progressive people here, in Serbia and in Yugoslavia. . . . Yugoslavia does not exist without Kosovo! Yugoslavia would disintegrate without Kosovo! Yugoslavia and Serbia are not going to give up Kosovo![1]

Soon after 1389 the Serbian Patriarch Danilo recorded what he claimed was a speech given by Prince Lazar to his men on the eve of combat:

> You, oh comrades and brothers, lords and nobles, soldiers and vojvodas [dukes] – great and small. You yourselves are witnesses and observers of that great goodness God has given us in this life. . . . But if the sword, if wounds, or if the darkness of death comes to us, we accept them sweetly for Christ and for the godliness of our homeland. It is better to die in

battle than to live in shame. Better it is for us to accept death from the sword in battle than to offer our shoulders to the enemy. We have lived a long time for the world; in the end we seek to accept the martyr's struggle and to live forever in heaven. We call ourselves Christian soldiers, martyrs for godliness to be recorded in the book of life. We do not spare our bodies in fighting in order that we may accept the holy wreaths from that One who judges all accomplishments. Sufferings beget glory and labors lead to peace.[2]

In all of European history it is impossible to find any comparison with the effect of Kosovo on the Serbian national psyche. The battle changed the course of Serbian history, but its immediate strategic impact was far less than many subsequently came to believe. Its real, lasting legacy lay in the myths and legends which came to be woven around it, enabling it to shape the nation's historical and national consciousness. This came about through a particular set of historical and political circumstances in the decades following the battle. A legend was created around the character of Lazar, primarily by monks, which was later preserved through the tradition of cycles of epic folk poetry. These provided a link to past glory and more importantly an inspiration for the Serbs in the nineteenth century and during the Balkan Wars when the time was ripe to shrug off Ottoman domination.

In the late 1980s, with Milošević acting as cup-bearer, the Serbs were again to drink from the Kosovo chalice and, fortified by its heady brew of nationalism, they marched confidently into war and disaster. The irony is that Milošević had predicted that 'Yugoslavia would disintegrate without Kosovo', yet it was Yugoslavia's fate to disintegrate *with* Kosovo, as the fissures that spread from the unhappy province managed to splinter the rest of the country. But Kosovo, against the will of most of its ethnic Albanian population, remains very much within the new Yugoslavia of Serbia and Montenegro.

The Battle and its Aftermath

Because it has become so central to the Serbian story, Kosovo can rightly be described as its historical crossroads. But for the Turks in the late 1380s it had no such metaphysical connotations. It was simply the next domino in their conquest of the Balkans. Much of it lay under the control of the powerful local lord Vuk Branković. Its plains were rich and fertile and its mines gave forth an abundance of minerals, especially gold and silver.

After the Battle on the Maritsa in 1371 the Turks spent time consolidating their rule in Bulgaria and Macedonia. By the mid-1380s, however, they began to raid Serbia itself. It was clear to all that a decisive battle was coming, especially if the Serbian lords did not submit and agree to become vassals beforehand. In 1389 Sultan Murad, acknowledging the importance of the coming conflict, not only led his troops personally but came to Kosovo with his two sons, Bayezid and Yakub. On the Serbian side the main contingents were led by Lazar and Vuk Branković. King Tvrtko of Bosnia had sent men under the command of Vlatko Vuković.

Considering the vast repercussions of the battle it is striking how little hard information there is about what actually happened. Later myth-makers and hagiographers were to compose histories crammed with a wealth of detail, such as Danilo's account of Lazar's eve-of-battle speech, but very little of this has any grounding in fact. All we know for sure is that Lazar and Sultan Murad died, along with many others. Vuk Branković, Vlatko Vuković and Bayezid survived, and immediately after the battle the Turks retreated to Edirne (Adrianople), their capital at that time. Today Kosovo is written and talked about as *the* great Serbian defeat, the end of empire and the beginning of centuries of Ottoman bondage. Yet none of this is strictly true. First, many of the initial reports from Kosovo, far from lamenting a great Christian catastrophe, celebrated a triumph over the Turks. Secondly, as we have seen, the Serbian Empire had begun to collapse as far back as 1355 after the death of Dušan. Thirdly, after the battle, a form of Serbian state, the so-called despotate, survived, on and off, for another seventy years. Despite the constant threat from the Turks, the despotate was to see a Serbian cultural renaissance, the most important monuments of which are the monasteries of the Morava valley.

The very first record of the battle that has come down to us was made by a Russian monk who was on Turkish territory at the time, close to Constantinople. Writing twelve days after the battle he noted the death of the sultan but said nothing of victory or defeat. By contrast King Tvrtko in Bosnia was soon trumpeting *his* victory. On 1 August 1389 he wrote to the senate of the Dalmatian town of Trogir informing them of the sultan's defeat. He then wrote to the Florentine senate. This letter has not been preserved, but their reply has been. In it he is congratu-lated on the victory and, significantly, reference is made to twelve men 'who broke through the enemy ranks and the camels tethered round about, opening a way with their swords, and reached Murad's tent. Blessed above the rest was he who, running his sword into the throat and skirt of the leader of such a great power, heroically killed him.'[3]

At the time the question of who had killed the sultan did not seem very important, but in later chronicles the man was named. He was Miloš Obilić, or in earlier writings Kobilić. No historian can say with absolute certainty whether Obilić was an historical character, but his name came to loom ever larger, not only in Serbian epic poems about the battle but also in the national pantheon of heroes.

Gradually reports of the battle began to filter across Europe but they were either unspecific about its outcome or they talked of a Christian victory. As in Chinese Whispers these reports also tended to become ever more distorted in the telling. By the time they reached Paris, for example, even the location of the battlefield had become hazy. The French chronicler Philippe Mesière recorded that the sultan 'had been completely defeated in the regions of Albania. Both he and his sons fell in the battle as well as the bravest of their army.'[4] These reports did not talk much about the death of Prince Lazar, who, at least in the west, was an obscure Balkan princeling.

A wealth of modern scholarship has examined scores of chronicles, Serbian, Turkish and others, written in the decades after the battle. What appears to have happened is that both sides, reeling from the loss of their leaders, now needed to consolidate power in the hands of their successors. On the Turkish side this was swift and bloody. After Murad's death Bayezid summoned his younger brother Yakub, murdered him and then hurried home to Edirne to secure his succession.

On the Serbian side it was the consolidation of power in the hands of Lazar's clan which gave birth to the myth of Kosovo. Lazar's widow Milica needed to secure the succession of their son Stefan, who in 1389 was still a young boy. Apart from retaining power, she had other urgent matters to attend to. Although it was not immediately evident that Kosovo was a military defeat, its implications were soon becoming clear. While Lazar's Serbia had been relatively wealthy and strong, it was no long-term match for the far more powerful Ottomans. If both armies had suffered heavy losses, only the Turks had a plentiful supply of fresh manpower to call upon when they returned home. No sooner had Bayezid secured his succession than the Turks were back demanding that Milica submit to his authority. With the Hungarians threatening the north, there was little choice. What had been Lazar's Serbia became a vassal state. Stefan and his brother Vuk were not yet old enough to lead troops for Bayezid, but tribute had to be paid – including the despatch of Lazar's fourteen-year-old daughter Olivera to grace Bayezid's harem.

In a bid to shore up her power-base against the potential threat of the other marauding Serbian lords who might now want to partition her lands, Milica put church scribes to work to sanctify Lazar in order to bolster Stefan's claim on power. So, as the scribes eulogised his 'saintly' father, young Stefan, like the Nemanjas, could also claim to be a 'sapling' from a 'holy root'. It would be too cynical to suggest that securing the position of young Stefan was the only reason for the canonisation of Lazar, but it was certainly a powerful motivation. In medieval society the church was the main source of news and information for ordinary people. As Lazar had been favoured by the church above the other Serbian lords of the time, its priests were happy to play their part.

Within a few years of the battle Stefan Lazarević was old enough to fulfil his obligations as a vassal – most importantly he was required to come to the Sultan's aid along with his soldiers. This led to a curious situation, but one which was then accepted as fate. While Lazar himself was being venerated as a saint and as the man who had given his life to save the Serbs from Murad's Turks, his son was now fighting for Murad's son Bayezid, who was also his brother-in-law.

Immediately after the battle, Bayezid had successfully consolidated his power, and there were ever fewer Balkan Slav leaders left who had not yet submitted to his authority. In 1396, however, the Turks had to confront the last serious crusade against them, but, in part thanks to Stefan's intervention, the Christians were defeated. In 1402, though, Bayezid's luck turned. This time the threat came from the east. Bayezid's army suffered a crushing defeat at Angora (Ankara) at the hands of Timur (Tamerlane), the Mongol leader who had begun to build up his empire in far-off Samarkand. Bayezid was captured and was said to have been carried around in a cage until he died. Timur's incursion into Asia Minor did not last long and his power crumbled after his death in 1405. However, the damage he wrought on the Ottomans was considerable and the episode managed to give a respite to the rump Byzantine Empire still lingering on in Constantinople. Stefan Lazarević, who had fought at Ankara with Bayezid, now seized his chance to slip the Ottoman leash. Escaping from the battlefield, where his men had defeated a Tartar unit, he collected his sister Olivera from Bayezid's harem and paid a visit to the emperor in Constantinople, Manuel II Palaeologus. He conferred on Stefan the title despot or ruler, which in Byzantine terminology does not have the negative connotations that it has in English.

Following the demise of Bayezid, his sons plunged into a bloody civil war in a bid to secure the succession. By 1413 it was over and Despot Stefan once again had to submit to Ottoman suzerainty. His nephew and successor Djuradj Branković (1427–56) tried to organise resistance with other Christian powers but, as usual, their own short-term interests came first. In 1427 the Hungarians made a deal with the Turks by which Djuradj Branković would be recognised as despot of a semi-independent buffer state which was to lie between them. It was not to last. The Turks occupied Serbia briefly in 1439 and again finally in 1459 when Smederevo, the purpose-built Danube fortress town and capital of the despotate, fell. On the map, Serbia as anything else but a far-flung Ottoman province ceased to exist. In the minds of the Serbs, however, Serbia was simply awaiting its resurrection.

Lazar's Choice: The Empire of Heaven

Vuk Karadžić (1787–1864) is remembered both as the great nineteenth-century reformer of the Serbian language and as the man who published the first major collection of Serbian epic songs. One of the best known is 'The Downfall of the Serbian Empire', in which Lazar makes his fateful choice between the eternal 'empire of heaven' and the temporal 'empire of the earth':

> Flying hawk, grey bird,
> out of the holy place, out of Jerusalem,
> holding a swallow, holding a bird.
> That is no hawk, grey bird,
> that is Elijah, holy one;
> holding no swallow, no bird
> but writing from the Mother of God
> to the Emperor at Kosovo.
> He drops that writing on his knee,
> it is speaking to the Emperor:
> 'Lazar, glorious Emperor,
> which is the empire of your choice?
> Is it the empire of heaven?
> Is it the empire of the earth?
> If it is the empire of the earth,
> saddle horses and tighten girth-straps,
> and, fighting-men, buckle on swords,
> attack the Turks,
> and all the Turkish army shall die.
> But if the empire of heaven
> weave a church on Kosovo,
> build its foundation not with marble stones,
> build it with pure silk and with crimson cloth,
> take the Sacrament, marshal the men,
> they shall all die,
> and you shall die among them as they die.'
> And when the Emperor heard those words,
> he considered, he considered and thought,
> 'Kind God, what shall I do, how shall I do it?
> What is the empire of my choice?
> Is it the empire of heaven?

> Is it the empire of the earth?
> And if I shall choose the empire of the earth,
> the empire of the earth is brief,
> heaven is everlasting.'
> And the emperor chose the empire of heaven
> above the empire of the earth.[5]

Central to many versions of the Lazar story is the dinner he holds on the eve of battle. In this version, which Vuk Karadžić wrote down, recollected from his father's recitations, Lazar drinks a toast to his knights until finally he comes to Miloš Obilić:

> Health to Milosh, the faithful traitor!
> first faithful, then a traitor!
> At Kosovo tomorrow you will desert me,
> you will run to Murad, the Emperor.

Angrily Obilić jumps up to defend himself and to lay bare the true traitor:

> I have never been any traitor,
> never shall be one,
> at Kosovo tomorrow I intend
> to die for the Christian faith.
> The traitor is sitting at your knee
> drinking cold wine under your skirts:
> Vuk Branković, I curse him.
> Tomorrow is lovely St Vitus day
> and we shall see in Kosovo field
> who is faithful, who is the traitor.
> The great God is my witness!
> Tomorrow I shall march on Kosovo,
> and I shall stab Murad, Tsar of Turkey,
> and stand up with his throat under my foot.
> And if God grants and my luck grants
> that I shall come home to Krushevats
> I shall take hold of Vuk Branković,
> and I shall tie him on my battle-lance
> like a woman's raw wool on a distaff,
> and carry him to Kosovo field.[6]

It was not to be. After killing Murad, Obilić is beheaded by the Turks. The Serbs, despite this shining example of self-sacrificial heroism from among their own ranks, go on to lose the battle as a result of the treachery of Vuk Branković. As an integral part of the myth, these key sequences have become central to Serbian historical and psychological consciousness – despite having no basis in historical fact. Let us take Branković first. Although in some early chronicles there were occasional hints that there might have been treachery at Kosovo, it was some two centuries before Branković was named as the traitor. Not until the nineteenth century did historians clear his name by studying direct sources. These showed that after the battle, despite tensions with Lazar's widow, the two had remained on good terms and that over the next few years Branković both submitted as a Turkish vassal and fought the Turks again. As far as myth was concerned, however, it was too late for Branković. When in 1847 Petar Petrović-Njegoš, the prince–bishop of Montenegro, published his seminal epic, *The Mountain Wreath*, he wrote that Kosovo had been lost because:

> Our Serbian chiefs, most miserable cowards,
> The Serbian stock did heinously betray.
> Thou, Branković, of stock despicable,
> Should one serve so his fatherland,
> Thus much is honesty esteem'd.[7]

As Rade Mihajlčić has written, 'Once legend, or one of its motifs, has found a way into literature in its original form then, even if it has not been perpetuated in the form of an epic poem, it becomes an integral part of the national cultural heritage.' In this way he argues that the Branković story is 'a legend which has become part of the reality, the foundation of a people's historical consciousness and awareness of its ethnic individuality'.[8] The Branković myth of treachery was needed as a way to explain the fall of the medieval state, and it has powerful seeds of self-replication contained within it. Throughout the war of 1991–5 no Serb ever ascribed a defeat to losing a battle fair and square. With monotonous regularity losses were always put down to secret deals – and treachery.

The Lazar story is only part of one of many epic tales which were told and retold through the ages. But because of the way it came to inspire the national struggle against the Turks beginning in 1804 and culminating with the end of the Balkan Wars in 1913, it is the most important. What was unique about the Lazar myth as opposed to others was its particular blend of history and Christian iconography. In this way Lazar becomes the Serbian Christ and Vuk Branković his Judas. Just as Jesus gathers his apostles around him at the Last Supper, so Lazar holds his own fateful last supper.

The idea that it is better to fight honourably and die than to live as slaves was not a Serbian invention and had existed in epic poetry since the times of classical antiquity. But it provided for the Serbs an explanation for their oppression by the Ottomans. It also identified the whole nation with the central guiding *raison d'être* of Christianity: resurrection. In other words Lazar opted for the empire of heaven, that is to say truth and justice, so that the state would one day be resurrected. An earthly kingdom was rejected in favour of nobler ideals – victimhood and sacrifice – and this choice is to be compared with the temptations of Christ. Professor Žarko Korać, professor of psychology at Belgrade University, believes that this point is so fundamental that 'it is not a metaphor, it is primordial':

> What it tells the Serbs is 'we are going to make a state again'. Just as Jesus is 'coming back' so is Lazar. It means that because we opted for the kingdom of heaven we cannot lose, and that is what people mean when they talk about the Serbs as a 'heavenly people'. In this way the Serbs identify themselves with the Jews. As victims, yes, but also with the idea of 'sacred soil'. The Jews said 'Next year in Jerusalem' and after 2000 years they recreated their state. The message is: 'We are victims, but we are going to survive.'

The Cult of Death

Today there is a tower on the field of Kosovo from which you can survey the surrounding countryside. In the distance there are hills, but a couple of kilometres from the tower there is a vast factory belching forth clouds of black smoke. It billows over the battlefield, so that even bright days are overshadowed by its grime. But the air of menace is not just above you. Nearby there is a military base, well barricaded to protect it from any surprise attack by ethnic Albanian militants. The soldiers from the base venture out, however, for manoeuvres and training. From the tower you can sometimes see tanks moving through the undergrowth over the medieval battlefield. Then thin lines of smoke spiral upwards as the Serbian soldiers settle down to cook their meals. You can also pick out the shapes of the men as they run, gather and take cover behind a domed, whitewashed *türbe* (a small Turkish mausoleum) in which, it is said, lie the remains of the sultan's standard-bearer. It is as though they are preparing for a new battle of Kosovo, which of course they may be. In recent years the tomb has been smashed and vandalised. Human excrement lies on the floor and bored conscripts have carved their names and thoughts on the walls.

In 1937 Rebecca West visited this *türbe* in which she says a man wearing 'a faded fez and neat but threadbare Western clothes' told her of the 'fame and gallantry' of the standard-bearer, 'in a set speech, unnaturally uttered from some brain-cell petrified by memory'. Asked who he was the man said that he was a descendant of the standard-bearer's servant 'in the sixteenth generation': 'My forefather was by him as he fell, he closed his dead master's eyes for him, he preserved his body and guarded it after it had been placed in this tomb. So have we all guarded him.' Contemptuously West noted that such people were 'sweet-sour phantoms, human wine gone to vinegar'.[9]

As for Sultan Murad, his entrails were extracted and his blood drained off. His body, suitably prepared for the journey, was then taken home to Bursa in Anatolia, where it was buried under a *türbe* which can be seen to this day. Likewise the entrails. They were entombed in Kosovo and a *türbe* erected to house them too. According to tradition the mausoleum was built on the precise spot where the sultan's tent stood during the battle and where he was supposed to have met his death. Unlike the *türbe* of his standard-bearer, this one remains in pristine condition. After the battle a family was brought from Bursa to take care of the monument. Incredibly, the Turbetari family, as they have inevitably come to be called, are still there – unlike the guardians of the battlefield's other *türbe*. The visitors' book is full of the signatures of passing Turks and also of local Albanians and Sandžak Muslims. Up until 1912 the Turbetaris were paid by Turkey, after which they passed on to the payroll of the Royal Yugoslav Government. After 1974 local politics intervened and the ethnic Turkish Turbetaris were displaced by Kosovo Albanians. In 1994, though, they reclaimed the work of their ancestors, and today Fahri Turbetari and his wife Sanija (a Sandžak Muslim) are employees of the Serbian Ministry of Culture.

Lazar's mortal remains were to be subject to an even more extra-ordinary life after death. The very first Serbian chronicles do not mention exactly how he died, but soon the priests were hard at work writing hagiographies about their new saint. The first records say no more than that Lazar, 'cut down by a sword blow, died a blissful death'.[10] Later the chroniclers began to say that he had been captured by the Turks, who had beheaded him. Some go so far as to claim that Murad himself or his son Bayezid chopped off Lazar's head. Some sources recount that Lazar's body was returned to Milica by Serbian vassal princes of the Turks who sought permission from Bayezid to perform this deed. Thereafter Lazar was laid to rest in nearby Priština, but in 1401 or 1402 Milica had his remains transferred to Ravanica, the monastery that Lazar had founded. His dried body was dressed in a coat adorned with lions rampant which he was reputed to have worn at the battle in which he met his death. He was also covered with a shroud of red cloth embroidered in gold with the prayer of the nun Jefimia: 'Don't forget your beloved children, who need your help, Oh Martyr!'[11]

At least in the early years of the despotate, Ravanica became the centre of a great cult which drew pilgrims from all over Serbia. Later the cult was to decline. But the bones were not to rest in peace. In 1690, Ravanica's monks fled with Patriarch Arsenije's great columns of refugees. Taking Lazar with them, they settled first in Szentendre (Sent Andreja) close to Buda (Budapest), but in 1697 they moved to a monastery in Srem, which they called Sremska Ravanica. There Lazar lay until 1942, when, after some Croatian Ustashas had stolen his golden rings, the Germans helped transfer the sacred bones to safety in Belgrade. There they stayed until 1987. During his years in Belgrade, Lazar's tomb in the patriarchate church became the focus of a modest pilgrimage, especially on St Vitus Day, or Vidovdan as the battle's anniversary is known, when candles were lit for him. In 1987 Lazar began his new great trek. As the prelude to their commemorations of the 600th anniversary of the battle, Lazar's bones were taken around Serbia and Bosnia from monastery to monastery, as Serbs again flocked in pilgrimage to pray before him. These were the beginnings of the years of euphoria which were to be followed so quickly by the war, the short-lived new Serbian Empire and its disastrous demise.

Today Lazar's shrivelled remains lie once more in Ravanica. On Sundays the coffin is opened but only his brown and withered hands peak out from under the new red and gold embroidered shroud. When the coffin is open it is covered with a plastic canopy to prevent people from touching the body. Despite this, the nun Mother Solomonija who watches over Lazar claims that 'He still makes miracles and cures diseases.' By the coffin is a large Serbian flag brought to Ravanica in 1989 by Serbs from Knin. It is, she says, a copy of Boško Jugović's banner.

Boško Jugović was the youngest of the nine sons of the old noble Jug Bogdan who all died at Kosovo, where, like their master, they would not bow down to the Turks. Boško Jugović has a special place in the epic tales. His sister was Milica, who sought permission from her husband Lazar to spare him from battle and keep him with her in Kruševac, from where the Serbian knights set out. She succeeded but Boško Jugović, carrying 'the flag with the cross', dismissed her, saying:

> Go home, sister, to the white tower;
> but I would never come back to you
> or give the flag of the cross out of my hands
> if the Tsar had given me Krushevats,
> so that my regiment would say:
> 'Look at that coward Boshko Jugovich,
> He dared not go down to Kosovo
> to spill his blood for the honourable cross
> and die for the faith of the Christians.'[12]

Or so says the tale. There is no historical evidence that Jug Bogdan or his sons existed.[13] This did not bother the Krajina Serbs, who with their gesture of copying the banner were paying homage to the mythic cause. Like Lazar, their leaders would not compromise or, as they saw it, bow down before the Croats, who in modern times were fulfilling the role once played by the Turks. With their utter defeat in 1995 the Krajina Serbs proved to their own satisfaction that it was 'better to die in battle' – or at least flee your ancestral home – than 'live in shame'. Mother Solomonija said she believed the Krajina Serbs had indeed made a Lazar's choice: 'They lost their possessions on earth but not in heaven. The Serbs are not vengeful, they can forgive. But I don't want to talk about Krajina. All those who have died will enjoy the kingdom of heaven, but those who tortured Serbs I wonder what will happen to them? We leave to the Lord to decide what happens to those who have committed crimes.'

Preserving the Message

Every generation of foreigners which has written about the Serbs has been surprised by the importance of the epic poem in Serbian cultural life and later on by the coincidence of the epic and history. As early as 1497 an Italian court poet wrote of exiled Slavs singing and 'jumping like goats' as they performed in a small Italian town during a visit of the Queen of Naples. In 1603 an English author discussed Serbian 'countrey songs' which sought to attribute the Ottoman conquest of Serbia to the treachery of some of its leaders.[14] In the 1840s the great German historian Leopold von Ranke became the first western historian to comment on the connection between poetry and Serbian history: 'the history of the nation, developed by its poetry, has through it been converted into a national property, and is thus preserved in the memory of the people'.[15] He also recorded that epics were performed both at home and publicly:

> At festivals and assemblies near the cloisters, parties stand forward who have devoted themselves exclusively to singing – including the blind; who, however – especially in Servia – are oftener singers than composers of songs. Men of real poetic talent, like Philip Wishnitsch [Filip Višnjić] from Bosnia, are occasionally met with, who collect a circle around them, and often move their audience to tears.[16]

Filip Višnjić not only regaled the revolutionaries of the first Serbian uprising of 1804–13 with tales of past heroes but wove them together with contemporary politics and fighting into his own poems. In this way he and other poets bridged an historical gap, binding the revolutionaries, in their minds, with Lazar's knights and the spirit of Kosovo. Such a connection was recorded by Sir Arthur Evans, the British archaeologist who was later to gain fame for his work at Knossos in Crete. Travelling in Bosnia during the uprisings against the Turks in 1875 he watched the performance of an epic which was accompanied by the one-string gusla, an instrument that survives to this day:

> what carried one back into epic days at once was a . . . gathering, form-ing a spacious ring lit up by a blazing fire, in the middle of which a Bosniac bard took his seat on a rough log, and tuning his ghuzla began to pour forth one of the grand sagas of his race. . . . Without a book or any aid to memory he rolled out the ballad for hour after hour. . . . perchance it told how Czar Dushan marched to seize the city of the Caesars; or of the finding of Knez Lazar and the sad day of Kossovo. . . . For in this land, without books, without history, it is these heroic lays . . . that keep alive from generation to generation the sacred traditions of the race. In the days of bondage these have been the one proud heirloom of the Serbian people from the Adriatic to the Danube. Their spirit has been continually refreshed from the perennial fount of epic song.

'An ecstatic thrill would run through the whole circle,' wrote Evans, 'and find utterance in inarticulate murmurs of delight.' Most remark-able, however, was an observation Evans made which has a resounding echo today. That is that the epic song makes 'the Bosnian Serb . . . forget the narrower traditions of his half alien kingdom in these more glorious legends, which override the cant of geographers and diplomatists, and make him see a brother in the Serb of the Black Mountain or Old Serbia, or the free Principality'.[17] The half-alien kingdom is Bosnia, while the Black Mountain is Montenegro, Old Serbia is Sandžak and Kosovo, and the principality is Serbia itself.

The tradition of epic poetry was to decline in Serbia after 1815 as the country gained first autonomy from the Turks and later independence. That did not mean that it vanished; it is simply that, unlike in Bosnia and other regions remaining under the Turks, a modern European society began to be introduced and its significance declined. For this reason the critic Svetozar Koljević has described the work of Filip Višnjić as the swansong of the epic tradition.[18] While modern politics and the Kosovo cycle were no longer mixed, it does not mean that the epics lost their power to inspire. In 1915 John Reed, the American journalist immortalised in the film *Reds*, which was based on his experiences during the Russian Revolution, wrote his accounts of wartime travel through the Balkans. He was clearly impressed by the Gypsy musicians who accompanied the Serbian troops:

Every regiment has two or three gypsies, who march with the troops, playing the Serbian fiddle or the bagpipes, and accompany the songs that are composed incessantly by the soldiers – love songs, celebrations of victory, epic chants. And all through Serbia they are the musicians of the people, travelling from one country festa to another, playing for dancing and singing.'[19]

Gypsies are still a mainstay of the modern Serbian musical scene and their bands can frequently be seen trailing through the streets as they move from party to party or restaurant to restaurant to earn their living. Serbs themselves still perform their own epic songs or traditional dances, but in recent decades they have inevitably become characterised as part of folklore. However, even this does not mean that their power is dead. A most graphic example was given in August 1991 when the war in Croatia was beginning to get under way. In the village of Strmica, which sits under the mountains on the borders of Bosnia, rebel Serbs of the Krajina region had organised a music and dance festival. As night fell, thunder rolled in the distance. On the stage, pigskin bagpipes wailed out into the night, accompanied by guslas and by singing and chanting. Some 2,500 came to listen to the music and to take courage from it. In the front row sat Milan Martić, the local police chief. Dressed in military fatigues he looked every inch the true warlord he was to become. At his feet sat a gaggle of little children. Henri Wijnaendts, the first of any number of European Community envoys, had just been to see him. Asked about the visit Martić said he could not remember the man's name but recalled dismissively that 'he was bald and had glasses'. On stage a singer whined out the lines: 'Krajina, our mother/We won't leave you to the Ustashas.'

Today no Serbs remain in Strmica, which was recaptured by the Croats in 1995. Back then, though, intoxicated by the music the Krajina Serbs were upbeat. 'It's the spirit of victory,' said Snežana, aged twenty-three. 'We'll beat the hell out of them,' said Jovan, her twenty-five-year-old husband. Asked if anyone was laying in stocks of food for the coming war one woman replied incredulously, 'Why should we? We'll defeat them in five days.'

In 1992 the film director Paul Pawlikowski made an extraordinary documentary for the BBC. He persuaded Radovan Karadžić, the Bosnian Serb leader, to play a gusla in the preserved house of Vuk Karadžić and to sing a favourite epic. In a later scene Karadžić looked down on a besieged Sarajevo with Eduard Limonov, a Russian writer, and told him about the poetry he had had published. He recounted how more than two decades ago he had written a poem beginning:

> I can hear disaster walking,
> The city is burning . . .

'Everything I saw in terms of a fight, in terms of war, in army terms,' said Karadžić.

Even more stunning were the soldier gusla players Pawlikowski found who were singing for a new generation of Serbian warriors. Not only did they sing the old songs: 'Oh, beautiful Turkish daughter/Our monks will soon baptise you,' but they also composed new ones to suit the situation: 'Sarajevo in the valley/The Serbs have encircled you.' As Karadžić prepared to depart for Geneva for peace talks, one gusla singer compared him to Karadjordje, who had led the first uprising against the Turks in 1804:

> Hey, Radovan, you man of steel!
> The greatest leader since Karadjordje!
> Defend our freedom and our faith,
> On the shores of Lake Geneva.[20]

The Heavenly State

While migrations scattered the Serbs and history and poetry struggled to keep them together, it was religion and language that set them apart from their neighbours. A village that spoke Albanian or Hungarian was clearly not a Serbian one, but such a distinction did not apply when the neighbours spoke more or less the same language. Such was the case in the lands where most Serbs came to live. What made them Serbs then was religion. Although there have been anomalies in history, the vast majority of Serbs have always identified themselves as such, or have even become Serbs, as a result of being Orthodox – as opposed to being Muslim or Catholic. In an age before nationalism Serbs would just as often identify themselves as Orthodox and Croats as Catholic; and in cases where their ethnic origins may have been neither Serb nor Croat but rather Vlach it was this religious identity which eventually made them Serbs and Croats. Today the vast majority of Serbs are not religious; but few would deny they were Orthodox.

The fact that the Serbs are Orthodox and the Croats Catholics is the result of historical accident. In 380 the Emperor Theodosius, who ruled the eastern half of the Roman Empire, decreed that his subjects would be Christians according to the formula laid down by the Council of Nicaea in 325. Henceforth the language of the Byzantine church was Greek, while that of the Roman church was Latin. When the empire was definitively split in 395, the line of division in Europe ran south along the Drina river. Roughly speaking modern Croatia and Bosnia lay to its west, with the regions of modern Serbia and Macedonia to its east. This division was to take place more than 200 years before the pagan

Slavs even migrated to the region, but so long-lasting was to be its legacy that we are still living with the results today.

The final break between the churches did not come until 1054. In the meantime another event had occurred that was to have a fundamental influence on the course of history. In the late eighth century the monks Cyril and Methodius developed a Slavic script called Glagolitic. Refined by their disciples, this alphabet, which later came to be called Cyrillic, was to be adopted by the Bulgarians, the Serbs and the Russians. For the Serbs, then, Cyrillic has always been another badge of Serbdom, which has complemented Orthodoxy and yet again set them apart from their Muslim and Catholic neighbours. In modern times nationalists bewailed the fact that many Serbs in Croatia were becoming assimilated because they did not know how to write in Cyrillic.

While it was the brilliance of St Sava which led to the foundation of the Serbian autocephalous church, it was the way the Turks ran their empire that gave that church a chance to survive. The *millet* system left to the local Christian leaders and the Jews many prerogatives of governance and taxation under the umbrella of the sultan. Though Christians and Jews were thus in all respects second-class subjects, they were regarded as 'peoples of the Book'. Anyone who converted to Islam became a first-class subject and could then hold public office and prosper within the system. How the Serbs fared under this religious dispensation varied with time.

After the conquest, Serbian society was to undergo radical changes. Above all, there was no longer an aristocratic class to dominate or lead the people, because its members had either fled or been killed. However, Sava had organised society to rest on two pillars, the state and the church. The first was gone, but the second survived. After 1459, however, the patriarchate at Peć fell into desuetude. But by 1557 another accident of history was radically to revive church and Serbian fortunes. The historian George Tomashevich has argued that after the great Hungarian defeat at Mohacs in 1527 Serbian clerics finally realised that:

> unwelcome Turkish domination was not to end in the foreseeable future. For this reason, and in order to secure their physical and cultural survival, the Serbian church and its flock had to prepare for the long haul ahead.
>
> The Balkan and Central European lands inhabited by the Serbs in the sixteenth century were of considerable economic and strategic importance to the Ottoman Empire. Isolated from the unconquered Christian countries from which no help was conceivable, the Serbs began to seek a new *modus vivendi*.[21]

In their bid to do this, Serbian churchmen began to campaign for the restoration of the Peć patriarchate. In this they came to be helped by a twist of fortune. Suleiman the Magnificent's grand vizier of the time was Mehmed Sokollu, born Sokolović, a Bosnian Serb. He had arrived at his exalted position because as a boy he had been taken, like tens of thousands of others, as a tribute by the Turks. These children, converted to Islam, were the men who made up the fearsome Janissary corps and also provided able civil servants for the empire. Sokollu kept in close touch with his homeland and his people and presumably felt that because of their strategic location 'a major gesture of reconciliation' was opportune.[22] Thanks to his interventions with the sultan, the patriarchate was restored in 1557 and Makarije, a member of the Sokolović clan, became its first new head.[23]

Under Makarije, the church was dramatically reorganised and rejuvenated. In this way it revived to play its historic role. So, as the medieval peasant went to church, he saw on the walls frescoes not just of religious themes but also of the Nemanjić kings, who, since they had almost all been canonised, found their places among the apostles. Many medieval churches, such as those at Peć, Studenica and Gračanica, were restored and many other new buildings were completed. Later, as the Ottoman state decayed and life became harder under more arbitrary and corrupt rule, the Nemanjić era was ever more remembered as a golden age. The harsh realities of feudalism were forgotten and the glories of Dušan's empire hallowed, as was the memory of Lazar and his noble knights.

Sokollu was assassinated in 1578, but it was some years before the situation in Serbia began to deteriorate. The church had just enough time to make its reforms. Between 1593 and 1606 the Habsburgs and the Turks were at war again and, fully expecting liberation, many Serbs threw themselves into the conflict. Especially in the north, in Hungary, in the Banat and around Timişoara, there was heavy fighting. Bishop Teodor of Vršac was in contact both with the Habsburgs and with the rebels. Ultimately Austria's peace with the Turks left the Serbs with nothing gained. Teodor was skinned alive and the patriarch hanged. As many of the rebels had painted St Sava's figure on to their flags, his remains were exhumed and brought to Vračar near Belgrade, where they were burned.

The church faced difficult years ahead, but it maintained its position as the sole institution keeping alive the idea of 'Serbdom' under the Turks. Thanks to this, most Serbs retained their Orthodox and thus Serbian identity. This contrasted with Bosnia, where, lacking a strong national church, many people had converted to Islam following the conquest in 1463.

There is a footnote to the Sokollu story: another member of the

Sokolović family, Ferhad Pasha, was to become the first pasha or governor of Bosnia, in 1580. Just before that, in 1579, he had built a magnificent mosque in Banja Luka with the ransom money he had extracted from the family of his Austrian prisoner Count Wolf Engelhard von Ausperg. When Serbian terror took hold of northern Bosnia in 1992, the Ferhad Pasha mosque and the adjoining community building became the centre for Muslim self-help and co-ordination. In what was to become a routine act of cultural vandalism, the mosque was blown up in 1993 and the rubble thrown on the municipal rubbish dump. The irony is that if it had not been for the Sokolović/Sokollu clan, there might have been no Serbs in Bosnia today.

Despite the setbacks of the early seventeenth century, not only did the church continue to preserve the Serbian national idea but its leaders saw their role as more than just serving God. The most famous example is that of Patriarch Arsenije, who welcomed the imperial army led by General Piccolomini which reached Kosovo and Skopje in 1689. When the imperial forces were routed, together with the Serbs who had risen in support, the patriarch led tens of thousands of his people into exile. The figure most often given is 30,000 families, but families were far larger then than they are today, perhaps as large as a small clan. At any rate, the numbers involved were considerable.

Although many believed that they would soon be returning home, the prudent patriarch refused to cross into Habsburg lands until he had received assurances that Orthodox religious rights would be guaranteed within the empire. This wish was granted and in this way the main focus of Serbian church and spiritual life was to shift from Kosovo in the south to Hungary in the north. After so many examples of Serbian disobedience towards the sultan, the Serbian church was eventually put under the control of Hellenising Greek Orthodox bishops known as the phanariots, but a 'pure' Serbian church was kept alive in what was to become the new patriarchate of Sremski Karlovci on the Danube in Habsburg southern Hungary.

It is impossible to underestimate the historical role of the church in keeping alive the idea of Serbia and its notion that one day the old state would, Christ-like, be resurrected. Under the Turks the Serbs tended to live in self-contained village and extended family communities called *zadrugas*, but it was the church, however weak it may have been at times, which gave people a glorious past to look back on and hence a hope for the future. Periodically the Turks would raid churches, hunt for gold and dig out the eyes of saints and Serbian kings immortalised in frescoes. For the people of these communities Serbia was a heavenly place, a place in the skies that they could dream of secretly in the darkest of times. And they were often dark. In the 1670s Edward Brown, the author of a *Brief Account of Some Travels in Divers Parts of Europe*, wrote this description after travelling through Serbia and Macedonia:

> I could not but pity the poor Christians, seeing under what fear they lived in those parts; and I observed them to make way as they perceived us coming toward them. In Macedonia the men and women would betake themselves into the woods to avoid us; and we took the pains sometimes to ride after them, to undeceive them of their folly and needless Frights. . . . But that which moved me most, was the spectacle of Captives and Slaves, which are often met in those countries.[24]

Although Bishop Jovan of Šabac-Valjevo in the 1980s made the following remark, it is not hard to imagine how, especially during times of strife and war, many Serbs would have thought in similar ways in times past, albeit with Turks taking the place of Croatian Ustashas:

> Since Prince Lazar and [the Battle of] Kosovo the Serbs, above all, have been creating HEAVENLY SERBIA, which today must certainly have grown, to become the largest state in heaven. If we only think of those innocent victims of the last war, millions and millions of Serbian men, women and children killed or tortured in the most terrible way or thrown into pits by Ustasha criminals, then we can understand that today's Serbian empire is in the heavens.[25]

4

RESURRECTION AND BEYOND

In 1664 a history published in England dismissed 'Servia', as it was then called, in a couple of contemptuous lines: 'The country was rich till the Turks got it, being stored with mines of Gold and Silver. . . . The people are rude and gross, and notable wine-bibbers; so false that little credit is to be given to them.'[1] A French encyclopaedia published in 1765 had even less to say and some of that was wrong: 'The whole of Servia is today depopulated, without culture or money. One may count there barely a thousand Christians, under a Latin [sic] archbishop that the Turks tolerate.'[2]

By contrast Edward Brown's account of his travels in the 1670s is far more valuable. He found Belgrade, at the confluence of the Danube and Sava rivers, a bustling Turkish city full of Armenian, Greek and Jewish traders. The Ragusans (Dubrovnikers) and the 'Eastern Merchants of Vienna' also had their 'factories' in Belgrade.[3] It is important here to note that he makes no mention of Serbs. The reason is that under Ottoman rule towns were mostly populated by Turks and other Muslims. The Serbs, being peasants, lived in the countryside. This phenomenon was not unusual. In other parts of eastern Europe, Jews and Germans were often the townspeople while the 'native' population lived in the villages. In Transylvania the majority Romanian population were the peasants, while the Hungarians and Saxon Germans dominated the towns.

In his account Brown describes how goods from central Serbia and parts of Bulgaria were brought by boat up the Morava river and then shipped along the Danube into which it flows. Coming the other way were goods from Austria, Hungary and other countries, salt in particular. As he moved south he found the land 'a fruitful and pleasant country' with 'stout men', good horses and wines. What a pity, he ruminated, that it was not in the hands of the Christians 'of the temper of those in the western part of Europe. . . . it might make a flourishing country'.[4]

Brown was writing in the years before a renewed outbreak of war between the Turks and the Austrians. In 1690 this was to lead to defeat and Patriarch Arsenije's famous migration. The next one hundred years were a period of alternating war and peace. They were also to set in train the developments which were to lead to the first Serbian uprising of 1804, to autonomy and ultimately to full independence in 1878. In July 1876, the reporter of the *Illustrated London News* gave a colourful account of Belgrade, which by now was an overwhelmingly Serbian city. But he found it a town which still hung between two worlds. 'Belgrade', he wrote, 'in its architecture is Cairo and Paris in equal proportions.' As in architecture, he noted, 'so in costume – the east and west meet in Belgrade':

> Look at the stately gentleman promenading. . . . he might be a hadji, with that fine dignified face of the genuine 'old Turk' type. He wears a red and yellow ephod-like waistcoat, a scarlet fez, a short, braided, brown jacket, with a cape to it, and a long voluminous kilt, or rather petticoat, of white flannel edged with black braid and slashed at the bottom.

By contrast soldiers were dressed in a uniform 'something between the French and Italian':

> They carry a sword-bayonet, and every man is armed with a pistol, carried in a leather case on the left side over sword-belt. Pistols seem the special weapons of the Servians; quite two thirds of the civilians go armed with them, and the great majority of those who cannot afford pistols carry long straight daggers that look extremely vicious.

At one point a soldier comes marching down a main street beating 'a bickering rub-a-dub' on a drum. This is to draw a crowd because the soldier is a 'military common crier, sent out into the highways with the duty of proclaiming the tidings from the front'. Among those who gather are 'ladies dressed in the western fashion' and 'women of the people . . . full fleshed, comely dames', sporting black fezzes and red tassels: 'Take them all in all, with their fezzes and their loose robes, these people of Belgrade have a wonderfully Turkish look about them. But how they hate the Turks!'[5]

From Pig Dealers to Princes

Djordje Petrović (*c.* 1768–1817), known as Karadjordje or Black George, the man who was to lead the first Serbian uprising of 1804, was violent, intrepid and brave. He had his stepfather killed during an earlier bout of fighting with the Turks for refusing to flee the enemy when it was deemed necessary to withdraw. During the rebellion he had his brother hung for rape: to drive the point home he then invited the Serbian leadership to dinner while the body dangled from his front gate. Today the figure of Karadjordje continues to brood over Serbia. Not only did this illiterate man of peasant stock beget a royal dynasty but, like all Serbian leaders ever since, he engaged in infighting to the detriment of the general good. He also began the tradition of attempting to play off the great powers one against the other while simultaneously seeking their support. Like many other future Serbian leaders he was to die a violent death. He was murdered by Miloš Obrenović, the founder of Serbia's rival royal family.

The Austro-Turkish wars of the eighteenth century saw tremendous upheaval in Serbian society, especially in the Ottoman Belgrade pashalik or province. Between 1718 and 1739 the Habsburgs had occupied the pashalik and, although they put it under a harsh form of martial law, a legal entity called the Kingdom of Serbia existed for the first time since the middle ages. During the Austro-Turkish war of 1788–91 the Austrians organised units of Serbian Freikorps or volunteers, who fought valiantly deep inside the country under Koča Andjelković. But following the French Revolution the Austrians signed the Treaty of Sistova, withdrew their troops and abandoned the Serbs to the Turks. This war-cum-rebellion, known to the Serbs as the Kočina Krajina after Andjelković, then collapsed. However, a new generation of Serbs from the Belgrade pashalik now had considerable military experience. Even more important, according to the historian Michael Petrovich, was the lesson drawn by the Serbs from the war: 'it convinced them that, however useful foreign support was, in the final analysis they had to look to themselves and their own resources'.[6]

Throughout this period the pashalik's demography was also changing. Serbs were migrating again. Although the wars meant that large numbers of people periodically fled to areas under Habsburg control, the relatively rich lands of the pashalik, described above by Brown, simultaneously acted as a magnet. Serbs came escaping poverty either from the mountains of Montenegro and Hercegovina or from Kosovo and Sandžak. Karadjordje's family, for example, originally came from Montenegro. Jovan Cvijić, Serbia's foremost geographer and anthropologist, estimated that during the eighteenth and nineteenth centuries as many as half a million Serbs arrived in that part of Serbia, which had become, or was to become, the nucleus of the Serbian state.

At the same time the Muslim population of the pashalik declined as it became an ever more insecure place for them to live. Muslims were referred to collectively as 'Turks', but most of them were not in fact ethnic Turks. Many were Bosnian Muslims, Albanians and Muslims from other parts of the Ottoman Empire.

Following the Treaty of Sistova, Sultan Selim was keen to appease the Serbs, but his power was waning. He introduced a highly liberal regime for the frontier province which amounted to giving it autonomy. However, his plans were scotched by the marauding Janissaries. Once the crack military men of the Ottoman Empire, they had by now degenerated into a mercenary corps putting themselves at the disposal of a number of rebellious Turkish warlords ruling their own fiefs in defiance of the sultan. The most important of these were Pasvanoglu of Vidin in Bulgaria and Ali Pasha of Janinna (Ionannina), now in northern Greece.

With the restoration of Ottoman rule in the pashalik, the Janissaries returned. They began to terrorise the Serbs and much of the Muslim population in their quest for plunder and taxes. The Serbian Hajduks – bandits-cum-outlaws-cum-freedom fighters – took to the hills, but soon the sultan approved the organisation of a Serbian army to fight the Janissaries. With Napoleon campaigning in Ottoman Egypt, however, he was soon forced to make peace with them. By 1802, the Dahis (the four top Janissary commanders) ruled the province. Local leaders, including Karadjordje, a swine dealer who had fought both in the Austrian Freikorps and in the Turkish-organised Serbian army, began to plot their removal. But the Dahis struck first. In early 1804 they executed up to 150 of the Serbian knezes or local leaders in an operation they called 'The Cutting Down of the Chiefs'. It was this that provoked the rebellion. At first the Serbs did not claim to be fighting to rid themselves of Ottoman domination but rather claimed to be rebelling in the name of the sultan against the repressive Dahis. Karadjordje was elected as leader of the uprising on 14 February 1804. He soon succeeded in liberating almost all of the pashalik, especially after the sultan ordered forces from Bosnia to intervene to finish off the Dahis.

At this early stage, the Serbs were joined by at least part of the pashalik's Muslim population, whom the Serbs called the 'Good Turks', and who were also keen to rid themselves of the rapacious Dahis. However, as the Serb aim soon changed to a demand for complete independence, co-operation rapidly turned to confrontation and massacre.

In the negotiations that followed the defeat of the Dahis, the Serbs demanded the restoration of their autonomy, but the Turks became alarmed. The rebels were making contact with Serbs in other parts of the Ottoman Empire and with semi-independent Montenegro. Karadjordje had also sent a delegation to Russia to appeal for help, and he was talking 'of throwing off the yoke that the Serb has borne since Kosovo'.[7] Another Ottoman army was sent to crush the rebels, but it was soundly beaten at Ivankovac on 18 August 1805. Meeting in Smederevo in 1805, the insurgents decided not only to repudiate the pashalik's annual tribute to the sultan but to take the struggle beyond the borders of the province. In reply a *jihad* or holy war was declared against them.

At the end of 1806, Russia went to war with the Ottomans, and the Serbs were encouraged to keep fighting. A modest Russian force was sent to fight alongside the Serbs. Within weeks, though, the Russians and the Turks signed the Treaty of Slobozia, in which neither side bothered to mention the Serbs. Talks between the Turks, Russians, Austrians and French followed. What was emerging was the beginning of the Serbian problem. This meant that every few decades the Serbs would burst back upon the international stage, causing uproar and what was regarded in the chancelleries of Europe as a general nuisance. The discussions in March 1808 between Caulaincourt, the French ambassador to St Petersburg, and Count Rumiantsev, the Russian chief minister, perfectly exemplify this attitude. At one point the Russian indicates that his country would like to control Serbia, but he informs Caulaincourt that this is not a very high priority. He then suggests that maybe Serbia could be given:

> to an archduke of a cadet branch or to some European prince, a Coburg for example . . . or to someone else entirely. If you wish to oblige us, give it as a dowry to one of our grand duchesses, even as the property of her husband, if you think this is necessary. As she would be of the Orthodox faith, she could win over for the prince whom she married all the inhab-itants of that country. They are more than fanatics and, as I propose this, I am convinced that I shall contribute to the cause of peace and indicate the only means of keeping order among those savages.

Caulaincourt thought the scheme a good one but observed that its glaring problem was that 'Serbia would be a poor dowry for a grand duchess who would be obliged to live in it.'[8] Nothing came of the idea, but it is not hard to see why, ever since then, the Serbs have regarded Russia with deep suspicion, despite its frequent extension of diplomatic protection to them. While the Russians have been happy to play the Orthodox or pan-Slav card when it has suited them the Serbs have always been conscious that there is no real love lost between the two countries. When push comes to shove Russia has always abandoned the 'savages'. During the war of 1991–5 much nonsense was written in the west about the great history of the Serbo-Russian alliance. But, as the Russians did virtually nothing to help the Serbs, it seems that the 'sav-ages' attitude has continued to prevail. Most memorably Vitali Churkin, a Russian special envoy, once stormed out of a meeting with Bosnian Serb leaders accusing them of being 'sick with the madness of war'.

In 1809, fighting between the Serbs and Turks resumed, with some

Russian help. However, Russia soon needed to muster all its strength to counter Napoleon's campaign of 1812, so a peace treaty was concluded in Bucharest with the Turks. It specified that Serbia would revert to Ottoman rule, with the proviso that there would be a general amnesty for participants in the insurrection. The Serbs rejected this, but their defences collapsed in the ensuing Turkish onslaught. Karadjordje fled, along with thousands of refugees, who sought protection in the Habsburg provinces, Wallachia and Russia. The Turkish vengeance was terrible. Villages were burned and thousands were sent into slavery. On 17 October 1813 alone, 1,800 women and children were sold as slaves in Belgrade.[9] Soon afterwards a halt was called to the reprisals, and many of the refugees began returning. Some of the former insurgent leaders, such as Miloš Obrenović from the Rudnik district (who had not fled), now made their peace with the Turks, who confirmed them in their local positions of power. It was an untenable situation, however. In 1814, one of Karadjordje's former commanders started a new rebellion, but it did not catch on. In the wake of the fresh reprisals following its defeat, however, preparations were made for yet another uprising. Led by Obrenović, the rebels had by mid-July 1815 succeeded in freeing a large part of the pashalik.

Just as before, it was the international situation which helped shape developments. With Napoleon defeated at Waterloo in 1815, the Turks were wary of the Russians in case they intervened again on behalf of the Serbs. So, after much negotiation, a deal was struck with Obrenović. The Belgrade pashalik was to become an autonomous province. Serbian chiefs were granted the right to collect taxes, but the Turks could remain only in the towns and forts of the province.

Obrenović was born in 1783 into a poor family which had originally come to Serbia from Hercegovina. As a child he tended cattle for his neighbours and later joined his brother, who had his own livestock business. He was a brave commander in the first uprising and after the second he proved himself a shrewd but brutal and murderous politician. He constantly sought increased concessions from the Turks while he gradually undermined their residual power in Serbia. In 1817, influenced by Philike Hetairia, the Greek revolutionary secret society, Karadjordje slipped back into Serbia. Sensing danger for both himself and his plans, Obrenović sent his agents who murdered Karadjordje with an axe. His skinned head was stuffed and sent to the sultan. This act was to spark off a feud between the families which was periodically to convulse Serbian politics until 1903. Then the last Obrenović and his wife were murdered by being thrown out of the palace windows in Belgrade. The hapless King Aleksandar allegedly grabbed the parapet, but he fell to his death after one of the conspirators used his sword to chop off his fingers.[10]

Miloš Obrenović was as rapacious as any Turk had been in collecting taxes. As his rule became ever more oppressive, there were seven rebellions against him including three major uprisings between 1815 and 1830. In 1830 the sultan nonetheless formally accepted Miloš' hereditary princeship. By 1833 autonomous Serbia's boundaries had been expanded and Miloš had secured an Ottoman commitment that the Turkish and Muslim population not connected to the Turkish garrisons would, in time, be compelled to leave.[11] Miloš was helped in his accumulation of power by the increasingly rapid decline in Ottoman authority. Turkish pashas in Bosnia and Albania were in revolt, there was an uprising in the Danubian principalities as well as the Greek revolution of 1821 and another round of Russo-Turkish fighting between 1828 and 1829. Treaties between the Russians and Turks in 1826 (Akkerman) and 1829 (Adrianople) reaffirmed Serbia's autonomy and Russia extended it some diplomatic protection among the European powers. Domestically a police force was introduced and, although a Serbian army was not permitted, Miloš retained a personal 'guard'. Every taxpayer was compelled to keep a gun and some military equipment, and some men were sent for military training to Russia.

Before 1804 the Austro-Turkish wars and the waves of Serbs in flight and of those immigrating from the mountain regions had already revolutionised society. Not only had the Serbs of the pashalik become highly militarised but agricultural patterns changed too. The most important of these was the custom of pig breeding, which the mountaineers brought with them. This led to increasing trade with Austria and the Habsburg Empire, which in turn contributed to the rise of a Serbian merchant class, both in Habsburg territories and in the pashalik itself. These men, travelling between Serbia and the Habsburg Empire, brought back with them not just trade and wealth but ideas and books too. Highly influential were Jovan Rajić's history of the Slavs published in 1768 and Hristofor Žefarović's *Stemmatographia* printed in Vienna in 1741. The latter was an adaptation of an existing collection of portraits and coats of arms of Slav saints, monarchs and bishops. As it linked them in one volume with the exiled Serbian Patriarch Arsenije IV Jovanović-Šakabenta, the suggestion was that he was the true heir of the Nemanjas, and as such the book was a major intellectual influence in the development and modernisation of the national idea.[12] Arsenije IV had taken refuge in Habsburg territory in 1737 after leading a second 'Great Migration', just like his predecessor in 1690.

An example of this influence can be found in the banners of Karadjordje's men, which were decorated with a coat of arms of a mysterious pre-Slavic tribe called the Tribalians taken from the *Stemmatographia*.[13] Its centrepiece was the image of a severed pig's head pierced through the eye with an arrow. Karadjordje picked for his personal seal the double-headed Nemanjić eagle, which was also found in the book. The modern coat of arms, which has been in use ever since the days of the principality, is also in Žefarović's book. It is a square cross flanked by four letters 'C', that is four Cyrillic 'S' characters. Originally they were meant to be not letters but representations of fire-lighting flints. Now, however, most Serbs believe that the four-'S' symbol stands for the motto 'Only Unity Saves the Serbs'.

Throughout the first uprising, many Serbian soldiers came from Srem and Vojvodina, Military Frontier areas close to the border, to fight for Karadjordje. Many exceptional and well-educated men also came to do their bit for the cause. Among them was Dositej Obradović, a former monk who had travelled as far as England. Vuk Karadžić, who although born in Serbia spent much of his life outside, also played a role. It was because of men like this that Serbia began to move from a war-ravaged peasant land to rejoin the European mainstream from which it had been cut off by centuries of Ottoman domination. Obradović was minister of education between 1808 and 1811 and under his patronage the Great School, the country's first institution of higher education, was opened in Belgrade. By 1813 there were forty schools in the province, attended by 1,500 pupils.

Vuk Karadžić's contribution was even more important. First, there was his collection of Serbian epic poems, which rendered them accessible to the emerging literate classes and enabled them to play an important role in the growth of the new nationalism. Karadžić's other contributions were in the fields of literary language reform and the development of a Cyrillic suitable for modern Serbian. Karadžić's work was also to have a fundamental impact on the development of the national idea as he began to reformulate the whole concept of nation and nationality.

In 1831 the first printing press opened. It printed not only books but all sorts of posters and poems too. Curiously one of the first things ever printed in the new Serbia was a flier inviting Belgradians to come and see an elephant which was being exhibited on a boat moored on the River Sava. Adorned with a picture and the word 'Elephant', a statement by one Emile Leserve in Serbian and Turkish told Belgrade: 'He has a big trunk, is very big and was seen in Paris, Vienna and Pest with the greatest of pleasure by the most distinguished of gentlemen. He is 12 foot high and 11 years old. He was born on a ship travelling from Ceylon to London. Since his youth he has been trained in the best way and he has become one of the most skilful elephants ever seen.'[14]

In 1837 the first bookshop was opened, and soon became a centre for literary activity. Until then the major Serbian newspaper, *Srpske Novine*, was published in Vienna, but gradually newspapers began to be published in the principality too. Belgrade was rapidly turning into a

Serbian town and losing its Turkish and Muslim character. Old prints of the city show an abundance of minarets breaking the skyline. The mosques were demolished and today only one remains.

From the 1830s Serbia began to develop an identity on the fringes of Central European society rather than as a subjugated province on the periphery of the rotting Ottoman Empire. Until 1903 the dynasty oscillated between heirs of Karadjordje and those of Miloš Obrenović, and although much energy was devoted to their political struggle much was also invested in building state institutions. The last Turkish soldiers were to leave in 1867 and the country was to receive full international recognition in 1878 at the Congress of Berlin.

From History into Ideology

Ilija Garašanin (1812–74) is one of the towering figures of Serbian history, because he was the first Serbian politician to articulate a national ideology. His father had been a fighter in the revolution of 1804 but had fallen foul of Mihailo Obrenović, who ruled (for the first time) between 1840 and 1842, after his father Miloš had been forced into exile. Accused of treachery, the eighty-year-old Milutin Garašanin had been beheaded and, in the traditional Turkish manner, had had his head impaled on a stake beside the road. Ilija's brother Luka suffered the same fate, but with the added indignity of having a lighted pipe stuffed into his mouth. After Mihailo was packed off into exile Aleksandar Karadjordjević, the lacklustre son of the revolutionary hero, was made prince. He was to rule until 1860.

Garašanin had been well educated and after beginning his career in the fledgling Serbian customs service he moved rapidly upwards. Between 1844 and 1852 he was minister of the interior. In this post he began transforming Serbia from a backward Turkish province, still nominally an Ottoman tributary, into a modern European state. Among his innovations was the introduction of a disciplined bureaucracy and police force. Above all Garašanin is remembered for his *Načertanije*, or draft plan, a document which laid out the Serbian principality's long-term foreign policy objectives. The text, which was kept secret until 1906, was submitted to Prince Aleksandar and for all of Garašanin's time in power, which included a second spell between 1861 and 1867, he did not cease to work for its fulfilment. Although Metropolitan Stefan Stratimirović of Sremski Karlovci had suggested the foundation of a great new 'Slavo-Serbian' empire in 1804, it was only under Garašanin that such ideas began to find concrete expression.

Načertanije is a blueprint for a Greater Serbia, and in the past few years Garašanin has been made out by Serbia's enemies to be some sort of diabolical figure intent on the conquest and subjugation of all non-Serbs in the Balkans. Such suggestions take Garašanin's ideas out of the context of his times. As Serbia was then the only emerging independent Slav Balkan state (excepting tiny Montenegro), Garašanin took it as read that it should dominate the region once the Ottoman Empire collapsed. This, he argued, was a necessity, because if the Serbs did not take clear steps to establish their predominance, the Balkans risked being partitioned between the Russians and the Austrians when Turkish power did finally fall. Failing that, small and weak Christian principalities might emerge which would be dominated by foreign powers. Garašanin argued that to escape this fate the Serbs had to take a lead in provoking rebellion in the Ottoman provinces – in this way Serbia would be in the best possible position to pick up the spoils of empire and so reunite the Serbs around Belgrade. He was less certain about the Habsburg lands but, as it happened, his first major challenge came in 1848 in Vojvodina, then part of southern Hungary.

Before writing *Načertanije*, Garašanin had been in contact with Polish and Czech émigrés who had hoped that the emerging Serbian state was going to be both the motor of liberation for Europe's Slavs and an alternative to Russian influence in the Balkans. The main leader of this movement was the Pole (and former Russian foreign minister) Adam Czartoryski, who lived in exile in Paris. In 1843 he wrote his *Advice on Conduct to be Followed by Serbia*. The next year Garašanin asked Czartoryski's agent, the Czech exile Frantisek Zah, to write him a document suggesting future policy outlines for Serbia. The main points of this were Slavic unity under a Karadjordjević dynasty, Bosnia joined to Serbia, Orthodox–Catholic accord and Serbia as the diplomatic and military nucleus of an emerging South Slav or 'Yugoslav' state. Zah was in contact with the so-called Illyrianists in Croatia and Dalmatia who also sought such a South Slav state, albeit within the confines of the Habsburg Empire. Garašanin and Prince Aleksandar absorbed many of Zah's ideas but were little interested in Illyrianism. They were resolutely Serbocentric and so Garašanin's *Načertanije* substituted such proto-Yugoslavism with the central theme of, first, a strong Serbian state and, second, the idea that it should come to dominate the regions gradually freed from the Turks and later from the Habsburgs. Like his contemporaries, Garašanin viewed Bosnia as inherently Serbian not least because the Serbs were then (as they were until the 1960s) the largest of its three communities. Although the Muslims identified with the ruling Turks, Garašanin argued that to achieve Serbian aims in Bosnia it was necessary to work with the Bosnian Croats and especially their spiritual leaders, the Franciscans. As for the Croats of historic Croatia, that part of the Habsburg lands centred on Zagreb, Garašanin was not antagonistic towards them; he was simply not much interested in them. Throughout his years in power, however, he would entertain consistent contacts with the Illyrianists. They included Ljudevit Gaj and Bishop Strossmayer as well as Ban Jelačić, the governor of Croatia who organised resistance to the Hungarians in 1848.

The main thrust of Garašanin's argument was that the Serbs had been building an empire during the middle ages, but that the arrival of the Turks had put a stop to this. As the empire had begun to collapse some twenty years before the Battle of Kosovo, this was not strictly true. However, for Garašanin, as for all nationalists, history was there to be used for the present, facts notwithstanding. As the Ottoman Empire was now close to collapse (or so he believed), the imperial mission had to be taken up once more. In this way, he wrote, the Serbs would be seen by the world as:

> The true heirs of our great forefathers, and they are engaged in nothing new but the restoration of their ancient homeland. Our present will not be without a tie with our past, but it will bring into being a connected, coherent, and congruous whole, and for this Serbdom, its nationality and its political existence as a state, stands under the protection of sacred historic right. Our aspiration cannot be accused of being something new, unfounded, out of revolution and rebellion, but everyone must admit that it is politically necessary, that it is founded upon the distant past, and that it has its root in the past political and national life of the Serbs, a root which is only bringing forth new branches and beginning to flourish anew.[15]

Consciously or not this last sentence recalls the Nemanjić idea of the 'holy root' bequeathed to posterity in family-tree frescoes in the medieval monasteries the Nemanjas had built.

Garašanin believed that achieving a new Serbian empire would not be difficult, because in no other European country was the memory of the historic past so 'steadfast'. Above all, it was important not to be parochial, but to think beyond the boundaries of the former pashalik principality. Serbian efforts should be concentrated on Bosnia, Hercegovina, Montenegro and northern Albania, which was important for the access to the sea that it would afford. Practical suggestions for achieving these aims included the setting up of a network of agents to gather information about the regions, to identify local leaders and to collect military intelligence. Forms of propaganda could include the printing of a history of Bosnia in which would be included 'the names of certain Bosnians who have gone over to the Mahomedan faith'. Garašanin thought that the book should be written in the 'spirit of national union of Serbs and Bosnians'.[16] He also wrote, 'One of the fundamental principles to underline: the principle of total religious freedom. This principle must be granted to all Christians and must be agreeable to them, and perhaps even, with time, to certain Mahomedans.'[17] As for the Montenegrins in their tiny mountain fastness, which had mostly escaped Ottoman rule, he suggested that an annual financial contribution to its budget would be enough to buy the loyalty of 10,000 hardy warriors.

During his periods in power Garašanin worked to implement his policies, but it was to be rather longer than he expected before they brought results. Austria, whom he regarded as the 'permanent enemy', occupied Bosnia in 1878 and it was not until the Balkan Wars of 1912–13 that Old Serbia, meaning Kosovo and Sandžak, was reconquered by the Serbs, along with a good part of Macedonia. The name Old Serbia was becoming increasingly current because it distinguished the areas that had been the core of the medieval state from the 'new' Serbia centred on Belgrade.

In the wake of the wreckage left behind by contemporary Serbian nationalism, *Načertanije* is a crucial link in understanding the development of the national idea. It is the document that synthesises centuries of Serbian dreams as preserved by the church and epic poetry and formulates them into a statement of modern nationalism. In this sense *Načertanije* was of enduring influence, guiding Serbian policymaking at least until 1918, when the south Slavs, apart from the Bulgarians, were finally united in a Serbian-dominated state. Garašanin can therefore be described as the father of modern Serbian nationalism – especially as, in the run-up to the Yugoslav collapse of 1991, Slobodan Milošević's idea of a Serbian-dominated rump Yugoslavia would have seemed eminently sensible to Garašanin. The problem was that while Garašanin's ideas had relevance in the nineteenth century, the world had changed by the late twentieth. To most people this is self-evident, but in the euphoria of the mass nationalism drummed up in the late 1980s many Serbs simply forgot or ignored this salient fact. In this way, they brought down disaster on themselves and all the people they had lived with in Yugoslavia.

Ultimately the central problem of Garašanin's proposal was the contradiction that has dogged Serbian political thinking ever since – the contradiction between the Serbs' desire for union with other south Slavs, with whom the Serbs were mixed in Bosnia and Croatia, and the desire of the strongest nation in the region to lead and dominate. Garašanin did not have to face this problem, but it was a central cause of the ruin of the first Yugoslavia in 1941 and of the second half a century later.

Just as striking as the legacy of Garašanin's ideas is the emulation of his methods by Slobodan Milošević in modern times. Just as Garašanin had prepared the ground for the Serbian rebellions with a network of agents and by identifying useful local leaders, so too did Slobodan Milošević. Even more noteworthy is the similarity between the methods which Garašanin sought to aid the Serbs in revolt in Vojvodina in 1848 and those used by Milošević, the JNA and its associated intelligence, police and militia services between 1991 and 1995. In 1848 the Vojvodina Serbs rose to demand autonomy to protect themselves against the fierce Magyarising policies of the Hungarians. Garašanin wrote:

> The Vojvodina Serbs . . . expect from all Serbdom a helping hand, so they can triumph over their traditional enemy. Since [these] Serbs view us as their closest brethren, I need not explain why. . . . But whether we wish to and are able to help them and how – about that we need to decide. Aside from sympathy, which as Serbs must attract us to our brethren and compels us as far as possible to assist them . . . the Magyars, if they defeat the Serbs there, will afterwards attack us and our fatherland. So keeping that circumstance in mind, we cannot remain wholly passive in their quarrel. But because of political factors we cannot aid them publicly, it only remains for us to aid them in secret.[18]

This was exactly the dilemma faced by Milošević, especially in Bosnia. Because of international sanctions and the fear of worse reprisals, aid had to be sent covertly although, as in Vojvodina in 1848, it ended as an open secret. Milošević pretended that there were no militias operating from Serbia and that his army officers were not involved in the war; Garašanin played the same game. So-called 'volunteers' were slipped in small numbers across the border, from where they made their way to mustering stations. Arms, ammunition and money were also sent. At the height of this covert operation there were some 8,000 'volunteers' from Serbia fighting the Hungarians. Just as in the early 1990s, though, after initial successes the operation began to go wrong. The Serbian leaders began to quarrel among themselves, the international situation changed and the 'volunteers' complained about their treatment by the Vojvodina Serbs. A Russian force defeated the Hungarians, and the Serbian troops had to be withdrawn. What Garašanin wrote then could have been written by Milošević in 1994 about Krajina and Bosnia: 'We have our worries besides our Vojvodina brethren. We decided to help them when they were in extreme need, feeling that we could not watch their destruction, but now we should not be condemned for thinking of ourselves.'[19]

Despite a brief period of autonomy for Serbs in parts of Vojvodina (until 1861), the adventure there was deemed a failure. However, it was also a turning point. It convinced Garašanin that from now on it was better for Serbia to concentrate on Old Serbia and Bosnia than on Habsburg lands. It also marked the emergence of the principality as a significant regional power. This meant that from now on Serbia had to be taken seriously in any diplomatic considerations. Even more importantly it meant that Belgrade began to be regarded by Serbs outside the principality, and also by many other south Slavs, as the beacon of liberty in the Balkans. In this respect it was significant that Serbs and Croats had opposed the Hungarians together and that joint services of celebration were held in both the Catholic cathedral and the Serbian Orthodox church of Zagreb. Like Piedmont in the struggle for Italy, Serbia began to see itself as the driving force for liberation and unity.

Creating the New Nationalism

History was not *the* motivating ideology when the insurrections began in 1804, but it was always present. Just as Bosnian Serb leaders in the war of 1991–5 decorated function rooms with portraits of Tsar Dušan and other Serbian kings, Austrian spies reported in 1809 that Dušan's portrait also hung in the building of the Sovjet or revolutionary council building. Both Karadjordje and Miloš Obrenović contributed funds for the restoration of medieval monasteries. However, it was only in the 1840s, following the consolidation of Serbian autonomy, that a culture imbued with the past and driving the nationalist future began to flower.

In the development of the new nationalism two direct contemporaries of Garašanin were to wield enormous influence. The first was Vuk Karadžić and the second was Petar Petrović-Njegoš, the prince–bishop of Montenegro.

Karadžić is best known for his collections of Serbian epic poetry and for the development of a Serbian literary standard based on the dialect of Hercegovina which was adopted by the principality in 1868. But Karadžić's linguistic work also led him to theorise about the nature and identity of the peoples of the southern Balkans. His ideas were to influence the development of a Greater Serbian ideology for many generations to come. The thrust of his argument was that the Slavs of the region were not different peoples but rather one people divided by religion – that is, Orthodoxy, Catholicism and Islam. While the Orthodox mostly called themselves Serbs, the problem with the people of the other confessions was that they would not recognise the fact that they too were Serbs. Karadžić conceded that those who lived around Zagreb and spoke its local dialect could claim to be Croats, but apart from some Adriatic islanders and people in Istria he argued that Catholics in Bosnia, Hercegovina, Dalmatia and many other regions were not

Croats at all but Serbs who refused to acknowledge the fact. This he surmised by analysing local dialects. Regarding this supposed division of the Serbs, Karadžić contrasted this state of affairs with that of the Albanians. He noted that their divisions between Orthodox, Catholic or Muslim mattered far less than what united them, which was their common Albanian nationality.

Not all Serbian intellectuals agreed with Karadžić, some of them preferring the more traditional guideline equating Serbdom with Orthodoxy. Nevertheless Karadžić's ideas were a powerful boost for the development of the ideology of Greater Serbia. Their direct application meant that, if dialect rather than religion was the core of nationality, all of Bosnia, Hercegovina and much of Dalmatia was really Serbian – even though much of their populations neither realised nor accepted this. So powerful was this imperial idea that it was even to play its part in the break-up of Yugoslavia in 1991 and 1992, when national as opposed to regional identities were far more pronounced. While most Serbian nationalists were prepared to concede that western Hercegovina with its own Croatian nationalist population was not a region they laid claim to, there were still even more hardline Serbian nationalists who did claim it, on both linguistic and historic grounds, reminding their audiences that in the early middle ages western Hercegovina had been predominantly Orthodox. So, they argued, its modern-day population of fanatically nationalistic Croats were actually Serbs, whether they liked it or not, and therefore they had to live in Greater Serbia.

One of the more bizarre episodes to develop out of this ideology in 1991 and 1992 was the idea of separating Dubrovnik from the rest of Croatia by attempting to turn the clock back to pre-Napoleonic days and declare it an 'independent' city state once more. Using various linguistic and historical arguments, a committee of Serbs from the city was wheeled out during the Serbian siege of the city. They rabbited on about Dubrovnik having always been a Serbian city, whether the population knew this or not. Evidently they did not. Some 'Republic of Dubrovnik' stickers were printed and stuck up in areas under Yugoslav Army occupation, but as soon as this was over the committee disappeared back into the obscurity it deserved.

The effect of Karadžić's ideas was to give intellectual backbone to Serbian or more particularly Greater Serbian nationalism. In this way he mocked the proto-Yugoslav ideology of Illyrianism that was being developed in the Habsburg lands. This ancient name had been revived because, being non-national, it could cover Croats, Serbs and Slovenes. Karadžić said that because it was a name revived from the dead it 'signified nothing'.

Karadžić's analysis was by no means exclusive. Equally virulent in rejecting Illyrianism were the Croatian nationalists Ante Starčević and

Eugen Kvaternik. Their Greater Croatian ideology met his Serbian one head on, holding that there were only two south Slav nations in the Balkans. They were the Croats and the Bulgarians. They also claimed that Serbia's medieval monarchs, the Nemanjas, were actually Croats. It was in this period that nationalists began the map game that they have continued to this day: claiming for their modern states the boundaries of short-lived medieval ones, all of which overlapped in time.

Just as important in reviving Serbian nationalism was the contribution of Montenegro and in particular its prince–bishop, Petar II Petrović-Njegoš (1813–51). His mountainous land had endured spells under the Turks, but from the end of the seventeenth century a small part centred on Cetinje and its Orthodox monastery had been effectively independent. In the middle ages the region had been as indubitably Serbian as had Kosovo or Raška. However, the Serbian exodus from Kosovo and a high rate of conversion to Islam meant that Cetinje and the minuscule area where the spirit of Serbian independence was kept alive were extremely isolated. Yet there was no question in the minds of these warrior people that they were Serbs, and the complex question of a Montenegrin national identity versus that of a Serbian one was only to raise its head much later.

Montenegrin men spent much of their lives sparring with the Turks and their Albanian and Montenegrin Muslim neighbours. While they like to claim that it was their military prowess which kept their land free, it is also true that the area was so poor that the Turks saw little point in expending blood and treasure trying to subdue it. The Montenegrins were also frequently embroiled in fighting one another, miring themselves in blood feuds and stealing one another's cattle. Society was highly tribalised, and life was so hard in the barren mountains that much of the population was emigrating to fertile Serbia. Although real power had traditionally lain with the tribes, authority became more centralised with the emergence in 1782 of the Petrović-Njegoš family, who acting as theocratic prince–bishops combined spiritual and (some) temporal power. The Prince–Bishop Petar II Petrović-Njegoš, generally known just as Njegoš, who ruled between 1830 and 1851, was to make as important a contribution to Serbian nationalism as Garašanin. In 1847 he published his great epic poem, *The Mountain Wreath*, which was to inspire generations of young Serbs and Montenegrins with its glorification of Miloš Obilić, the legendary hero of Kosovo who was said to have killed the sultan:

> Who, Miloš, would not envy thee?
> A victim thou to thine own truth and worth!
> All-puissant spirit in the things of War;

> A thunder mighty which did shatter thrones!
> The deeds thy knightly soul hath wrought,
> Outshine all lustre of the Past, –
> The fame of Sparta and of mighty Rome!
> Their valiant and heroic feats
> Are all surpass'd by thy proud arm.[20]

What Njegoš demanded in his epic was nothing less than the resurrection of the Kosovo spirit to free the Serbs from alien rule. The poem was to capture the spirit of the age, and its glorification of regicide or tyrannicide was something that a later generation of nationalist youths could respond to. Their dream was to culminate in the person of Gavrilo Princip. He was the nineteen-year-old Bosnian Serb who assassinated the Archduke Franz Ferdinand in Sarajevo on the anniversary of the Battle of Kosovo in 1914, so sparking off the First World War. Like many of his contemporaries Princip knew the lengthy *Mountain Wreath* off by heart. Just before the assassination, Nedeljko Čabrinović, a member of the conspiracy, had thrown a bomb at the Archduke but had missed. His identification with Obilić was all the greater as he too had been suspected of treachery because his father was a police informer. At his investigation he expressed outrage that Franz Ferdinand was visiting Sarajevo on St Vitus Day, Vidovdan, the Kosovo anniversary:

> this fact fired me with zeal to carry out the attempt. Our folklore tradition tells how Miloš Obilić was accused before Vidovdan that he was a traitor, and how he answered: 'On Vidovdan we shall see who is and who is not a traitor.' And Obilić became the first assassin who went into the enemy camp and murdered Sultan Murad. The local Socialists have called me a spy like my father.[21]

If the glorification of murder, for however noble a purpose, seems incongruous coming from a churchman, the context in which Njegoš wrote should not be forgotten. Outside his monastery window were arrayed the impaled heads of slain Turks.[22] In similar vein John Reed, during his travels through the Balkans in 1915, was asked by a Serbian priest in the ranks of the Serbian Army, 'Have you heard the story of how the Serbian Bishop, Duchitch, shocked the Bishop of London?'

> 'You are fortunate', said the Bishop of London, 'in your people. I am told they are very devout.'
> 'Yes,' said Mr Duchitch, 'in Serbia we do not trust too much to God. We prayed God five centuries to free us from the Turks, and finally took guns and did it ourselves!'[23]

There was another side to *The Mountain Wreath* far more sinister than its praise of tyrannicide. With its call for the extermination of those Montenegrins who had converted to Islam, the poem was also a paean to ethnic cleansing.

Just as Serbia came to see itself as the Piedmont of the Serbs, the Montenegrins came to view themselves as the Serbian Sparta. So keen on this idea and on 'avenging Kosovo' was Njegoš that after having persuaded Montenegrins to abandon their Turkish fezzes and adopt a style of cap favoured on the Bay of Kotor he began to explain the band of black which encircled them as representing mourning for Kosovo and their red centres as the blood which had flowed ever since then.[24] 'When you talk to these people,' wrote Ljubomir Nenadović, the Serbian writer, in 1878, 'you have the impression that the Battle of Kosovo took place yesterday.'[25] Under Njegoš, the Obilić medal for valour was instituted and it became the country's highest military decoration. Curiously the ruler of medieval Montenegro, or Zeta as it was called, had in 1389 pointedly failed to send his soldiers to the Battle of Kosovo because his own lands were not directly threatened. What mattered in the nineteenth century though, as now, was what people *believed* to be true. In this spirit the Montenegrin national anthem, written by Prince, later King, Nikola (1841–1921), also evokes Kosovo:

> Over there, o'er there, beyond those hills,
> Where the heavens bend the blue sky,
> Toward Serb fields, toward martial fields,
> Over there, brothers, let's prepare to go!
>
> Over there, o'er there, beyond those hills,
> One can find they say, Milos's tomb . . .
> Over there! . . . My soul will receive its rest
> When the Serb no longer will be a slave.[26]

It was such a martial spirit that Jovan Cvijić came to identify with his most famous concept, that of Dinaric man. Analysing the peoples of the Balkans he broke them down into certain types. Those Slavs, three-quarters of them Serbs, who lived in the shadow of the Dinaric Mountains he identified as Dinarics, whom he said were energetic, impulsive and imbued with a patriotic ardour for which they were prepared to die. The mountains run from Montenegro through Hercegovina and Bosnia up to Lika and Kordun in what later and briefly became the Republic of Serbian Krajina. Cvijić became well known internationally, taught at the Sorbonne and, just as Karadžić and Njegoš had influenced ideas at home, he was to influence generations of scholars abroad. At the core of his ideas about Dinaric man was the concept of 'avenging Kosovo' which was to play such a prominent role in Serbian history up until the end of the Balkan Wars in 1913:

> The Dinaric is consumed with a burning desire to avenge Kosovo, where he lost his independence, and to revive the Serbian Empire about which he has never ceased to dream even in the most desperate circumstances in which a man of pure reason would have despaired. . . . This tenacity, this absolute faith in the national ideal, is the essential fact of his history. He considers himself chosen by destiny to accomplish the national mission.
>
> . . . [he] feels a profound tie to his ancestors. . . . he considers himself a part of a line . . . that of the kings or *tsars*, of his celebrated heroes of the Nemanjić times and Kosovo. . . . each Dinaric peasant feels as his own ancestors the heroes of his nation's history. . . . He knows not only the names of the heroes of Kosovo, but their qualities and faults; he is from regions where he can all but feel their wounds. To kill lots of Turks is for him not only a way of avenging his ancestors but of assuaging their pain which he shares.[27]

If the spirit of Serbdom had been kept alive by the church and epic poetry, and if the commonplaces of Balkan history were war, violence and cruelty, one still has to wonder at what stage some of Cvijić's notions were overplayed. In Bosnia, for example, inter-communal violence in the nineteenth century would flare frequently, just as it has in this century, but in between these periods of conflict came times of peace. Just as the average Bosnian Serb did not wake up every morning between 1945 and 1990 with a burning desire to 'avenge Kosovo' by killing a Bosnian Muslim, the same was true during peaceful periods of the nineteenth century. Cvijić, however, was a man of his times. He was the product of an age of nationalism in Europe which was especially keenly felt among the Serbs because so much of the nation remained under Ottoman or Habsburg rule. For these reasons the ideology of liberation became increasingly important in making policy, even if it did not always bear fruit. After uprisings by Christian peasants in Hercegovina and then Bosnia in 1875, Serbia and Montenegro felt compelled to intervene. In 1876 they went to war with the Ottoman Empire. 'This time we have to avenge Kosovo!' said Montenegro's Prince Nikola. 'Under Murad I the Serbian empire was destroyed – now during the reign of Murad V it has to rise again.'[28]

Although the Montenegrins did well, the Serbs did not. A Russian general, M. G. Cherniaev, came to command the Serbian Army along with 5,000 Russian volunteers fired by pan-Slav convictions. Like the handful of Russians who helped the Bosnian Serbs after 1992, they were often drunk and had little or no military experience. By March

1877, Serbia had suffered 15,000 casualties in a disastrous conflict. Things changed for the better when the next month Russia itself went to war with the Turks. Such a general conflagration was just what European diplomats feared. It was the dreaded Eastern Question, or what to do with Turkey's European possessions once the empire collapsed. Serbia was reluctant to fight again, but, fearing that Niš and Skopje would be lost to Bulgaria, it joined in the fray. The Treaty of San Stefano of March 1878 created a Russian satellite, Greater Bulgaria, incorporating much of Macedonia. This was rejected by the other European powers, so diplomats from Russia, Britain, France, Italy, Germany, Austria–Hungary and the Ottoman Empire met at the Congress of Berlin, which opened in June of the same year. The Balkan states were not invited to participate beyond presenting their views. The decisions of the Congress were to have a tremendous historical impact. Greater Bulgaria never came about. Serbia and Montenegro had their territories expanded and they were recognised for the first time as *de jure* independent states. However, in a great blow to Serbia, the provinces of Bosnia and Hercegovina were given to Austria–Hungary to administer. The Habsburg Empire also received the Sandžak – so a foreign power still occupied that strip of land between Serbia and Montenegro. Not wishing to live under Christian rule, many Muslims left Bosnia. Albanians and Muslims were forced out of Serbia's newly acquired territories. In return many Serbs left Kosovo because of the pressure put on them by these same refugees.

The Austro–Hungarian occupation of Bosnia–Hercegovina contained within it the seeds of the First World War, yet Habsburg diplomats initially and sensibly tried to channel Serbian nationalist energy southwards. In 1881 a secret agreement was signed by which Austria–Hungary sanctioned Serbia's expansion southwards into Ottoman territory on the condition that it did not agitate among the Habsburg Serbs: 'Serbia will not tolerate political, religious or other intrigues which, taking its territory as a point of departure, might be directed against the Austro-Hungarian monarchy, including therein Bosnia, Hercegovina and the Sandžak of Novi Pazar.' Its most stringent stipulation, however, was that 'without a previous understanding with Austria–Hungary, Serbia will neither negotiate nor conclude any political treaty with another government, and will not admit to her territory a foreign armed force, regular or irregular, even as volunteers'.[29]

Tempered by defeat in war and diplomacy Serbia was taking a step backwards. Although the rhetoric remained that of 'avenging Kosovo', the treaty represented a serious restriction on Serbia's sovereignty. But part of the growing pains of a small Balkan state was the need for politicians to consider things like economics and domestic politics rather than to concentrate solely on liberating other Serbs or restoring a medieval empire.

These were years of economic growth, and Serbia was keen that the Orient Express railway should pass through Belgrade, knowing full well the benefits it would bring. The railway was indeed constructed through Serbia, which also signed economic agreements with Austria–Hungary.

In 1882 Milan Obrenović, the reigning prince, upgraded his and the country's status by proclaiming himself king. In 1883 the government was forced to suppress peasant uprisings and in 1885 it launched a war against the Bulgarians – who, to general surprise, crushed the Serbian invaders. Milan grew unpopular, and in 1887 his wife, whom he had divorced, left the country taking the heir to the throne with her. Unlike other countries with similar problems the Serbs had the option of restoring the Karadjordjević dynasty and an attractive candidate, Peter Karadjordjević, lurked in the background. In 1888, however, Milan abdicated and a regency council ruled in favour of his thirteen-year-old son Aleksandar.

After such a miserable period of defeat, humiliation and weak governance it is not surprising that Serbian officials seized upon the 500th anniversary of the Battle of Kosovo in 1889 to revive the national spirit. Like Slobodan Milošević one hundred years later, they invoked Prince Lazar's ghost to come to their aid. At one of many events organised that year, Čedomil Mijatović, Serbia's foreign minister, told the Royal Academy that:

> An inexhaustible source of national pride was discovered on Kosovo. More important than language and stronger than the Church, this pride unites all Serbs in a single nation. . . . The glory of the Kosovo heroes shone like a radiant star in that dark night of almost five hundred years. . . . Our people continued the battle in the sixteenth, seventeenth and eighteenth centuries when they tried to recover their freedom through countless uprisings. There was never a war for freedom – and when was there no war? – in which the spirit of the Kosovo heroes did not participate. The new history of Serbia begins with Kosovo – a history of valiant efforts, long suffering, endless wars, and unquenchable glory. . . . Karadjordje breathed with the breath of Kosovo, and the Obrenovići placed Kosovo in the coat of arms of their dynasty. We bless Kosovo because the memory of the Kosovo heroes upheld us, encouraged us, taught us, and guided us.[30]

The Royal Academy is now the Serbian Academy of Arts and Sciences, which in the 1980s was to play a key role in reviving Serbian nationalism. In 1889 requiem masses were said for the knights who had died 500 years before and a Prince Lazar medal was struck. At Sremski Ravanica, in Habsburg territory, some 30,000 pilgrims came to pay homage to the bones of Lazar, and in Zagreb there were a number of commemorative events. Naturally there were services in the Orthodox churches, especially in areas that, a century later, were to be the scenes of the bitterest fighting – Vukovar, Vinkovci and Pakrac.[31]

This period, which ended with the First World War in 1914, also saw an outpouring of literature, theatre and art infused with patriotic themes. Serbian playwrights competed with one another to write dramas about Lazar and the Nemanjić kings, and the most famous national–romantic historical art was now produced. Paja Jovanović was among the most prominent artists, painting massive canvases on historical themes such as the Coronation of Tsar Dušan. In this way Paja Jovanović was doing for Serbian art what Jacques-Louis David had done for France a hundred years before with pictures such as *The Coronation of Napoleon*. Jovanović also painted pictures depicting the uprisings against the Turks. One of the best known of these is that of Miloš Obrenović being declared leader of the uprising of 1815. Dressed in the full Turkish style of the period, the turban-wearing Miloš raises a flag while a priest gives his blessing. He is acclaimed by Serbian fighters, all wearing fezzes, some of whom raise their swords in salute. Kosovo was, of course, another great inspiration. The most famous of this series is the slightly belated *Kosovo Girl*, finished in 1919, by Uroš Predić. In a scene from one of the best-known Kosovo epic poems, the girl holds the head of Lazar's dying standard-bearer while she gives him wine to drink from a golden jug. Strewn around them are the bodies of the dead, and the warrior himself lies propped up on the corpse of a slain Turk. It is an image that has become imprinted on the Serbian mind and is so well known that it can be turned against the Serbs in parody. After the signing of the Dayton Accord in November 1995, which ended the war in Bosnia, an adapted *Kosovo Girl* was published by a magazine in Sarajevo. The beautiful maiden had become Biljana Plavšić, the diehard Bosnian Serb politician, and the dying warrior Radovan Karadžić, the wartime Bosnian Serb leader.

Curious though it now seems, some of the most important works of the period celebrating or commemorating Kosovo were executed by Croats. The best known was Ivan Meštrović, the sculptor from Dalmatia. In his political life he exemplified the common experience of a Croatian intellectual who began as a philo-Serb and pro-Yugoslav and ended as a disillusioned Croat in the post-1918 era. In 1911 Meštrović, along with other artists from Croatia, was the main attraction in the Serbian pavilion at the Rome Exhibition of International Art.[32]

Today Meštrović's brooding and powerful *Miloš Obilić* stands in the main hall of Belgrade's National Museum. Meštrović's great project was the Kosovo temple, a massive pantheon which he hoped would rise on the battlefield to commemorate the suffering of all the south Slavs. It was to be a cathedral-like building of domes and columns centring on a giant statue of Obilić. To reach the Kosovo altar one would pass through a triumphal arch topped by figures of the Kosovo heroes before proceeding down a walkway dominated by a bell tower supported by five layers of caryatids. In 1911 in Rome the idea was reported to have caused a 'real sensation in the artistic world'.[33] R. W. Seton-Watson, the historian of the Balkans, writing in 1917 recalled the Rome exhibitions:

> In the midst of the usual depressing collection of the trivial and the banal that constitutes the bulk of our much advertised international art exhibitions. . . [was] the strong, sombre little building erected by Serbia to contain Meštrović's statues of the fierce warriors and mourning women of his race. Meštrović stands pre-eminent amongst the sculptors of the modern world, in that he has had in the tragic story of his indomitable nation subject matter worthy and consonant with the almost overwhelming force of his powers of expression, and in his solemn pre-occupation with the high themes of the martyrdom of his race and the sufferings of humanity has resisted all temptation to dissipate his powers in producing the clever trivialities that alone secured popular recognition with the light-minded, cosmopolitan public of Europe before the war.[34]

The Kosovo temple was never built, but the scale model that was made to show it off still lies mouldering in the Serbian provincial museum of Kruševac, Lazar's medieval capital. Unfortunately most of the little model caryatids have been picked off by souvenir hunters.[35]

The one real monument to this period of Serbian history that was built is the church of St George at Oplenac. This tall, stark white church built in Serbo-Byzantine style sits on top of a wooded hill and its domes can be seen for miles around. Begun in 1910 the church was built by King Peter Karadjordjević, who came to the throne after the murder of King Aleksandar Obrenović in 1903. Oplenac lies close to Topola, the home village of Karadjordje Petrović, the founder of the dynasty. No expense was spared in the construction of this memorial church. Karadjordje and King Peter lie under white marble sarcophagi, while a crypt was built in which the remains of most of the rest of the Karadjordjević clan were gathered.

Ideas for decorating the inside of the church changed while it was being built. King Peter thought to inscribe its walls with the names of those who had died in the Balkan Wars, but events overtook him. With the outbreak of the First World War, Serbia was occupied and by the time it was over so many had died that it was thought impossible to cover the walls with all their names. Instead artists were sent out to all the medieval monasteries and churches of Serbia and Mount Athos to copy frescoes of historic kings and saints. These were faithfully reproduced in 725 mosaic compositions made up of forty million pieces. The centrepiece, hanging under the central dome, is a candelabrum made of the bronze of melted cannons. Within it is a massive inverted crown symbolising the end of the medieval empire and the Battle of Kosovo.

The terrible irony is that this sombre and final monument to Serbia's past was completed too late. It was finished when the Karadjordjevićs were no longer kings of Serbia but kings of Yugoslavia, and so the church came to symbolise all that was wrong with the new kingdom. Instead of using the opportunity to turn it into a shrine for all Yugoslavs it was completed as it was intended: a church for Serbia and its Karadjordjević dynasty.

Although the building of Oplenac was finished after the First World War, in its conception it summarised the national–romantic and patriotic atmosphere of the years leading up to the Balkan Wars. In 1912 Serbia, Montenegro, Greece and Bulgaria formed an alliance to expel the Turks from the Balkans. The lightning campaign was a dazzling success, but in 1913 the aggrieved Bulgarians attacked their former allies because they felt cheated over the territorial spoils. For the Serbs the crowning moment of the two wars was the return of Serbian rule to Kosovo. Such was the religious fervour of the first campaign that when the Serbian Army reached Prilep in Macedonia, the home of Kraljević Marko, one of the legendary figures of the Serbian epics, the whole regiment is reported to have suffered from a collective hallucination and to have seen him lead their charge. One of the soldiers who had taken part in the advance on Kosovo recalled the overwhelming sense of emotion as Serbian troops finally returned to the holy battlefield:

> The single sound of that word – Kosovo – caused an indescribable excitement. This one word pointed to the black past – five centuries. In it exists the whole of our sad past – the tragedy of Prince Lazar and the entire Serbian people. . . .
>
> Each of us created for himself a picture of Kosovo while we were still in the cradle. Our mothers lulled us to sleep with the songs of Kosovo, and in our schools our teachers never ceased in their stories of Lazar and Miloš. . . .
>
> My God, what awaited us! To see a liberated Kosovo. The words of the commander were like music to us and soothed our souls like the miraculous balsam.

When we arrived on Kosovo and the battalions were placed in order, our commander spoke: 'Brothers, my children, my sons!' His voice breaks. 'This place on which we stand is the graveyard of our glory. We bow to the shadows of fallen ancestors and pray God for the salvation of their souls.' His voice gives out and tears flow in streams down his cheeks and grey beard and fall to the ground. He actually shakes from some kind of inner pain and excitement.

The spirits of Lazar, Miloš, and all the Kosovo martyrs gaze on us. We feel strong and proud, for we are the generation which will realize the centuries-old dream of the whole nation: that we with the sword will regain the freedom that was lost with the sword.[36]

For the Serbs the decisive battle of the First Balkan War took place at Kumanovo in northern Macedonia. From then on Kosovo was deemed to have been 'avenged'. The slogan of victory was 'For Kosovo – Kumanovo'. None of the region's majority Albanian population saw the return of the Serbs as a liberation, however, and uprisings against Serbian rule were put down with the utmost brutality. Serbia's triumph was short-lived. In 1915 the Serbian Army was in flight. As the soldiers escaped across the old battlefield, Rebecca West recorded that 'Above them circled enemy aeroplanes, evil's newest instrument.'[37]

5

CUTTING THE TURKS INTO PIECES

Nena Mejra was a hundred years old. She was dressed in traditional Bosnian Muslim baggy pants and sat on the sofa next to the body of Selma Hodžić, her seven-year-old great-granddaughter. 'Please sit down,' she said. A relative hissed, 'She has seen three wars.' The day before, on 3 May 1992, a Bosnian Serb militia had spent their Sunday torching Hranča, Nena Mejra's eastern Bosnian village. Selma, worried about her pet lamb, had slipped out while the masked Serbs poured petrol into buildings and then set them on fire with grenades. She was shot dead.

In the next house Hanija Hodžić, aged fifty, kept a silent vigil over the body of her husband. 'I didn't see how he was shot,' she said quietly. A neighbour lifted the shroud: 'They bayoneted him.' His entrails were tumbling out.

The two other men to die that Sunday were Osman Ramić, aged twenty-two, and his uncle Samir Ramić, aged thirty-five. Čamil Ramić, the father and brother of the men, said, 'They hauled them from the cellar where we had been hiding. There were at least ten of them. They screamed, "Give us the guns." They kicked them, they beat them with their rifle butts.' Osman's skull had caved in from the blows. Near the house pools of drying blood were still visible where they had been killed. 'Why, why? You ask "why"?' screamed a woman, tears streaming down her cheeks. 'There is no food or drink . . . all our stores are burned. They want to ethnically clean the area. . . . There is no why . . . it is because we are Muslims.'

Many of Hranča's men had fled the village into the hills in the hours and days before the attack. The week before, JNA troops had driven past and threatened them, saying that their vehicles had been fired on. 'It was not true,' said a survivor. The day before the attack the villagers had handed in their hunting rifles to the Bosnian Serb authorities, so when the killers came they were defenceless. Before they left the village the Serbs tied up and abducted some ten men. The next day Hajrija

Hodžić, whose sixteen-year-old son had been taken, went to the Serbian police station in the nearby town of Bratunac but was told that they knew 'nothing'.

One man pushed forward an hysterical woman trailing five small children. 'Take her with you,' he begged. 'They have taken my husband,' she cried.

Many of those who were kidnapped may have died in Bratunac school, where a large number of men were murdered. The rest, if they managed to escape, fled to the nearby hilltop town of Srebrenica, which was to hold out until July 1995. In the annals of the Bosnian war Hranča was just an anonymous hamlet, just another village cleared of its Muslim population. But it was also the beginning of a bloody trail which was to culminate in the massacre of thousands of men from Srebrenica when it finally fell. Penned inside what was to become an enclave, the Muslims retaliated and raided Serbian villages in search of food. On 14 December 1992, during one such raid, they burned two villages and massacred sixty-three of those who could not run fast enough. Ljubo Simić, the mayor of Bratunac, kept a video of the bodies which showed that some of them had been mutilated – hacked about with blunt objects and knives. One man seemed to have been castrated. The victims were buried in Bratunac cemetery, which grew relentlessly over the years. In accordance with custom the crosses were dressed with men's shirts or women's shawls. Small toys lay on the graves of the children. The hatred blazed ever more fiercely. 'Many want revenge,' said Simić. 'We cannot wait until the last village is burned and its people massacred. . . . We'll neutralise them.'

On a gutted Muslim house on the banks of the nearby Drina river someone had painted the words, 'There will be death but no remorse, because there will be the sign of the cross and no bowing down.' It was 1992, but the religious symbolism of past wars had come back to haunt this unhappy country.

'The burning of villages and the exodus of the defeated population is a normal and traditional incident of all Balkan wars and insurrections. It is the habit of all these peoples. What they have suffered themselves, they inflict in turn upon others.'[1] During the Bosnian war such a view was considered politically incorrect by western liberal circles. Serbia and the Serbs were the aggressors and to make reference to history in this way was considered the sin of 'moral relativism'. According to this theory, observations such as the one just quoted attempted to make all sides equally guilty and therefore absolved the west of its duty to intervene. This was wrong. Reference to history is essential because otherwise all the crimes that were committed seem as random as those of a mad sniper taking pot shots in a western city. It does not, however, absolve anyone of guilt. In the war that began in 1991, the Serbian leadership must take the lion's share of the blame. But they could not have organised militias who knew from the experience of generations exactly what to do unless their own forefathers had been as practised in the art of village-burning as they were in fleeing from their own flaming hamlets. Militias-cum-bandit gangs, official or not, have always been a feature of war in the Balkans, and the last war was no different from any that went before it. The astute lines cited above were not written in 1992, although they could have been. They are from the findings of an international observer mission sent by the American Carnegie Endowment to report on the Balkan Wars of 1912 and 1913.

The Burning Tradition

Village-burning and ethnic cleansing have, as the Carnegie Endowment pointed out, traditionally accompanied Balkan wars. The Serbs have no monopoly on this evil. However, it is important to trace the heritage of this practice among them. Vuk Karadžić makes use of the word 'cleansed' in describing what had happened to the Turks of Belgrade when the city was taken by Karadjordje's revolutionary forces in 1806. Konstantin Nenadović, who wrote a biography of the Serbian leader, published in 1883, noted that after the fighting 'the Serbs, in their bitterness, slit the throats of the Turks everywhere they found them, sparing neither the wounded, nor the women, nor the Turkish children'.[2] In the documents by which the sultan formally granted autonomy to Miloš Obrenović's Serbia, specific clauses spelt out that the Muslims of the principality, who were not connected to the Ottoman garrisons, would have to sell their property and leave. There was no question of this being an act of undesirable discrimination; it was simply accepted as normal for the time and place. How widespread was the massacre of Muslims during the insurrection is unclear, yet there was no doubt that such a practice was deemed a laudable aim worth singing about. Filip Višnjić, the bard of the 1804 revolution, did just that:

> In the middle of the field [Kara] George drew his sword
> and cut away the heads of oppressors.
> When he had cut the Turks into pieces,
> when he had cut the Turks, the oppressors,
> then George went in and entered the cities,
> he cut whatever Turk was for cutting,
> what was for handing over he gave out,
> what was for christening, he christened it.[3]

That forcible conversion was considered an alternative to death shows how much poison lay at the bottom of the stagnant Ottoman pool. Then as today the matter of religion was far more than a simple question of belief. It was a question of identity, and the fact that Islam was the faith of the conqueror made it a political question too. The Ottoman Empire was not a colonial empire as we understand such things in the west. It was not a Turkish imperial exercise, but an *Islamic* one in which non-Muslims could live as *rayah* or second-class subjects and converts could become full subjects with full rights and privileges. For Christians, then, those who converted to Islam were worse than Turks – they were traitors to the faith of their forefathers and, in times of war, apostates who deserved to die. Civil wars are always bitter, but in the Balkans this religious twist has made them all the more brutal.

In Njegoš' 1847 epic *The Mountain Wreath* Metropolitan Danilo agonises over the question of what to do about Montenegrins who had converted to Islam. There was a duty to protect one's brother and one's clan, but there was also a duty to one's faith and nation. Ideally the renegades could be persuaded to return to the true faith, but, if they would not, they would have to be extirpated. The historical Danilo, who officiated between 1700 and 1735, did take action but it is not known exactly when and to what extent Muslims were killed or simply driven out. However, more than a century later, when Njegoš came to write his epic, it was clear that he regarded Danilo's blow as one for Christ and Serbdom. In this passage Vojvoda Batrić tries to persuade the Muslim leaders to convert . . . or else:

> Have done with minarets and mosques!
> Let flare the Serbian Christmas-log;
> Paint gaily too the eggs for Easter-tide;
> Observe with care the Lent and Autumn Fasts,
> And for the rest – do what is dear to thee!
> If ye take not the counsel that I give,
> Why, then, I swear by name of Obilitch,
> And by these arms in which I put my trust,
> That both our faiths – they *both* shall swim in blood:
> And that which better is – it surely shall not drown!
> Bairam agrees not with our sweet Noel –
> Brothers Montenegrin, is't not so?
>   (*All cry:* "Tis so! 'Tis so!')[4]

In the end it comes to war, and Vojvoda Batrić reports to Danilo what has taken place:

> Though broad enough Cetinje's Plain,
> No single seeing eye, no tongue of Turk,

> Escap'd to tell his tale another day!
> We put them all unto the sword,
> All those who would not be baptiz'd;
> But who paid homage to the Holy Child
> Were all baptiz'd with sign of Christian Cross,
> And as brother each was hail'd and greeted.
> We put to fire the Turkish houses,
> That there might be nor stick nor trace
> Of these true servants of the Devil!
> From Cetinje to Tcheklitche we hied,
> There in full flight the Turks espied;
> A certain number were by us mown down,
> And all their houses we did set ablaze;
> Of all their mosques both great and small
> We left but one accursed heap,
> For passing folk to cast their glance of scorn.

Joyfully the Metropolitan responds:

> Great gladness this for me, my falcons,
> Great joy for me! Heroic liberty
> Has resurrection morn to-day,
> From every tomb of our ancestors dear![5]

It is hard to underestimate the influence of *The Mountain Wreath*. Today it is still celebrated as one of the pinnacles of Serbian literary achievement. But, in the wake of another Balkan war, its significance is that of a missing link. It helps explain how the Serbian national consciousness has been moulded and how ideas of national liberation became inextricably intertwined with the act of killing your neighbour and burning his village. In 1930, the Serbian academic Vladeta Popović wrote a preface to the standard English translation of *The Mountain Wreath* in which none of these considerations was raised. What he wrote was not an apologia, since it did not occur to anyone that there was anything to apologise for. All that was needed was some kind of explanatory background:

What the Turks could not do by military power, thanks to the inaccessibility of the Montenegrin land, their religion began to do. The spread of Mohammedanism among the Montenegrin tribes became a serious danger. Christianity went, national questions went with it. Language would remain, but the people would be cut away from the bulk of the Serbian nation, and would feel like men in a fog. That is what may be seen to-day in Bosnia: the Mohammedans speak Serbian and consider themselves as Serbs, but the stream of their energy has been blocked, and, not mingling with the current of Christian Serbia, it is flowing nowhere and is stagnating. The racial instinct of the Montenegrins was in mortal opposition to Mohammedanism.[6]

It was not just Serbs who in the 1930s thought little wrong with paeans of praise to mass murder. Rebecca West wrote that she was 'on the side of the brothers Martinovitch' who in Njegoš' epic carry out the bidding of Danilo:

> Having seen what Turkish conquest meant to the Slav, it is certain they were justified in their crime. A man is not a man if he will not save his seed. But the destiny is abhorrent that compelled the brothers, who may be assumed to have been of flawless and inhuman beauty, like the Montenegrins of to-day, to go out into the night and murder the renegades, who also would be beautiful.[7]

Today Rebecca West might have moderated her views if she had seen villages like Hranča on television. But it is essential to understand that many Bosnian Serbs went to war in 1992 elated and in the spirit of Njegoš and *The Mountain Wreath*. Or at least they were incited to do so. It is encouraging that some Serbian academics have by now realised the connection between the poetry and hate. Aleksa Djilas, an historian and the son of the Yugoslav dissident Milovan Djilas who had among other things written a biography of Njegoš, recounts the reaction of his cousin when asked about *The Mountain Wreath*. Aleksa Djilas says that the Montenegrin cousin had just arrived in Belgrade to study and so he asked him, 'How did the Muslims in your class react when they had to read *The Mountain Wreath* and learn parts of it by heart?' His cousin was dumbstruck: 'It had never crossed his mind to ask his Muslim classmates such a question – even though some were his close friends. Clearly he did not connect them with the Muslims against whom Njegoš wrote.'[8] It may not have occurred to him, but it is in this way that, for generations, literature that elsewhere would have long been banned from schools is still, subconsciously or not, shaping the worldview of Serbian children. It is inconceivable that in Germany, for example, poetry inciting the murder of Jews and the burning of synagogues would be considered acceptable today, however noble its literary pedigree.

Bosnia's Sulphurous Vapours

Throughout the Ottoman Balkans there were converts to Islam and in some areas there was also settlement of Anatolian Turks. In Bulgaria, for instance, there are today pockets of *pomaks*, the descendants of converted Bulgarians, and 10 per cent of Bulgaria's population is of ethnic Turkish stock. In the former Yugoslav republic of Macedonia there is a small Macedonian-speaking Muslim population and an ethnic Turkish one, but since the Balkan Wars there have been major migrations, especially of Turks to Turkey. Sandžak too was and is an area with a substantial Slav Muslim population. Despite these groups, there are only two populations which converted *en masse* to Islam. These were the Bosnians and the Albanians.

Vuk Drašković began his professional life as a journalist. He then became a novelist, a hardline nationalist politician and, next, Serbia's main opposition leader hostile to the war. In 1982 he published a novel called *The Knife*. It caused a sensation partly because of its graphic descriptions of Bosnian Muslim violence against Serbs during the Second World War. Such topics were strictly taboo in the communist Yugoslavia of 'brotherhood and unity'. In the field of literature Drašković was thus among the first to break the mould shaped by Tito, who had dominated the country until his death two years before. In retrospect its insight into the Serbian nationalist view of Bosnia was telling. In this passage an old Muslim explains the Muslim tragedy to a young man. When the Turks began their invasion of Europe, he says:

> two young men by the name of Ljubović, Serbian nobles from Hercegovina, were killed in a battle against the invader on the Maritsa. That was in 1371. In 1875, at the time of the Serbian insurrection in Nevesinje, five Islamicised Ljubovićs, who were direct descendants of the two nobles killed on the Maritsa, found death . . . but this time fighting the Serbs. They were the last defenders in a desperate struggle. . . . They died without even understanding the tragedy and the absurdity of the role they had to play, and which prevented them from seeing, even at the moment that they perished, that they were falling under the blows of their own kind to defend the power of foreigners.[9]

Following the logic of Vuk Karadžić, Drašković was expounding the common Serbian belief that Bosnia's Muslims are treacherous Serbs whose ancestors were converted to Islam. By implication they have no right to an independent national identity of their own, let alone a state. Not only is this mostly unhistorical, but it is also one of the many myths that have fuelled the episodic eruptions of violence that have characterised the country's history. While in many areas there were conversions of Serbs to Islam, the bulk of Bosnia's Muslim population derives its origin from the people who lived in Bosnia before the Ottoman conquest – that is to say, people who were neither Serbs nor Croats but simply Slavs who lived in the land that lay between those of their Orthodox and Catholic cousins. When it comes to discussing this question, though, like that of Kosovo, many otherwise rational and sane Serbs simply cease to function as such. They prefer their own long-held convictions to facts which would force them to rethink everything they hold dear.

In the first weeks of the Bosnian war in 1992 it was sometimes hard to know who controlled which area, as the first militias did not always have uniforms or clearly identifiable insignias. Asked if their patch of territory was Serb-held, a column of armed men replied that it was. But one man said no, it was not. 'This is Serbia,' he said baldly. It was common enough at the time to see this slogan sprayed over the country's walls, but to hear it spoken was to discover the urgency of the emotion.[10] It was said confidently, but the fact that it had to be said at all proved the point. Bosnia, even those parts inhabited by Serbs for centuries, is not Serbia and has never been part of Serbia. That a soldier needed to tell a foreigner that a village deep in Bosnia was in fact in Serbia betrayed his own fear, even if only subconsciously at the time. For, if it was not in Serbia, the war would be in vain.

Even in the heyday of Dušan's empire, which by 1355 stretched from Hungary deep into Greece, Bosnia was not part of Serbia. By contrast, predominantly Orthodox Hercegovina did, during the middle ages, lie firmly within the ambit of what could be described as the Serbian lands. In Bosnia proper the Orthodox presence, except in some peripheral areas, dates mainly to the period following the Turkish conquest. There are no great medieval monasteries in Bosnia to bear testament to the Nemanjićs and, though Serbian, Croatian and Hungarian influences and power periodically asserted themselves over the region, it was always recognised as a land apart. Around 1180, the first Bosnian kingdom under Ban Kulin emerged and it was to remain until the Turkish conquest of 1463. Between 1353 and 1391 the country was ruled by Tvrtko Kotromanić, whose lands took in Hercegovina, central Dalmatia and parts of Serbia itself. It was he who sent troops to Kosovo to fight alongside Lazar against the Turks and who had himself crowned King of the Serbs and of Bosnia. Tvrtko's coat of arms was adorned with the fleur-de-lys. After his death, although the Kotromanić family retained the throne, the country was riven by quarrelling nobles and threatened by Venetian raids and by the Turks and the Hungarians, who claimed suzerain rights over Bosnia.

When on a foggy night in 1992 a new militia appeared on the streets of Sarajevo, some of them had Tvrtko's coat of arms sewn on their berets or pinned to their coats. This was the first public appearance of the Patriotic League, the Muslim-dominated army in embryo. Few people knew where this coat of arms had sprung from or what it meant. Many said that the two groups of three lilies symbolised the three peoples of

Bosnia. Soon afterwards the coat of arms became the Bosnian flag, recognised only by Muslims or by those Serbs and Croats brave enough to fight for the multi-ethnic ideal in which they believed. The irony is that there were obviously no native Muslims in pre-conquest Bosnia and that then, as now, it was riven by hatred and religious persecution.

Even today many otherwise well-informed people, including Bosnian Muslims, claim the Bogomils, a medieval heretical Christian sect, for the ancestors of the Bosnian Muslims. Like the Cathars in France, the Bogomils were ascetic dualists who rejected the power of the established church. During the middle ages their influence was widespread in Bulgaria and Macedonia and parts of Serbia too. However, modern historical research has shown that the monastic-based Bosnian church, which wielded a strong influence in the medieval state, was not the same as Bogomilism and appears to have developed out of a cross-fertilisation of Catholic and Orthodox traditions. Thanks to the proselytising work of the Franciscans, who had arrived in the 1350s, and Hungarian-led persecutions it seems that the Bosnian church had more or less ceased to exist by the time of the Turkish conquest. So the theory that it was the Bogomils who converted *en masse* to Islam falls flat. By contrast, it is now argued that the legacy of the Bosnian church and the frequently high levels of tolerance afforded it by the Kotromanićs ensured that after the conquest the Bosnians were weak in terms of religious faith and so ripe for conversion. While Sava's legacy in Serbia was a strong church which identified itself with the nation, no such equivalent existed in Bosnia, nor was Catholicism so firmly impressed on people as it was in Croatia. Many medieval Bosnians may have also regarded Catholicism with suspicion, as it was the religion of the persecutors of their own Bosnian church.[11]

One legacy of widespread Islamic conversion in Bosnia was that most Orthodox Serbs lived in the countryside, while a greater proportion of the Muslim population lived in the towns and owned the land that these peasants worked. Over time this led to a mix of resentments. There was the resentment of the oppressed peasant, which was similar in other parts of eastern Europe, but here it was combined with bitter religious, national and emotional grievances. By the nineteenth century, these factors were exacerbated by the rise of nationalism in both Serbia and among the Croats and by the intense conservatism of Bosnia's Muslim lords, who feared that any reform would undermine their position. The situation exploded in 1875 when Christian peasants rose in rebellion in Hercegovina, an insurrection which soon spread to Bosnia. Arthur Evans, who was travelling through the Ottoman provinces at the time, soon witnessed many of the same barbarities as we have seen in our times and he came to the same conclusions as many today:

At the moment that I write this, nearly 3,000 Bosnian and Herzegovinian villages and scattered hamlets are blackened ruins and over 200,000 Christian refugees are starving among the inhospitable ravines of the Dalmatian Alps. In the interests of humanity as well as of European peace, in discharge of responsibilities which no adroitness of European statesmanship can disavow, an armed occupation of Bosnia by civilized forces has become indispensable.

In 1996 the armed occupation by 'civilized forces' took the form of 60,000 NATO-led troops; in 1878 it was the army of the Austro-Hungarian Empire which the international community sanctioned to do the job. While in 1992 it was the Muslims who were the main victims of what Evans described as 'the robber bands of fanaticism', then it was the Christians, meaning Serbs and Croats, who were the victims of the Muslims. This did not mean that Evans could not take a balanced view: 'Discordant as are the political materials in Bosnia, fanatic as are the Christians as well as the Mahometans, I feel convinced that there exist elements of union in that unhappy country which might be moulded together by wise hands.'[12]

It is curious that, despite the bloodbath he was witnessing, Evans could come to the same optimistic conclusions about Bosnia that many were to reach more than a century later. Even more interesting in the wake of the ethnic cleansing of 1992–5 is Evans' description of what today we call militias. He wrote that the uprising had released upon the land marauding bands. 'The long restrained savagery of the old dominant caste has burst forth like a caged lion for the defence of Islam.' In Sarajevo he watched the arrival of groups of Muslim volunteers, Bashi-Bazouks, who had come to wreak vengeance on the Christian infidels or Giaours.

> We met a party of them defiling through the street, and the leader of the gang, as he passed, glared savagely at the Giaour. They are, from what we hear, mere organised brigands headed by irresponsible partizans, and at the present are committing the wildest atrocities – cutting down women, children and old men who come in their way, and burning the crops and homesteads of the rayah.[13]

Watching the mist fall over 'Serajavo' or 'the Serai', as the Bosnian capital was then known, Evans wrote a passage which is eerily familiar to the generation which witnessed the outbreak of war in 1992:

> It was, indeed, portentous of the present state of Serajevo; nothing but the present certain; her nearest future overclouded; forebodings of internecine struggles within; the sulphurous vapours of civil and reli-

gious war rising around her – doubly awful in the uncertain light of rumour. 'It is the beginning of the end,' said a foreign representative to us, 'do not be surprised if you are surveying the last days of Ottoman rule in the Serai.'[14]

They Are Not Human Beings: The Balkan Wars

Although Ottoman rule duly ended in Bosnia in 1878, it was to linger in much of the rest of the Balkans until 1912. Following the assassination of Aleksandar Obrenović in 1903, Peter Karadjordjević had become king of Serbia. He was the grandson of the leader of the 1804 rebellion and had lived most of his life in exile in France, Switzerland and Montenegro. He had graduated from the French military academy of Saint Cyr, and had had a distinguished military career. He earned the Légion d'Honneur during the Franco-Prussian war and fought in Bosnia during the rising of 1875–6 under the name Petar Mrkonjić. Already almost sixty by the time he came to the throne, he was popularly known as Čika Pera – Uncle Pete. Under the tutelage of the Radical Party, the government now broke away from the Austrian influence which had circumscribed its freedom under Aleksandar Obrenović. This soon led to Serbia's first experience of economic sanctions. Objecting to Serbian moves to free up trade with Bulgaria, the Habsburg monarchy banned the import of livestock, Serbia's main export, in a move that became known as the Pig War. This lasted until 1911. Serbia was able to find other outlets for its pigs and began processing more of its own meat domestically. Comic as its name may be, the Pig War was to have an enduring legacy. In the light of the sanctions placed on Yugoslavia by Stalin's Soviet bloc in 1948, the imposition of sanctions by the United Nations on Serbia in 1992 meant that many people happily assumed that history was repeating itself and that embargoes were par for the course when taking on the superpowers of the day. By adopting this David and Goliath attitude, they of course also assumed the justice of their cause.

After the Habsburg Empire, King Peter was determined to take on the Turks and finally 'avenge Kosovo'. There had been attempts under the Obrenovićs to organise an alliance of Balkan states against the Turks, but these had come to nothing. By 1912, though, Greece, Serbia, Montenegro and Bulgaria were ready for war. Together they massed 720,000 troops against an Ottoman force of 307,000. Serbia's contribution was 286,000 soldiers. After an imperial interlude of some 500 years the Turks were rapidly driven back, almost to the gates of Constantinople. The Serbs and Greeks had assumed they would partition Albania, but when the great powers met in London they dictated that an Albanian state should be formed. This had the effect of concentrating minds on Macedonia, about which no firm prior agreements had been made. The Serbs and the Greeks now made a deal to divide it between them. Bulgaria, fearing that it would become the great loser in a territory in which most of the Slav population fell within the Bulgarian religious and linguistic ambit, went to war with its former allies. The campaign was a disaster and, apart from the small area of Pirin Macedonia, the province was duly carved up by Serbia and Greece.

The Balkan Wars were to set the precedent in this century for massive waves of ethnic cleansing and the forced migrations of hundreds of thousands of people. All the worst evils that were witnessed in the former Yugoslavia between 1991 and 1995 were present in the Balkan Wars, including large-scale massacres of civilians, the destruction of whole towns and the gross manipulation of the media. This book has discussed only Serbian history, but it is important to remember that the Serbs do not live on an island. Despite each Balkan nation's historical peculiarities, there are as many similarities and shared values as there are differences. An example from the Carnegie Endowment report relates to the vilification of the Bulgarians by the Greeks during the Second Balkan War; it is worth quoting in full because precisely the same techniques were used in Serbia and Croatia to incite hatred in the early 1990s. The Carnegie report wryly notes that when the Bulgarians were massacring Turks little was said. Now that Greeks and Bulgarians were heading towards war with each other things were different:

Day after day the Bulgarians were represented as a race of monsters, and public feeling was roused to a pitch of chauvinism which made it inevitable that war, when it should come, should be ruthless. In talk and in print one phrase summed up the general feeling of the Greeks towards the Bulgarians, 'Dhen einai anthropoi!' (They are not human beings). In their excitement and indignation the Greeks came to think of themselves as the appointed avengers of civilization against a race which stood outside the pale of humanity.

When an excitable southern race, which has been schooled in Balkan conceptions of vengeance, begins to reason in this way, it is easy to predict the consequences. Deny that your enemies are men, and presently you will treat them as vermin. Only half realizing the full meaning of what he said, a Greek officer remarked to the writer, 'When you have to deal with barbarians, you must behave like a barbarian yourself. It is the only thing they understand.' The Greek army went to war, its mind inflamed with anger and contempt. A gaudily coloured print, which we saw in the streets of Salonica and the Pireus, eagerly bought by the Greek soldiers returning to their homes, reveals the depth of the brutality to which this race hatred had sunk them. It shows a Greek *evzone* (highlander) holding a living Bulgarian soldier with both hands, while he gnaws the face of the victim with his teeth, like some beast of prey. It is entitled *Bulgarophagos* (Bulgar-eater), and is adorned with the following verses:

> The sea of fire which boils in my breast
> And calls for vengeance with the savage waves of my soul,
> Will be quenched when the monsters of Sofia are still,
> And thy life blood extinguishes my hate.[15]

The Carnegie Endowment's account of the crushing of the Albanian revolt in Kosovo is also important because in 1913 as in 1941 or the 1990s it was quite clear to all involved what the purpose of ethnic cleansing was:

> Houses and whole villages are reduced to ashes, unarmed and innocent populations massacred *en masse*, incredible acts of violence, pillage and brutality of every kind – such were the means which were employed by the Serbo-Montenegrin soldiery, with a view to the entire transformation of the ethnic character of regions inhabited exclusively by Albanians.
>
> We thus arrive at the second characteristic feature of the Balkan wars, a feature which is the necessary correlative of the first. Since the population of the countries about to be occupied knew, by tradition, instinct and experience, what they had to expect from the armies of the enemy and from the neighboring countries to which these armies belonged, they did not await their arrival, but fled. Thus generally speaking, the army of the enemy found on its way nothing but villages which were either half deserted or entirely abandoned. To execute the orders for extermination, it was only necessary to set fire to them. The population, warned by the glow from these fires, fled all in haste. There followed a veritable migration of peoples, for in Macedonia, as in Thrace, there was hardly a spot which was not, at a given moment, on the line of march of some army or other. The Commission everywhere encountered this second fact. All along the railways interminable trains of carts drawn by oxen followed one another; behind them came emigrant families and, in the neighborhood of the big towns, bodies of refugees were found encamped.[16]

Just as conversion had been accepted as a means to escape death in earlier times, in some places it once again became an issue. When the Montenegrins captured the village of Plav, Rebecca West, whose pro-Serbian bent somewhat undermines her otherwise masterly account of

Yugoslavia in the 1930s, characteristically dismisses a major massacre as an 'unfortunate *contretemps*'. During this little misunderstanding a former Muslim cleric, now converted to Orthodoxy and a major in the Montenegrin Army, demanded that his former congregation convert. They refused and so 500 of them were shot.[17] In another incident, some Macedonian villagers had their church surrounded by Serbian soldiers during the Sunday service. On emerging they found that a table had been set up on which was a piece of paper and a revolver. Either they could sign that they were Serbs rather than Bulgarians – or they could die. They chose the former option.[18]

The Serbs used extreme force in their attempt to Serbianise Macedonia. As a consequence they were plagued with violence in the land they had rechristened Southern Serbia right up until the Second World War. The assassin of King Alexander in Marseilles in 1934 was a Macedonian who was working in league with the exiled Croatian extreme nationalist Ustashas of Ante Pavelić and the Italians.

Under the Turks, Macedonian nationalists had been divided between a pro-Bulgarian wing and those who favoured autonomy within a Balkan federation. At least in theory, in what became its Yugoslav part this was what was finally granted by the communists. In the wake of the Second World War a Macedonian Republic was set up. While in its early years its political autonomy was restricted, its outcome has been the development of a firm sense of Macedonian ethnic identity among the Slav population, where it had been weak before. It is also noteworthy that, having had their rights recognised, the Yugoslav Macedonians were mostly in favour of preserving Yugoslavia and voted to leave only once it was clear that their sole alternative would be to remain in a Serb-dominated rump state.

Instinct and Experience: How Many?

Though the world has been appalled by the vast movements of populations provoked by the war of 1991–5, it is certain that the unstable history of the Balkans has taught its peoples precisely when is the right moment to flee. As the Carnegie Endowment succinctly puts it: 'instinct and experience'. To underline this point it is worth examining some of the figures which demonstrate just how massive were the migrations and population exchanges in the Balkans in the period which began with the Serbian insurrection of 1804.

In the pashalik of Belgrade, Karadjordje's revolution resulted in the almost complete cleansing of the Muslim population. Turks fled or emigrated via the island of Ada Kale in the Danube, while Bosnian Muslims made their way home. Before the revolt there were estimated

1815–1913: Serbia and Montenegro Expand

to be some 40,000 Muslims in the Belgrade pashalik and perhaps 250,000 Serbs. Karadjordje's Serbia proved to be a powerful magnet for Serbs living in Ottoman and also Habsburg territories and a place of refuge for thousands who fled in the wake of Serbian military defeats. When the Turks finally put down Karadjordje's insurrection, 100,000 Serbs left for Habsburg territory – but many subsequently returned. The renewal of Turkish authority also saw the return of some Muslims, but under Miloš Obrenović the Serbian population is believed to have doubled in the period 1815–33. This was partly due to his policy of distributing land to immigrants and refugees. In 1844 the population of the principality was reckoned to be 849,236, but by 1874 it had climbed to 1,350,000.

According to the Serbian historian Milan St. Protić, the Serbian–Turkish wars of 1876–8 'caused the most massive migration process in the Balkans in the course of the 19th century'.[19] By his reckoning, some two million people, equally divided between Serbs and Muslims, fled their original homes. These included Muslim Albanians who were driven from Niš and other areas taken by the Serbs and more than a quarter of a million Serbs who fled from Kosovo to Serbia and Montenegro. Between 1878 and 1884 the Ottoman government had to absorb some 812,193 refugees, who were either in flight for their life or who would not live under the new Christian authorities, for example in Bosnia or Bulgaria. For the period 1884 to 1897 the figure was 202,822.[20] Turks and Muslims were also emigrating from Greece and from insecurity in Macedonia and Albania, although the Ottomans did attempt to settle refugees in Macedonia.

The next great spasms in the Balkans were the Balkan Wars, which may have dislodged up to 500,000 people; the dynamics thus begun in 1912 were to continue until 1923, when Greece and Turkey formally agreed under the Treaty of Lausanne to exchange most of their remaining minority populations. Bulgaria in agreements with both Turkey and Greece had already moved towards such formal population exchanges, which would today be denounced as legalised international ethnic cleansing. By one estimation, some two and a half million people in the Balkans were shifted from their homes during the period 1912–23 thanks to wars and population exchanges.[21] Between 1924 and 1933, 100,000 people, mostly ethnic Turks, also emigrated to Turkey, mainly from Yugoslav Macedonia, also as the result of inter-governmental agreements.[22] In February 1938 at a conference in Istanbul, Turkey, Romania and Yugoslavia met to discuss ways of encouraging emigration to Turkey. The Turkish government wanted Muslim settlers for its empty regions and to repopulate those areas which Greeks had left. The Balkan states were happy to encourage the emigration of their non-Christian populations. A meeting was also held in June and a convention foreseeing the migration of 200,000 'Turkish Muslims' from southern Serbia, many of whom would have been ethnic Albanians, was initialled but not ratified by the Yugoslav and Turkish governments.[23] Between 1952 and 1967 inter-governmental agreements resulted in the further emigration of 175,000 Muslims from Yugoslavia to Turkey. Nominally the emigrants should have been ethnic Turks, but a worried Turkish government was forced to send a circular note to its embassy in Belgrade and to its consulate in Skopje when it found considerable numbers of ethnic Albanians also entering the country this way.[24]

Dimitrije Djordjević of the University of California has written that for Greece, Bulgaria and Turkey the population exchanges of the earlier part of the century, 'although a curse for contemporary generations', have proved to be 'a blessing in the long run of history. It transformed them into predominantly nationally homogeneous states. It stabilized their frontiers along which refugees were mainly settled.' With regard to Greece, he says, it marked 'the end of the emotional but unrealistic

Megali Idea which dominated national politics for more than a century'.[25]

The Megali Idea, the 'Great Idea', was the dream of recreating a Greek Byzantine Empire, taking in not just Greece and Constantinople but much of Anatolia too. The fact that Serbs, Croats, Albanians and others remained scattered across the southern Balkans meant that, unlike the Greeks, whose nationalistic aspirations were now shattered, their own 'emotional' and 'unrealistic' national dreams were to remain either unfulfilled or satisfied only at the expense of another.

6

UNION OR DEATH

There is no better place to contemplate Serbia's changing fortune in the world than at the top of the Grand Staircase of the Foreign Office in London. During the First World War the artist Sigismund Goetze painted a series of large murals representing the triumphs of Britannia. The central painting is that of Britannia Pacificatrix. She stands resplendent alongside America and France, the colonies and other suitably bosomy or bemuscled allies. While Britannia grasps the hand of America with one hand, with the other she 'encloses within the folds of her royal mantle' those whom she had hastened to protect in 1914. Here is Belgium, a 'Psyche-like figure of pure girlhood', alongside Serbia, who in turn comforts little Montenegro.[1]

In the wake of all that has happened since, it is difficult now to imagine just how glorious was the Serbian name during and after the First World War. The Serbian Relief Fund in Britain boasted no lesser a figure than Queen Mary as its patroness, and its president was the Bishop of London. In 1917 an appeal for funds appeared with a grim depiction of Serbia's fate at the hands of the occupying Austro-Hungarian forces, the Germans and Bulgarians:

'Watchman, what of the night? Watchman, what of the night?' Such is the far, faint cry which reaches us from Serbia, while Armageddon's midnight settles on the world, and we her strongest ally, can but answer her as the prophet answered that same wistful cry of old: 'The morning cometh, and also the night.' And it is a rayless night indeed. Her land is drowned in blood and tears, the prey of four invasions in one year. Her women are flogged and violated in the open streets; her wee, wan ghosts of children gnaw weeds by the wayside, and forage in refuse-heaps for filthy bones. Her churches reek of profanation, and her priests are either murdered or deported. Her timber, her cattle, her harvests, are the enemy's so that within the war-zone a quarter of the population has already perished.[2]

Much later the historian Edward Crankshaw penned this iconoclastic opinion:

> The legend of 'gallant little Serbia' . . . which sprang to life as soon as England found herself at war with Germany and Austria–Hungary in August 1914, at once obscured the fact that for the previous decade Serbia had been regarded generally as a thorough-going nuisance, a nest of violent barbarians whose megalomania would sooner or later meet the punishment it deserved. There had been several occasions when the rest of Europe fully expected to see Austria lash out and wipe Serbia off the map.[3]

'It is necessary to be clear about the Serbs,' fulminated Crankshaw, in whose 1963 book *The Fall of the House of Habsburg* these trenchant views were expressed:

> This nation of proud and often splendid individuals has become familiar to us now. Everything in us which is attracted by the primitive, the unbending and the brave, responds to the appeal of these mountain warriors from the medieval Serbian heartland and their magnificent and heroic women who for centuries have borne the yoke as though it were a crown. But it takes more than an aggregation of splendid individuals to make a civilized society; and the extremes of bravery and self-reliance go all too easily with the extremes of treachery and cruelty. Centuries of existence under oppression may bring out the best in a people, but it may also magnify the worst. The manners of the oppressed are all too likely to take their colour from the manners of the oppressors; when the oppressors are Turkish Janissaries the results are likely to be bad. Further, the habit of conspiratorial violence which may be just the thing in a resistance movement operating against a tyranny is apt to be continued, with undesirable consequences, when the tyranny has been overthrown.[4]

Crankshaw was writing about the origins of the First World War at a time when memories of the Second were still fresh. But, in the wake of the demise of communism and another treacherous and cruel war brought about thanks to the habits of 'conspiratorial violence', one has to wonder whether any more proof is needed of man's predilection to repeat history.

Narodno Jedinstvo: The Birth of 'National Unity'?

Although Austria–Hungary had occupied Bosnia and Hercegovina and the Sandžak in 1878, the provinces were not formally annexed until

1908, after which the Sandžak was restored to the Ottoman Empire. This strategic strip of territory dividing Serbia and Montenegro was to remain in its possession only until the First Balkan War of 1912. The occupation of Bosnia and Hercegovina, while welcomed by the Catholic Croats, was opposed by the Orthodox Serbs, who being the largest of the three peoples in the two provinces wanted to join Serbia. The Muslims, who had no desire to be ruled by an alien Christian power, also opposed the occupation, and so both Serbs and Muslims resisted Austro-Hungarian forces. At the time the Serbs constituted 43 per cent of the population, the Muslims one-third and the Croats 20 per cent.[5] It took the imperial army three months to subdue the provinces and cost it 5,198 men killed, wounded or missing. The northern town of Brčko, the site of fierce fighting in 1992, was also burned down in 1878 'in consequence of the treacherous conduct of the inhabitants towards the Austrian troops'.[6]

Bosnia was quickly pacified after the occupation, but the political fallout was immense. Serbia was now constrained by the Habsburgs to channel its expansionist energies southwards, but this was a policy that could not endure. King Peter had, as we have seen, fought with the Bosnian rebels in 1875 and took a keen interest in what he and his countrymen universally regarded as unredeemed Serbian land. As a consequence the annexation of 1908 was greeted with outrage in Serbia, where the Austro-Hungarian flag was burned during demonstrations. In the ensuing crisis Serbia looked for international support but received none, and so war was narrowly averted. Although Serbian politicians were angry about the annexation, they were also quite capable of calculating the odds in a conflict that would have pitted the resources of a state of 2.9 million souls against an empire of 50 million. However, as Serbia did not receive even the Sandžak in compensation, the residue of bitterness was immense. In Vienna and Budapest, independent Serbia was regarded with similar suspicion, seen as a dangerous pole of attraction for the Serbs of the empire and increasingly for Croats too.

The Habsburg authorities had every reason to fear the influence of Serbia. Just as many nationalist Serbs in Serbia saw the country as the Piedmont of Serbian unification, so too did increasing numbers of Serbs within the empire, especially those in Bosnia who felt the most bitter about the annexation. These *prečani* or 'across the river' Serbs had to be careful about expressing such opinions, though, lest they be accused of treachery. In Croatia, Slavonia and Dalmatia, however, the Serbs were at the same time becoming a political force to be reckoned with. This was because, after the occupation of Bosnia, the old Military Frontier regions lost their *raison d'être* and by 1881 they had been abolished. For the first time, significant numbers of Serbs entered the

Croatian political mainstream. In Croatia and Slavonia, they made up a quarter of the population, while in Dalmatia they accounted for 16 per cent.[7]

The great controversies of the years before 1914 within the Habsburg south Slav lands centred on two questions. The first was the status of the south Slavs within the monarchy and the second was the related question of Bosnia.

Apart from the historical argument, whereby both Serbs and Croats claimed Bosnia for themselves, the Croats were in favour of the annexation because of the weight it would give to Slav claims within the monarchy. While the Croatian nationalists saw the annexation as the means of achieving a Greater Croatian state, a growing number of Croats also saw merit in the pursuit of 'Trialism'. This foresaw a unified south Slav state within the empire rather than numerous Slav provinces divided between Austria and Hungary. But first it was necessary to strive for the recreation of the Triune Kingdom, that is to say the political reunification of Croatia, Slavonia and Dalmatia. While the former were subject to Hungary, Dalmatia was subject to Austrian jurisdiction. Within the Habsburg lands the politics of the years leading up to the First World War saw a good deal of antagonism between Serbs and Croats. There were disagreements over Bosnia and sometimes quarrels which became violent. In 1903 for example there were anti-Serb riots in Zagreb following anti-Croat polemics in a local Serbian newspaper. Despite disagreements, there was also an increasing level of political co-operation between the two communities.

In the latter years of the nineteenth century, ideas of Illyrianism or Yugoslavism in the Habsburg lands had undergone something of a decline. It was Hungarian attempts to play off Serbs and Croats, however, and the continued division of Dalmatia from Croatia and Slavonia that helped revive the ideology. The single most important development here was the founding of the Croatian–Serbian Coalition of political parties in Croatia in 1905. Part of the understanding that led to this was that, if the Serbs would support Dalmatian unification with Croatia and Slavonia, which were being subjected to increasing Magyarisation, the Croats would support the principle of Serbian political equality within Croatia. In 1906 the Croatian–Serbian Coalition won the elections in Croatia–Slavonia. Central to its ideology was *narodno jedinstvo*, or Croat–Serb 'national unity', which was a precursor to the idea that Serbs, Croats, Slovenes and the other south Slavs were simply different names for parts of the same 'Yugoslav' nation.[8]

The Austrian and Hungarian authorities, who governed according to the principle of divide and rule, took fright at these developments and attempts were made to discredit the Croatian–Serbian Coalition. In

1909, a great treason trial of fifty-three Serbs was held in Zagreb, at which they were accused of having treasonous contacts with Belgrade. Evidence included the singing of Serbian epic poetry and the owning of portraits of King Peter, which were popular among the Serbs of Croatia.[9] Although the trial ended in convictions, the charges were so widely seen as having been trumped up that the emperor was forced to issue pardons. Hard on the heels of this came a case in Vienna against Dr Heinrich Friedjung. The eminent historian was accused of libel, having written an article claiming that leaders of the Croatian–Serbian Coalition were being funded by the authorities in Belgrade. What Friedjung had not known, however, was that the documents he had been given, which came from the Austro-Hungarian Foreign Ministry, were forgeries. The net result of both these cases was to alienate both Croats and Serbs from the Habsburgs and so to further the Yugoslav cause.[10]

In Serbia the idea of Yugoslavism was far less attractive than it was in the Habsburg lands. It was seen as one of three political options which governed thoughts about the future. The first and most prevalent was the creation of a Greater Serbia, including Bosnia and perhaps those lands in Croatia, Slavonia and Dalmatia inhabited by large numbers of Serbs. The second was the formation of a somehow united Slav Balkans. This would include the Bulgarians, who were seen as no less south Slav than the Croats or the Slovenes. With the Bulgarian attack on the Serbs in 1913, though, this option was foreclosed. The third idea, that of Yugoslavism, while becoming increasingly prominent in academic circles, remained of little interest among politicians. In 1904, however, intellectuals and students founded Slovenski Jug (Slavonic South), a society which aimed at uniting the south Slavs.

Over the next few years, there were increasing numbers of proto-Yugoslav congresses and exhibitions held in Belgrade. In September 1904, King Peter opened the First Yugoslav Art Exhibition. On display were 458 pieces by Serbian, Croatian, Slovenian and Bulgarian artists. In 1906, some 800 gathered for a conference of teachers from all of the lands that would later become Yugoslavia.[11]

It was only in the wake of the Balkan Wars and during the First World War that the idea of Yugoslavism, that is uniting the Habsburg south Slav lands with Serbia, began to be considered as a serious possibility. Until then, within the Habsburg possessions, the main Yugoslav thrust had been to create a south Slav state within the empire and only later, maybe, unite with Serbia. As the Habsburg monarchy was still very much a going concern, a Yugoslavia from Skopje to Ljubljana seemed then little more than a fantasy. In Serbia too politicians were more interested in a pan-Serbian creation but were still loath to go to war with Austria–Hungary to realise this dream. But by 1913 things had changed. The outcome of the Balkan Wars was that Serbia had almost doubled in size and its population had leapt from 2.9 million to 4.4 million.[12] This did not mean that Serbian politicians were suddenly keen on war with the Habsburgs, but it did mean that Serbia's stock with the monarchy's south Slavs rose to new heights. It was no longer simply a beacon of Serb and south Slav freedom but a glorious liberating military power which demanded respect. If King Peter was the first Serbian monarch to pay homage to the fallen of Kosovo Field in 523 years, surely it would not be long before the rest of the Serbs were liberated. It is hardly surprising, then, that in this climate belligerent parties in Austria–Hungary demanded the annihilation of Serbia before it was too late. On 28 June 1914, they were handed the excuse they were looking for. In Sarajevo, the young Serb Gavrilo Princip assassinated Archduke Franz Ferdinand, the heir apparent to the Habsburg throne.

Sarajevo, 1914

Following Austria–Hungary's annexation of Bosnia and Hercegovina in 1908, Narodna Odbrana (National Defence), a semi-secret society, had been set up in Serbia to organise volunteers to fight in what was believed to be the coming war. It also established a network of agents throughout the south Slav Habsburg lands. With many senior civilian and military figures involved, its aim was a Greater Serbia. In 1909, however, when it became clear that not even Russia would support Serbia in its quarrel with the Habsburgs, the Serbian government was forced to make a humiliating climbdown. A statement proclaimed that henceforth the government would 'disarm and disband volunteers and their companies', and would 'not permit the formation of irregular units on her territory'.[13] Narodna Odbrana's units were dissolved and the organisation turned to cultural issues, although its espionage network was maintained. By 1911, however, preparations had been made for the foundation of another semi-secret society called Ujedinjenje ili Smrt (Union or Death). It was conceived by hardline nationalists, many of them army officers, who held the civilian authorities in disdain for what they believed had been their treacherous capitulation after 1908. One of them was Colonel Dragutin Dimitrijević, always known by his codename Apis. By 1913, he had risen to the position of head of military intelligence of the Serbian Army. Apis had been a leading member of the regicides who had hunted down and killed Aleksandar Obrenović and his wife in 1903.

Ujedinjenje ili Smrt was behind the nationalist newspaper *Pijemont*

(Piedmont), and in the secret part of its statutes the organisation proclaimed that its aim was 'the unification of Serbdom'. It added that 'all Serbs, regardless of sex, religion or place of birth, can become members, and anyone else who is prepared to serve this ideal faithfully'. Cocking a snook at Narodna Odbrana, the statutes also declared that the organisation 'chooses revolutionary action rather than cultural' and that it would 'fight with all the means available to it those outside the frontiers who are enemies of the ideal'. Known by its enemies as the Black Hand, the organisation had an elaborate initiation ceremony. This involved masked men in hooded cloaks swearing in new members at a table covered with a black cloth on which lay a cross, a dagger and a revolver. The oath proclaimed:

> I [so and so], becoming a member of the organization Ujedinjenje ili Smrt, swear by the sun which is shining on me, by the earth which is feeding me, by God, by the blood of my ancestors, by my honour and my life, that from this moment until my death I will serve faithfully the cause of this organization and will always be ready to undergo any sacrifices for it. I swear by God, by honour and my life, that I will carry out all orders and commands unconditionally. I swear by God, honour and life, that I shall take to the grave all secrets of this organization. May God and my comrades in this organization judge me, if intentionally or unintentionally, I break or fail to observe this act of allegiance.[14]

The exact nature of the links between Apis, Ujedinjenje ili Smrt and the group who successfully plotted to kill the heir to the Habsburg throne in Sarajevo in 1914 has been the subject of vast amounts of academic research. While there is no absolutely conclusive evidence, it appears that Gavrilo Princip and other members of a group of revolutionarily inclined Bosnian students and schoolboys were in contact, at least indirectly, with Ujedinjenje ili Smrt. It supplied them with weapons and helped smuggle them back from Serbia into Bosnia using Narodna Odbrana's network. Apis himself, although the most important member of the ten-man Ujedinjenje ili Smrt committee, may have had little to do with the plotters, unlike his associate Major Vojin Tankosić. The Serbian government of premier Nikola Pašić, which at the time was involved in a general election campaign, found out that something was afoot and tried to stop it, although either it was too late or Princip refused to back down. There was also a vague warning delivered by Jovan Jovanović-Pižon, the Serbian minister in Vienna, who told the Austro-Hungarian minister of finance, Count Bilinski, who had responsibility for Bosnia, that the archduke's trip was inadvisable. In 1924, he told a Viennese newspaper that he had visited the count on his own initiative to say that 'among the Serb youths there might be one who will put a ball cartridge in his rifle and he may fire it'.[15]

On 13 July, a special emissary of the foreign ministry in Vienna reported from Sarajevo that 'There is nothing to show the complicity of the Serbian government in the direction of the assassination or in its preparations or in the supplying of weapons. Nor is there anything to lead one even to conjecture such a thing. On the contrary, there is evidence that would appear to show that such complicity is out of the question.'[16] The Germans came to the same conclusion. The former chancellor Bernhard von Bülow recorded in his memoirs that 'Although the horrible murder was the work of a Serbian society with branches all over the country, many details prove that the Serbian government had neither instigated it nor desired it.'[17] The Austro-Hungarians, however, were determined to use the assassination as an excuse to eliminate Serbia and sent it an ultimatum which was designed to be rejected. The Serbian government, fearing war, accepted the ultimatum except for one point, which demanded that it 'open a judicial inquiry against those implicated in the murder, and allow delegates of Austria–Hungary to take part in this'.[18] Despite this, the government said that it was willing to put the question to arbitration. This reservation was enough for Vienna to consider that the Serbs had rejected the ultimatum, and war was declared on 28 July.

Within weeks the whole of Europe was at war. Serbia was completely occupied by 1915. In 1917 Apis was tried in Salonika and executed, having been accused of treason and conspiring to kill Alexander Karadjordjević, the Serbian prince regent. Gavrilo Princip escaped the death penalty at his trial because he was just under the legal age at which he could be executed. He died in the Austrian fortress prison of Theresienstadt in April 1918 after enduring years of manacles, solitary confinement and execrable conditions.

Although Princip had acted with the help of men who believed in a Greater Serbia, and although the majority of his Young Bosnia group were Serbs who had been inspired by the Obilić story and the Kosovo myth, he said at his trial that he had not committed his act in the name of Serbdom: 'I am a Yugoslav nationalist, aiming for the unification of all Yugoslavs, and I do not care what form of state, but it must be free of Austria.'[19]

Agony and Resurrection

Immediately after the assassination of Franz Ferdinand, Croatian and Muslim mobs rampaged through Bosnian towns destroying Serbian shops and property. Soon afterwards, special armed units of Muslims and Croats called *Schutzkorps* were formed by the authorities and given 'full powers to deal with the Serbian population'.[20] By the end of July 5,000 Serbs were in prison, and the *Schutzkorps* often dispensed their rough justice without recourse to courts or other such legal niceties. Cyrillic was banned in Bosnia, Serbian schools closed down and property confiscated if members of a particular family had fled – for example, to fight in the Serbian Army. In 1915 a trial of 156 Serbian intellectuals was begun in Banja Luka. In eastern Bosnia, in an early version of ethnic cleansing in the region, 5,200 Serb families living along the Serbian border were resettled in north-west Bosnia. By far the worst collective punishment, though, was the opening of concentration camps in Hungary, to which some 150,000 Serbs were sent during the war and from which many did not return, owing to disease and poor conditions. These prisoners were not just from Bosnia but also from Serbia itself.[21]

Given the might of the Austro-Hungarian Empire compared to Serbia, it was widely expected that the imperial forces would soon overrun the kingdom. In fact two offensives were quickly repulsed by the Serbs, who even launched counter-attacks into Bosnia. Nonetheless, by December 1914 Belgrade had fallen. Soon afterwards, however, Austro-Hungarian forces deep inside Serbia found themselves overstretched and were crushed in a stunning Serbian victory at a battle on the Kolubara river. The Serbian Army then recaptured Belgrade.

In a strange echo of the days when Serbs fought each other as frontiersmen for both the Habsburgs and the Ottoman Turks, some of the Austro-Hungarian units pitted against the Serbian Army consisted of up to 25 per cent Serbs. The historian Vladimir Dedijer records the loyalty of these men to their emperor:

> In the battle of Mačkov Kamen in September 1914, fighting on one side was the Fourth Regiment of Užice [Serbian] and on the other a regiment from Lika including a large number of Serbs from that area whose forebears had for centuries been the most faithful soldiers of the Habsburg emperors. Commander Purić of the Užice regiment led his men in fourteen charges, to which the men from Lika responded with lightning-like countercharges. In one of these Purić shouted to them, 'Surrender, don't die so stupidly,' and they replied, 'Have you ever heard of Serbs surrendering?'[22]

Despite its initial victories the Serbian Army was no longer able to hold back its enemies after Bulgaria was tempted into the war with a promise of Macedonia. In October 1915, combined forces from Austria–Hungary, Germany and Bulgaria took six weeks to occupy the country. It was then divided between Austria–Hungary and Bulgaria. Conditions under occupation were appalling. In addition to those despatched to concentration camps in Hungary, some 30,000 Serbs were sent to Austrian camps or used as forced labour. Factories were plundered of their machinery and a devastating typhus epidemic stalked the land. Just as the Serbs had forced Macedonian Slavs to affirm that they were Serbs, the Bulgarians now forced Serbs to say that they were Bulgarians. Thousands died in desperate uprisings, and in some cases Bulgarian policy was so rigid that it even provoked mutinies among its own soldiers.[23]

If Serbia had simply been occupied and had laboured under extreme conditions, there would be little more to say on the subject. But this was not the case. In an extraordinary development, the Serbian government, the army, its high command, deputies, government officials, King Peter, the prince regent Alexander and thousands of civilians began an historic retreat through Kosovo, Montenegro and Albania. The ageing King Peter, who had yielded his royal duties to his second son Alexander in 1914, was hauled on carts into exile. Generals were carried in sedan chairs. As if to exult in the idea that Serbia would soon be resurrected, the soldiers also carried with them the casket and remains of Stefan Prvovenčani, the so-called 'First Crowned' Nemanjić monarch who had died 700 years before.

The Serbian aim was to reach the Adriatic coast, from where they could be rescued by Allied forces. As the Austro-Hungarians, Germans and Bulgarians were closing in and the Serbian escape route to Salonika in the south had been cut, the only hope was to trek across the snow-clad mountains. The retreat was as remarkable as any single event in Serbian history. It falls into the tradition of the great migration of 1690 or the flight of the Krajina Serbs in 1995, but is even more remarkable because in 1915 the army had every intention of returning and eventually succeeded in doing so.

The order for a general retreat was given on 12 October 1915. The authorities organised mustering stations, and before pulling out of towns and villages, public and even private property was put to the torch. 'What poet of genius, what writer could ever evoke the tragic scenes which were about to unroll,'[24] wrote Nikola Petrović, a Serbian captain who recorded his experiences in a book published after the war in France called *Agonie et résurrection*: 'Priests, teachers and their pupils followed the army. And behind it came the immense crowd of women carrying their children in their arms and young girls who did not want to remain under the domination of the conquerors.'[25]

At first the main problem was that roads were crowded with the sheer mass of humanity attempting to flee. Soon, though, conditions deteriorated dramatically. Roads turned to mud tracks impassable by car, laden cart or artillery hauled by yoked oxen. Cars were doused with petrol and set on fire while ammunition was destroyed and artillery thrown off steep mountain passes. With every passing mile, food was in ever shorter supply and the weather became colder and colder. Men began to freeze to death where they lay down to sleep. The price of horses, normally 100 or 120 francs, shot up to 700 or 800, and even saddle bags normally worth 6 to 10 francs went for 100 to 150. But the cold, the dreadful conditions and the lack of food were not the only problems.

The route to the Albanian coast taken by Petrović's regiment led through Kosovo, which had been liberated, or occupied, by the Serbs and the Montenegrins in 1912. The occupation had been followed by harsh repression against the majority Albanian population, which deeply resented its forced incorporation into these two Slav monarchies and desired instead union with the emerging Albanian state. The Serbian retreat presented the perfect opportunity for revenge. Petrović records that the local Albanians, 'whose feelings were violently . . . hostile to Serbs', mounted guerrilla actions to pick off weak detachments. 'The whole Serbian Army suffered . . . suffered horribly from the cold,' he wrote,

> . . . and the worst thing was that unlike the enemy it could not take refuge in the houses of Albanian villages, because if one of ours dared to venture into one of these houses to warm up or rest, he would be pretty sure to die there. The Albanians killed those who had become isolated, chopping their heads off with axe blows. Then they seized the uniform of the dead man and, disguised as Serbian soldiers so as to allay any suspicion, they killed other unhappy men by luring them into ambushes.[26]

Large numbers of soldiers began to desert before the army made it to the Albanian coast. Typhus and dysentery were rife. Military baggage was burned to warm cups of tea and in some of the most horrific scenes Petrović describes pathways strewn with the corpses of soldiers mingled with the carcasses of horses and oxen. There was worse to come, as starving soldiers, refugees and prisoners of war who had also been forced on the great march began ripping off 'sticky' flesh from dead horses: 'hunger was stronger than disgust'.[27]

By the second half of December the Serbs began to arrive in northern Albania, making initially for Shkodër, where the Serbian government had taken refuge. Because the area was exposed to Austro-Hungarian naval attacks from nearby Kotor Bay, however, it was impossible either to send provisions or to evacuate Serbian forces from there. They began to march again, this time to Durrës and Vlorë. From there, they were evacuated by the French to Corfu. But the agony was not yet over.

Epidemics swept through the Serbian camps and in an effort to contain them the sick were quarantined on two little islands off the coast. In the two months to March 1916, 11,000 soldiers died of disease and 7,000 of them had to be buried at sea.[28] 'The bodies were piled up one on top of the other until the heap was sometimes three metres deep. The night fell, they were put on barges and thrown into the open sea.'[29]

Within months the surviving army of some 120,000 men was taken to Bizerte in French Tunisia and from there to the front which the Allies had opened at Salonika. Civilians too were taken to north Africa and to France itself, especially to Corsica. Petrović, who finished writing his account just before the Serbs began to fight at Salonika in September 1916, recorded the spirit in the army, the 'debris' that little by little had reassembled itself. Impatient for action, it was a force driven by an 'implacable' lust for vengeance waiting only for the 'moment when the hour of Revenge would at last sound on the pitiless clock of history'.[30]

Along the Salonika front the Serbian Army fought valiantly, but after its victory at Kajmakčalan peak in 1916 and some other relatively modest advances the Allied lines remained stable until the end of the war. It was this that prompted the French premier Georges Clemenceau to dub the Allied and Serbian troops there 'the gardeners of Salonika'.

Today, just south of the present Macedonian frontier with Greece, there remains a simple, unkempt and windswept memorial overlooking the plain on which are inscribed the words: 'To the heroic youths of Great Britain, France, Italy and Serbia, who, faithful to the commands of their ancestors, fought in these places and died for freedom and world peace 1916–1918.'

During the Balkan Wars Serbia lost some 30,000 men. The First World War cost it 275,000 men and wartime diseases another 800,000 civilians. These losses amounted to a quarter of the population and two-thirds of its male population between the ages of fifteen and fifty-five.[31]

Over There, Far Away: Corfu 1917

In the early 1990s Serbian television sometimes showed a documentary that had been made on Corfu. The filmmakers had taken some of the veterans of the retreat and the survivors of the epidemics back to the island, where they talked about their experiences. Then, to the faint strains of the wartime song 'Tamo Daleko' ('Over There, Far Away'), which recalled their distant country, the old men tossed flowers into the sea. More than seventy years before, in what they called this 'blue grave', they had tipped the bodies of their dead comrades-in-arms.

State-controlled Serbian television never showed anything of such a nature without a reason, even if the film itself had been made in good faith. The subliminal message was the continuity of Serbian history. While veterans mourned the dead of one war, a new generation was condemned to fight another. But there was another way of looking at the film. The flowers were not just for the dead, but for a Serbia that was lost on Corfu too.

Although the army had left the island in 1916, the Serbian government of the white-bearded Nikola Pašić and the Prince Regent Alexander remained there. From Corfu they plotted the future not just of Serbia but of all of what was to become Yugoslavia. While Serbia was occupied, the position of its government was weak but plans still had to be made on the assumption of an Allied victory. Pašić was mainly interested in the creation of a Greater Serbia, combining, at a minimum, Bosnia, Hercegovina and Montenegro, which was also now under Austrian occupation. However, Pašić soon found that he was not the only exile thinking about the future. While most south Slav politicians within Austria–Hungary remained loyal to the Habsburgs, a number of important figures did not. They included two of the most important leaders of the Croatian–Serbian Coalition, the Dalmatian Croats Frano Supilo and Ante Trumbić and also Ivan Meštrović, the sculptor. In November 1914 they began work on forming the Yugoslav Committee, which was formally constituted in April 1915 by seventeen Serb, Croat and Slovene exiles and émigrés. They chose London as their headquarters, and their mission was to represent the south Slavs of the empire.

The Yugoslav Committee began to raise funds, especially among Yugoslavs living in the Americas, and even to recruit troops. Because of their stature, the members of the Yugoslav Committee were able to make their views known to the Allied governments, which began to take them increasingly seriously, especially as the fate of the Austro-Hungarian Empire looked more uncertain. While the Committee's basic aim was the unification of the Habsburg south Slav lands with Serbia, its more immediate concern was to head off Italian claims in Istria and Dalmatia. This was a very real concern. In 1915, the Allies had lured the Italians into the war with the promise of substantial territorial gains in exchange. According to the secret Treaty of London, which was made public by the Bolsheviks in 1918, these included Istria and large parts of Dalmatia, where relatively small numbers of Italians lived compared to the surrounding Slavs. Although in 1915 the Serbian Assembly had pledged itself to work for the liberation of all Serbs, Croats and Slovenes, the Yugoslav Committee was nervous that *Realpolitik* would intervene and that Serbia would abandon this stance in favour of a Greater Serbia. Indeed, in a bid to appease the Serbs, the Allies, who were also trying to lure Bulgaria into changing sides with promises of territory in Macedonia, were offering them Bosnia, Hercegovina, Slavonia, Bačka and those bits of Dalmatia not reserved for the Italians.[32] Croats such as Supilo became deeply alarmed, fearing a carve-up of Croatia between Serbia and Italy. There were also quarrels about the designation and command of units of south Slav POWs in Russia now being mobilised to fight with the Allies. The Yugoslav Committee wanted them to fight in the Yugoslav name, while Pašić, seeing in this a 'Croat Army', wanted them to fight under the Serbian flag.[33] The Serbian government also demanded that the officers create units 'imbued with Serbian ideas, and which are willing to die for the liberation of the Serbian hearth and for the unification of Serbdom and the Yugoslavs'.[34] Disillusioned, thousands of Croat and Slovene soldiers deserted. They were among the first to see that, if there was to be a Yugoslavia, as far as Pašić was concerned it was to be on his terms, especially as in the new state there would be twice as many Serbs as Croats. In 1918 he wrote, 'Serbia wants to liberate and unite the Yugoslavs and does not want to drown in the sea of some kind of Yugoslavia. Serbia does not want to drown in Yugoslavia, but to have Yugoslavia drown in her.'[35]

In the summer of 1917, however, Pašić was in a more conciliatory mood. Diplomatically the Serbian position had been severely weakened by the March revolution in Russia. King Nikola of Montenegro was also opposing union with Serbia, and there were fears that Bulgaria would take up the Allied offer in exchange for those parts of Macedonia that it coveted. Relations with the Yugoslav Committee were bad and within the empire a Yugoslav caucus had been formed in parliament which declared loyalty to the throne but demanded a state for Slovenes, Croats and Serbs under the Habsburg 'sceptre'. Meeting on Corfu in June and July the Serbian government and the Yugoslav Committee hammered out a declaration which was issued on 20 July and which was to lay the foundation of the post-war state. The preamble stated that the Serbs, Croats and Slovenes were 'the same by blood, by language, both spoken and written, by the feelings of their unity, by the continuity and integrity of the territory which they inhabit undividedly, and by the common vital interests of their national survival and the manifold development of their moral and material life'.[36] The future state was to be called the Kingdom of the Serbs, Croats and Slovenes and was to be a constitutional monarchy under the Karadjordjević dynasty.

While what happened at Corfu was to presage the future Yugoslav state, the declaration also bore within it the seeds of the same state's eventual self-destruction. For the sake of political expediency, given the need to present a united front to the Allies, or out of wishful thinking, it created a country on the basis of a lie. The Serbs, Croats and Slovenes were closely related, but there was as much which divided them as united them. Serbs were Orthodox, Croats and Slovenes were Catholics. The Slovene language was not the same as Serbo-Croatian, the Serbs of Serbia and Croats and Slovenes had no experience of living together in a common state, and above all their representatives were deeply divided about the future organisation of the country. The Croats had spent hundreds of years fighting for their 'state right' within the Habsburg monarchy, and the centralising tendencies of the Serbs were to be the cause of increasing hostility. Ever since 1804, Serbia had been growing, but always as a centralised state. In the new country the Serbs would be the largest single people, which led many of them to ask why they should make concessions to the Croats. This was the central political problem which was to paralyse the state between 1918 and 1941. It is also significant that the Yugoslavs, the so-called 'three-named people' of the declaration, were no more than that. The majority of Montenegrins considered themselves Serbs, but they had their own state and were not represented on Corfu. The Macedonian Slavs, Albanians and Muslims were simply not recognised as peoples in their own right or were ignored. This was not just arrogance but foolhardiness, for which the people of the former Yugoslavia are still paying today.

The Empire Restored

Before the collapse of the second Yugoslavia in 1991, its politicians spent years squabbling about what sort of state, federation or confederation the country emerging from communism should be. The Serbs demanded a strong centralist state. This made economic and political sense, they argued, because a confederal Yugoslavia was really a halfway house towards its disintegration. This they could not countenance because it would leave so many Serbs outside Serbia. The Croats and Slovenes countered that a strong centralised state was really a mask for Serbian domination, hence their demand for a loose federation or confederation. The greatest tragedy of all was that none of these arguments were new. As the shackles of communism loosened in the late 1980s, instead of finding new ideas and compromises which could have benefited everyone, politicians simply reverted to all the old arguments which had so sapped the Yugoslavia born in 1918.

As the Habsburg Empire dissolved, a National Council of Slovenes, Croats and Serbs took power in Zagreb on 6 October 1918. On 29 October, the Croatian Sabor or parliament declared independence and vested its sovereignty in the new State of the Slovenes, Croats and Serbs. The Yugoslav Committee was given the task of representing the new state abroad. Quarrels broke out immediately about the terms of the proposed union with Serbia. Svetozar Pribićević, a Croatian Serb, a leader of the Croatian–Serbian Coalition and vice-president of the state, wanted an immediate and unconditional union. Others, who favoured a federal Yugoslavia, were more hesitant. They feared, as Trumbić did, that Nikola Pašić's Serbia would simply 'annex' the former Habsburg territories.[37] There was good reason for this. Most Montenegrins, for example, were in favour of union with Serbia but, with the Serbian Army in occupation of the country in 1918, an uncompromising takeover was effected. King Nikola was deposed, and Montenegro ceased to exist as a juridical entity. Any demands for a federal Yugoslavia were simply brushed aside. For many, this left a bitter taste. Milovan Djilas wrote in *Land without Justice*, a book about his youth, that 'Some Serbians called the Montenegrins traitors and threw into their faces that they, the Serbians, had liberated them. The Serbians sang mocking songs, one about how the wives of each greeted the Austrians – the Serbian women with bombs, and the Montenegrin women with breasts. All this gave offense and caused confusion.'[38]

In Croatia the problem was far greater. Communist rebellions were brewing and law and order was breaking down in several areas. The National Council's authority was limited and the Italians were moving to take more territory than they had been allotted in an agreement with the Yugoslav Committee. Political opinion was divided and, despite talks in Geneva, exasperated Serbian ministers began to threaten that if the Croats insisted on a republic or a relationship with Belgrade which was similar to that which had existed between Austria and Hungary then Serbia would simply take areas already occupied by the Serbian Army and other regions inhabited by Serbs. After much debate the National Council agreed to unification with Serbia, although its declaration stated that the final organisation of the state should be left to the future Constituent Assembly. The most prominent opponent of this decision was Stjepan Radić, the leader of the Croatian Peasant Party.[39] In a speech that foreshadowed the bitter polemics of the years to come he told the National Council:

Gentlemen, your mouths are full of words like '*narodno jedinstvo*, one unitary state, one kingdom under the Karadjordjević dynasty'. And you think it is enough to say we Croats, Serbs, and Slovenes are one people because we speak one language and that on account of this we must also have a unitary centralist state, moreover a kingdom, and that only such a linguistic and state unity can make us happy. . . . Gentlemen, you evidently do not care a whit that our peasant in general, and especially our Croat peasant, does not wish to hear one more thing about kings or emperors, nor about a state which you are imposing on him by force. . . .

You think that you can frighten the people [with the Italian menace] and that in this way you will win the people to your politics. Maybe you will win the Slovenes, I do not know. Maybe you will also win the Serbs. But I am certain that you will never win the Croats ... because the whole Croat peasant people are equally against your centralism as against militarism, equally for a republic as for a popular agreement with the Serbs. And should you want to impose your centralism by force, this will happen. We Croats shall say openly and clearly: If the Serbs really want to have such a centralist state and government, may God bless them with it, but we Croats do not want any state organization except a confederated federal republic.[40]

Radić was excluded from the party that travelled to Belgrade, where the Kingdom of Serbs, Croats and Slovenes was declared on 1 December 1918. The name of the state was only changed after King Alexander's royal coup in 1929, although it was commonly referred to as Yugoslavia from the beginning. Of the country's 12 million people, 4.6 million or 38.8 per cent were Serbs and 2.8 million or 23.77 per cent were Croats.[41] This figure includes Montenegrins, but excludes more than half a million Macedonian Slavs, then almost 5 per cent of the population, who at that time were counted as Serbs.

It is not clear that the union was as unpopular in Croatia as Radić made out, but the relentless drive of Serbian politicians to impose a centralised and thus Serbian-dominated state over the next few years certainly alienated many waverers. Above all was the resentment felt by the Croats that they were not being treated as equals. For example, their former officers from the old Austro-Hungarian Army had to apply to join the new Yugoslav one, while Serbs did not. The army in effect remained a Serbian Army and in many other walks of life there was anger that the new Yugoslavia was not a state of *narodno jedinstvo* but a Greater Serbia in all but name. While the Serbian parliament was called upon to ratify the unification, Yugoslavia's first minister of the interior, Svetozar Pribićević, used his influence to prevent the Croatian Sabor from doing the same. He wanted to avoid problems being raised by federalists or those who opposed the union. However, like all such Serbian centralising and unitarist measures, this move, in the words of the historian Ivo Banac, 'rebounded with a vengeance, since the Croatian opposition ... could henceforth challenge the legality of the union'.[42] Likewise, using the Serbian-dominated gendarmerie Pribićević cracked down hard on manifestations of Croatian and other separatisms. He also had Radić thrown in jail, only to be released on 28 November 1920, the very day of the elections to the Constituent Assembly.[43]

It was not only in Croatia that there were problems. In Montenegro there was unrest among those opposed to the form of union imposed on

1918: The Formation of the Kingdom of Yugoslavia

Legend:
- Former Habsburg lands
- Provincial borders in Austria–Hungary
- Acquired from Bulgaria, 1919
- Frontiers of the kingdoms of Serbia and Montenegro, 1913
- Zadar, Italian enclave, fixed by treaty, 1920

0   Km   100

the country. In Kosovo, the army put down uprisings with the utmost force. There the Albanians were angry at the return of the Serbs, especially because, during the Austrian occupation, Albanian nationalism had been encouraged. In November 1918 some 800 Albanians were reported massacred around Djakovica.[44] No doubt for many of the soldiers involved it was a question of revenge for the toll exacted on the Serbian Army by the Albanians in 1915. Despite brutal repression and military intervention in Albania itself, the region was to be plagued for years to come by the activities of anti-Serb insurgents known as *kaçaks* who enjoyed widespread support. They were mostly directed by the Kosovo Committee, an exile group based in Albania. Their activities ended when, with Belgrade's help, Ahmet Zogu (later King Zog) returned to power in Tirana in 1924 after a violent domestic struggle in which the *kaçaks* and the Kosovo Committee were involved. The inter-war period also saw an influx of Serb administrators, police and colonists, especially from poor regions such as Lika, Montenegro and Hercegovina.

In Bosnia the situation developed differently. As Habsburg power ebbed away, Serbian militias began to take revenge for the wartime misdeeds of the *Schutzkorps*. But this violence also had an agrarian character, as had the uprisings that had begun in 1875. The 1910 census recorded that, while 91.15 per cent of all landowners were Muslims, 73.92 per cent of tenants were Orthodox and 21.49 per cent were Catholic.[45] The vast majority of these Muslim landlords, however, owned relatively small holdings. Because of this, the Yugoslav Muslim Organisation, the Bosnian Muslim party founded in 1919, was able to carve out a political role for itself in the new state. While it lent support to the main Serbian centralist parties it also extracted concessions from them. These protected the rights of landowners, Muslim traditions and institutions and the borders of Bosnia–Hercegovina, which were initially protected from any redrawing of regional boundaries.[46]

Slovenes too were able to extract gains from the central Serbo-Croat dispute. Half a million of them also lived under Italian rule and the Slovenes understood that it was only as part of Yugoslavia that they would be able to free these people in Istria. This duly came about in 1945. After 1918, however, the Yugoslav Slovenes benefited from the new state, receiving, in the words of their leader Anton Korošec, 'all they had previously lacked, high schools and a university to boot'.[47] As there was no native Serb population there, Slovenia had never been of interest to the partisans of Greater Serbia, and Slovene being a sufficiently different language from Serbo-Croatian the Slovenes were left to administer themselves with little interference from Belgrade. Unlike the Croats, the Slovenes in the Austro-Hungarian Empire had no historic claim to statehood, so there was no sense of loss to Belgrade.

The elections for the Constituent Assembly in November 1920 brought victory for the two main Serbian parties by virtue of there being more Serbs in the new state than other nationalities. Of 419 members, 92 were from Pribićević's new and mostly Serb Democratic Party, which garnered Serbian votes from across the kingdom. Nikola Pašić's solidly nationalist Radicals got ninety-one seats, having done well in Serbia, Vojvodina and Bosnia. The third largest party was the communists with fifty-eight seats. The fourth was Radić's Croatian Peasant Party, which swept Croatia and gained fifty seats. The new government was a coalition of the two Serbian parties led by Pašić. They were determined to push through a centralist constitution. In response Radić's party prepared a draft constitution for a Neutral Peasant Republic of Croatia which mentioned the concept of a confederated Yugoslavia.[48] The Serbs would have none of this, and so a dialogue of the deaf began. Thanks to horse-trading with the minor parties, including the Yugoslav Muslim Organisation, the centralist constitution was pushed through parliament on 28 June 1921.

Because it was the anniversary of the Battle of Kosovo, the 1914 assassination and Vidovdan, St Vitus Day, it became known as the Vidovdan constitution. With 285 deputies present – the Communists were absent and Radić's party was boycotting the assembly – 223 voted for the constitution. An editorial in the newspaper of Pašić's Radical Party celebrated, 'This year's Vidovdan restored an empire to us.' But, as Banac has pointed out, 'The restored empire was small and short-lived, like the terrestrial empire that, according to the Serbian folk epic, Prince Lazar abjured on the eve of the first Vidovdan in exchange for the celestial empire that is always and forever.'[49] For the Croats, Vladko Maček, Radić's successor, summed up his people's resentment in equally millenarian terms. The constitution 'eliminated the historic provinces' and 'made way for a royal governor whose chief duty was to liquidate the remains of Croatia by transferring authority in all matters to ministries in Belgrade. Thus, Croatia, a nation for a thousand years, had been wiped off the map, but continued to live on, ineffaceable, in the souls of its people, the Croats.'[50]

Shortly after the constitution was passed, old King Peter died. He was succeeded by Prince Alexander.

The Yugoslavia that tottered through the 1920s and 1930s was a poor, unstable and mostly sullen country. Macedonians, Albanians and Croats all harboured grievances against the Serbs, who dominated the state in every respect. In political life the Serbo-Croat national question prevailed over all other issues, and Radić and the Serbs zigzagged in their strategies for dealing with it. In 1925 for example Radić announced he would accept the constitution, work within it and even support Pašić's government. Radić became minister of education, but by 1926 this experiment in co-operation had failed. In almost as spectacular a reversal, Pribićević switched from a centralist position to supporting the federalist line. Maček attributed Pribićević's switch to his realisation that only by recognising 'the Croats and all other historical provinces on a level of parity with the former Kingdom of Serbia' could Yugoslavia be saved.[51]

It was not to be saved in parliament though. On 20 June 1928, after months of rowing and even fist-fights in parliament, Puniša Račić, a Montenegrin deputy, leapt up in the chamber and shot two Croats dead and wounded three others, including Stjepan Radić. In the ensuing weeks it seemed as though Radić had escaped death, but he finally died on 8 August. During those fateful weeks Pribićević held a number of extraordinary conversations with King Alexander. Since then, these talks have mostly been ignored by historians or mentioned only in passing. Given the Serbian attempt to carve out a Greater Serbia in 1990 it seems time to re-evaluate them. The first talk was about history itself. Pribićević told the king that in the wake of the assassination elections had to be held. Alexander rejected this, saying that he did not want the Croats to 'exploit the corpses' during an election campaign. Pribićević replied that if he did not want them to do this there should have been no corpses to exploit, and anyway 'was not all our history a campaign with corpses? Have not the Serbs in their campaigns been using for centuries the head of the martyr prince Tsar Lazar and the ashes of St Sava who was burned by the Turks? And did not the Karadjordjević dynasty campaign for a whole century on the head of Karadjordje?'[52]

Following this, Alexander promised to mull over the elections idea. He then called Radić from his sickbed for an audience, but Radić asked Pribićević to go in his place. He went on 7 July, the day before Radić was due to return to Zagreb. The king thereupon suggested that Pribićević should tell Radić that once he got home he should proclaim Croatian independence: 'Since we cannot live together it is better to separate. The best is to separate in peace like Sweden and Norway. If Radić accepts my proposition, tomorrow he can proclaim the separation.'[53]

'I was stupefied,' wrote Pribićević in his memoirs. He then proceeded to tell the king that such a suggestion was pure treason. The king responded by saying that he would prefer separatism to federalism. 'If you are thinking of amputation,' said Pribićević, 'the question arises: who will hold the handle of the knife by which the state must be cut?' The king replied, 'This will not be as difficult as you think. The bulk of the Serbs will remain in their state, which will be small but homogeneous and much stronger than now.'[54]

These premises were of course the very same ones on which Serbian President Slobodan Milošević was to base his disastrous policy of amputation or the 'cutting off' of Croatia in 1990.[55] Pribićević's account is not undisputed, but it is clear that there was serious discussion at the time about whether or not to cut Croatia adrift.[56] What is unknown is whether Alexander was serious or bluffing. For the Croats, it would have meant leaving large numbers of their people inside a Greater Serbia, while what was left would be a small rump state, most likely under Italian domination. Radić, who died soon afterwards, rejected the proposal and Alexander dropped the idea too. Despite this, the political crisis continued. Rumours swept Croatia to the effect that Radić had been murdered on the orders of the king, and Maček, who had witnessed the shooting, talked darkly of a 'doubtless premeditated plot'.[57] In December 1928, on the tenth anniversary of the founding of the state, there were riots in Zagreb, where students unfurled black flags on the cathedral. Exasperated, King Alexander finally acted. In January 1929 in a royal coup he seized full power and abolished parliament.

Far from attempting to create a physical Greater Serbia, Alexander now launched into an attempt to create a genuine Yugoslavia – by

1 Paja Jovanović, *Migration of the Serbs*, 1896: the Serbian patriarch leads his people away from the promised land, 1690.

2 St Sava and Stefan (Simeon) Nemanja.

3 Tsar Dušan and King Uroš from the fresco showing the
Nemanjić family tree in the monastery of Visoki Dečani.

4 Slobodan Milošević, 28 June 1989, six-hundredth anniversary
of the Battle of Kosovo.

5 Stefan Lazarević, from a fifteenth-century fresco in
Resava monastery.

6 In myth and memory: Lazar, the hero of
Kosovo, celebrated on a modern-day bottle
of (very cheap) wine.

7 Obilić kills the Sultan. Print of 1871.

8 1989, Gračanica monastery: elderly Serb in peasant costume bends down
to kiss the open coffin of Lazar, who died at nearby Kosovo Polje in 1389.

9 Handing down Serbian epics from generation to generation: Serbian peasant house with man playing the gusla. Line drawing, 1888.

10 The church of the Peć patriarchate in Kosovo, for centuries the seat of the
Serbian patriarchs and the centre of the Serbian Orthodox Church.

11 (*above*) Karadjordje, leader of the 1804 revolution and founder of the Karadjordjević dynasty.

12 (*right*) Miloš Obrenović, leader of the second Serbian uprising of 1815 and first prince since the Middle Ages.

13 (*right*) Ilija Garašanin (1812–74), the first Serbian politician to articulate a national ideology.

14 (*below left*) Njegoš, Prince-Bishop of Montenegro, author of *The Mountain Wreath*, 1847.

15 (*below right*) 1991: a Montenegrin soldier on the Dubrovnik campaign trail sports a 'Njegoš-style' cap.

16 Uros Predić, *The Kosovo Girl*, 1919, perhaps Serbia's most famous painting.

17 1915: in the footsteps of its ancestors, the Serbian Army retreats across the battlefield of Kosovo Polje.

18 Nena Mejra, one hundred years old, sitting next to the body of her dead, seven-year-old great granddaughter killed the day before by a Bosnian Serb militia. Hranča, eastern Bosnia, May 1992.

19 Shkodër 1913: the original caption to this picture reads, 'Montenegrins stone a Turk'.

20 Herding pigs – nineteenth-century Serbia's main export. Print of 1888.

21 Serbian infantry pass a Muslim cemetary as they enter Skopje in Macedonia, just liberated from the Turks, 1912.

22 1915: Vizir's Bridge, Albania. Serbian troops in retreat. The first group is carrying the famous General, Vojvoda Mišić, in a sedan chair. In the front of the chair is a little window for him to see out.

23 Serbian cavalry crossing the Black Drin river during their retreat across Albania, 1915.

24 The Serbian premier Nikola Pašić,
(1845–1926).

25 King Alexander Karadjordjević,
(1888–1934).

force. He decided to abolish Yugoslavia's historic regions. New internal boundaries were drawn for provinces or *banovinas* which, apart from the Slovene one, cut across the old historical borders. The *banovinas* were mostly named after rivers. Regional parties were outlawed. Many opposition politicians such as Maček were jailed, held under house arrest or kept under tight police surveillance. The effect of Alexander's dictatorship was further to alienate the non-Serbs of the kingdom, because the country remained Serb-dominated.

The repression, however, also turned a good many Serbs against the king. In 1934 he was assassinated in Marseilles, along with the French foreign minister Louis Barthou. The assassin, a Macedonian, was contracted to the Ustasha (Uprising) party of one Ante Pavelić, a hardline Croatian nationalist and parliamentary deputy who had fled in 1929 and now enjoyed the support of Mussolini and the Hungarians. Just before leaving for France, Alexander sent a message to the jailed Maček telling him that he would be released on his return and that they would then discuss the future together.[58]

Alexander was succeeded by his eleven-year-old son Peter II and a regency council headed by his cousin Prince Paul. Under the new regime, repression relaxed and Maček and other prominent political prisoners, including Serbs, were released from jail. Despite gestures to win over the Croats, however, the government of the Serb Milan Stojadinović, which took over in 1935 with the support of the Slovenes and Bosnian Muslims, did little to find a *modus vivendi* with the Croats. Stojadinović became increasingly concerned with securing Yugo-slavia's future after France and Britain consented at Munich in 1938 to Hitler's territorial demands in Czechoslovakia. The Austrian Anschluss of the same year made matters all the more urgent as the German Reich now had a frontier with Yugoslavia. Mussolini had for years also been plotting various schemes to weaken Yugoslavia, as he had territorial designs on Dalmatia. After visiting *Il Duce*, Stojadinović himself began flirting with fascism, introducing Yugoslav 'greenshirts', a fascist-style salute and the title *vodja*. But this last had to be dropped, because when chanted the words ran together and came out sounding like *djavo* or devil.[59]

The 1938 elections were won by Stojadinović's government party, but 44 per cent of the vote went to a broad opposition list headed by Maček and including Serbian parties. However, over the previous few months and at the prompting of Prince Paul, Maček had been having serious talks with the Serbian minister Dragiša Cvetković in a bid to find an enduring solution to Croatian grievances. The fact that there was support for this, among Serbs in general and Croatian Serbs too, was demonstrated by the fact that some 650,000 Serbs voted for the Maček list in the polls.[60]

Stojadinović was soon removed from office, and by the end of August 1939 Cvetković, now the premier, and Maček came to their historic Sporazum (Agreement). That both sides had been able to compromise after twenty years of bitter polemics and repression was entirely thanks to the international situation. For their part the Serbs feared that if and when Yugoslavia became embroiled in the coming war it would simply fall apart unless something was done to appease the Croats. There was good reason to fear this. In May 1939, at the height of the negotiations with Cvetković, the Italians proposed to Maček that 'in the event of war' the Croatian Peasant Party should declare Croatian independence under Italian protection. Maček says in his memoirs that he 'declined unconditionally', but the accounts given by Count Ciano, Mussolini's foreign minister, are very different and certainly helped concentrate minds in Belgrade.[61] In his diaries Ciano wrote on 18 May 1939 that he was informed that Maček 'no longer intends to come to any agreement with Belgrade . . . will continue his separatist movement . . . asks for a loan of 20,000,000 dinars. . . . within six months at our request, he will be ready to start an uprising'.[62]

The Sporazum created an autonomous Croatia within Yugoslavia, to include not only Croatia, Slavonia and Dalmatia but a large part of Bosnia. Of its population of 4.4 million, some 866,000 were Serbs. The agreement was not supposed to be the end of the matter but rather the beginning of a thoroughgoing reorganisation of Yugoslavia. So, although Serbian nationalists were enraged by the Sporazum, Cvetković began thinking about how to transform the rest of the country. These ideas included the creation of a Slovene federal unit and a Serbian *banovina*, based in Skopje.[63] Bosnian Muslim anger at the utter disregard for their interests in the Sporazum's division of Bosnia was of no interest to the Serbian or Croatian parties concerned. On 26 August 1939, parliament was dissolved but the Sporazum's provisions were enacted by decree using emergency powers reserved for the crown under the constitution. Prince Paul hoped that by settling the Croatian question Yugoslavia would be strong enough to weather the war, which started six days later.

7

WE CHOSE THE HEAVENLY KINGDOM

Was it the spirit of Kosovo, sheer folly or bungling that led to the military coup in Belgrade on the night of 26–27 March 1941? That night the government and the regency of Prince Paul were overthrown less than forty-eight hours after they had succumbed to Hitler's threats and signed up to the Axis Tripartite Pact. In London, Winston Churchill exulted:

> Early this morning the Yugoslav nation found its soul. A revolution has taken place in Belgrade, and the Ministers who but yesterday signed away the honour and freedom of the country are reported to be under arrest. This patriotic movement arises from the wrath of a valiant and warlike race at the betrayal of their country by the weakness of their rulers and the foul intrigues of the Axis Powers.[1]

On the streets of Belgrade and of several other cities, exuberant crowds chanted, 'Bolje rat nego pakt!' and 'Bolje grob nego rob!' ('Better war than pact! Better graves than slaves!'). Patriarch Gavrilo, who had been staunchly against the signing, clearly saw the coup in terms of the epic tradition. On the radio he said, 'Before our nation in these days the question of our fate again presents itself. This morning at dawn the question received its answer. We chose the heavenly kingdom – the kingdom of truth, justice, national strength, and freedom. That eternal idea is carried in the hearts of all Serbs, preserved in the shrines of our churches, and written on our banners.'[2]

On 6 April, Hitler began Operation Punishment. Belgrade was subjected to massive air raids, and the invasion and dismemberment of Yugoslavia began.[3] The war was to cost the lives of hundreds of thousands. In Croatia and Bosnia above all, but also in Kosovo, Serbs were hunted down and slaughtered and, in between fighting the occupying armies, the Serbs fought a civil war among themselves. In a perhaps unintentionally metaphorical passage, Churchill wrote of the aftermath of the 6 April Belgrade bombing: 'Out of the nightmare of smoke and fire came the maddened animals released from their shattered cages in the zoological gardens. A stricken stork hobbled past the main hotel, which was a mass of flames. A bear, dazed and uncomprehending, shuffled through the inferno with slow and awkward gait down towards the Danube. He was not the only bear who did not understand.'[4]

Decline and Fall

Until the spring of 1941 Yugoslavia had managed to steer clear of the war. However, by then Mussolini's troops had become bogged down in Greece, and Hitler was keen to begin his invasion of Russia. Bulgaria, Hungary and Romania had all signed up to the Axis Tripartite Pact and Albania had been conquered by the Italians in 1939. The noose was tightening around Yugoslavia. Prince Paul and the government, both Serbs and Croats, had little sympathy with Nazism and on the whole were Anglophiles who believed that, in the end, the Allies would win the war. But in 1941 Britain was in no position to send aid and Hitler was effectively telling Prince Paul and his ministers that, unless they subscribed to the Pact, Yugoslavia would be invaded. Most senior army officers, who were Serbs, told the Prince that in view of Germany's massive military muscle the country stood little chance of surviving an attack. For months the Prince prevaricated, and eventually his ministers managed to secure what they believed was the best deal possible.

Under the terms of Yugoslavia's accession to the Tripartite Pact, Hitler and Mussolini agreed that the country's borders would be respected and that it would not be compelled to give the Axis military support nor would Yugoslavia be forced to let Axis troops cross the country. As a sweetener the Yugoslavs were also promised that their interest in acquiring Salonika would be taken into account after the war. With a heavy heart, and believing that there was little more that could be done, Prince Paul agreed to Yugoslavia's accession to the Pact.

Hitler's main interest in forcing Yugoslavia to sign was to neutralise it and deny its territory to the Allies. Britain, for example, was trying to tempt Belgrade to stay aloof from the Axis by promising it the then Italian Istria. Importantly Hitler wanted to assure himself that the Allies could not gain airbases in Yugoslavia from which the oil wells of Romania, vital to the German war-effort, would be within bombing range.

Because of the experience of occupation during the First World War and of the Salonika front, there was, among Serbs at least, an instinctive reaction against signing up to the Pact. However, as the historian Jozo Tomasevich has pointed out, 'a large proportion of the population, in Serbia and especially in other areas, accepted the signing as the lesser of two evils, just as Prince Paul and his government did'.[5] To this day, the circumstances surrounding the coup remain not just a mystery but the subject of intense debate among scholars.

The main figures in the coup were the commander of the air force General Dušan Simović and his deputy General Bora Mirković. Immediately after assuming power, the plotters declared that King Peter, aged seventeen and a half, had come of age. They also implored Maček to join their new government, as they did a wide spectrum of politicians. Then, rather oddly considering that their prime motivation had been hatred of the Pact, they announced that they subscribed to it and that the Germans had nothing to fear. Without a doubt the British intelligence services played some role in the plot, but how much is uncertain. What is clearer though is that only after the coup did the plotters realise that despite all Britain's hints that it would help it was quite unable to deliver anything. It is also possible that the Símović government was forced to declare its loyalty to the Pact because otherwise Maček would not join it – which, with Yugoslavia on the edge of disintegration, would have encouraged an Axis invasion. It was all too late anyway. Enraged, Hitler vowed on 27 March to destroy Yugoslavia and demanded that the blow 'be carried out with inexorable severity and that the military destruction be carried out in a lightning-like operation'.[6]

Advancing on several fronts, German and Italian troops supported by Hungarians and Bulgarians quickly smashed what little resistance there was. Some Croatian regiments refused to fight, while the almost entirely Serb senior officer corps saw little point in shedding blood in the face of such an overwhelming offensive. The Yugoslav government fled. Before ending up in London it passed through Jerusalem, from where, it was pointed out, the grey hawk had once set out with its fateful message for Prince Lazar. Maček decided not to go into exile and returned home to Croatia. An act of capitulation was signed on 17 April.

Yugoslavia was now carved up. As Maček refused to head the new quisling state in Croatia, Ante Pavelić was brought back from Italy to lead the so-called Nezavisna Država Hrvatska, the Independent State of Croatia, which is most commonly referred to by its initials, NDH. As many Croats blamed the Serbs for the coup and for Yugoslavia's subsequent collapse, Maček noted that the declaration of the NDH on 10 April was greeted with 'a wave of enthusiasm' in Zagreb 'not unlike that which had swept through the town in 1918 when the ties with Hungary were severed'.[7] It did not last long. On 18 May, Pavelić's new state was compelled to cede to Italy large parts of Dalmatia. Hungary

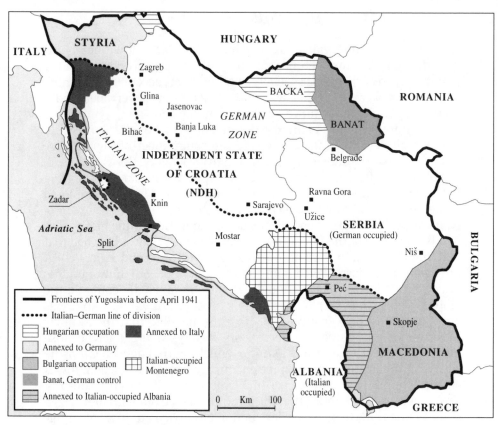

1941: The Destruction and Occupation of Yugoslavia

took Bačka, Baranja and part of Slovenia. The rest of Slovenia was divided between Germany and Italy. Although Bosnia was annexed to the NDH, a dividing line split both Bosnia and Croatia into German and Italian zones.

As for the rest of Yugoslavia, Bulgaria was awarded most of Macedonia, while Italian Albania became a Greater Albania, taking in most of Kosovo, western Macedonia and some parts of Montenegro. Montenegro itself fell under Italian rule. The Germans took the Banat for themselves, partly to avoid conflict there between Romania and Hungary. It was run by local ethnic Germans who constituted less than one-fifth of the population. What was left was Serbia, more or less within its 1912 boundaries. Answering to the German occupation authorities, a Serbian caretaker regime was installed under General Milan Nedić, a former minister of the army and navy and chief of the General Staff. He believed his role to be on a par with that of Pétain in France and his task to be to save as many Serbian lives as possible.

The collapse of Yugoslavia was so rapid that, although some

375,000 soldiers and officers fell into Axis hands and became POWs, hundreds of thousands did not.[8] In the main they just went home. But the speed of the collapse meant that most of Yugoslavia, especially the areas outside towns and cities, was not actually occupied, so no disarmament could take place. This was to have profound consequences. Hitler's original idea had been to dismember Yugoslavia and, once reliable regimes had been installed, to move on to finish off Greece and then attack the Soviet Union. His failure to do this meant that, within months, occupied Yugoslavia was in utter chaos. In Serbia rebellions were breaking out and in Croatia and Bosnia fanatical Serb-hating Ustashas were on the loose, perpetrating appalling massacres which quickly led to Serbian uprisings and the loss of control over large areas.

After the takeover of Serbia Hitler's frontline troops did indeed move off, leaving security in the hands of Nedić and smaller numbers of German soldiers. Nedić was allowed to create a small Serbian State Guard and he was also backed up by 3,600 men from Zbor (Rally). This was a pro-Nazi militia led by the Serbian fascist Dimitrije Ljotić. Also operating were a White Russian militia and the Chetnik units of Kosta Pećanac, which in May 1942 reached a peak strength of 13,400 men. Deriving their name from the guerrillas who had fought behind Turkish and enemy lines between 1904 and 1914, Pećanac's Chetniks were born out of the Serbian patriotic organisations of the same name which had existed in Serbia in the 1930s. Pećanac's Chetniks were not, however, the same as those of Colonel, later General, Dragoljub-Draža Mihailović, who formed his own resistance movement soon after the Yugoslav collapse.

Into the Whirlwind

At his trial for collaboration and war crimes in 1946 Draža Mihailović said, 'Destiny was merciless towards me when it threw me into the most difficult whirlwinds. I wanted much, I began much, but the whirlwind, the world whirlwind, carried me and my work away.'[9] A former military attaché and General Staff officer, Mihailović was stationed in northern Bosnia when the war broke out. Refusing to accept the surrender, he trekked to Serbia with a small group of followers expecting to link up with the main lines of Yugoslav military resistance. He discovered that there were none. Choosing the isolated Ravna Gora area of western Serbia as a base, he began to build up a following, starting with only twenty-six men.

Mihailović was an officer of the old school. He had survived the 1915 retreat across Albania and the Salonika front. Typical of his generation of Serbian officer, he was an ardent nationalist. A photo from an open-air Chetnik church service shows it being conducted beneath a cross, at the centre of which is a picture of King Peter. As if to emphasise their roots, many of Mihailović's followers affected beards and long hair like the Hajduks of earlier generations. They also adopted not just the old Serbian symbols but skull-and-crossbone flags adorned with the slogan 'Freedom or Death'.

Like many of his generation who had survived the horrors of the First World War, Mihailović was terrified lest this new war should precipitate the Serbs towards 'national suicide'. So the question arose of which was the best way to fight the enemy. Mihailović felt that it was to build up his forces and, though certainly launching sabotage actions, guard their resources until such time as a national uprising could have a real chance of success. At first, this was also what the British and the Yugoslav government in exile told him to do. However, Mihailović was not acting alone, even though in 1942 he was appointed the Yugoslav government's minister of war and chief of staff of the Yugoslav Army's Supreme Command. In the nearby Serbian town of Užice, communist Partisans had also started operating.

On 22 June 1941, the Germans attacked the Soviet Union. Stalin then appealed for communists to attack the Nazis wherever possible, in a bid to weaken their onslaught on the USSR. While Yugoslavia's communists had been relatively strong in 1920, domestic repression and the Moscow purges had decimated the movement. By 1941, though, a small but unified team operating under the leadership of the half-Croat, half-Slovene Josip Broz, known as Tito, was at the helm. In the First World War, Tito had fought in the Austro-Hungarian Army, even briefly fighting against Serbia. Later he was taken prisoner and lived through the revolution in Russia. Throughout the 1920s, he had been a trade union and party activist and he also spent time in jail. In November 1928, he had been imprisoned after bombs that he had been hiding for the party were found in his flat. During the period of Stalin's great purges, Tito was in Moscow. By 1940, he was back in Zagreb, where he was appointed party leader.[10]

Responding to the call from Moscow, Tito's men began attacking the Germans in Serbia in early July. Chetniks, eager for action, also began to fight the enemy. By August it became clear that the Germans had a severe problem on their hands. In September they reacted by ordering the execution of one hundred hostages for every German soldier killed and fifty for every German wounded. In reprisals for some twenty German deaths in mid-October, they proceeded to execute some 5,000 civilians, including schoolboys in Kragujevac and Kraljevo.[11] It was precisely savagery like this that Mihailović had feared. He could not control the situation, and it was rapidly becoming clear that the

Germans were not his only enemy.

The Germans' failure to occupy the whole country and the fact that so many of their best troops had quickly been moved off to attack the Soviet Union meant that by September Tito's Partisans were in control of Užice and a large area around it. From here Tito engaged in discussions with Mihailović about fighting together, but neither side was prepared to subordinate itself to the other. Tito also had none of the reservations about safeguarding lives that Mihailović had. He operated on the principle of 'the worse the better': every German reprisal brought more people, volunteers or refugees, into Partisan ranks. The ideological gulf was also far too great. Mihailović was committed to the restoration of the royal and Serbian-dominated Yugoslavia. Tito was committed to the seizure of power at war's end and a socialist revolution. Relations rapidly deteriorated and a civil war within the wider war broke out. Because at this stage almost all the Partisans were Serbs, in effect a Serbian civil war had broken out.

Confronted by the communists, Mihailović held talks with the Germans with a view to collaborating against their common enemy. The Germans were not keen, but it was the beginning of a complex relationship typical of the conflict that was now to be played out across wartime Yugoslavia. In 1943, for example, Tito's deputies likewise engaged in discussions with the Germans in Zagreb, but nothing came of these talks.

By early January 1942, the Partisans had been driven out not only of western Serbia but of Montenegro too, where there had been an initially successful uprising against the Italians. Despite Mihailović's offer not to fight the Germans, they turned on him as well, especially as on 15 November General Simović, broadcasting on the BBC, had described him as the 'commander of all Yugoslav armed forces that are fighting in the country'.[12] The British too soon made a decision that military aid would be sent to him exclusively. For the next three years, both Mihailović and Tito were to move with their forces across the nominally occupied or NDH territories locked in combat with one another, with the Germans, with the Italians, with the Ustashas, or in some form of triangular combination. At various times both held large areas of territory. After Užice, for example, the communists went to Foča in eastern Bosnia, while the Chetniks held an area of some 500 villages to the north in the Mount Majevica region.

While Tito and Mihailović initially disagreed on strategy and tactics, ideology was in the end to seal the Chetniks' fate. For while Mihailović's Greater Serbian patriotism appealed to the conservative peasantry of Serbia and his men helped organise protection for the Serbs of Bosnia and Croatia, his was not an idea around which the other peoples of Yugoslavia could rally. Although the Serbs constituted at most 40 per cent of the population and so were the largest single nation in Yugoslavia, this still left them a minority. By contrast, the Partisans learned to play down communism in favour of a Popular Front approach which appealed to all Yugoslavs to come forward and fight the enemy together. In Bosnia, for example, the Partisan rallying cry was for a country which was to be 'neither Serbian nor Croatian, nor Moslem, but Serbian and Moslem and Croatian'. It was to be 'a free and brotherly Bosnia and Herzegovina, in which full equality of all Serbs, Moslems and Croats will be ensured'.[13] At his trial in 1946 Mihailović said, 'Politics never interested me.'[14] This lack of inspiration is evident in the Serbian exclusivist messages such as that contained in Directive No. 1 of the Chetnik Supreme Command of January 1943. This declared that 'Partisan units are composed of a motley of rascals, such as the Ustashas, the most blood-thirsty enemies of the Serbian people, Jews, Croats, Dalmatians, Bulgarians, Turks [Muslims], Hungarians, and all other nations of the world. . . . Because of this mixture, the fighting value of the Partisan units is very low, a fact partly due to their poor armament.'[15]

In the Sandžak and Bosnia, then, the Chetniks were soon involved in bloody inter-ethnic strife with Muslims, many of whom had been enrolled into Italian and Ustasha units. The familiar cycle of massacres and village-burning began, becoming more bloody at every turn. Historians are divided over Mihailović's own role here. There exists one document, for example, apparently signed by Mihailović, in which he talks specifically about an 'ethnically pure' Greater Serbia and about the need for 'cleansing the Moslem population from Sandjak and the Moslem and Croat populations from Bosnia and Herzegovina'. Its authenticity is heavily disputed, though, and it may well have been forged by a local Chetnik leader in a bid to bolster his own authority.[16]

In 1946, the new Yugoslav communist authorities put Mihailović on trial. It was, of course, a show trial. Nevertheless, in the wake of the war of 1991–5, the atrocities committed during the conflict and the setting up of the UN International War Crimes Tribunal in The Hague, it is interesting to look again at some of the evidence presented there. For example, on 1 January 1943, according to the prosecution, Mihailović was informed by his commander Pavle Djurišić that in Plevlje in Sandžak and in Čajnice and Foča in eastern Bosnia his Chetniks had carried out operations against the Muslims there:

The operations were executed exactly according to orders. . . . All the commanders and units carried out their tasks satisfactorily. . . . All Moslem villages in the three above mentioned districts are entirely burnt, so that not one of their houses has remained undamaged. All property has been destroyed except cattle, corn and hay. In certain places the collection of fodder and food has been ordered so that we can set up warehouses for reserve food for the units which have remained on the terrain in order to purge it and to search the wooded areas as well as establish and strengthen the organization on the liberated territory. During operations complete annihilation of the Moslem population was undertaken, regardless of sex and age.

Victims . . . among the Moslems, about 1,200 fighters and up to 8,000 other victims: women, old men and children. . . .[17]

Mihailović told the court only that Djurišić had told him that he would 'settle accounts' on his way somewhere else and 'I also had reasons for wanting this terrain cleared up, but I never thought he would clear it up in this way. . . .'[18] Mihailović specifically told the court that he had never issued orders for massacres and insisted that they had hindered his work. He explained that at one point he had taken a Muslim to talk to a group of Serbs: 'He rose to speak and said: "Brothers, I am a Moslem. The Moslems have suffered enough. But there are three ways to solve this question. The first is to slaughter them all." All the people at the meeting, male and female, shouted: "Let us slaughter them!" We were flabbergasted.'[19]

The prosecutor then stated that Mihailović had incited the Serbs, but he denied it: 'Never in my life did I go in for this way of killing.' In what was, however, 'a typical case' he lamented that: 'Entire regions were destroyed by Moslems, but this had repercussions afterwards. The men revenged themselves in battle. The Drina carried away large numbers of corpses from all three sides. It was a river of blood. The people revenged themselves for the crimes the Ustashas [mostly Muslim in that area] had committed.'[20]

It remains to be seen whether the same line of defence will be used by the new generation of Serbian leaders if and when they come to trial. But, even if there are no documents to prove that during the war that began in Bosnia in 1992 Bosnian Serb leaders gave orders for massacres, it would seem abundantly clear that they did even less than Mihailović to put a stop to them.

As for the post-war settlement, apart from the objective of winning the war Mihailović seems to have had few clear ideas. He was of course also counting on the return of the government in exile. This was not true of the few intellectuals that Mihailović managed to gather around him. They did not mince their words when it came to elaborating their vision of what they called the Ravna Gora Movement. The most famous statement of this is the document called 'Homogeneous Serbia' written in 1941 by Stevan Moljević, a Bosnian Serb lawyer who was among Mihailović's top advisers. Central to this was the idea that the Serbs were to dominate the future Yugoslavia by 'creating a homogeneous

Serbia which has to include the entire ethnic area populated by Serbs'. On the map of this Greater Serbia, Croatia is reduced to a small rump divided in two parts. Slovenia is enlarged with the addition of territories in Italy and Austria. Serbia consists of everything that is left plus territory taken from Albania, Hungary, Romania and Bulgaria. A part of Dalmatia and Hercegovina would have a special status within Serbia but major population transfers would be necessary, 'especially of Croats from the Serbian and Serbs from the Croatian areas'.[21] Judging by the maps there would have been precious few of the latter.

In the wake of the 1992–5 war in Bosnia it should come as little surprise that, despite such Chetnik thinking, nothing was really as simple as it seemed. In some areas Muslim Ustashas had fallen on their Serbian neighbours at the beginning of the war, and in 1942 and 1943 there were large massacres of Muslims by Chetniks, especially in the eastern Bosnia and the Foča region. However, in some places there were actually groups or villages of Muslim Chetniks and in the west a small number of ethnic Croat Chetniks. At the end of 1943, some 4,000 of Mihailović's men or 8 per cent were estimated to be Muslims.[22] The prevailing chaos is captured in this account of his wartime experiences by a Serb from the eastern Bosnian village of Kitovnice who was nineteen when the war broke out in 1941:

> The Muslims from the neighbouring village had a militia and they came up to our village wearing Ustasha symbols. They arrested, took away and killed thirteen people. Then we were called to Zvornik to be mobilised into the Ustasha army and had to swear an oath of loyalty to Ante Pavelić. After this they said they had no uniforms for us and to go home and wait until we were called. The Muslims then came and tried to catch people, so we escaped to Majevica, which was free Chetnik territory. The Muslims had to leave that area. In 1942 the Chetniks and the Ustashas made an agreement to fight against the Partisans, so the Muslims came back. I could not go back to my village, though, because then I would have had to join the Ustashas. Until 1944 I fought the Partisans, but then I joined them. There were forty-eight of us who joined at the same time. We were in Serbia at that point and the Partisans surrounded us and called on us to surrender. It was obvious by then that the Chetniks would lose the war and that there was no future for them. So, as Partisans now, we crossed back to Bosnia to fight the Chetniks. There were no more Ustashas in our area then. At this point many Muslims joined us too. They had been part of the Green Cadres, who had just been protecting their villages.[23]

The man who told this story was sitting in a house not far from the front line in 1995. The difference between this war and the Second World

War in Bosnia was that then there were very few frontlines and there were far more pockets and ethnic enclaves that survived throughout the conflict. Nevertheless, after he told his story, a younger man, a Bosnian Serb soldier, said that among recently captured men from the Muslim side was a Serb anti-aircraft gunner. He said the Muslims were offering several Serb prisoners to get him back because they valued his skills so highly. Besides, he said, the Serb wanted to go back, because his family were on the Muslim side. 'I'd kill him,' opined a venerable Serbian grandmother in the corner.

Despite the fighting, Tito and his Partisans laid the foundations for the future Yugoslavia at their historic congresses held in Bihać in November 1942 and in Jajce a year later. It was to be a left-wing federal state. At the time it was deemed opportune to play up the Popular Front approach and not to emphasise that the real aim was a fully fledged communist state. As the Chetniks, operating either under Mihailović's control or independently, slid progressively into ever deeper relationships of dependence with the Germans or the Italians or into various tactical alliances, the British made their fateful decision to drop Mihailović and switch their support to Tito. In part this was under the influence of liaison officers such as Fitzroy Maclean who had Churchill's ear and were impressed by what they had seen of Tito and the Partisans. As defined by Churchill in the summer of 1943, Maclean's task 'was simply to find out who was killing the most Germans and suggest means by which we could help them to kill more'.[24] Because the Partisans were killing more Germans, Mihailović was dropped in the spring of 1944 and his movement began to crumble away. As the fateful decision was being made, Maclean told Churchill that, whether Britain helped the Partisans or not, they would be 'the decisive political factor' in Yugoslavia after the war 'and that the system which they would establish would inevitably be on Soviet lines and, in all probability, strongly oriented towards the Soviet Union'.

> The Prime Minister's reply resolved my doubts.
> 'Do you intend', he asked, 'to make Jugoslavia your home after the war?'
> 'No, Sir,' I replied.
> 'Neither do I,' he said. 'And that being so, the less you and I worry about the form of Government they set up, the better. That is for them to decide. What interests us is, which of them is doing most harm to the Germans?'[25]

In 1943 Italy had collapsed, which enabled the Partisans in Yugoslavia to seize a large amount of their weaponry. After this, the Allied decision to supply Tito, the inexorable advance of the Allies, the

German retreat and the gradual melting away or defeat of Mihailović's Chetniks put the Partisans in a strong position to inherit the whole of Yugoslavia at war's end. In October 1944 the Partisans and the Soviet Red Army took Belgrade, but the war in Yugoslavia did not end until May 1945, when the NDH collapsed.

Although Mihailović was hunted down and captured, many Chetniks, especially those from western Bosnia and the Serbian areas of Croatia and Dalmatia, retreated and gave themselves up to the Allies. Some who passed through Croat-held territory were killed by the Ustashas and many of those who managed to get to Austria were sent back by the British. In Italy, however, policy was different and at the end of the war the British had some 20,000 former Chetniks in their care. They were sent to a camp at Eboli in southern Italy. Technically they were 'Surrendered Enemy Personnel', but they were mostly looked on with considerable sympathy. They were seen as being basically pro-Allied and so were put in British uniforms and given non-combatant duties throughout Italy such as guarding munitions and supplies. In 1947 they were moved to Germany for screening, and although 104 were deemed to be possible war criminals none was sent back to Yugoslavia. About 8,000 of the men now came to settle in Britain, while the rest went mainly to the US, Canada and Australia. A curious landmark of this minor Serbian migration is the Ravna Gora Hotel, which doubles as a Serbian social club on London's Holland Park Avenue.[26]

Croatia, Kaputt

When Ante Pavelić was returned from Italian exile to become the Croatian Poglavnik (Führer) he came with no more 300 supporters. Naturally he also had followers within the country, but the extreme nationalist Ustasha movement had never had any mass support within Croatia. Certainly it found its roots in the nineteenth-century nationalist politics of Ante Starčević, but throughout the inter-war period Croatian politics had been dominated by the Croatian Peasant Party. The installation of the NDH regime meant that fanatics were now in power in a state where law and order rapidly collapsed and whose population was barely 50 per cent Croat. Together with Bosnia the NDH was composed of 6.5 million people, of whom about one-third were Serbs and 12 per cent Muslims. While the Muslims were declared the 'flower of the Croatian nation', that is Muslim Croats, the implacable anti-Serb ideologues now in power sought to exterminate the Serbs of the NDH.

Svetozar Babić was a fourteen-year-old Serb from Glina in Croatia when the NDH was proclaimed on 10 April 1941. Glina was a mixed town of Serbs, Croats and some Jews. These are his recollections of the first weeks of the NDH:

> When the war began I remember the German troops passing through. There was no defence, no fighting, they just passed through. Then the Croats nationalised our shop and those of the other Serbs and Jews without any right to compensation. But there was no threat to anyone's life. Early in May they took away the five or six Jewish families. We thought 'Okay, they are against the Jews, but we are Christians.' We did not think they were against us. Then came the night of the 10–11 May. Ustashas, not locals, men with guns came knocking on doors at midnight asking who was in the house. They took my father and my brother. My mother lied and said I was twelve which saved my life. They said it was for an investigation, and there was already a line of people outside on the street. On the next day we were allowed to bring food to the prisoners, but on the 13th they told us that they had all been taken away to Germany to work. A few days later we heard that they had all been killed.[27]

More than 300 died in this first Glina massacre.

As we saw earlier, Alberto Fortis writing in the 1780s had recorded the 'most perfect discord' which had reigned between the Catholics and Orthodox of Morlacchia.[28] During the intervening years the identities of these communities had matured into Croatian and Serbian national consciousnesses. In the early years of this century there had been antagonism between Serbs and Croats but there had also been political co-operation. Between 1918 and 1941 many Croats resented Serbian domination in the new Yugoslav state and welcomed the birth of the NDH, but there was no reason for Serbs or the vast majority of Croats for that matter to have any inkling of the fanatical hatred that was about to be unleashed by the Ustashas. Whereas there had been a long history of bloodshed between Serbs and Muslims and Serbs and Albanians, the genocidal wave begun by the Ustashas in 1941 was an aberration and a break with history. For that reason the sequence of events described by Babić is unsurprising. In the new Croatian state Serbs would have had good reason to suspect they would be second-class citizens but not that their lives were in danger. As Babić describes it, the realisation came quickly.

The Glina massacre was not the first, though. On 28 April, 187 people from the village of Gudovac and its surroundings were killed. The campaign soon picked up speed, but not seemingly in any organised fashion. For example, at the beginning of June appalling pogroms were launched against Serbs in Hercegovina; Maček recalls in his memoirs that at the same time frightened Serbian peasants freely came to see him and asked him what they should do. Should they for example convert to Roman Catholicism?

The most oft quoted statement of Ustasha intentions is that of Mile Budak, the Croatian writer who became the NDH minister of education. On 22 June he is alleged to have said that in the NDH one-third of the Serbs would be killed, one-third expelled and one-third converted to Catholicism.[29] In September an Italian military report recorded that Budak and others were giving speeches about the 'Serbian Orthodox question' in which 'they have not hesitated to define the aim of the Ustasha struggle . . . [as] the extermination of the Serbs'.[30] The Cyrillic script was banned, Orthodox church schools were closed and Serbs were ordered to wear identifying armbands. Deportations to Serbia began and by 1943 the Serbian Orthodox church estimated that there were some 300,000 refugees in Serbia alone from the NDH.[31] Of course there were a good deal more refugees in the areas which soon rose in rebellion and turned themselves into enclaves from which NDH power was expelled.

For the Catholic church one of the most controversial demands of the NDH was the conversion of Serbs to Catholicism. The bishops were uncomfortable with this direct conversion, without the converts first passing through the Uniate phase (loyalty to Rome but Slavonic liturgy), and some of course were disturbed by the fact that this whole process was achieved under duress. While some priests naturally welcomed the chance to convert the Serbs, many honest ones also saw it as a way of saving lives. In his memoirs Maček recalls a priest from Sarajevo who had told Serbs, 'Children, you see that your mother (the Orthodox Church) is in grave distress and she cannot take care of you. Come to your aunt (the Catholic Church) and when your mother recovers, you will return to her.'[32]

The exact number who 'converted' is unknown but is believed to be between 200,000 and 300,000. In October 1941 the Italian consulate in Sarajevo recorded not only that the propaganda in favour of Serbian (and Jewish) conversion had been stepped up but that the tax payable had been slashed from 500 to 50 kunas. It said that 'whole villages' in Bosnia had converted, though there had been few requests to do so from urban Serbs. Those who converted incurred the wrath of those who wanted to 'maintain their purity'. There was, said the consulate's report, 'little sincerity' in these conversions, but those who did pass from 'one faith to the other' were 'left in peace', which was 'enough' in these 'grave times'. In many cases even this was to prove wishful thinking.[33]

In the spring of 1943 the NDH tried another tack: the creation of a Croatian Orthodox church. It was headed by Bishop Hermogen, an émigré Russian Orthodox priest and it had little success.

Among the most infamous of the early massacres was one which took place, again in Glina, on 5 August 1941. Some 1,200 Serbs dressed in their Sunday best were called to the church from surrounding villages to be 'converted' to Catholicism. Instead they were locked inside the church and murdered. In November, Bishop Mišić of Mostar wrote to Archbishop Stepinac, the head of the church in Croatia:

> At one time it seemed that a large number of schismatics [that is, Orthodox Serbs] would be converted to the Catholic Church. However [the Ustasha officials] . . . have abused their positions . . . with the result that a reign of terror has come to pass. . . . Men are captured like animals, they are slaughtered, murdered, living men are thrown off cliffs. The under-prefect in Mostar, Bajić, a Moslem, has said – it would be better if he kept silent instead of saying such things – that at Ljubinje, in a single day 700 schismatics were thrown into their graves. From Mostar and from Čapljina a train took six carloads of mothers, young girls, and children . . . to Šurmanci. . . . they were led up the mountains and the mothers together with their children were thrown alive off the precipices. . . . In the town of Mostar itself they have been bound by the hundreds, taken in wagons outside the town and shot down like animals.[34]

Professor Milorad Ekmečić, a historian who helped found the Serbian Democratic Party (SDS), the Bosnian Serb political party, in 1990, recalled what happened in his village of Prebilovci, which like Mostar is in Hercegovina: 'In 1941 when the great massacres started a neighbour killed my father, my uncles and others. Seventy-eight members of my family were killed. The youngest was Andjelina aged four months and the oldest was my seventy-seven-year-old grandfather. Those who remained created the first Partisan unit.'[35]

Hitler's intention, as in Serbia, had been to install a friendly regime, or in the Italian zone leave Mussolini's men in charge. He had not counted on the fanaticism of the Ustashas, which, although successfully killing unknown hundreds of thousands, rapidly led to Serbian revolts, first in Hercegovina and then in the old Military Frontier districts of Kordun and Lika. The SS quickly understood the nature of the problem, which was to end up by diverting German troops away from the fronts. One of their reports stated that:

> The atrocities perpetrated by the Ustasha units against the Orthodox in Croatian territory must be regarded as the most important reason for the blazing up of guerrilla activities. The Ustasha units have carried out their atrocities not only against male Orthodox of military age, but in

particular in the most bestial fashion against unarmed old men, women and children. . . . because of these atrocities innumerable Orthodox have fled to rump Serbia and their reports have roused the Serbian population to great indignation.[36]

While the Partisans soon managed to take control of the Serbian uprising in Lika and Kordun, the situation developed very differently in Italian-controlled Dalmatia and Hercegovina. Revolted by the massacres that were taking place, the Italian military began to extend protection to Serbs and to reoccupy areas which they had earlier relinquished to the NDH. Ordinary Italian soldiers came to the aid of beleaguered Serbs and there were even cases of the Italians having certain senior Ustashas arrested and shot. General Mario Roatta, the Italian commander for the region, wrote that the NDH should not be seen as 'an independent state' but as 'a sick man who has brought himself to the brink of his own grave'.[37]

Italian policy had several consequences. Serbs and Jews began to flee to Italian-controlled territory.[38] Serbian villagers living in terror of Ustasha depredations began to plead with the Italians for their protection. An Italian military report stated that on 29 September twenty-four representatives of different villages in western Bosnia met Italian officers and told them that 'they would be disposed to an intensive collaboration with Italian troops, either to fight, to repair roads or to act as guides, on the condition that they [the Italians] occupy their villages'.[39] This, commented the report, was not just in order to escape further attacks but also to save the harvest, which could not be gathered in the present conditions. Under Italian protection, Chetnik groups now began operating or secured their territory, and they subsequently came to be armed by the Italians. Of course they were armed not just to protect Serbs but also to fight the Partisans. This became increasingly necessary. Although in the German zone of operations the Partisans were at first almost all Serbs, Mussolini's policy of forced Italianisation in Dalmatia ensured that it was here that the first significant numbers of Croats began to flock to Tito's colours. Given that Mussolini's long-term strategy was to take the whole region under Italian control, another remark by Roatta is telling: 'It must not be forgotten that, during the time in Yugoslavia, our real, natural and irreconcilable enemies were the Croats and not the Serbs.'[40]

The Italian–Chetnik collaboration led to bizarre scenes. The Germans were horrified when Italian troops reoccupying Mostar marched into town shoulder to shoulder with the Chetniks, who carried black flags and placards reading 'Down with the Ustashas' and 'Down with Adolf Hitler'.[41] Ekmečić recalls that when the Italians reimposed their authority in the region 'it was a kind of liberation'. The policies pursued by the Italians were fondly remembered by the Serbs of Croatia. Indeed Milan Martić, who after 1990 became the leader of the breakaway Krajina Serbs, told a press conference held with a visiting Italian parliamentarian during the war with Croatia that he looked forward to the day when Serbian and Italian soldiers would once again march together. He suggested that a future goal should be to 'liberate Zadar', the Dalmatian port known to the Italians as Zara. During the inter-war years Zadar had been Italian territory, albeit an enclave surrounded by Yugoslavia.

The Italians' collaboration with the Chetniks was of course remembered by Croats in a far less favourable light. Several thousand Croats died at the hands of Chetniks in Croatia and Dalmatia, although the death tolls here were much lower than in areas such as eastern Bosnia. In one of the most infamous massacres, up to 200 people from the village and surroundings of Gata near Split were killed by Chetniks under the command of the priest Momcilo Djujić. They arrived at the end of September 1942 in trucks provided by the Italians, who were furious when they found out what had happened. After the war Pop ('Father') Djujić went to live in California.

In an apparent attempt to ape the Germans, the Ustashas set up a number of concentration camps. Being far less organised than their mentors, or lacking the technology, they often resorted in these camps to knives with which to murder Serbs, Jews, Gypsies and undesirable Croats. The most infamous camp was at Jasenovac on the Sava river, on the border of Bosnia. No one knows exactly how many died there, but today the name Jasenovac has the same meaning for Serbs as that of Auschwitz has for Jews.

For many Serbs the most enduring image of this holocaust is the scene described by Curzio Malaparte, the Italian journalist and writer, in his book *Kaputt*. Malaparte was a genuine war correspondent who at first supported and then opposed fascism. *Kaputt* was a semi-fictionalised account of his wartime experiences, so whether the following actually happened or was concocted from the rumours then circulating in Italian officers' messes is unknown. Given the grisly realities, however, the scene has become so well known among Serbs that the vast majority believe that it is a description of a real event. Several months after the founding of the NDH Malaparte goes to interview Pavelić. He is joined by the Italian minister in Zagreb, Raffaele Casertano:

While he spoke, I gazed at a wicker basket on the Poglavnik's desk. The lid was raised and the basket seemed to be filled with mussels, or shelled oysters – as they are occasionally displayed in the windows of Fortnum and Mason in Piccadilly in London. Casertano looked at me and winked,

'Would you like a nice oyster stew?'

'Are they Dalmatian oysters?' I asked the Poglavnik.

Ante Pavelić removed the lid from the basket and revealed the mussels, that slimy and jelly-like mass, and he said smiling, with that tired good-natured smile of his, 'It is a present from my loyal *ustashis*. Forty pounds of human eyes.'[42]

The NDH, which by the end of the war controlled very little of its territory, was to linger on until 9 May 1945, two days after the German surrender. Tens of thousands of Croats fled, fearing the advent of communism or convinced that, having served the regime in one capacity or another, they would be marked for execution by the Partisans. They were right. On 15 May they surrendered to the British at Bleiburg, just over the Slovene border in Austria. Returned by the British, between 20,000 and 40,000 of them were executed by the Partisans. They were not just Croats though. Their numbers included Slovenes and some Chetniks who were also trying to escape.

Kosovo: Land of Revenge

Because the scale of the wartime atrocities in Bosnia and Croatia so overshadowed those that took place in Vojvodina and in Kosovo, there has been a lack of serious research into what happened in these regions, especially the latter. This is a pity, because the reincorporation of Kosovo into Serbia in 1944 was to be the equivalent of reincorporating a cancer into the Serbian body politic. The lack of research is notable when one examines work by otherwise trustworthy scholars. So poisoned is the whole subject of Kosovo that when Albanian or Serbian academics come to discuss its history, especially its modern history, all pretence of impartiality is lost. This often makes their work utterly unreliable, especially when it comes to figures. For example, while the official census of 1921 reported an ethnic Albanian population of 439,657, Albanians believe the number to have been far higher.[43] This lack of undisputed data enables 'scholars' intent on scoring nationalistic points to state whatever they want in support of their fellow nationals' claims to the area. In this way the Albanian school claims that 'hundreds of thousands' of Albanians were deported to 'desolate regions of Turkey between 1919 and 1941'.[44] By contrast, a Serbian academic writing about the same period mentions in passing that 'some 35,000 people emigrated, but these were mainly rich landowners, Turkish feudalists and others with close economic and emotional ties with the former Turkish and Imperial systems'.[45]

Following the collapse of Yugoslavia in 1941, Kosovo and the

Albanian-populated areas of western Macedonia were divided between the Italians, the Germans and the Bulgarians. While the Germans took the zone which included the important Trepča mines and the Bulgarians were awarded a relatively small area, the bulk of these regions became part of Italian-ruled Greater Albania. Pogroms against Serbs began immediately and the Italians were often forced to intervene. These massacres could hardly have come as a surprise, as the appalling state of inter-communal relations was evident even to foreigners in the years before the war. Rebecca West recounted how in 1937 her Albanian cab driver and his friend in Peć gave her a dramatic description of their feelings:

> They both agreed that they would thoroughly enjoy another war if only it would give them the chance of shooting a lot of Serbs. They held up their left arms and looked along them and twitched their right thumbs against their left elbows and said 'Boom! boom! A Serb is dead!' I said, 'But what have you against the Serbs?' They said, 'After the war they ill-treated us and took our land from us.'[46]

In 1941 the wrath of the Kosovo Albanians was directed primarily against Serbian and Montenegrin settlers, almost all of whom fled. Serb sources talk of some 100,000 Serbs fleeing, of whom 40,000–60,000 were of settler stock. Albanian sources unsurprisingly say little or nothing about this subject. By April 1942, the authorities in Belgrade had registered more than 70,000 refugees from Kosovo. Another 10,000 Serbs are said to have been killed.[47] Albanian sources talk of Chetnik reprisals, but how many Albanians were killed is unknown.

Carlo Umilta, an Italian civilian commissioner in the region, recorded in his memoirs some of the appalling scenes that took place at the beginning of the occupation, in villages where the Italian forces had not yet established their control. He wrote, 'The Albanians are out to exterminate the Slavs' and added that people were begging passing Italian lorries and vehicles to take them to safety. In one region he found villages where 'not a single house has a roof; everything has been burned down. . . . There are headless bodies of men and women strewn on the ground.'[48]

At the monastery of Visoki Dečani, the Serbian monks still remember the Italians with gratitude. According to Father Sava, the monastery found itself in great danger several times during the war and at one point members of the Albanian nationalist resistance, the Balli Kombëtar, had threatened to destroy it: 'A Father was sent to get the Italians, who saved us. We had no bad experiences with them. The regular army were very friendly but the [fascist] blackshirts were aggressive.'[49] Other historic monasteries were not so fortunate.

Sopoćani had been without a roof for 240 years until King Alexander began restoring it in 1929. The Germans used it as a stable.

After the Italian capitulation in 1943, the Germans moved into the former Italian zone and proceeded to recruit an SS division named after Skenderbeg, the great Albanian medieval hero.

As the war progressed the inevitable debate arose in Partisan circles about who should control the resistance. Tito's representative in the region, Svetozar Vukmanović-Tempo, was disappointed to find that 'The Albanian population is suspicious of all those who struggle for Yugoslavia.'[50] The Yugoslav Partisans, as opposed to those from Albania, began to recruit Kosovo Albanians with the promise that Kosovo would stay within Albania after the war. When, in 1944, it was discovered that Kosovo was again to be part of Yugoslavia, insurrections began and Tito was forced to send some 30,000 troops to pacify the region. Atrocities occurred once again; in one of the worst cases several hundred Albanians imprisoned in a tunnel in Tivat in Montenegro were asphyxiated. As Miranda Vickers has written in her history of Albania, 'Official accounts spoke of Fascists and collaborators being punished but what was really happening was a repetition of the hideous massacres that had occurred between Serbs and Albanians during the Balkan Wars.'[51] Not to mention 1915, 1918 and 1941.

In 1981 the Albanian newspaper *Zeri-i-Popullit* claimed that in 1946 Tito had told Enver Hoxha, the Albanian communist leader, that 'Kosovo and other Albanian regions belong to Albania and we shall return them to you, but not now because the Great Serb reaction would not accept such a thing.'[52]

Frankenstein's Monster

For many, the war did not end in 1945. In the interests of restoring Yugoslavia, Tito's policy was to draw a line under the past. Everyone who had died in the Second World War had either been a collaborator or a Partisan or a victim of the Axis powers and their satellites. For the sake of balance, Chetniks and Ustashas were condemned equally by the new regime as the evil twins of the Serbs and Croats. Jasenovac was commemorated as a memorial to 'victims of fascism' rather than a shrine for its principal victims, the Serbs. Pits down which bodies had been tossed were sealed up and academic work on how many people of which nationality had died was not encouraged. The effect of this was not to make people forget, as was the intention, but to leave the wounds unhealed. Milorad Ekmečić, the historian whose family died at Prebilovci in 1941, says that the memory of what had happened there never faded during the communist era: 'Over the years when I came to visit Prebilovci for weddings and funerals the stories they told were about the massacres during the war. They were possessed by the memories of 1941–5. Probably it was the same with the Muslims and Croats.'

As communism crumbled in the late 1980s, Serbs, Croats and Slovenes began to dig up their dead and rebury them. Ekmečić took a leading role in the ceremonies at Prebilovci. The Croats and Slovenes likewise reburied the bones of the victims of Bleiburg and other massacres committed by the Partisans. There was nothing unusual about this, but the atmosphere of the times was such that these events inevitably fed the growing nationalist hysteria and was used by nationalist politicians to further their aims. In Serbia, another way in which the war was used to inflame passions was the screening of endless documentaries about the NDH which sought after 1990 to demonstrate an alleged continuity between it and Croatia's newly elected government under President Franjo Tudjman.

Perhaps the most grotesque way in which nationalists pressed the dead of the Second World War into service was the debate over numbers. In the immediate post-war period, the Yugoslav government claimed that 1.7 million Yugoslavs of all nationalities had died. In fact the number was too high. It later emerged that this figure, which was needed to claim post-war reparations, included not only the dead but total demographic losses, including shortfalls in births. The lack of reliable documentation then meant that nationalist historians and fellow-travelling journalists could claim all sorts of outrageous figures to back their arguments. For example, some Serbs claimed that more than one million Serbs had died in Jasenovac alone, while Tudjman, who had worked as an historian, put the number at about 30,000.

What the nationalists were happy to ignore, however, was that, although under Tito there had been no reliable data on wartime deaths, by 1989 two sets of serious figures had been published which gave remarkably similar results. One was published by a Serb and the other by a Croat. Their work was the fruit of much scientific labour based on census returns and computer projections.[53] They estimated that the total number of wartime deaths was about one million, out of a pre-war population of sixteen million, and that about half of them were Serbs (see Table 1, p.134).

If there had been rational discussion using figures such as those in Table 1, a real cause of war could have been avoided. Milorad Ekmečić was one of the hitherto distinguished historians who, under the influence of his own experiences, sought to claim far higher Serbian figures than was suggested by the numbers above. He claimed, for example, that during the Second World War 25 per cent of Bosnia's population was killed (or fled), and that of this figure of 687,000 people

Table 1   *Wartime Casualties by Republic, 1941–5 (000s)*

	Serbs	Croats	Muslims	Total
Bosnia	170	66	78	328
Montenegro	6	1	4	37
Croatia	137	118	2	295
Macedonia	6	0	4	24
Slovenia	0	0	0	40
Serbia	211	7	15	303
Total	530	192	103	1,027

Source: Figures of Vladimir Žerjavić cited in Sabrina P. Ramet: *Nationalism and Federalism in Yugoslavia, 1962–1991.* 2nd edn (Bloomington and Indianapolis, 1992), p.255.

630,000 were Serbs. In 1990, he became an important figure in Bosnian Serb politics. Five years later, he claimed that he had warned all along that nationalist politics could lead to civil war:

> I do not know why I was not listened to. I said our history is not a nice history, it is one of bloody misunderstandings. I said nationalism begins with epic folk songs and finishes with great wars. It begins with Hansel and Gretel and becomes Frankenstein's Monster. I should know as I lectured on the history of nationalism. The first who said this was Hegel, who said violence was the founding father, Marx said that human progress came through bloody civil wars.

What he omitted to say was that 'bloody misunderstandings' also began with lying with statistics and playing with history.

8

YOU USED TO WARM US LIKE THE SUN

It was one of the strangest events to have taken place in Belgrade for decades. Marshal Josip Broz Tito, the man who had ruled Yugoslavia until his death in 1980, had returned saying that he was back to see 'what's going on'. Resurrected for two days in 1994, the man who had reunified Yugoslavia in 1945 strolled around the city to be greeted by adoring crowds and also by angry individuals who accused him of being responsible for the misfortunes that had befallen the country since his death.

As he toured Belgrade, women crowded around the dead leader to give him flowers. One told him that she had cried when he had died at the age of eighty-seven. 'So did I,' replied Tito, who was wearing military uniform and looking none the worse for his death. Scores engaged their former leader in conversation. 'I am a Serb and you are a Croat,' said one man, 'but I used to admire you.' Another said that after his death he had been part of his honour guard. 'Yes, I remember you,' said Tito encouragingly. The man said, 'You were everything for us, you used to warm us like the sun.' Another disagreed, telling the former communist leader that he was 'guilty', a 'bandit', and accused him of hating Serbs. 'I used to be one of your soldiers,' said another, 'but now there is no bread in the shops.' Another said that during his time there was only one Tito: 'Now there are fifty-five.'

'We thought of it as a joke,' said Aleksandar Vasović, of the independent radio station B-92 which sponsored the film, 'but as you see it turned out rather serious.' *Tito: For the Second Time among the Serbs* was the brainchild of film-maker Želimir Žilnik. He dressed up an actor as Marshal Tito, let him wander Belgrade and filmed people's reactions. Amazingly, far from seeing the funny side of Žilnik's prank, people reacted as though the actor was the real Tito. In front of Belgrade station, a Gypsy accordionist struck up a Tito-era tune and the crowd grew so big that the police had to intervene. According to Žilnik, 'First they told the cameraman to move, and then me, but I told them to tell Tito. They said, "No, leave him out of it."'

One man explained to Tito that nowadays 'everyone has their own flag, state and coat of arms – for only one hill two or three hundred boys must die'. An old man stopped to accuse him of being pro-American and betraying the Soviet Union in 1948. Another said that while he was in power, 'I built a house – now I couldn't even build an out-house.'

Reflecting on this bizarre interaction, Slobodan Stupar, the deputy director of B-92, said he thought it was a terrible reflection of contemporary Serbia: 'It shows that the common people have lost touch with reality. Everything you tell them through the media they absorb like a sponge. So you have a situation where Tito is resurrected and people believe that.' Žilnik said, 'It's obvious that today, for the majority of people, there is a strong need to compare Tito's time and today, but people are not looking so much at Tito as a symbol as at their own past.'

In the most pathetic scene of all, Tito finds an old man sitting alone by the tombs of the Marshal's old comrades-in-arms. Their busts have been removed. 'Who was bothered by them?' asks Tito. 'Those who don't like order, those who don't respect the past . . . those who are irresponsible,' says the old man. He does not look up. Tito asks him where he is from and he replies that he is a refugee from the war in Bosnia. 'When will it end?' asks Tito. 'There is no end, my friend,' says the old man.

White Lines and Marble Columns

In 1945, when the old man was young, it had looked very much like the beginning of something new and the end of the fratricidal conflicts of the past. Phoenix-like, a new Yugoslavia was rising from the ashes and, in contrast to *narodno jedinstvo*, the mythical national unity of the 1918 state, the new Yugoslavia was to be based on a new concept. This was *bratsvo i jedinstvo*, meaning 'brotherhood and unity'. It was crucially different from *narodno jedinstvo* because it proceeded from the starting point that Yugoslavia would be strong, not because its peoples were one, but because they were many, and that strength was born of unity. However, just as the fundamental underpinning of the kingdom had been flawed, it was the contradictions inherent in brotherhood and unity which were eventually to tear apart its successor. While it sought to accommodate the national interests of most of Yugoslavia's peoples in a federal system, it also assumed an unchanging unity of interests. Until Tito's death this contradiction could be papered over, especially as Tito dictated what these interests were. After his death the cracks became too wide and, without the goodwill necessary to repair them, the Yugoslav edifice collapsed.

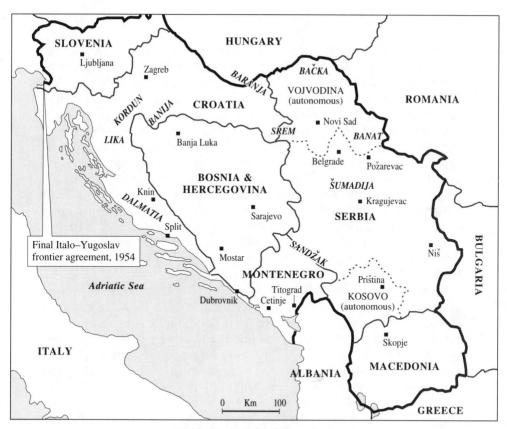

1945: Tito's Federal Yugoslavia

Based on the wartime decisions of the communists, the new Yugoslavia was made up of six republics and two autonomous regions. The republics were Serbia, Croatia, Bosnia–Hercegovina, Montenegro, Macedonia and Slovenia. Serbia contained the two autonomous regions. These were Kosovo and Vojvodina. Bosnia was restored, with its historic 1878 frontiers, in recognition of its mixed population and to prevent it becoming the renewed object of dispute between Serbs and Croats. The decision to form a Macedonian republic out of the lands which, between the Balkan Wars and 1941, had been called Southern Serbia was made because it was recognised that the region's Macedonian Slavs were distinct from Serbs and (except in Bulgarian eyes) from Bulgarians too. By creating this republic, the communists also wanted to prevent Macedonia from again becoming a source of conflict between Serbs and Bulgarians. In addition, until 1948, there was serious talk of a Balkan federation, within which Macedonia, perhaps reunited with its Bulgarian and Greek portions, would become a larger entity.

Montenegro was made a republic in recognition of its historic status and so partly to satisfy that portion of the population which resented being relegated to the position of a far-flung province of Serbia. Kosovo had to be given an autonomous status in recognition of its ethnic Albanian majority. Vojvodina, with its mixed population, about a quarter of whom were Hungarians, was also given autonomy. It had never been part of historic Serbia, despite the pivotal role it had played in Serbian history, although after the war half its population was Serb. Another area which had historically not belonged to Serbia but which became part of the Serbian republic, mostly within Vojvodina, was eastern Srem, that stretch of the old Habsburg lands which ran along the pre-1918 northern border of Serbia right up to Zemun, which is now a suburb of Belgrade. Much of its population was Serb, although there was a significant Croatian minority and, until its members fled or were expelled in 1945, a German community too.

Most of the republican borders were drawn up taking ethnic, historic and economic factors into consideration. While there were some disputes, for example over eastern Srem, in the main the division was uncontested. This was not a testament to the fact that most people considered them fair, which they may or may not have done. The reason was that the decisions were implemented at a time when the communists were shooting any opposition and when Stalin was considered the model leader. There was also the consideration that the borders were not seen at the time as particularly important. After all, the communists were drawing frontiers not between independent states but between different parts of Yugoslavia, which for all its much trumpeted federalism was going to be ruled by a communist party and by Tito in particular.

Later, Serbian nationalists began to articulate the kind of opinions that might have been heard in the 1940s if free expression had been permitted. Their first noticeable champion in the late 1960s was Dobrica Ćosić, a communist and novelist turned human rights activist and nationalist. They centred on his obsession that Serbia 'won its wars but always lost the peace'. With regard to the 1945 settlement it was argued that, in a bid to allay fears of Serbian domination in the new state, the Serbs had been forced to give up Macedonia, Montenegro and Kosovo. The nationalists also pointed out that it was only Serbia which contained autonomous regions; there was not one for Serbs in Croatia, for example. In this way they argued that Serbia had been compelled to give up the most to recreate Yugoslavia, even though in their view the Serbs had been on the winning side in the war and had suffered genocide at the hands of Croatian and Albanian quislings who were now being rewarded. Another source of resentment for many Serbs was the communist abolition of the monarchy, which having sprung from the Serbian peasantry had retained its popularity.

In the immediate post-war years arguments about borders in particular, apart from being dangerous for the individual concerned, were not particularly relevant. Politically Bosnia was still Serb-dominated and in 1945 the Serbs were still its largest single community, despite the ravages of the Ustashas. Because of its wartime history and the anti-Yugoslav uprising of 1944–5, Kosovo was run by Serbs, and in Croatia the fact that more Serbs had been Partisans for longer meant that Serbs were over-represented in the republican and local communist hierarchies and security organs. Besides, in theory at least, it was not Serbs that ruled anywhere but communists. For this reason it was not necessary to square the circle of the constitutional contradiction that was eventually to undermine the new state.

The heart of the contradiction in post-1945 Yugoslavia was that of nation or state. Yugoslavia was not itself a nation-state, but within it it was important to blur the distinction between nation *and* state, or federal unit. Only in the case of Slovenia were the two coterminous. The federal constitution which was adopted in 1946 was based on the decisions made in Jajce in November 1943. There, the meeting of the Second Anti-Fascist Council for the National Liberation of Yugoslavia, known by its initials as AVNOJ, laid down the formulation that the new state was founded 'on the basis of the right of every people to self-determination, including the right to secede or unite with other peoples, and in conformity with the true aspirations of all the peoples of Yugoslavia'.[1] So Yugoslavia seemed to be a union of *peoples*. However, an examination of the other contemporary documents reveals not just that each people was being told something slightly different but that this principle that Yugoslavia was made up of peoples rather than states was less clear than it appeared. For example, in July 1944 the declaration on the rights of citizens of Bosnia–Hercegovina stated that for the 'first time in history' its people had 'begun building their common home whose foundation has been cemented by the blood of their best sons'. This home was to be 'a common state' which in turn was to be an 'equal federated unit of democratic federal Yugoslavia'. Even more important, though, for Bosnian ears was the need to emphasise that their republic was to be one of 'equality, freedom, peace and prosperity'.[2]

For Serbia, it was important to underline different things. A declaration of November 1944 began with the statement that 'The Serbian people have always aspired to the creation of a common state of the Southern Slavs in which all Southern Slavs would be united on a basis of fraternal equality.' Although the 'always' part was patently false, the statement served to paper over the problem of the Serbs outside Serbia. According to the declaration:

It is through this common struggle waged jointly by the Serbs and the other Southern Slav nationalities, and especially the Serbs living outside Serbia on the same territory with their Croat and Moslem brothers, that for the first time in the history of the Southern Slavs, true brotherhood and unity have been forged, so strong and solid that no power on earth will ever be able to shatter this.[3]

In other words, to calm Serb fears for the Serbs outside Serbia they were assured that the fate that they had suffered at the hands of the NDH could never happen again as the new state would never again be broken up.

One of the most explicit explanations of the meaning of federalism came from Tito himself in Zagreb in May 1945. To calm Croatian fears that they were being incorporated into a new Serb- and Belgrade-dominated Yugoslavia, it was necessary to talk up the element of home rule that was to accrue to the new sovereign Croatian state. But it was also important to make clear that 'the name "federal Yugoslavia" does not imply some sort of separatism'. Tito explained that borders did not mean:

> drawing a boundary line between this federal unit and the other, and now you on the other side shall do as you please, and I shall do as I please on my side of the boundary. No! These boundaries, figuratively speaking, should resemble the white lines on a marble column. The boundaries of the federated units within the federal state of Yugoslavia do not denote separatism but unity.[4]

Yugoslavia then was 'now a conglomerate of small states', the federation was 'invested with . . . an administrative character', and what was important was 'the independence of each federal unit . . . full independence in the sphere of free cultural and economic development'. However, lest anyone misunderstand him, Tito said on another occasion: 'I warn you there can be no chauvinism, no negative local patriotism in the new federal Yugoslavia as this would be detrimental not only to the respective federal unit but also to the country as a whole. The question of chauvinism and negative local patriotism should be superseded once for all, it simply must not exist.'[5]

Even more explicit was the explanation of why the question of self-determination was really a dead letter:

> Let me tell those who say that the present achievements can still change: nothing can be changed any more. There can be no change because the new federal Yugoslavia has been accepted by the overwhelming majority of all Yugoslav nations. Nothing can be changed because we are all

aware that this is an historic necessity. There can be no change because we know that the Yugoslav nations cannot exist without genuine unity, that they would be unable to develop on the economic and social plane.[6]

In other words the right to self-determination had already been exercised by the pooling of sovereignty into Yugoslavia and it could never be exercised again by seceding from it. To meet the demands of changing political circumstances the constitution was to evolve through several versions until 1974, and it was only a small minority who ever took the theoretical question of self-determination seriously. But there was one way in which the question did change: although still unclear, the constitutional bias in favour of self-determination shifted over the years to favour republics rather than nations.

Blind Alleys

Anyone who has browsed through the literature on the Yugoslavia of 1945 to 1990 cannot fail to be struck by just how inconsequential some of the great debates of the past have turned out to be. While some of them were extremely important at the time, other developments which eventually turned out to have far-reaching consequences, especially demographic changes, tended to be seen as less interesting. There were hundreds of books written about the policies of non-alignment and socialist self-management of the economy, but there are few if any serious and above all impartial studies of Serbian emigration from Kosovo and Bosnia. In the wake of the conflict which enveloped Yugoslavia after 1991, it now becomes important to unravel the modern history of Yugoslavia. This means not only giving less emphasis to those subjects that once dominated Yugoslav studies but also tracing those threads which led to the re-emergence of Serbian nationalism. These threads remain inextricably tangled, however, with those of Croatian, Kosovo Albanian and Bosnian Muslim nationalism. For this reason, the history of all these peoples in the second Yugoslavia remains *Yugoslav* history; so for this period a Serbian or Croatian or Muslim history alone would be impossible if not dishonest.

The most important event in the life of the young communist state was the split with Stalin and the Soviet Union in 1948. Tito and his entourage had always been loyal supporters of the Soviet state and looked to Moscow as the centre of the communist world. This did not mean that they would blindly obey orders, and Yugoslavs began to resent what they saw as attempts by the USSR to exploit Yugoslavia economically. Much has been written about the 1948 expulsion of Yugoslavia from the Cominform, the successor to the international communist party grouping, the Comintern. Suffice to say here that Stalin was deeply suspicious of Tito and his men because, despite some Soviet help, they had not ridden to power on the back of Soviet tanks and did not remain in power thanks to Soviet support. Plans to create a Balkan federation with Bulgaria, Albania, perhaps Romania and even Greece if the communists won the civil war also increased Soviet doubts about Tito, whom they feared might set up a rival centre of power. One of the results of the excommunication of the Yugoslavs from the Soviet bloc was the purging of cominformists, thousands of whom were sent to the Adriatic prison camp of Goli Otok. These were people who either were, or were feared to be, communists loyal to Stalin. In terms of foreign relations, an economic embargo of Yugoslavia by the rest of communist Europe soon forced Yugoslavia not just into opening up trade with the west but also into accepting financial and military aid from western countries keen to exploit the split. Two further consequences of Yugoslavia's expulsion from the Soviet fold were the evolution of the socialist self-managing economy and the development of non-alignment.

The essence of socialist self-management was that Yugoslavia was moving ahead of the Soviet model by decentralising economic power. At its simplest, this meant that companies were no longer owned by the state but directly by their workers. Increasingly power to make economic and financial decisions was also to be devolved away from the centre down to the republics and to smaller territorial units. In agriculture, the first effect of the split was that the Yugoslav government moved quickly to collectivise land. After droughts and much passive and sometimes even active peasant resistance to collectivisation, the ever flexible Yugoslav communists decided to reverse the policy. This meant that most land returned to private ownership, although there were restrictions on the size of individual holdings.

Between 1945 and 1990 the Yugoslav economy lurched from crisis to crisis, but it was better off than any of its communist neighbours. Between crises, it experienced periods of growth, and in general Yugoslavs prospered even though there were wide regional disparities. Slovenia, Croatia and Vojvodina were the richest areas, while Kosovo and Macedonia were the poorest. 'Inner' Serbia, that is Serbia without the provinces, fell within the middle income bracket. The fluctuations of the economy meant that Yugoslavia, unlike other communist countries, was afflicted by bouts of inflation and high unemployment. Irrational planning, encouraged by decentralisation and the policy of redistributing wealth from richer to poorer areas, also led to the construction of 'political factories', which were plants built for political reasons rather than for economic ones. Above all, though, Yugoslavia's economy was able to survive thanks to western financial support.

There were two other crucial aspects to the economy which must be taken into account. The first was the decision to abolish visa restrictions and to encourage mass tourism, which was to bring in large amounts of hard currency. The second was to allow the free movement of Yugoslavs out of the country. By the 1980s this meant that up to one million were working abroad; known as gastarbeiters ('guest-workers' in German), they were sending home considerable sums of money.

On the international plane, Yugoslavia's relations with the Soviet Union went up and down, but the initial split had established the hitherto heretical concept that there could be differing paths to socialism. The split was to be the initial spur, however, to Tito's development of relations with the Third World which was to blossom into the non-aligned movement. As a founding father of this grouping, which was supposed to represent a third way in international politics, Tito was to gain immense international prestige both for himself and for Yugoslavia. By the late 1970s, though, the movement had become discredited, especially following Cuban attempts to steer it in a pro-Soviet direction.

With the exception of Kosovo, the years until 1966 were really the golden age of Yugoslavia. This does not mean that they were a particularly happy period, only that the experiences of most people were relatively uniform. This was also the time in which the idea of a 'socialist Yugoslav patriotism' was fostered, a notion which was not to be pursued with any great vigour in later years.

Ranković and Beyond

The year 1966 marked the end of Yugoslavia's post-war consolidation and the beginning of the unravelling of the state. As we now know, it also ushered in what was to be a new and long pre-war period. The key event was the fall of Aleksandar Ranković, Yugoslavia's vice-president and Tito's heir apparent. He had fought alongside Tito during the war and was devoted to him. Until 1963 he was minister of the interior and head of UDBa, the secret police. After his promotion to the newly created position of vice-president, he remained close to UDBa, even its *de facto* head.

Ranković was a Serb and, although his association with the secret police made him a hate-figure, he was also seen by many Serbs as their representative in Tito's inner circle. There is nothing to suggest, however, that he was a closet Serbian nationalist; rather he was an old-style communist who believed in tight control and who tended to confer trust on fellow Serbs more than on individuals from other nations who might be more susceptible to 'separatist' inclinations.

During the early 1960s Yugoslavia's top politicians and economists were involved in a series of important debates which tended to split leaderships along national lines. They centred around the question of decentralisation, the introduction of certain market mechanisms and the related issue of increasing republican autonomy. In general, Slovenia and Croatia, being the richer republics, were in favour of increased decentralisation and more republican authority. They wanted to keep a larger proportion of their incomes for themselves rather than yield more to the federal authorities in Belgrade to be disbursed to the less developed regions. By contrast, the poorer regions were in favour of centralisation because they benefited from these funds. The reformers also wanted to break the power of the banks and other financial institutions which were based in Belgrade. Entangled with this debate was the question of tourism. The Croats in particular demanded that visa restrictions be abolished so that more foreign tourists would come to the coast. Ranković was suspicious of this, believing that the absence of visa controls would lead to the infiltration into the country of all sorts of spies and undesirable émigrés. There was also an economic disadvantage: to attract more tourists the authorities would have to invest in hotels and other facilities, which would in turn mean less cash for the poorer regions.

It is possible that Ranković may have always supported the centralists because he was a Serb, and, just as Russians saw the Soviet Union and Russia as inseparable, he may have seen the interests of the Serbs and Yugoslavia in the same way. It is equally possible that he understood that decentralisation meant the loss of central control and consequently of his own power. One of his most bitter opponents was the Slovene Edvard Kardelj, who not only favoured decentralisation but was also a potential candidate to succeed Tito. It is worth noting, though, that while most Serb politicians were against decentralisation the divisions within the Yugoslav leaderships were by no means rigid. Petar Stambolić, the Serbian prime minister who participated in the moves to have Ranković stripped of his powers, was then considered a liberal.

Tito was not particularly interested in economics and, unless required to make a decision, he far preferred others to deal with such tedious matters. But deadlock meant that he was drawn into the debates more and more, and in the end he decided to support the decentralisers. This was the beginning of the end for Ranković. Tito may well also have become angered at discovering that Ranković had been threatening people who had argued for decentralisation and was increasingly controlling access to him. An investigation was ordered and, after it reported that UDBa had been bugging Tito's personal telephones, Ranković was ordered into retirement.

It is impossible to underestimate the effect of the fall of Ranković. It marked a definitive point in Yugoslav history and the beginning of a period of liberalism previously unimaginable in a communist country. It was also the beginning of real decentralisation, which in the end was to go so far that after the passing of the 1974 constitution many Serbs at least believed that Yugoslavia was ceasing to be one country and becoming eight statelets under a Yugoslav umbrella. In the 1960s, however, most people welcomed the relaxation that followed the end of the Ranković era, and the twenty or so years after his fall are remembered fondly by many as good years. But not by everyone. Many of the grievances which were to surface in the 1980s, especially Serbian ones over Kosovo, have their roots in the post-Ranković period. The irony of the liberal years is that in the absence of democracy the strongest and most enduring ideas were to be illiberal, intolerant and mutually exclusive ones which, used by politicians, were eventually to destroy the country.

Croatian Spring

A key part of Tito's strategy to rebuild Yugoslavia had been, as we saw at the end of the last chapter, a decision to draw a line under recent history and to equalise guilt in a bid to neutralise it. While this later meant that all sorts of outlandish historical distortions and grotesque debates were to emerge, it also ensured that after 1945 there was neither catharsis nor grief. Likewise, the expression of national interests had to take place in a peculiarly circumscribed fashion. While the Croats were haunted by the Ustasha ghost, the Serbs were haunted by the spectre of the accusation of 'Great Serb Hegemonism'. The Serbs might privately complain about the post-war settlement, but in general they had less to be discontented about than most. Bosnia was run almost as an extension of Serbia, and Kosovo was kept under strict control. Centralism suited Serbian interests. Although it was the economic debate which had begun to unsettle Serbo-Croat relations, in the wake of Ranković's fall all sorts of other grievances began to be voiced.

In 1967, the first blow was struck when a group of Croatian writers published a declaration asserting that Croatian was a distinct language from Serbian. The implication was that Serbo-Croatian and attempts to harmonise the languages were really attempts at Serbianising it. The writers also demanded that all those with official functions in Croatia use only Croatian. This was interpreted as an anti-Serbian jibe because of the high proportion of Serb, albeit Croatian Serb, civil servants in employment. Serbian intellectuals hit back by insisting that Serbian children in Croatia be taught in Serbian and not Croatian. They also demanded that they use the Cyrillic alphabet. The question of the difference between Serbian and Croatian was essentially a political one, because the difference between the mainstream dialects is significantly less than say that between English English and accented Scottish English. In Croatia itself, however, there was almost no difference at all between the language spoken by the republic's Serbs and Croats.

In this atmosphere, all sorts of accusations began to be exchanged. One of the most prominent was the idea that Croatia was economically exploited and that its interests were subordinated to those of Serbia. Also, in the view of Petar Segedin, the president of the Croatian Literary Society, 'the Croatian nation has, by various nefarious means, been portrayed as criminal. . . . Croatia is still being equated with the Ustashas . . . [and] Belgrade is attempting to assimilate the Croats, that is, to Serbianize Croatia'.[7] A specific example was the question of the Croatian population. The republic had the lowest birthrate of the whole of Yugoslavia, the highest proportion of gastarbeiters working abroad and also a large émigré community. Consequently, Croatia had a slow rate of population growth. Whatever the real reasons for this, nationalists began to allege that this was a 'Serbian plot'.[8]

Behind much of the increasing national debate was Matica Hrvatska, a Croatian intellectual organisation originally founded in 1844 and revived in 1967. For the next few years Matica Hrvatska was in the vanguard of what eventually became known as the Croatian Spring or, by Serbs especially, as the Mass Movement or Maspok.

The Croatian renaissance was initially confined to intellectual circles. In 1970, however, the Croatian communists, led by the young liberals Savka Dabčević-Kučar and Miko Tripalo, came down firmly on the side of the nationalists, and by the following year Croatia was being swept by waves of popular national euphoria. Stjepan Radić, for example, the assassinated leader of the Croatian Peasant Party, who as Tito remembered had despised communists, was reinstated as a Croatian hero. The newspapers published columns to help people weed out Serbian words from their everyday speech.[9] There was also a fierce debate about Croatia's constitution and what role the Serbs should play in it. The question was whether Croatia should be defined as the state of the Croatian nation or as the 'national state of the Croatian nation, the state of the Serbian nation in Croatia and the state of the nationalities inhabiting it'.[10] Such things may seem arcane, but they were really window dressing for fundamental questions concerning power and the perennial issue of Serbo-Croat relations. In the wake of the collapse of Yugoslavia, it can now be seen that many of the debates of the period 1970–1 in Croatia were simply a dress rehearsal for those of the late 1980s. Without Tito to draw everyone back from the brink, the second time around the national questions were pushed relentlessly to their bloody conclusions.

The best example of this is the question of Krajina, Croatia's breakaway Serbian area in the early 1990s. Although it was set up with strong help from Belgrade, this did not mean to say that it did not have an intellectual pedigree of its own. In the 1920s there had been discussion of an autonomous region for Lika, Kordun, Banija and north-west Bosnia. It was to be named after the Una river which flows through these parts. In 1939 Serbian nationalists who were angered that so many Serbs in Croatia and northern Bosnia were to be included in the Sporazum's Croatian *banovina* suggested they be part of a Serbian *banovina*. After the Ustasha murders of Serbs, the Partisans toyed with the idea of a Serbian autonomous region here, but this idea was rejected. In 1970, as Croatian nationalism was on the rise once more, the notion of a separate Serbian province resurfaced.[11] Over Bosnia too some of the debate was to foreshadow the events of the Bosnian war. Matica Hrvatska began to rally support in Bosnia and produced statistics to show how the republic was politically dominated by Serbs. This soon led to a demand for the annexation of part of Bosnia by Croatia, a demand which was answered by Serb nationalists calling for the annexation of Serb-inhabited areas by Serbia.[12] Pushing ever further, Matica Hrvatska and the intellectuals clustered around it eventually began to raise the question of Croatian independence. This was too much, as the Croatian League of Communists (as the Croatian communist party was called) had become closely identified with Matica Hrvatska.

Tito hesitated for many months before he took action. He saw Tripalo in June 1971, but their conversation yielded nothing. After this, Soviet leader Leonid Brezhnev offered to intervene militarily if Tito asked for such help. Tito did not want it, but the offer was something which could be used to threaten the Croats. In July he declared, 'Under the cover of "national interest" all Hell is assembling. . . . It may go as far as counter-revolution. . . . In some villages the Serbs, out of fear, are drilling and arming themselves. . . . Do we want to have 1941 again?'[13] In September Tito declared that he did not believe that there was a problem in Croatia. Several weeks later, though, he was convinced by the army that he was mistaken. He called a meeting at the old royal hunting lodge of Karadjordjevo in Vojvodina, where the decision was taken to crush the nationalist movement in Croatia. The meeting began on 1 December, the anniversary of the founding of the first Serb-dominated Yugoslavia in 1918. Many Croats were also insulted by the fact that the meeting had taken place in Serbia.

Today the significance of Karadjordjevo has changed. Twenty years later the Serbian and Croatian presidents met in the same place to discuss the partitioning of Bosnia – one of the very notions which had eventually forced Tito to act in 1971. Croatian President Franjo Tudjman was a former Partisan and JNA general who was among those purged and imprisoned for his activities during the events of the Croatian Spring, so the irony of the 1991 Karadjordjevo summit cannot have been lost on him.

The full-scale purging of Croatia had several long-term consequences. Within Croatia, the most important was that it drove Croatian nationalist feeling underground but did not extinguish it. With the end of communism, it was to re-emerge. Whereas the Croatian communists, the successors to Dabčević-Kučar and Tripalo, were discredited by the part they played in helping to reassert control over Croatia, many of those who had been in the forefront of Maspok were to set up Croatia's new political parties in 1989. The most successful was the Croatian Democratic Union (HDZ) of Franjo Tudjman, which was to win the elections in the republic in 1990.

Serbian Summer

Serbian intellectuals were of course involved in the Croatian debates, and the press in Serbia was deeply suspicious of the events in Croatia, but the main developments in the wake of the fall of Ranković in Serbia were of a different nature.

In June 1968 there was turmoil at Belgrade University just as there was in Paris, Prague and elsewhere that summer. The university strike in Belgrade began over conditions, but soon took on a political flavour. There were denunciations of authoritarianism, unemployment and the Vietnam war. There was no hint of Serbian nationalism here, and much inspiration came from the philosophy faculty. This was the department of Mihailo Marković and others who were identified with the liberal Marxist journal *Praxis*, which was much admired in western Marxist circles. The university strike lasted a week, with clashes between the police and students. The Serbian leader Petar Stambolić demanded that the university be attacked and extra troops were moved closer to Belgrade. In a characteristic stroke of genius, however, Tito suddenly appeared on television and declared that not only did he support the students but he had been obstructed in his work by the country's bureaucracy and if he did not achieve their *common* aims, he would resign. There was jubilation in the university and the students went home. Two weeks later Tito demanded that the philosophy faculty be purged of men like Marković who were 'corrupting' the nation's youth.

Three years later Petar Stambolić was no longer in power and, as in Croatia, young liberals had come to the fore. Unlike in Croatia, however, there was no nationalistic wave to ride and indeed the new Serbian leaders, the economic modernisers Latinka Perović and Marko

Nikezić, were deeply anti-nationalist. It was during their period in power, for example, that Mihailo Djurić, a Belgrade law professor, went to jail. He had suggested that the Serbs of Croatia and other republics should be given special protection. Even more radical, however, were his reactions to the constitutional changes in 1971 which increased the power of the republics *vis-à-vis* the centre. He said that, if the republics were becoming sovereign states, Tito's AVNOJ borders, which were not international frontiers, should be reconsidered.

Perović and Nikezić regarded Tito as rather old; they did not try and flatter him and were rather reserved towards him. Following the purges in Croatia, Tito decided that they should be sacrificed too. Possibly he mistrusted them, but more importantly he felt it necessary to purge them and their followers for the sake of balance. Power in Serbia was then delivered back into the hands of the older, Partisan generation. Petar Stambolić, who had commanded Partisan forces in Serbia, returned. With him was Draža Marković, another senior figure of the wartime generation. Nikola Ljubičić, Yugoslavia's defence minister, was also to play an important role in Serbian politics.

While ideology, religion, emotion and economics are the staple of history, it sometimes takes one aback to see how extraordinary a role pure fate can play. The change of power in Serbia offers an example. Draža Marković had a young niece called Mira, who had grown up in provincial Požarevac. She was married to a man called Slobodan Milošević. The couple's best friend was Ivan Stambolić, the nephew of Petar Stambolić. In the former Yugoslavia the initials VIP stand for *veza i protekcija* – connections and protection. Mira Marković and her husband had plenty of VIP.

Kosovo: Use Brute Force

Vaso Čubrilović, one of the young Bosnians who had taken part in the plot to kill the Archduke Franz Ferdinand, later became a distinguished historian and a member of the Serbian Academy of Arts and Sciences. One of his interests was Kosovo and the question of how to secure the land for the Serbs for ever. In 1937 he declared that the only way to cope with the majority Albanian population was to 'use the brute force of an organized state. . . . if we do not settle accounts with them at the proper time, within 20–30 years we shall have to cope with a terrible irredentism'. They should be driven out, he opined, adding that:

> the world today has grown used to such things much worse than this and is so preoccupied with day to day problems that this . . . should not be a cause for concern. At a time when Germany can expel tens of

thousands of Jews and Russia can shift millions of people from one part of the continent to another, the shifting of a few hundred thousand Albanians will not lead to the outbreak of a world war.[14]

Apart from arming Serb gangs and enforcing a highly repressive regime, Čubrilović noted that there remained one more method to rid Serbia and Yugoslavia of Albanians, which 'Serbia employed with great practical effect after 1878, that is by secretly burning down Albanian villages and city quarters'.[15] The war intervened and in the wake of the pogroms of Serbs during the period 1941–4 Čubrilović again suggested, this time to the new communist authorities, that the Albanians should be expelled from Yugoslavia. At the time such an idea was not quite as radical as it seems now because it was at precisely the same moment that ethnic Germans and many Hungarians were being expelled or put to flight; Čubrilović had indeed suggested that they too should be chased out.

Čubrilović's suggestions about the Albanians were ignored, but in the light of the poison the Kosovo issue was to spread throughout the lifetime of the second Yugoslavia they put an interesting gloss on at least one strand of academic life. Marginal though it may have been, it was precisely this thinking that reappeared among the former academics who led the Bosnian Serbs to war in 1992.

No ethnic Albanians participated in the Jajce meeting of 1943 which laid the foundations of the new Yugoslavia and, as we have seen, there was an uprising in 1944 as Yugoslav rule returned. Tito and his colleagues were well aware of the sensitive nature of the problem, and they hoped that it would be solved within the framework of the proposed Balkan federation. As a concession to the Albanians, the Serbian settlers who had been expelled after 1941 were not allowed to return after the war. The Yugoslav authorities also took no steps to expel Albanian settlers who had come to the region while it was under Italian rule. Many of these people had themselves been forced from their original homes in Albania during the brief period of Italian colonisation, especially along the coast. There are no reliable statistics for how many Albanian settlers there were, but many years later Serbian nationalists claimed, in what were certainly wild exaggerations, that from 1941 hundreds of thousands of Albanians had come from Albania both during the years of Italian rule and to escape the Stalinist regime of Enver Hoxha. No less wildly, Albanian nationalists claimed that following the reimposition of Yugoslav rule in Kosovo hundreds of thousands of Albanians were 'deported'.[16]

Although Kosovo was ostensibly autonomous, this was largely theoretical until the fall of Ranković, who ran it as a police state. In 1956 there were trials in Prizren of Albanians charged with espionage and subversion, and violence was used by the police in frequent arms-collection raids. Serbs dominated the security and police forces and indeed held all important positions, although they made up only about a quarter of the population. The fall of Ranković was to bring about a rapid change of atmosphere. In 1968 those who had been convicted in the 1956 Prizren trials were rehabilitated.[17] In November there were demonstrations by ethnic Albanians who demanded that the province be upgraded to a republic and that an Albanian-language university be established. The demonstrations spread to Albanian-populated areas of western Macedonia, and some demanded union with Albania.[18]

Although there were arrests and trials of some of the rioters, the response of the government in the years that followed was to conciliate the Albanians. In 1969 an Albanian-language university began functioning in Priština and the Albanianisation of the province began in earnest. Contacts with Albania were opened and various agreements resulted in textbooks and other educational materials being supplied for use in Kosovo by Albania. Close contacts were also established between the universities of Priština and Tirana. While the Yugoslav authorities hoped that these measures would help diminish the attraction of the poverty-stricken orthodox Stalinist state next door, they in fact did quite the opposite. As Anton Logoreci, a writer and broadcaster on Albanian affairs, has written:

> The main reason that things turned out the way they did was because, having been denied for many generations everything that helped to nourish a people's national consciousness and identity, the Albanians living in Yugoslavia, especially the post-war generation, were by the 1960s like a very parched sponge, immensely avid to absorb anything that helped to illuminate their past history and made some sense of their current situation.[19]

Throughout the 1970s the authorities kept turning up alleged groups of separatists. Although ethnic Albanians were increasingly in control of the province, there were frequent arrests and trials of people charged with subversion. In 1979 hundreds were arrested. In 1981 a new round of violent rioting began and the army, commandos and special police units were deployed to put down the protests.

Economically, Kosovo was one of the poorest regions of Yugoslavia. While it had made great strides in terms of real income after the war, in comparative terms it was slipping ever further behind the richer parts of the country. After 1974 the province became a republic in all but name, and politically its leaders often made common cause against the Serbian leadership in Belgrade. However, while the Croats and Slovenes exploited this, they were increasingly loath to pay the large subsidies

which the federal authorities channelled to Kosovo. Not only was much
of this money wasted but, under Albanian control, the province had a
rapidly expanding bureaucracy. It grew in part because Priština
University began to churn out ever larger numbers of graduates, many
of whom had no jobs to go to.

More than any other part of the former Yugoslavia, the polemics over
Kosovo are fought with statistics. Both Albanians and Serbs have a
predilection for trying to prove one point or another with figures. As
Yugoslavia entered the 1980s, Albanians produced numbers to show
just how many people had been arrested and charged with subversion
in a bid to 'prove' that they were increasingly coming to live under a
regime of police repression. Serbs would use the same figures to 'prove'
that the Albanians wanted to secede. The Albanians would use
economic statistics to 'prove' that Kosovo was either exploited or not
getting its fair share of development money, while the Serbs or
Yugoslav authorities would use the same figures to show just how
much money was being lavished on the region. In the 1980s, however,
the bitterest statistics war was waged over the question of population
and emigration.

Although both sides question the official statistics when they do not
suit their arguments, they both use them, for example the census
returns, when they do. An examination of these figures, then, is a good
place to start (see Table 2).

Table 2   *Population of Kosovo, 1948–81*

Year	Albanians		Serbs		Montenegrins	
	No.	%	No.	%	No.	%
1948	498,242	68.5	171,914	23.6	28,050	3.9
1953	524,559	64.9	189,869	23.5	31,343	3.9
1961	646,605	67.2	227,016	23.6	37,588	3.9
1971	916,167	73.7	228,261	18.4	31,555	2.5
1981	1,226,736	77.4	209,497	13.2	27,028	1.7

Source: Dr Hivzi Islami, *Demographic Reality in Kosova* (Kosova Information
Centre, n.d.), p. 31.

Although the number of Serbs and Montenegrins fell in the period
1971–81, overall their population had increased in real terms since
1948. However, their numbers as a *proportion* of the population
dropped from a combined 27.5 per cent in 1948 to 14.9 per cent in
1981. By contrast, the Albanians, with one of the highest birthrates in
Europe, more than doubled their numbers, which explains the halving
of the Serbian and Montenegrin share of the population. During the

1970s and 1980s, as the administration and just about everything else in the province was progressively Albanianised, Serbs (henceforth the name covers Montenegrins too) began to leave. Intercommunal relations worsened as the Serbs lost their privileged status and became convinced that the Albanians wanted to secede and join Albania. If such a thing had ever become a real possibility, many might have balked at union with Enver Hoxha's grim country, as the attraction of Albania was above all emotional. It is important not to forget, however, that the Albanians of the former Yugoslavia were the biggest non-Slav minority in the South Slav state and were there by dint of conquest in 1912 and, as far as they were concerned, in 1944 as well. Their demand for a republic after the fall of Ranković was also aimed at redressing what they saw as a communist and Serbian con-trick. By designating ethnic Albanians a *nationality* rather than a *nation* (like Serbs and Croats), the federation withheld from them the right to self-determination. Serbs argued that the nationalities, which included ethnic Hungarians, did not have this right because, unlike nations, they had a mother state outside the borders of Yugoslavia.

Hostility between the communities was fuelled by poverty, which in turn became increasingly difficult to redress because of the Albanian population explosion coupled with Yugoslavia's mounting economic crisis. Growing numbers of Serbs sought their fortune elsewhere, and in villages with small Serb populations the more Serbs that left the more insecure were those that remained behind. They felt uncomfortable surrounded by a hostile Albanian population. Albanians claim that Serbs began to leave for economic reasons, and Serbs that they did so because they were chased out, threatened and even attacked. There is truth in both these arguments. Anti-Serb graffiti were daubed on the walls along with demands for a republic. Although the Yugoslav police and army clamped down harshly when angry unemployed Albanian youths or students demonstrated, it was clear that something had to be done to resolve the problem. But within the constraints of 'brotherhood and unity' – which had never in any sense existed in Kosovo – it was not clear what. In the end it was Kosovo, the uncompromising nature of mutually exclusive nationalisms and the power of the Serbian Kosovo spirit, conjured back to life in the late 1980s, which were to begin to destroy Yugoslavia.

Bosnian Spirit

Just as everywhere else, it was the fall of Ranković that was to ring the changes in Bosnia too. After 1966 Serbian dominance of the administration and the Bosnian communist party began to wane. Increasingly

Bosnia's Muslims began to make themselves felt in the running of the republic and in the shaping of its future.

In the pre-communist era and especially before the late nineteenth century, Serbs and Croats in Bosnia would just as often identify themselves as Orthodox and Catholic. In the context of religious definitions of identities, then, there was no need for the Muslims to be anything else but Muslims. Although Serbian and Croatian nationalists spent a lot of energy in the century before 1945 trying to prove that Bosnia's Muslims were really Serbs or Croats, the fact that they mostly voted for the Yugoslav Muslim Party in the inter-war years points to a more developed sense of nationality than many Serbs or Croats like to admit. After the Second World War the communists shrank from declaring the Muslims a nation with the same standing as Serbs and Croats. In part this was because the recognition of Muslim nationhood would create problems arising out of the (theoretical) right to self-determination conferred on nations by the constitution.

Throughout the war which began in 1992, almost every single analysis of Bosnia began with the premise that the Muslims were the most numerous people in the republic. What was not often realised was just how new this phenomenon was. In fact, the Muslims only overtook the Serbs as the largest nation in Bosnia some time in the late 1960s. There are several reasons for this. After the war large numbers of Bosnian Serbs (and Croats) were encouraged to move from poor areas to the rich farmlands of Vojvodina and eastern Croatia, where they were needed to replace the 350,000 Germans who had fled in 1945.[20] Industrialisation in Croatia and Serbia also exerted a pull, and in the 1950s and 1960s some 16,000 Serbs a year were calculated to be leaving Bosnia.[21] For many young Serbs Belgrade was also a far more attractive and exciting place to make a career than provincial Sarajevo. The same held true for young Croats, moving perhaps from the rocky wastelands of western Hercegovina to Zagreb or the Croatian coast, which was undergoing a boom thanks to tourism. By contrast, while Serbs were leaving the Sandžak (in Serbia and Montenegro) and moving to Serbia's cities, Muslims from the same area gravitated towards Bosnia. Once one brother was established, another would come, and then more and more of the family. These were natural economic and demographic pull factors which were changing the ethnic map of Bosnia. The statistics also show that the Muslims had a far higher birthrate than the Serbs or Croats (see Table 3).

Interestingly these statistics also show that the number of Serbs killed during the Second World War did not affect their proportion of the population, because so many Muslims and Croats died too.[22]

Demography was not the only way in which Bosnia changed. As the debate between the Croatian and Serbian nationalists in 1971 showed,

Table 3   *Populations of Bosnia–Hercegovina, 1875–1991 (%)*

	1879(a)	1910	1948(b)	1961(c)	1971(d)	1981	1991
Serbs	42.9	43.5	44.0	42.9	37.2	32.0	31.3
Croats	18.1	22.9	24.0	21.7	20.6	18.4	17.3
Muslims	38.7	32.2	31.0	25.7	39.6	39.5	43.7
Others	0.3	1.4	1.0	9.7	2.6	10.1	7.0

Sources: (a) For 1879 and 1910: Alexandre Popovic, *L'Islam balkanique: les musulmans du sud-est européen dans la période post-ottomane* (Berlin, 1986), p. 271. (b) Stevan K. Pavlowitch, *Yugoslavia* (London, 1971), p. 186. Muslims listed as nationally 'undecided'. (c) Sabrina P. Ramet, *Nationalism and Federalism in Yugoslavia 1962–1991*, 2nd edn (Bloomington and Indianapolis, 1992), p. 124. The lower number of Muslims indicates a higher number declaring themselves 'Yugoslavs'. (d) Figures for 1971–91 from 'Ethnic Map of Bosnia–Herzegovina' by Prof. Dr Ante Markotić, Ejub Sijerčić and Asim Abdurahmanović in *Why* (Sarajevo), February 1992. 1971 was the first year in which Muslims were listed as a nation in their own right. In 1991 Bosnia's population was 4,354,911.

extremists on both sides remained unreconciled to 'losing' Bosnia. The recreation of a Bosnian entity in Tito's Yugoslavia had been done in large measure to prevent it becoming a renewed object of conflict between Serbs and Croats. On the whole, Bosnia's Muslims were happy with this premise, and until the very end they were the most pro-Yugoslav of the country's peoples.

After the Second World War the communists hoped that in a post-religious era the Muslims would increasingly identify themselves as Serbs or Croats or as plain Yugoslavs. By the early 1960s, however, there were signs that this policy was being quietly abandoned.[23] Besides, Tito's policy of non-alignment was having the unforeseen effect of stimulating interest among Muslims in their Islamic heritage and in opening contacts, commercial and academic, with Muslim countries. This was something that Tito chose to exploit, and these contacts were to flower in the 1970s and 1980s. One of the side-effects of these new relations was the construction of mosques throughout Bosnia, often using money from Islamic countries. Although this alarmed Serbs and Croats, the vast majority of Muslims were not particularly religious. But these developments in turn spurred academic debate on the nature of what it meant to be a Muslim in Bosnia. While the future president Alija Izetbegović wrote a pamphlet on Islam in general, the *Islamic Declaration*, in which he did not talk about Bosnia, another school of thought was emerging.

In February 1967 Muhamed Filipović, a philosophy professor, later the Bosnian ambassador in London, published a seminal piece in *Život*, Sarajevo's leading literary journal, entitled 'The Bosnian Spirit'. He argued that Bosnia's Muslims, whom he wanted to call specifically

Bošnjaks, had their own separate tradition and culture. The idea was to reinforce Muslim identity not through religion but in an ethnic sense. At first this got him into trouble and he was expelled from the communist party and from all his other positions. By 1969, however, the Bosnian party's central committee adopted the main thrust of his ideas and they became the new orthodoxy. In 1971 the ideas were 'legalised' because by the Bosnian Muslims' inclusion as Muslims (but not Bošnjaks) in that year's census they were effectively declared a *nation* on a par with Serbs and Croats.

The Bosnian Spirit was an idea whose time had come. In the wake of the events in Croatia, Tito, who had never been particularly interested in Yugoslavia's Muslims, saw the benefit of promoting them not only to underline that Bosnia should be out of bounds in Serbo-Croat disputes but to cultivate a grateful, loyal and pro-Yugoslav population. This he succeeded in doing, and Bosnia's Muslims were forced out of Yugoslavia reluctantly when it collapsed. During the Bosnian War, Tito's portrait remained in offices and shops throughout Muslim-controlled areas of the country, and more than any other nation the Muslims mourned the passing of the old country.

A Proposal for Hopelessness

'After Tito – Tito!' This was the slogan that described what was supposed to happen after the leader's death. There was to be no single successor but a complicated system involving a rotating federal presidency of eight members – six from the republics and two from Serbia's provinces. At first this unwieldy system seemed to work, and the much feared transition of power was smooth. It seemed that Yugoslavia would pull through and that, with goodwill, the country would be able to meet the challenges of the years ahead. This proved a forlorn hope. With power thoroughly devolved to the republics and provinces by the 1974 constitution, decision-making without a final arbiter ultimately proved impossible. Republican and provincial hierarchies put their local and ethnic national interests above that of the country as a whole and, given the lack of democracy in the country, it was eventually to crack under the strain.

The greatest source of political instability in Yugoslavia was Kosovo. After the 1981 riots the numbers of Serbs leaving the province began to pick up. Stories began to circulate about the 'persecution' of Kosovo Serbs, the destruction of their churches and graveyards and frequent acts of violence. For every real incident, though, the rumour mill could fabricate a thousand more. It became a commonplace that 'the rape of little Serbian girls was an everyday occurrence'.[24] In 1982 a man was murdered by his Albanian neighbours and there was another murder the next year. In one of the most bizarre and notorious of occurrences, a farmer called Djordje Martinović somehow emerged from an incident with a bottle rammed up his rear. Slowly the historical demons were beginning to stir. The Martinović case was said even by eminent academics to recall the old Turkish practice of impalement. There was increasing gossip about Serb 'refugees' from Kosovo – and less mention of the fact that many of them had sold their houses for large sums of money thanks to the housing shortage in the crowded province.

The first sign that the Kosovo problem was beginning to have a deeply corrosive effect within 'inner' Serbia occurred in 1983. The occasion was the funeral in Belgrade of Aleksandar Ranković, who had lived in obscure retirement since his fall from power in 1966. Everyone was taken aback, then, when tens of thousands turned out to mourn him, some of them shouting nationalist slogans such as 'Serbia is Rising!' Ranković may have been bad, reasoned these people, but at least he kept the hated Shiptars or Albanians in their place.

An earlier sign of disquiet over events in Kosovo, at least among the political classes, had come in 1968 when the matter had been raised by Dobrica Ćosić. Until 1968 Ćosić had been close to the centre of power. However, he was expelled from the central committee after warning that Kosovo's Albanian leaders were separatists. In the same year he had also taken up the cudgels against Hungarians in Vojvodina and attacked moves to promote Yugoslavia's Muslims to the status of a nation. This was 'senseless', he declared.[25] Despite being cast out from the party, the novelist–politician did not disappear from the political scene. According to Vojislav Šešelj, later to be the leader of Serbia's extreme nationalists, he became a role model 'for all us younger dissidents'. Ćosić was never arrested and he gathered around him a circle of reform-minded intellectuals. During the 1970s he and others who had been in trouble with the authorities, such as Mihailo Marković, organised the 'Free University', through which they would give talks in private flats on various, mostly philosophical topics.

The former communist began to argue that the only way in which Yugoslavia could be preserved was to introduce social democratic reforms. Later he claimed that this had proved impossible because the Slovenes and Croats had been 'so nationalist'. However, despite his self-proclaimed reformist bent, some were not so certain that Ćosić himself was not simply an old-fashioned nationalist in dissident's clothing. The party magazine *Komunist* condemned him in 1977 for saying that the Serbs were being 'exploited and denigrated by other Yugoslav nationalities' and for making other 'inflammatory nationalistic statements'.[26]

In 1984 Ćosić became a leading light in the Committee for the

Freedom of Speech, which had been formed to protect dissidents. Curiously its most famous cases turned out to feature some of the main actors in the drama of Yugoslavia's demise, including Franjo Tudjman, Alija Izetbegović, Vojislav Šešelj and his Croatian opposite number, the extreme nationalist Dobroslav Paraga. At the same time Ćosić was also giving discreet help to a small group of Serbs from Kosovo who had sought him out and asked for his advice. He told them to send a petition to the government.[27] At first they had little success, but in October 1985 they collected 2,016 signatures. In January 1986, 200 prominent Serbian intellectuals signed another one demanding action over the 'unbearable condition of the Serb nation in Kosovo'.[28] Later in the year yet another petition was signed by 50,000 people.

With communist power slowly beginning to dissipate, it was not just the question of Kosovo which showed how things were changing in Serbia. In 1985 Veselin Djuretić, a Serbian historian who worked under the aegis of the Serbian Academy, published the first book since the war to reappraise the Chetnik leader Draža Mihailović and to question the official communist version of wartime history. The book caused a storm, but the Academy stood by Djuretić.[29] The reason was that the Academy itself was now involved in a radical reappraisal of Yugoslavia, focusing on the Serbian relationship with the state, the republics and the provinces. Sixteen prominent academics, including economists, scientists and historians, began work in June 1985. The year before Ćosić had suggested that the Academy discuss various national and social problems, but in fact he played only a very minor role in the composition of what became known as the *Memorandum*.[30] By contrast it is clear that the work that was produced was to a great extent the inspiration of the man who came to be called the 'father of the nation'.

On 24 and 25 September 1986 the whole of Yugoslavia was shaken by a political earthquake. The Belgrade newspaper *Večernje Novosti* published leaked extracts of the unfinished *Memorandum* and launched into a major attack on the document, which it called 'A Proposal for Hopelessness'. Photocopied editions of the typed document began to circulate. While the first part of the *Memorandum* asserted that decentralisation was leading to the disintegration of Yugoslavia and attacked the various economic policies which had been pursued since the 1960s, it was the parts concerning the condition of the Serbs in Kosovo and Croatia which caused the real shock. While most of the document was written in trenchant language, these parts suddenly took on a tone of shrill hysteria. Although the census returns showed that Kosovo's Serbian population had hovered around the 200,000 mark since the war (see Table 2, p. 152), the *Memorandum* asserted that over the last twenty years 200,000 Serbs had already been 'forced to leave' Kosovo: 'It is not just that the last of the remnants of the Serbian

1991: Ethnic Yugoslavia before the War

nation are leaving their homes at an unabated rate, but according to all evidence, faced with a physical, moral and psychological reign of terror, they seem to be preparing for their final exodus.'[31] A direct line was drawn from the migrations led by Patriarch Arsenije in 1690 to the present, and the *Memorandum* declared, 'The physical, political, legal and cultural genocide of the Serbian population in Kosovo and Metohija is a worse historical defeat than any experienced in the liberation wars waged by Serbia from the First Serbian Uprising in 1804 to the uprising of 1941.'[32]

As for the Serbs of Croatia the *Memorandum* argued that assimilation and emigration meant that 'Except for the time under the Independent State of Croatia, the Serbs in Croatia have never before been as jeopardized as they are today. A resolution of their national status is a question of overriding political importance. If solutions are not found, the consequences might well be disastrous, not only for Croatia, but for the whole of Yugoslavia.'[33] The *Memorandum* went on to point out that according to the 1981 census (whose figures it ignored when it was arguing about Kosovo), 24 per cent of Serbs lived outside Serbia and 40.3 per cent outside 'inner' Serbia:

> A nation which after a long and bloody struggle regained its own state, which fought for and achieved a civil democracy, and which in the last two wars lost 2.5 million of its members, has lived to see the day when a Party committee of apparatchiks decrees that after four decades in the new Yugoslavia it alone is not allowed to have its own state. A worse historical defeat in peacetime cannot be imagined.[34]

Such language from so august a body as the Serbian Academy had never been heard before in communist Yugoslavia. Genuine grievances suddenly became genocide, Croatia was compared to the NDH, Serbia's leaders were apparatchiks and then came the conclusion: 'The Serbian people cannot stand idly by and wait for the future in such a state of uncertainty. . . . Naturally, Serbia must not be passive and wait and see what the others will say, as it has done so often in the past.'[35]

The blue touch-paper had been lit.

Antique God

One can but wonder whether Slobodan Milošević, then the Serbian communist party leader, has come to rue his words about the *Memorandum*:

> The appearance of the Memorandum of the Serbian Academy of Arts and Sciences represents nothing else but the darkest nationalism. It means the liquidation of the current socialist system of our country, that is the disintegration after which there is no survival for any nation or nationality. . . . Tito's policy of brotherhood and unity . . . is the only basis on which Yugoslavia's survival can be secured.[36]

It is widely believed that Milošević cleverly avoided saying anything about the *Memorandum*, and that he soon came to take complete power in Serbia by nonetheless adopting its ideas. In fact, luckily for him, the speech in which he condemned the *Memorandum* received no publicity because it was made to a select group of secret policemen. What is curious, though, is that he made it in June 1987, after adopting the Kosovo cause as his own, which goes to show that he was an opportunist telling different audiences different things in order to garner their support.

Slobodan Milošević was born in Požarevac in 1941, the second son of recent Montenegrin immigrants. His father Svetozar had trained to be an Orthodox priest but ended up as a teacher. The Milošević home was not a happy one and soon after the war Svetozar went back to Montenegro where, in 1962, he committed suicide. The Milošević boys were brought up by their mother Stanislava, a strait-laced communist activist and teacher who in 1972 also committed suicide. According to Slavoljub Djukić, Milošević's (unofficial) biographer, young Slobodan was regarded as 'untypical'. He was 'not interested in sports, avoided excursions and used to come to school dressed in the old-fashioned way – white shirt and tie'. He also 'preached' to his classmates that they were not suitably attired. He was regarded as 'a restrained and diligent pupil'. Djukić quotes one of his old friends as saying that he 'could imagine him as a station-master or punctilious civil servant'.[37]

The curious thing is that Milošević might indeed have become a station-master had he not, while at school, fallen in love with school-mate Mirjana Marković. The couple were extraordinarily close and it is widely believed that Mirjana was the driving force behind her future husband's career. As noted earlier Mirjana, who preferred to be known by her mother's wartime and partisan *nom de guerre* of Mira, was not just any pupil in the Požarevac school. Her uncle, Draža Marković, was one of Serbia's leading politicians. Her father Moma Marković had been the political commissar of Partisan units in Serbia during the war, and another close relation, Davorjanka (Zdenka) Paunović, had been Tito's wartime secretary and lover.[38] Her mother, who had died during the war, had been secretary of the Belgrade Communist Party, but had been denounced as a traitor for her 'unheroic attitude'. Possibly she had given the names of other communists under torture, but her daughter resented and rejected the accusations of treachery.

At university in Belgrade, Slobodan headed the ideology section of its party branch and had a hardline reputation. It was also at university that Mira and Slobodan met Ivan Stambolić, the nephew of Petar Stambolić, one of the grandees of Serbian politics. Ivan became their best friend and was Slobodan's best man when he married Mira. Although Ivan worked in a factory while studying, it was clear that what Yugoslavs call his 'biography' meant that he was not going to disappear into obscurity on graduating. He began the long march through the institutions, all the while taking Slobodan with him. In 1968 Milošević got a job in the Tehnogas company where Ivan was already working. By 1973 Milošević was head of Tehnogas. In 1978 he became president of Beobanka, a major Belgrade bank. These positions, plus Ivan's patronage, provided stature for Milošević's move into politics. By 1984 Stambolić was head of Serbia's Central Committee and as such he arranged for his friend to become head of the Belgrade party branch. In 1986 Stambolić moved up to become president of Serbia and passed on his old job to Slobodan.

Until this time Milošević was not seen as a particularly interesting politician in his own right; he was no more than a sidekick of Stambolić. Politically Stambolić had been voicing Serbian grievances over Kosovo and the resentment felt about the 1974 constitution which gave Serbia's provinces the right to participate in legislating in 'inner' Serbia while 'inner' Serbia itself did not have the same rights in its own provinces. Stambolić felt caught between two stools. He wanted to improve Serbia's position, but he did not want to fan the flames of nationalism. In other words he was a classic example of the 'apparatchik' castigated by the *Memorandum*. Milošević himself generally expressed no particular interest in the national question except to attack nationalism and praise Tito's policies.

Although Milošević had a rather dull reputation, it is telling that he became a major politician in his own right as the result of a stunning act of treachery. In April 1987 Stambolić asked him to go to Kosovo to meet local leaders because angry Kosovo Serbs were threatening to come and protest in Belgrade. Outside the building in Kosovo Polje, which is on the outskirts of Priština, the demonstrators clashed with the (predominantly Albanian) police. Milošević came out. 'No one should dare to beat you,' he told the crowd. 'This sentence enthroned him as a Tsar,' said the Kosovo Serb leader Miroslav Šoljević.[39] From this point on Milošević, using the issue of the Kosovo Serbs, was brutally to shove aside his old friend Stambolić as he began to consolidate all power in Serbia for himself. For many years it was thought that Milošević's dramatic gesture at Kosovo Polje had been completely spontaneous. Later it became known that he had been to Kosovo four days earlier to prepare for his fateful trip.[40] Šoljević was in fact not a Kosovo Serb at all, but a man from Niš who was working in Kosovo. He and his comrades, now working in tandem with Milošević's men, would turn out large numbers of Kosovo Serbs to dramatise their plight throughout the country and, of course, drum up support for their newfound leader. When this job was finished Šoljević went home to Niš. Clearly he was not as worried about the Serbian flight from its ancestral heartland as he had once made out.

Over the next few years Milošević was to emerge as the triumphant and undisputed leader of Serbia. With the help of Mira, now a professor of Marxism at Belgrade University, he was able to gather around him a group of supportive intellectuals, many of whom seemed to see in him a Serbian messiah. Milošević's greatest skills were organisational. This meant that he promoted to senior positions people whose main attribute was personal loyalty. He also understood the power of the media, and this was gradually brought under his control by the judicious placing of friends and allies in all the top editorial jobs. They were skilled propaganda experts and were able to turn all sorts of events and even tragedy to their advantage. In September 1987, for example, an Albanian conscript in the JNA went berserk. He shot dead four fellow conscripts and wounded six others before killing himself. Only one of the dead was a Serb, all of the other casualties were of different nationalities. There was no doubt that the killer was mentally disturbed, but the Serbian media seized the opportunity to indulge in an orgy of anti-Albanian propaganda. As a result 10,000 people turned out for the funeral of the hapless dead Serb, Srdjan Simić. The affair could not have come at a better time, for at precisely the same moment Milošević was involved in a struggle to get rid of one of his enemies who had alluded to Milošević's nationalism.

Milošević and his allies were to use mass rallies and demonstrations more and more over the next two years to promote the new Serbian leader. Kosovo Serbs provided the shock troops and they were joined by local people and workers bussed in for 'Meetings of Truth' summoned to confirm Milošević's support. It was as though the Serbs were going through an exercise of mass catharsis. All the old fears and the old banned nationalist songs bubbled back up to the surface. Milošević rode ever higher on this wave of nationalist euphoria. But to keep popular support he actually had to do something. By manipulating crowds and demonstrators he moved to abolish the autonomy of Vojvodina and then Kosovo. In Montenegro too the old regime was toppled in favour of his supporters. 'This is no time for sorrow; it is a time for struggle,' he told hundreds of thousands at a Belgrade rally in November 1988:

> We entered both world wars with nothing but the conviction that we would fight for freedom, and we won both wars. . . . We shall win the battle for Kosovo regardless of the obstacles facing us inside and outside the country. We shall win despite the fact that Serbia's enemies outside the country are plotting against it, along with those in the country. We tell them that we enter every battle . . . with the aim of winning it.[41]

On 20 February 1989 Albanian miners in Kosovo staged a last-ditch struggle to stop the reimposition of Serbian rule in Kosovo. It failed but, in the midst of the Serbian euphoria, came a sudden shot across the bows. Although the Slovenes and Serbs had been wrangling over the future of Yugoslavia, Serbs liked Slovenes. They had no historic quarrel with them and thousands of Slovene children had been welcomed as refugees in Serbia during the war. Suddenly Serbs were horrified to find not only that all of the Slovene leadership had gathered to denounce Serbian policies at a meeting in the Cankarjev Dom, a concert hall in Ljubljana, but that Milan Kućan, the Slovene president, had asserted that Yugoslavia was being 'defended' by the Albanian miners.

Undeterred, Milošević moved towards his coronation. He assumed the presidency of Serbia on 8 May 1989, but the real ceremony was timed to coincide with the 600th anniversary of the Battle of Kosovo. On 28 June, all of Yugoslavia's top politicians were assembled at the very battlefield, at the part called Gazimestan. Milošević arrived by helicopter and in front of one million people he declared:

Serbs in their history have never conquered or exploited others. Through two world wars, they have liberated themselves and, when they could, they also helped others to liberate themselves. . . . The Kosovo heroism does not allow us to forget that, at one time, we were brave and dignified and one of the few who went into battle undefeated. . . . Six centuries later, again we are in battles and quarrels. They are not armed battles, though such things should not be excluded yet. . . .[42]

Many years later, Father Sava, a monk at Visoki Dečani in Kosovo, said:

In the late eighties we felt the national change and thought it would be a good thing. But I was at the meeting at Gazimestan in 1989 and then I saw it was the wrong way. We thought he would come to [the church of] Gračanica to bow down to the ideals of the past, the good, spiritual, moral traditions, but he did not. He appeared like an antique god by helicopter. I saw at that moment that the change was going in the wrong direction.

Six hundred years after the battle, Lazar's bones were lying in state at Gračanica. Milošević wanted Lazar's glory, but he did not believe that, like Serbia's greatest hero, he was going to lose the coming battles. In fact he believed that having secured power in Serbia, the provinces and Montenegro he could now move on to browbeat the rest of Yugoslavia's republican leaderships into submitting to his authority. The immediate result was a grotesque rerun of all the old debates of the 1920s and 1930s. Milošević argued that more centralisation made sense. To the Croats and the Slovenes, already horrified by the abolition of Serbia's provincial autonomy and the use of the police and army in Kosovo, this was just an excuse for a new Serb-run Yugoslavia. And, of course, Yugoslavia did not exist in an international vacuum. Everywhere else communism was crumbling. In January 1990 the Slovenes walked out of the Yugoslav Communist Party. Ante Marković, the federal prime minister, said that, despite this, Yugoslavia would 'continue'. He was optimistic that the multi-party elections that were now to take place would result in the peaceful transformation of the communist state into a new country, willing and able to take its place in the new Europe.

Bolshevism Is Bad But Nationalism Is Worse
(Radovan Karadžić)

The Slovene elections, held in April 1990, led to the victory of a centre–right coalition and to Milan Kučan, the republic's former communist president, returning to power as the first democratically elected leader within Yugoslavia since 1945. In Croatia in May, the communists were swept from office by Franjo Tudjman's new party, the HDZ, which came to power on a wave of nationalist euphoria. One of its first major acts was to 'demote' the Serbs (about 600,000 people and some 12 per cent of the population) from the Croatian constitution. Croatia was now the 'national state of the Croatian people' and only then of the other nations who lived in it. As we have seen, this subject had been at the core of the quarrels of 1971 and by this act the HDZ in essence tore up the ideological basis of Serbo-Croatian co-operation which had been born in 1905 with the political understanding that underpinned the Croatian–Serbian Coalition. For Serbs and Croats the move was of enormous emotional significance. Milošević's Serbian nationalism was the greatest boost to Tudjman's Croatian nationalism, but now that the Pandora's box had been opened there was no shutting it. The result of the Croatian elections fuelled the next round of Serbian nationalism, both within Croatia and within Serbia, where in December 1990 Milošević and the old Serbian Communist Party, now the Socialist Party of Serbia (SPS), was returned to power.

Milošević's adoption of nationalism and of the mantle of Kosovo meant that the communist parties of Serbia and Montenegro were the only ones in the whole of the communist world which were able to survive the first round of post-communist elections.

Given Yugoslavia's peculiar history, one nationalism had to be answered by another. For every call that 'all Serbs should live in one state', there was another that Croatia or Slovenia should not live in this same state. The irony of this period, given what followed, is that in Bosnia, as opposed to Croatia, Slovenia and Serbia, the political parties were still talking about keeping Yugoslavia together. In its November elections, the population had voted broadly along national lines, although a significant minority, 28 per cent of those who voted, cast their ballots against the three ethnically based parties.

The Bosnian Croats voted mostly for a branch of the HDZ which at the time was led by a moderate pro-Bosnia as opposed to pro-Greater Croatia faction. Most Muslims voted for the Party of Democratic Action (SDA), which was led by Alija Izetbegović. At the time it wanted to preserve Yugoslavia, as did the main Bosnian Serb party, the Serbian Democratic Party (SDS). After the elections, the three national parties formed a coalition government. They had all encouraged Bosnians to vote for their respective parties, not on the basis of a nationalist ticket but rather on an anti-communist one.

The SDS was led by a Sarajevo psychiatrist and poet, Dr Radovan Karadžić. He was born in Montenegro and had previously flirted with Bosnia's Green Party. During his spell as an ecologist he had declared that 'Bolshevism is bad, but nationalism is even worse,' and was remembered for making suggestions about food labelling. In 1985 he had been imprisoned for fraud, along with Momčilo Krajišnik. This sinister-looking bushy-eyebrowed man later became the speaker of the Bosnian Serb parliament, one of the most important Bosnian Serb powerbrokers. In 1996 he was elected as the Serbian delegate for Bosnia's first post-war presidency. In 1968 Karadžić had been involved in student protests at Sarajevo University, but there were suspicions later that he had been a police informer. In 1990 he was the psychiatrist of Sarajevo's football team, which was trailing badly in the national league.[43] He had had some books of poetry published and taught poetry at a workers' night-school. There was nothing in his past which suggested that he was a radical nationalist. He was not first choice to head the SDS as a number of other people had turned down the post. He was chosen at the suggestion of Jovan Rašković, a fellow psychiatrist and friend of Dobrica Ćosić, who earlier in 1990 had founded the SDS of Croatia, in Knin.

Apart from Karadžić and Krajišnik, the two other top leaders of the SDS were Nikola Koljević and Biljana Plavšić. Both were teachers at Sarajevo University. Plavšić was a biologist by profession who had studied earlier in her career in the United States. Tall and stern, she later evolved into a hardliner and this, coupled with her trademark handbag, meant that she was often compared to Britain's Mrs Thatcher. In September 1996 she was elected the first post-war president of the Republika Srpska, that is the Serbian entity that was to emerge during the Bosnian war.

Nikola Koljević was Yugoslavia's foremost Shakespeare scholar. Short, bespectacled and cardigan-wearing, Koljević exuded a pleasant, moderate air, which belied his involvement in an increasingly radicalising party. He was the younger brother of Svetozar Koljević, a renowned scholar who had written extensively on Serbian epic poetry. Some have suggested that Koljević went into politics because he resented the fact that throughout his whole life he had had to live in the shadow of his famous elder brother. His involvement in Serbian nationalist politics shocked his Muslim students, many of whom had remained good friends after graduating, because he had never before shown the slightest trace of prejudice. Koljević's son had died in an accident a few years before the war, and some believed that as a result of that trauma Koljević had become intent on playing out a full-blown

Shakespearean tragedy of his own with himself in a starring role.

In the long run, co-operation in Bosnia proved impossible. The main republican leaders, Milošević, Tudjman and Kućan, were all playing an uncompromising political game, all the while beginning their preparations for war. The professed desire of Bosnia's Serbian leaders to co-operate was either insincere or short-lived, for they soon began to turn the SDS into a clandestine armed force.

Yugoslavia's leaders were gambling for big stakes, but many ordinary people did not believe it would come to war. They just thought that everything would come right in the end, that somehow their leaders would draw back from the brink. In fact Tito's words from 1945 seemed to echo down the passages of the massive and increasingly empty Federation Palace building in Belgrade, home of the fading federal government:

> We have seen the results of the national oppression in the past; we have seen them when, in 1941, Yugoslavia collapsed like a house of cards. Essentially what did this mean? That the peoples did not like this Yugoslavia such as it was, not only that the Croats and Slovenes did not like it, that the Serbs did not like it either, particularly not in the way all our nations love the new Yugoslavia.[44]

9

FRANKIE AND BADGER GO TO WAR

'There'll be war, by God,' said Slobodan Milošević. Borisav Jović, Milošević's ally, confidant and Serbia's representative on the Yugoslav federal presidency, begged to differ: 'We won't allow it, by God. We have had enough war and death in two World Wars. Now we shall avoid war by all means!' General Veljko Kadijević, Yugoslavia's defence minister, added his own view: 'There will not be the kind of war which they want . . . but it will be the kind of war which it must be, and that is that we shall not allow them to beat us.'[1]

It was 13 February 1990. The alleged conversation took place during an informal chat after a meeting of the federal presidency and is recorded in Jović's diary. Four days later the SDS was born in Knin, later to become the capital of the Republic of Serbian Krajina (RSK), the Serbian breakaway state in Croatia.

There may not be a direct connection between the two events, but they showed which way the political wind was blowing. Alarmed by the rising tide of Croatian nationalism and seeing a need for a party to represent Serbian interests in Croatia, psychiatrist Dr Jovan Rašković and others had formed the SDS in time to take part in Croatia's first multi-party elections in May. The party did well in Knin and some other areas of compact Serbian settlement, but overall it did not do particularly well among the republic's Serbian population. However, the election result, the triumph of the HDZ, shocked many Serbs. Rašković was a moderate compared to those leaders who were to follow him. He wanted to assure Serbian rights, not found a separatist state, but then he did not want Croatia to become independent either; he said, 'If the Croatian people want their own state, then the Serbs will decide their own fate.'[2] Even after the elections he declared, 'This is an uprising of the Serb people . . . but it is an uprising without weapons.'[3]

As the situation became ever more embittered, Rašković was sidelined. He was discredited after Tudjman leaked a recording of him to the press in which he described the Serbs of Croatia as 'crazy people'. He was pushed aside by Milan Babić, a power-hungry young politician who before 1990 had been a Knin dentist. It was under his direction that the party began to take action, shifting from talk about Serbian cultural and personal autonomy to territorial demands. The first steps towards implementing this policy was the formation of a league of Serbian municipal councils. This began to give a physical definition to the land claimed by the SDS within Croatia.

Framing the Serbs

Jović's diaries disclose that on 28 June 1990 (the fateful Vidovdan–Kosovo anniversary again) he was already discussing with Milošević not just the 'ejection' of Croatia and Slovenia from Yugoslavia but the ways in which predominantly Serbian-inhabited areas could be carved out of Croatia. He says that Milošević put forward two ideas, the first of which shows that he was already thinking of doing what King Alexander had not done in 1928: that is, effecting the 'amputation' of Croatia while keeping the rest of Yugoslavia, minus Slovenia, but including the Serbian-populated areas of Croatia. Milošević suggested to Jović that the:

> 'cutting off' of Croatia be carried out in such a way that the municipalities of Lika, Banija and Kordun, which have created an association, should decide in a referendum whether they wanted to stay or leave; second, that the members of the SFRY [Socialist Federative Republic of Yugoslavia] presidency from Slovenia and Croatia be excluded from the vote on this issue, because they do not represent that part of Yugoslavia taking the decision.[4]

Likewise General Kadijević has written that some time after April 1990 the JNA was already considering 'how to defend the right of the peoples which want to live in the mutual state of Yugoslavia'.[5] Only later were the Serbs and Montenegrins specifically identified as those peoples, because it was not yet clear that both the Bosnian Muslims and the Macedonians would feel compelled to follow the Croatian and Slovene example.

It may be that even at this stage Milošević did not really intend to carry out his plan, perhaps believing that the Croats, as in 1928, could be frightened into staying in a Yugoslavia dominated by himself. What he did know for sure, though, was that arming the Serbs outside Serbia was a good idea. It was, at the very least, a contingency plan. For this the SDS was a suitable vehicle, first in Croatia and then in Bosnia. The reason for this was the military structure of the Territorial Defence (TO) organisation that had been evolved over the years in Yugoslavia. Based on the Partisan experience, the Yugoslav military had developed the concept of Total National Defence. This meant that, apart from the regular army, each republic had reserve forces to call upon in the event of war. These were to be local forces which, in the event of a breakdown in communications, would be able to continue functioning on their own. For political guidance they would work closely with the leadership of the local Communist Party. By substituting the Communist Party with the SDS, the Serbian leadership was able to make use of the TO system for mass mobilisations of Serbs in what was to become Krajina and then in Bosnia.

Milošević gave the task of laying the groundwork to his most trusted lieutenants. They were Radmilo Bogdanović, Jovica Stanišić and Mihalj Kertes. Until 1991 Bogdanović was Serbia's minister of the interior, after which he remained a powerful figure, mostly behind the scenes. Kertes was a former Yugoslav deputy interior minister who became a Serbian minister without portfolio. Despite some ethnic Hungarian antecedents, he was an SPS deputy and an agent of Serbia's secret police, the SDB, which had played a key role in organising the rallies which had secured the Serbian president's power in Vojvodina. Stanišić was the head of the SDB. Below them were the SDB's two top men, Frano Simatović, known as Frenki, and Radovan Stojičić, known as Badža, a deputy interior minister of Serbia. (Badža, pronounced Badger, is the Serbo-Croatian name for the bully in the Popeye cartoons.)

The SDB could not prepare a Serbian insurrection alone, however. It needed help from within the military. Because of the communist and Yugoslav orientation of many of the top brass, the high command could still not be trusted, so selected generals had to be recruited. They included General Andrija Biorčević, the commander of the Novi Sad Corps, and Colonel Ratko Mladić, the commander of the Knin garrison. A clandestine network was developed. It was not a formal group but rather a small number of people who met over dinner to discuss their plans. It became known as the Vojna Linija – the Military Line – and its main idea was simple. In the words of one source it was: 'Let's arm our people first in Croatia, then Bosnia. So if Croatia and Slovenia want to get out we won't let them take what we take before them.' The plan they evolved over 1990 was called RAM, an acronym which spells out the word frame. It is not known exactly what the letters stand for, but the purpose of the plan was the organisation of the Serbs outside Serbia, taking control of the fledgling SDS parties and the prepositioning of arms and ammunition.

During 1990 Frenki and Badža were frequent visitors to Knin and other areas with predominantly Serbian populations. Their job was to help organise the SDS, to enhance its emerging police-cum-military capability and to distribute arms. While the driving force behind this organisation was the SDB, there were many other individuals, usually already with a secret police track record, who could be called upon to help. There were many Serbs for example within Croatia's own SDB. There were also individuals within the Yugoslav (hence less trustworthy) SDB, and there was KOS, Yugoslav military counter-intelligence, too.

Goran Hadžić was a typical product of their work. He was a classic man from nowhere who became the leader of the Serbs in eastern Slavonia and for a time Krajina's president. He was often mocked because, in his past life, he had been a warehouse manager. In fact, in the former Yugoslavia, this job was rather powerful because of the opportunities for corruption that it presented. The payoff, though, was that it often went hand in hand with being an SDB informer, which is what Hadžić was. He proved to be a pliant political tool for Milošević's men. Another example of how the preparatory work was done was the despatch to Knin of Brana Crnčević, a poet and columnist for the magazine *Duga*. If, in this capacity, he was not a paid-up SDB agent then he certainly played his role as though he were. His function was to write rousing pieces to help prepare the Serbs for war. Even more important though was Crnčević's role as head of Matica Iseljenika Srbije. This venerable but more or less moribund cultural organisation and publishing house was revived under Slobodan Milošević. It did not however seek out up and coming young poets. Its humanitarian aid department was widely believed to be a cover for dispensing money and arms in preparation for events to come.

This was also the period when Serbian television played its part by the constant screening of documentaries about the Ustashas and Jasenovac, implying all along that President Tudjman was the heir of Ante Pavelić. The effect of all of this was profound and did much to terrify and soften up the Serbs, especially those in the rural Krajina regions. These programmes made them susceptible to the suggestion that their only course of action was to take up arms and so to be prepared – unlike 1941.

Frenki and Badža's first weapons came from police stocks in Serbia and then from the TO and JNA. On the early convoys were Thompson sub-machine guns probably from stocks provided by the US government to Yugoslavia in the 1950s and stored away ever since. They did their job well. By July 1990, only two months after the Croatian elections, Milan Martić, Knin's police chief and the man who built the so-called Krajina Militia, boasted that he could call upon the services of some 12,000 men. The core of this army was Serb policemen in Serbian majority areas, but they were supplemented by TO reservists and volunteers. By the middle of August, areas around Knin had slipped away from Croatian control. Serbian militias built road-blocks with logs, hence the name of their insurrection – the log revolution. A Croatian attempt to fly police into Knin by helicopter was thwarted when the Yugoslav Air Force was scrambled and the jets warned the policemen to turn back or die.

In March 1991, before fighting had begun in earnest, Milošević outlined his strategy to a gathering of Serbian municipal leaders in Belgrade. His assessment was, first, that although Yugoslavia was doomed the Bosnian Muslims would opt to stay within the new state. He reasoned that, just as the Serbs should stay together in one state, Yugoslavia's Muslims would opt for the same solution. Like the Serbs they were scattered across the republics: not just in Bosnia, but in Serbia, Montenegro and Macedonia too. Milošević thus believed that it was in their interests to side with the Serbs in the coming conflict. Logical as this may have been, it proved to be one of the most fundamental errors of his political life. He then told the assembled group that unity was essential because if the Serbs wanted to 'dictate the outcome of events', and that meant frontiers, they had to be powerful. 'And it is always the powerful and never the weak who dictate frontiers.' To this end he explained that reserve police forces had been mobilised and that new forces were being created, that is to say units which 'will give us the capability to defend the interests of our republic and, as well, the interests of the Serbian people outside Serbia. . . . I have been in contact with our people from Knin, from Bosnia, the pressures are enormous.' He then said, 'Are we going to announce on the radio everything that we intend to do? I don't think we could do that. And if we have to fight, well, we'll fight! But, I hope that they will not be so stupid as to fight us. Because if we don't know how to work well and manage the economy at least we know how to fight well.'[6]

During this period neither the Croats nor the Slovenes had been idle. After the elections in Slovenia and Croatia, the JNA had confiscated most of their TO weapons, so they had had to begin clandestine rearming operations. General Martin Špegelj, the former head of the JNA's Fifth Military Region, was put in charge of building Croatian forces. He began with the police in June 1990 and at the end of the year formed the National Guard Corps, which was to become the nucleus of the Croatian Army. At the beginning of 1991, he also began to organise civil defence units. Arms were bought in five different countries, including Hungary, which delivered a large consignment of Kalashnikov AK-47 assault rifles. The Croats also came into possession of considerable quantities of arms after they laid siege to JNA barracks, particularly in Zagreb, Varaždin and Djakovo, in mid-September. But these preparations and military successes were not enough to counter the work already done by Serbia's SDB, the JNA and the SDS. They had access to the arms and ammunition of one of the best-armed states in Europe, and these would stand them in good stead.

In an attempt to disarm the Croats completely before any fighting began, General Kadijević demanded in January 1991 that the JNA be given the authorisation to disarm 'illegal paramilitaries'. As the collective presidency still functioned, this had to be debated and the Croats argued that their units were legal while the only illegal paramilitaries were those of the Serbs in Krajina. In a singularly spectacular coup, Milošević then had shown on television a tape of General Špegelj that had been made by KOS in which he discussed arms and a supposed plan to murder Serbian army officers. Its effect was to terrify. Many Yugoslavs, who had up until now dismissed the possibility of war, realised for the first time that conflict was inevitable.

Over the months that followed public wrangling continued between the republics. We now know, however, that a tacit secret deal was struck in January 1991 between Serbia and Slovenia. Milošević signalled to Kučan that the Slovenes were free to leave Yugoslavia so long as they did not oppose Serbia's plans for the rest of the country. According to Kučan:

> It was obvious at that meeting that the Serbs would not insist on keeping Slovenia within Yugoslavia. . . . We Slovenes said that we wanted the right to have our own state. Milošević said the Serbs wanted the recognition of this right for themselves, too – that is all Serbs in Yugoslavia in one state. My reply, of course, was that the Serbs also had this right, but in the same way as the Slovenes, without hurting the rights of other nations. Milošević replied 'Yes of course, this is clear' and with that we flew home to Ljubljana.[7]

This was the rub, of course. The Yugoslav constitution was, as we have seen, unclear on the question of secession. Although the *republics* were the declared subjects of the 1974 constitution, the constitution itself provided that 'The nations of Yugoslavia, proceeding from the right of every nation to self-determination, including the right to secession . . . have . . . united in a federal republic of free and equal nations and nationalities and founded a socialist federal community.'[8] As Slovenia had no native-born minorities and there were no pockets of Slovenes outside the republic, the issue was clear-cut: republic and nation were the same thing. By contrast, Milošević argued that the Croats had a right to self-determination, but that they could not take Serbs out of Yugoslavia against their will. The problem, as Kučan implied, was that Serbian self-determination was not possible without hurting the other nations, mainly the Croats and Muslims among whom they lived. Likewise Croatian and Muslim self-determination without hurting others was also impossible. Determined to ignore this, however, Milošević and Tudjman pressed on with their preparations for conflict. Indeed, they went further. In March 1991 they met in Karadjordjevo, the old royal hunting lodge in Vojvodina, to discuss the partition of Bosnia. They agreed in principle but failed to reach any firm decisions.[9]

Milošević's attention was now momentarily distracted by events at home. On 9 March riots rocked central Belgrade as student demonstrators took to the streets demanding his removal. Milošević was shaken, but he put tanks on to the streets and quickly restored order. At the time the large demonstrations, in which the opposition leader Vuk Drašković played a major role, appeared to signal that Serbia was unstable and that anger against the regime was welling up beneath the surface. In fact it proved just the opposite. Demonstrations in the years that followed always proved ineffectual and rallied mostly the same metropolitan Belgrade middle classes who saw Milošević not as a nationalist or even as a political opportunist but rather as an unrepentant communist.

With very few exceptions these demonstrations were not directed against the war and most opposition leaders such as Drašković could never make up their mind whether Milošević's greatest crime was starting the war or losing it, or whether to oppose him from an anti-nationalist standpoint or from a hyper-nationalist one. Drašković, who eventually came to oppose the war, originally garnered support with his public espousal of the old Chetnik cause, the adulation of Draža Mihailović and the drawing of lines on maps designed to show how big Serbia really should be.

With events moving quickly now, a fateful meeting of the presidency was held between 12 and 15 March. General Kadijević, together with Serbia, demanded that the JNA effectively be allowed to take power. The presidency failed to agree, but on 16 March Milošević declared:

> Yugoslavia has entered into the final phase of its agony. The Presidency ... has not functioned for a long time, and the illusion of the functioning of the Presidency of Yugoslavia and its powers, which in reality do not exist, has since last night finally expired.
>
> The Republic of Serbia will no longer recognize a single decision of the Presidency under the existing circumstances because it would be illegal.[10]

Simultaneously the by now self-proclaimed SAO – Serbian Autonomous Region – of Krajina declared its independence from

Croatia, although stating that it remained within Yugoslavia. In this fashion its emerging armed forces could claim to remain under the control of the authorities in Belgrade.

After the meeting on 15 March the JNA declared that it would consider what measures to take after its recommendations aimed at preventing inter-ethnic armed conflict and civil war were voted down by the presidency with a majority of votes'.[11] General Kadijević later revealed that that meant organising the 'protection and defence of the Serbian people outside Croatia and the gathering of the JNA within the borders of the future Yugoslavia'.[12] More specifically it meant the 'intensive organisation and preparation of Serbian rebels in Croatia' and the preparation of a unified operation 'to defeat the Croatian Army'.[13]

In his memoirs, *My View of the Break-Up: Army without a State*, Kadijević is unclear about when exactly the army ceased to be a Yugoslav one and became a Serbian one, but in an interview he said, 'There were no precise dates, because decisions were ripening with events.' However, he added that, after the fateful March presidency meeting, 'it was definitely clear' that from then on 'it would be hard to preserve Yugoslavia in her existing borders, and those who wanted Yugoslavia in those borders were not making the decisions'.[14] In other words, Milošević, was making the decisions and Kadijević was going to follow them. After this meeting there was no question that the Serbian-dominated top brass still believed a Yugoslavia from Ljubljana to Skopje could survive. A political and psychological Rubicon had been crossed.

The descent into all-out war was gradual. Already in February armed Serbs had taken over the police station in Pakrac, a town in western Slavonia, in which the Serbs were the largest community. They were ejected by Croatian police. That same month men from Milan Martić's Krajina Militia took over the Plitvice National Park, a region of massive tumbling waterfalls which, in 1990, had attracted 800,000 tourists. On 31 March the Croatian police attempted to reassert their authority. In the ensuing fire-fight one Croat and one Serb died, the first casualties of war. Most ominously, though, the Battle of Plitvice was to establish a precedent for the months to come. In the name of separating the belligerent ethnic groups, the JNA moved in, in force, to Plitvice. The plan was simple and was followed throughout Croatia. It was that Serbian rebels, or even better Croatian police, would begin a fight and then the JNA would move in to separate the parties. In what was to become a typical explanation of what was happening, General Andrija Rašeta, the JNA commander of the Plitvice operation, said that his men were 'protecting neither side', that they were there to prevent 'ethnic confrontations' and that they intended only to remain 'as long as necessary'. In fact they were moving in to establish a western Serb frontier. It was not only the army which was adept at lying. The SDB's Goran Hadžić was caught by the Croats in Plitvice and beaten up. In his home village of Pačetin in eastern Slavonia his sister Goranka Hadžić told anyone who would listen that innocent Goran had just happened to be 'passing through Plitvice' when he was caught. But it helped to frighten eastern Slavonia's Serbs. Barricades were thrown up around Pačetin and Goranka declared, 'the Ustashas are all around us . . . but we're ready for action, we'll fight'.

Milan Martić said, 'We've done our bit, now it's up to Milošević to keep his promise and supply us with arms.' He should have said 'more arms'.

The fighting in Plitvice also set the pattern of misery. The Serb who died was called Rajko Vukadinović and he came from the nearby town of Titova Korenica. A butcher, he had been brought up in the shadow of the genocide of the Second World War. Ten minutes' walk from his little shop were the walls of the old Serbian Orthodox church destroyed during the war but never rebuilt. Standing opposite the cemetery, they were a mute reminder to Serbs that they could not remain passive in the event of a new Croatian threat. Or so it seemed to them. What was not clear to them was how intransigent politicians were pushing people into war. The SDB's involvement was clandestine, the arming of Croatia likewise. But the increasingly hate-filled rhetoric was encouraging a climate of fear and violence which was taking on a life of its own. This was exactly what the SDB had envisaged.

In the rain a black flag of mourning and a Serbian flag hung limply over Vukadinović's shop while memorial candles spluttered in the damp. Across the road the town's hotel was already full of frightened and angry Serbian refugees who had been chased from their homes in outlying villages by local Croats working, the newcomers claimed, together with the police. One woman said, 'We are almost more afraid of the people we used to call our neighbours than their special police units.' Another woman, Koviljka Mirić, said, 'In 1941 it was almost the same. We all fled the village and from the age of six I spent three years living in the woods with my family. It seems as though it is going to happen again.'

And of course it was not just Serbs who were beginning to flee. The Croats too had their memories of the Chetniks, and so they too were either chased from their homes or ran in terror as Serbian militias backed by the JNA moved to consolidate power in the areas they wanted. This was a planned Serbian attempt to seize control of areas, mostly but not all of which had a predominantly Serbian population frightened by the prospect of Croatian independence. This led directly to war as the Croats mobilised to defend their frontiers. It was the logical conclusion of the unresolved debate about whether nations or republics had the right to self-determination.

A week after Vukadinović's death, Croatian civilians were being invited to enroll in 'Voluntary Units of National Protection', whose slogan was 'Everything for Croatia! All for Croatia!'

After Plitvice the action soon moved to eastern Croatia, where conflict began around Serbian villages along the Serbian–Croatian border. Barricades were thrown up, most notably around the village of Borovo Selo, close to the Danube town of Vukovar. The Serbs of Borovo Selo, who apart from their own hunting rifles had been armed by the SDB, had set up formidable defences. These included barricades of lorries, felled trees, rubble and oil on the road, which armed village guards said they would set alight if the Croatian police attempted to enter the village. The events in the village were also to introduce a new element into the conflict. It was at Borovo Selo that paramilitary forces armed, organised and sent by the Serbian authorities themselves made their first appearance. The most prominent was that of the radical nationalist Vojislav Šešelj.

Dr Mladen Jović, a leader of the Borovo uprising, waved his pistol about as he explained that the barricades would stay up until either 'we are incorporated into Serbia or we die . . . it's Serbia or death'. He also expounded what was becoming, in the minds of the Croatian Serbs, the *raison d'être* of their rebellion: 'It seems as though Croatian leaders are just the same as the fascists who murdered the Serbs here during the war . . . we don't want to be ruled by such men.'

In the middle of April, Gojko Sušak, later to be the Croatian defence minister, led a group of men who fired three missiles at Borovo Selo.[15] Four Croatian policemen tried to get in on the night of 1 May and were shot at. The next day a group of Croatian policemen drove into an ambush. Twelve of them died in the centre of Borovo Selo along with five Serbs. It was a watershed. In the subsequent propaganda war, the Croats claimed that the Serbs had gouged the eyes out of a young Croatian policeman. The Serbs denied it. However, the story of the eyes had its effect. The JNA moved into the village. Peaceful pigs snouted around the tanks, but there was no disguising that something was changing. The links that bound ordinary people together were cracking under pressure. One villager said that his best friend was a Croat: 'A few days ago he called me and said that if a political settlement was not found all Serbs would be killed. I cannot consider him a friend any more. Friendship between Croats and Serbs is now impossible. As a people we must separate.'

It was the type of conversation that was to be repeated a million times over the next year. But, importantly, some friendships were nonetheless maintained in the most difficult of circumstances, even if people had to be discreet about them.

Goodbye Slovenia, Hello Croatia

Fed up with the eternal wrangling and desperate to desert the sinking ship, Slovenia declared independence on 25 June. The celebrations were muted. Within forty-eight hours the JNA moved to reassert control over the country's international border. Some believe that this was a charade, that for some reason it seemed to be necessary to be seen to be 'doing something'. In fact, as Milošević and Kučan had already agreed that Slovenia should leave the old federation, it now looks as if it was some form of blunder: if Milošević did not oppose Slovene secession, why send in the army? The answer appears to be that, although he had acted to take control of as many of the structures of the state as he possibly could, he still did not have complete power. It was Ante Marković, the Yugoslav prime minister, a Croat who still believed that Yugoslavia could survive, who ordered the troops to move. While the borders were successfully retaken hundreds of confused and weeping conscripts found themselves blocked on the roads by the Slovene TO. Forty-four JNA troops died in this ten-day 'war' plus a handful of Slovenes. Marković then tried to distance himself from the army's actions. On 30 June General Kadijević explained to Serbian leaders the options that lay before them. Later he wrote: 'The Army did not want to stay in Slovenia and be insulted. The only solution was to leave . . . the question was how to do that.'[16]

According to Kadijević, the army top brass wanted to defeat the Slovene 'armed formations' before leaving. However, Borisav Jović pointed out that, as the Serbs saw no reason to oppose Slovene secession, it might as well pull out without further ado. This solution was opposed by the Croats because they knew that the retreat of the JNA would really be tantamount to a redeployment in Croatia and Bosnia. Over the next few weeks and months there was much coming and going as European Community foreign ministers attempted to secure a diplomatic solution. What they did not know was that Milošević had everything planned in advance. He made fools of them, using them as messengers. The army was going to leave Slovenia anyway and carry on the job that it had already begun, which was the carving out of a Greater Serbian border.

The meeting of 30 June was simply the last nail in Yugoslavia's coffin. The fact that the army had got involved in fighting in Slovenia was at the time seen by some as proof that nostalgic communist generals were desperate to preserve the old country. In fact it was nothing of the kind. Many people were of course deeply confused and loyalties were divided, but in the end men like Kadijević had already made the decision that as Yugoslavia was dying they had little choice but to seize as much of it as they could for the Serbs. The Slovene fighting, then, was not a charade or a last-ditch gamble, but simply part of the idiotic chaos in which the state died. It was avoidable because Milošević and Kučan had already decided on the secession of Slovenia, but as is the nature with such tacit deals nothing is written down, few people know and so confusion results. In Kadijević's version of events the JNA did 'not attack Slovenia':

> we just wanted to re-establish control of the borders, and we did that. What happened was that all Slovenia attacked us, not just the Slovene Army. Then the Supreme Command did not suggest keeping Slovenia under conditions of terror. They said why should Serbia and Montenegro send troops to keep Slovenia only to leave it later – then it was clear to me that this was the definitive end of Yugoslavia. From that point on we moved to the second concept of creating the new Yugoslavia. When the Croats started to attack the Serbian people in Croatia we co-operated with the TO in those areas and gave the people weapons and so on . . . as for borders there was a clear idea, that is that they should be where there was a majority of Serbian people. If Croatia wanted to go that was okay but they could not take the Serbs with them.[17]

As more and more incidents were deliberately created in Croatia by Serbian militias, the JNA took up position to solidify the new frontier. Meanwhile with Croatian, Slovenian, Muslim and Macedonian officers and men streaming out of the army, many believed it would collapse. Far from it. In fact the JNA encouraged them to go. In this way the Serbs inherited a Serbian Army in all but name.

As Croatia slipped towards war, there were many events and dates that, at the time, seemed tremendously significant. There was for example the quarrel over whether Stipe Mesić, the Croatian delegate on the collective federal presidency, should be allowed to become its president, a post which should have been his thanks to Yugoslavia's system of automatically rotating jobs among the republics. In retrospect it seems incredible that such a lot of media and foreign diplomatic interest should have been generated by what was, by then, an irrelevant question. Given that Milošević had decided to carve out a Serbian territory from Croatia, that Croatia and Slovenia had decided on full independence and that there was no will to find an equitable solution or compromise, war was inevitable. It is easy to say this with hindsight, but at the time there still remained a hope that Yugoslavia was run by responsible people who knew what they were doing and who had the best interests of their people at heart. Unfortunately this was not the case.

In public the presidents of the six republics were still arguing about whether some form of Yugoslavia could be preserved. Milošević wanted a 'modern federation', which was code for Serbian domination. Kučan and Tudjman wanted 'an asymmetric federation', which was code for independence while still enjoying the benefits of Yugoslavia without paying for them. Alija Izetbegović of Bosnia and Kiro Gligorov of Macedonia argued for a compromise, but having little political clout they were ignored. The reality was the RAM plan, the arming of Croatia, the firebombing of Serbian shops and houses in Split and other Croatian towns and the same treatment meted out to Croats remaining in Knin and other areas now under the authority of the Krajina Militia.

You Must Have Bloodshed to Make a Country

On 12 May 1991 Serbs in Krajina were invited to vote on whether they wanted to become part of the Republic of Serbia 'and thus remain in Yugoslavia with Serbia, Montenegro and others that want to preserve Yugoslavia'. It was one of many Serbian referendums that were to punctuate the political landscape over the next few years. It was a farce dressed up as democracy, by which people who had been bombarded by a single media message were herded to the polls to turn in the requisite popular mandate for the authorities. There was never any public debate on the question and it could be assumed that if you were not going to vote as the authorities wanted then you were not a Serb and hence had no right still to be living where you were.

Forming the backdrop to the Krajina poll were the two types of shop in Knin. There were those which were festooned with Yugoslav and Serbian flags and those, owned by Croats, which had recently been smashed and looted. The names of towns on sign-posts under Croatian government control had been spray-painted out. At polling station number four the niceties of democracy, such as private polling booths, had been dispensed with and replaced by a cosy atmosphere of fresh garlic and biscuits served to voters under the Serbian flag. Not so cosy for everyone of course. Jelena, for example, a girl about to finish high school, talked of her discomfort and fear. According to Radio Knin, Croatian doctors and nurses had been 'planning to kill Serbian patients'. Her friend Valentina said that local Croats had not been fleeing town because they were being bombed out but because 'they are organised. Many of them had guns.' Passing a looted watch shop, she said of its owner, 'He had a radio with which to interfere with the broadcasts of Radio Knin.' In such times it seems that people are simply willing to surrender all critical faculties and be led by the mad simply because it is the easy option.

During this period, Krajina's all-important propaganda chief was Lazar Macura. He was deputy mayor of Knin, an English teacher and director of Knin's radio station. He was in ebullient mood and clearly believed everything he said. With Milošević, the SDB and the JNA underpinning Krajina's rebellion, however, this was not so naive at the time. It only seems so in retrospect, as it becomes clear that Macura and the 600,000 Serbs who made up 12 per cent of Croatia's population were, to use Lenin's phrase, 'useful idiots' who could be discarded when they were no longer useful to Milošević. On the day of the referendum Macura opened up a map to show off the vast areas of Croatia he claimed for the Serbs, saying, 'I don't expect war because the Croats would have no chance of winning. . . . You must have bloodshed to make a country.' In these last words he encapsulated the arrogance of the entire Serbian leadership, who assumed that after a knock-out blow neither the Croats nor Bosnia's Muslims would fight. How they could have miscalculated so badly about the people with whom they had lived for so long remains a mystery.

A week later, under leaden skies, the rest of Croatia went to the polls to vote for a 'sovereign and independent' state. It was a surprisingly sombre affair, contrasting with the festive mood in Knin. Like Krajina's poll a vast majority voted as requested by the authorities. There was something unsettling about the affair; it was not just that war was coming, it was a deeper sense of unease. Irena Tomić, a Croatian student, said, 'The people from Krajina are making Croats hate their ordinary Serbian neighbours and friends. This morning, very early, I was woken up by shouting in the street. People were going past my window shouting "NDH! NDH!" It made my flesh creep.'

We've Been Here Before!

Until 2 January 1992, when a ceasefire was signed in Sarajevo, the war raged in Croatia. It was a dirty war in the republic which almost incidentally had declared independence a few hours before Slovenia. Using their overwhelming firepower, the Serbs managed to carve out between a quarter and one-third of Croatia's landmass and hold it until, abandoned by Serbia, it was reconquered by Croats in 1995.

Incidents such as the ones at Plitvice and Borovo Selo multiplied, and soon the army gave up any pretence of being a neutral force. The JNA was deployed massively in the east, where it bombarded and eventually

flattened the town of Vukovar. It also blundered into a siege of
Dubrovnik, the magnificent medieval and renaissance port known to
millions of westerners who had holidayed there over the years. It was to
be the worst public relations disaster for the Serbs during the entire war
with Croatia.

Following a plan devised by General Špegelj, the still lightly armed
Croatian forces besieged JNA barracks in Zagreb and other towns well
away from areas that the Serbs intended to capture for themselves.
Maddened by this impudence the JNA responded massively in
vulnerable areas such as the tapering southern tip of Croatia. Here
troops were wheeled in from Montenegro to capture the strategic
Prevlaka Peninsula commanding the mouth of the magnificent Kotor
Bay in Montenegro, which was to become the new home of the
Yugoslav Navy. It was the first week of October 1991. The troops were
mature reservists, not young conscripts, who had been drafted into the
Sava Kovačević Fifth Proletarian Brigade. They came from the hard
industrial town of Nikšić and the war they fought came to typify the
arrogance of their commanders and the way in which the Serbian
leadership believed that by fighting a war just as you had always done
you would win. Although General Kadijević later claimed that regional
military commanders had disobeyed his orders and crossed a line on the
map that he had expressly told them not to, it only goes to show that the
Serbian leadership were so incompetent that they could not have done
a better job for Croatia's image if they had been paid to do so.

The Montenegrins went to war in the firm belief that this was
something that you did once a generation and that as soon as the
fighting was done you went on a looting spree and then returned home.
Under the benign gaze of their officers, this was exactly what they
proceeded to do. They were happy to remind visitors that they had been
this way before. 'You don't understand,' they clamoured, 'our fathers
fought the Italians, the Germans and the Croats. Our grandfathers
fought the Turks and the Albanians.' And in 1806, in exactly the same
place, some of their ancestors had fought the French too. In alliance
with the Russians they had besieged the then French-occupied
Dubrovnik, failed to take it, plundered its surroundings and stomped off
home. 'All the houses round town were razed to the ground,' wrote
Luigi Villari in a history of Dubrovnik published in 1914, 'the villas of
the rich nobles were plundered, the more valuable contents being seized
by the Russian officers, and the rest left to the Montenegrins . . .
Bosnians and even Turks, who had swarmed down in the hope of loot.
The inhabitants who did not get away in time were murdered and even
tortured.'[18]

Jabbing the air, the new generation shouted that it was thanks to
Britain that the Montenegrin Army had been forced to abandon

Shkodër, the northern Albanian port, in 1913. Having sacrificed thousands of men during their seven-month siege of the town, the statesmen of Europe ordered the 'Serbian Sparta' to withdraw. It refused and so an international naval blockade was ordered. Reluctantly the Montenegrins turned Shkodër over to the British Royal Navy in mid-May 1913. What the angry Montenegrins of 1991 forgot to mention was another factor which had helped prise their army out of Shkodër – a six-million-franc loan-cum-bribe to King Nikola.

Seven months after the beginning of the 1991 siege of Dubrovnik, the UN imposed sanctions on Serbia and Montenegro. The combination of this and the policing of the UN arms embargo on former Yugoslavia meant that history, at least in part, began to repeat itself. A latter-day naval blockade, again involving the Royal Navy, was duly installed.

While goats and cattle may have been the prize pillage after the 1806 siege, this was no longer the case in 1991. On the day of a ceasefire, troops drew back their tanks and some men settled down to roast lamb on the spit in the traditional fashion. Meanwhile, down the road from Dubrovnik airport, their friends gingerly trundled baggage trolleys marked 'Donated by Thomson Holidays'. With their AK-47s balancing on the top basket, their loot consisted of duty-free cigarettes, whisky, brandy, chocolate, soft drinks, perfume, toys and, in one case, a Barbie doll. Despite this, a valiant effort was still made to try and convince sceptical visitors that what they were really doing was fighting the just reunited German 'Fourth Reich' and the Croatian fascist phoenix. 'And what do you think of this then?' demanded a soldier presenting a crinkled brown NDH-era banknote he had found, presumably while looting. 'What can we conclude about a man who kept this hidden for fifty years?'

In another scene from the beginning of the siege, a group of soldiers clustered around a rocket unit whooping with joy as houses exploded into dust. A soldier wiggled a joy-stick, pressed a button and the lethal 'wire-guided' rocket shot off, dancing down over the rocky hillside contours like a demented firework. They were aiming at houses on a bay just south of the ancient city. As each home exploded they would all point at different buildings yelling, 'Hit that one!' or 'Take that one out!' as if this was the greatest video game ever invented.

On the same day the mood turned sombre and angry after a soldier was killed. Five Croats were captured and dragged up the hill, bloodied and frightened. One was barefoot, one grey haired and all in civilian clothes. Jostling them, the soldiers demanded their immediate execution. Simultaneously, and as if in a different world, three trembling pensioners were escorted away from danger. With one hand and the utmost care a soldier helped guide an old lady wearing a little straw hat. In his other hand he carried a modest prize. It was a picture of Franjo Tudjman.

Afterwards it was burned by a girl soldier. The fate of the five Croats was not revealed to outsiders, but the omens did not look good.

After the bay was taken, the soldiers closed in on Dubrovnik itself. It was hard to know how to explain the sheer lack of Croatian defenders: was it because the republic was so poorly prepared for war or because the authorities were luring the JNA into the trap that it proved to be. Young Croatian guardsmen set up mortar positions just outside the walls of the old city and hard Hercegovinian warriors fought rocket duels with the Montenegrins over the ancient walls. The world, watching on television, was transfixed. Here it seemed as though the JNA had stooped to the lowest depths, that it was about to destroy the 'pearl of the Adriatic', one of the greatest architectural and historical jewels of the Mediterranean. Several shells fell on the old city, but the damage here, as opposed to the modern outskirts of town, was never as bad as the Croats made it out to be. Spectacular film was made one sunset of columns of smoke appearing to rise from within the walls. 'They are destroying it stone by stone!' shrieked the Croats. 'The Croats are lighting tyres!' cried the JNA. Neither was true. The JNA had hit a car park by the walls which burned with an abundance of black smoke.

Strangely the Serbian leadership never seemed to realise that they had fallen into a trap and that with every shot they were turning the Serbs into international pariahs. It was too late anyway. They could not pull back while there was fighting because this would be celebrated by the Croats as a morale-boosting military victory. Next came Vukovar and then Sarajevo. The JNA and then the Krajina and Bosnian Serb armies believed that they were fighting a traditional Balkan war. They consistently failed to understand that since 1941 an extra dimension had been added to war – international opinion as guided by television and the media.

Rusty Shoehorns

It was not only the Serbs who made mistakes. One of the greatest mistakes the Croats ever made was to let Željko Ražnatović, also known as Arkan, slip through their fingers. The leader of one of the most feared, brutal and efficient paramilitaries to emerge during the war, Arkan was arrested by the Croatian police in November 1990. He had been in Croatia, allegedly discussing the logistics of Serbia's clandestine arming of the Krajina rebellion. Caught by the police with a car full of arms and ammunition he was tried, convicted and released pending an appeal. He told the Croatian court that he had been in the area out of 'pure curiosity'. Having fled back to the safety of Belgrade, Arkan taunted the Croats, 'You will never catch me alive!'

Goran Vuković, an infamous gangster later to be gunned down on a Belgrade street corner, reminisced about the good old days when he and Arkan and a number of others had spent their youth touring western Europe:

Of all of us Arkan robbed the most banks: He walked into them almost like they were self-service stores. No one can quarrel with that fact about him. I don't know about politics, but as far as robbery is concerned, he was really unsurpassed. That is all he has done his entire life. Banks were his speciality, as well as escapes from prison. He managed to escape from the same prison two or three times. He even escaped from the Germans.[19]

In 1994 a UN report identified eighty-three paramilitary groups fighting in Bosnia and Croatia, of which fifty-six were Serb, thirteen Croat and fourteen Bosnian Muslim.[20] On the Serbian side, most were small and, although murderous, not particularly significant. Two, however, deserve special mention. They are Arkan's Tigers and the Chetniks of extreme nationalist politician Vojislav Šešelj. These groups played major roles as shock troops of 'ethnic cleansing' both in the autumn and winter of 1991 in eastern Slavonia and at the beginning of the war in Bosnia. The reason they became a necessity was twofold. First, Arkan's men especially were used as a form of brutal commando force whose incentive to venture where others feared to tread was the promise of loot. Šešelj's men were also fighting for pillage but, less specialised than Arkan's troops, they were used to make up dwindling numbers in the JNA. This was because, as the war in Croatia ground on, the number of desertions and failures to report for duty rose dramatically. Tens of thousands of young men, especially from Belgrade, began to escape abroad rather than go to the front. As the military police hunted for those that remained, they slept in different places every night until such time as the authorities began to lose interest in them. In eastern Serbia, reserve units began to mutiny in protest against going to Vukovar, and General Kadijević complained that many of those units which reached the front soon 'abandoned it'. In the most famous desertion, a man drove his armoured personnel carrier away from the front and down the motorway, and refused to come to a stop until he reached the federal parliament building in the centre of Belgrade. Serbian nationalism had lost its appeal in the mud and gore of eastern Slavonia.

That Arkan had been arrested by the Croats in November 1990 proves that Milošević's various secret services not only foresaw a role for the former bank-robber but knew him well. His record was, as Vuković noted, absolutely spectacular. He had robbed banks in Sweden and been convicted of armed robbery in Belgium, Holland and Germany, but had always managed to escape from prison. The Italian police still want him for an alleged murder in 1974. Clearly Arkan was no ordinary thief. Born in 1950, he was the son of an air force officer. A teenage delinquent, he devoted himself early to a life of crime. It is believed that his father, despairing of his son, asked contacts inside the Yugoslav Federal Secretariat for Internal Affairs (SSUP) if they could sort the boy out. Apparently they could. The SSUP ran an espionage network for which Ražnatović, when not robbing banks, is widely reputed to have worked as a hitman carrying out political assassinations abroad. It was during this time that Arkan picked up his nickname which was derived from one of his early forged foreign passports. He also came to the attention of Stane Dolanc, the head of the SSUP. With a powerful patron like this, Arkan's multiple prison escapes begin to look less remarkable.

Arkan returned to Belgrade in the 1980s, where he kept up his criminal activities and his work for the SSUP. While officially a simple pastry-shop owner, he suddenly emerged at the end of 1990 as the head of Delije, the official fan club of Belgrade's Red Star football team. Until Arkan was put in charge, the fans had become increasingly prone to uncontrolled outbursts of nationalist chanting. Milošević's men needed to control this. They did not want any surplus energy being harnessed by Vuk Drašković's nationalist and opposition Serbian Renewal Party. Simultaneously, but rather more discreetly, Arkan founded the Serbian Volunteer Guard, known as the Tigers. The core of this new militia was none other than a select group of young men from Delije. 'We fans . . . trained without weapons,' said Arkan, which may or may not be true. 'I insisted on discipline from the beginning. You know our fans, they are noisy, they like to drink, to joke about. I stopped all that in one go, I made them cut their hair, shave regularly, not drink – and so it began the way it should be.'[21]

Arkan's contacts were Radmilo Bogdanović, Frenki and Badža. The Tigers set up a training camp in Erdut in Serb-held eastern Slavonia from which they fought and co-ordinated their pillage. (All the best Belgrade restaurants suddenly began serving Erdut wine.) Later, Arkan was to enter politics and he served a term as a Kosovo deputy, elected on a hardline Serbian nationalist ticket. Many voters believed that he would carry out his threats and be as efficient at driving out Albanians from the province as he had been at expelling Croats from eastern Slavonia. No such luck. They were disappointed to find that Arkan's main interest in Kosovo was grabbing a slice of the black market which the local Albanian mafias were forced to share with him. After the Croatian ceasefire, Arkan's thousand-odd troops seemed at a loose end, but with the outbreak of fighting in Bosnia they were to play a vitally important role on the Serbian side in the first few weeks of the war.

Vojislav Šešelj's background could not have been more different. Born in 1950, he had been a brilliant Bosnian Serb student, the youngest PhD in Yugoslavia (his thesis was on Marxism and guerrilla warfare), and in the early 1980s he was a teacher at Sarajevo University. In 1984 he was arrested and, convicted of counter-revolutionary activities on the basis of an unpublished manuscript found in his desk drawer, sentenced to eight years in prison. According to Šešelj the manuscript advocated not just a multi-party system for Yugoslavia but the country's complete reorganisation. Instead of six republics he proposed a large and dominating Serbian republic plus Croatia, Slovenia and Macedonia. Thus Bosnia, dominated he believed by closet Islamic fundamentalists and the home of the 'bogus' Bosnian Muslim nation, was to be abolished. So was Montenegro, home of another 'invented' nation. He served twenty-two months in Zenica jail, where he was reputed to have been tortured. In Belgrade he became a *cause célèbre* among the small group of human rights activists clustered around Dobrica Ćosić. After his release many began to believe that his treatment in jail had left him less than sane. He became extremely close to Vuk Drašković and in 1990, in the run-up to the first multi-party elections in December, they formed a political party together. They fell out, however, and Šešelj then organised the Serbian Chetnik Movement. He came fourth in the presidential poll.

Although at first on the fringes of politics, Šešelj, with his brand of extreme nationalism, began to attract more and more support. Milošević's men noticed him and concluded that he could be used to mop up the hardline nationalist vote. Thus they 'parachuted' him into parliament at a by-election in Rakovica, an industrial suburb of Belgrade, in June 1991. The Chetnik Movement, now renamed the Serbian Radical Party, was given a huge amount of prime-time television coverage and in this way Milošević boosted Šešelj from relative obscurity. In return Šešelj supported Milošević. But it was not just political support that was required. The men from the Military Line also had plans for Šešelj and his wild men of the extreme right.

After the fatal shootings in Borovo Selo at the beginning of May 1991, Šešelj boasted that his men had been present. Not only that but he helped fan the fires of hatred by joining the gruesome debate about the gouged-out eyes. He claimed that the eyes of the Croatian policeman, which he said were hanging from the sockets by their stalks, had been forced out by the pressure exerted by a bullet from a Thompson sub-machine gun penetrating the brain. Asked on a popular Serbian television show if his Chetniks, like their Second World War namesakes, still killed with the knife he replied no, they had graduated to rusty shoehorns which they intended to use on Croatian eyeballs. 'It was black humour,' he protested afterwards.

Later Radmilo Bogdanović was to boast of the connection between the Serbian secret services and the seminal events in Borovo. 'If we had not equipped our Serbs, who knows how they would have fared in the attack by the Croatian National Guard?'[22]

Unlike Arkan's disciplined, clean-shaven 'kill 'n' loot' shock troops, Šešelj's men were often drunk and shabby. Nevertheless, Šešelj was frequently seen on television and this, combined with Milošević's patronage, meant that his party began to grow powerful. The result was that he started to believe that he could command power in his own right and that he was even strong enough to challenge Milošević. He was wrong. In September 1993 Milošević's SPS turned on him. With the Serbs vilified the world over as war criminals, it was decided that Šešelj would make the perfect scapegoat. A party statement called him 'the personification of violence and primitivity' and accused him of 'war crimes, abetting war profiteers and criminals'. It also said that he was involved in 'crimes committed by paramilitary groups against Muslim, Croat and Serb civilians'. Šešelj then became a non-person, hardly ever seen again on state television or quoted in the pro-government press. Consequently his support began to wither.

There is little doubt that all the charges levelled against Šešelj are true. He was frequently arrested and charged with minor infractions such as causing an affray and spitting at the speaker of parliament. However, it is clear why Šešelj was never formally charged with the crimes he was accused of by the SPS. The reason was simple and Šešelj is willing to tell anyone prepared to listen:

Milošević organised everything. We gathered the volunteers and he gave us a special barracks, Bubanj Potok, all our uniforms, arms, military technology and buses. All our units were always under the command of the Krajina or [Bosnian Serb] Republika Srpska Army or the JNA. Of course I don't believe he signed anything, these were verbal orders. None of our talks was taped and I never took a paper and pencil when I talked with him. His key people were the commanders. Nothing could happen on the Serbian side without Milošević's order or his knowledge.

While Arkan's men came under the command of the Ministry of the Interior, Šešelj's lot, by his own admission, were under the wing of the JNA, along with a cluster of smaller paramilitaries. By the end of 1993 veterans of the Croatian campaign were complaining that the authorities were trying to duck their responsibilities when it came to invalid pensions, orphans, widows and so on. Colonel Milan Milivojević, president of the War Veterans Association, told the magazine *Vreme* that his organisation was:

a non-party association which rallies all soldiers equally – JNA . . . the Territorial Defence, as well as all sorts of volunteers. All volunteers were armed and sent to the front by the JNA and the State Security of the Serbian Interior Ministry; they all served in formations under the direct command of the JNA, the Republic of Serbian Krajina and the Serb Republic in Bosnia, or received orders from officers of these armies in the field. We now meet resistance in spite of these facts. The state of Serbia is now trying to prove that the Serbs have never been at war because of the phrase of one man, Slobodan Milošević, which reads *Serbia is not at war*. All other officials, who are nothing but executioners of his policies, seem to fear talking to us. . . . We've sent three letters to Slobodan Milošević, but he didn't find it necessary to see us.[23]

Half-Time

After Vukovar fell in November 1991, both the Croats and Milošević were willing to listen to the entreaties of foreign statesmen to stop fighting. Tudjman feared that if he did not stop the war he would lose more territory. It was better to call a halt until such time as his army was ready to retake the lost territories. As for Milošević, the JNA was plagued with increasing mutinies and desertions, but the Serbs had managed to secure almost everything they wanted in Croatia. It was better to stop while ahead of the game. The United Nations had appointed Cyrus Vance, a former US secretary of state, to try and secure a peace deal. His plan, the so-called Vance plan, envisaged the withdrawal of the JNA from Croatia, but accepted that it could stay on the borders in case of trouble. The plan anticipated the return of all refugees and the reconstruction of the police forces in what were to become the four UN Protected Areas (UNPAs) in the same proportions as the ethnic make-up of the localities before the war. The Krajina Serbs were to disarm and to put their weapons in store under a 'dual lock' system to be supervised jointly with the UN. Despite these provisions, the Vance plan declared that it did not prejudge the final outcome of any political settlement.[24]

In Krajina, Milan Babić ferociously opposed Vance's plan. He feared that without the JNA to safeguard Krajina's future it would sooner or later be attacked and overwhelmed. He was to be proved right, but Milošević wanted to end the war and Babić was forced to give way. No Croatian refugees were allowed to return to Krajina, and there was no question of the Serbs conceding any police powers. Indeed the number of policemen soared as soldiers changed from green camouflage uniforms to blue police ones. In many cases they were responsible for terrorising the remaining Croats, and the UN found that instead of supervising the return of refugees they were helping new ones to flee. Politically the Serbian aim was to freeze the frontlines and create a situation like that in Cyprus. If the creation of a *de jure* Greater Serbia was not yet possible, a *de facto* one would have to do for the moment. Signing the Vance plan was the right thing to do, wrote General Kadijević later, because 'given the international circumstances' it made possible the realisation of the Serbian leadership's goals, albeit 'in a longer term'.[25] In a mood for self-congratulation he wrote that:

> all Serbian areas in Croatia, except one part of western Slavonia, were liberated in close cooperation with Serbian rebels. That makes approximately one third of the territory of the former Croatia. The future army of the RSK was practically built through combat and the JNA equipped that army with arms and military equipment. . . . With the results of the war in Croatia the JNA completely and under conditions unrecorded by history fulfilled . . . [its] task – to militarily defend the right of the Serbian and Montenegrin people for a united state.[26]

10

WE ARE THE STRONGEST

Frustrated, angry and politically impotent, Ante Marković, the last prime minister of the old Yugoslavia, told his cabinet in September 1991 what he had gleaned from a wiretap that had come into his possession:

> The line has been clearly established [between the Serbian government, the army and Serb politicians in Bosnia]. I know because I heard Milošević give the order to Karadžić to get in contact with General Uzelac and to order, following the decisions of the meeting of the military hierarchy, that arms should be distributed and that the TO of Krajina and Bosnia be armed and utilised in the realisation of the RAM plan.[1]

General Nikola Uzelac was the JNA commander in Banja Luka, which was to become the main Serb-held town in northern Bosnia. The transcript of the tape that was leaked to the press runs as follows:

> Milošević: Go to Uzelac, he'll tell you everything. If you have any problems, telephone me.
> Karadžić: I've got problems down in Kupres. Some Serbs there are rather disobedient.
> Milošević: We can deal with that. Just call Uzelac. Don't worry, you'll have everything. We are the strongest.
> Karadžić: Yes, yes.
> Milošević: Don't worry. As long as there is the army no one can touch us. . . . Don't worry about Hercegovina. Momir [Bulatović, president of Montenegro] said to his men: 'Whoever is not ready to die in Bosnia, step forward five paces.' No one did so.
> Karadžić: That's good . . . But what's going on with the bombing in –
> Milošević: Today is not a good day for the air force. The European Community is in session.[2]

By the autumn of 1991 the SDS in Bosnia had begun to declare large parts of the republic that they coveted as SAOs or Serbian Autonomous Regions. These were the first organisational moves towards declaring a Serbian state in Bosnia. The SDS leadership, which at first had talked of co-operating with Bosnia's Muslims, was making preparations for war. The war in Croatia had destabilised Bosnia, and the SDS leadership had rapidly fallen under the spell of Milošević. Frenki and Badža had been active in Bosnia, but the SDB network was much weaker there than in Croatia. It had assumed that the republic would probably fall into Serbian hands anyway and so it left much of the organisation of its SDS to the locals. This was to prove a grave mistake. It meant that later, when conflicts arose with Belgrade, Milošević had far less control over its affairs than he wanted.

During 1991, apart from the distribution of arms to the Bosnian SDS, the priority was assuring a smooth flow of weapons and supplies to the Serbs in Krajina. This could only be done through Bosnia, because other supply routes led through Croatia. In securing co-operation for this the lead role was taken not by the SDB but rather by KOS, Yugoslav military counter-intelligence.

Which Side Will You Be On?

After the Bosnian elections of November 1990, in which the republic's 4.3 million people voted more or less on ethnic grounds, a coalition government of the three ethnically based parties had been set up. Fikret Abdić, a popular entrepreneur from Velika Kladuša, received the most votes in the presidential poll but ceded his place as president of the Bosnian presidency to Alija Izetbegović. The reasons for this were never quite clear, but as part of the deal Abdić's nominee, Alija Delimustafić, became minister of the interior. This was one of the most important jobs in the government because of the control it gave over the police.

Abdić was a complex character who, despite having been a candidate for the Muslim Party of Democratic Action (SDA), was rather more interested in business than in politics. He had made his name as a commercial genius and communist tycoon, building from nothing an agricultural and food-processing firm which became well known throughout Yugoslavia in the 1980s. The effect of Agrokomerc on the economy of Velika Kladuša and the wider north western Bihać region where it was based was striking and it brought comparative wealth to a traditionally poor peasant area. To the locals Abdić became known as Babo (Daddy). But disaster struck in 1987 when it was revealed that Agrokomerc had actually financed a large part of its expansion by issuing worthless promissory notes which were juggled from company to company and bank to bank until the system collapsed. Abdić went to jail but was later released, only to become a leading light in the SDA.

As the situation in Bosnia began to deteriorate, Abdić played a key role in trying to prevent war and was decidedly lukewarm about independence. When the war broke out, he left Sarajevo and in mid-1993 returned to his fief in Velika Kladuša. He later declared the autonomy of this isolated region, which had become known as the Bihać Pocket, and which was completely surrounded by Serbian forces. Alija Delimustafić fled abroad. Their involvement with KOS had been considerable. To what extent Delimustafić had been an agent, double agent or an honourable man trying to save Bosnia from war is unknown and remains one of the great secrets of the beginning of the war.

Unlike the SDB in Serbia, KOS was a federal or Yugoslav organisation. Hence it was less partial to Serbian nationalism and, at least at the beginning of the period of disintegration, more concerned with keeping the old country together than with creating a new Greater Serbia. It was a professional outfit and one of its greatest coups was obtaining the film of General Špegelj, the Croatian minister of defence, apparently discussing the murder of Serbian army officers. The leadership of KOS wanted to use this in order to arrest Špegelj and clamp down on illegal arming in order to save Yugoslavia. But Milošević refused because he wanted to use the film for his own purposes at a time which suited him. During the 1990–1 period KOS was increasingly penetrated by agents of the Military Line, and, sensing the way things were going, it became increasingly willing to pursue its policies. But its head, General Aleksandar Vasiljević, was uncertain. Milošević invited him to a private dinner, but Vasiljević refused on the ground that it would be improper for the head of a federal organisation to meet with the president of one of the republics without the permission of his federal superiors. Milošević was later to get his revenge. Vasiljević was arrested and spent a few months in jail owing to a KOS-related scandal.

Before this, and despite his pro-Yugoslav sympathies, Vasiljević was still prepared to do business with Milošević. After all, the Serbian president still said that he wanted either a 'modern federation' or a small Yugoslavia including Bosnia and Macedonia. To that extent, and given the shrinking chances of saving the whole of old Yugoslavia, Vasiljević was prepared to co-operate. Abdić and Delimustafić were recruited. Abdić's role was to secure food supplies for Krajina and the JNA during the war in Croatia. Because of its location, surrounded on two sides by what was to become Krajina Serb territory, Agrokomerc was ideally situated for the job. The deal was also to provide work and cash for Abdić's company and its workers, who practically worshipped their boss. Delimustafić's role was even more contentious. Bosnia's

Muslims were utterly unprepared for war, so he tried to sup with the devil in order to avoid conflict. He came to an agreement with Vasiljević by which the Bosnian police would not hamper the shipments of arms either to Krajina or to the Bosnian Serbs. In return Vasiljević provided Delimustafić with flak jackets and pistols and may even have had a direct hand in conceiving the Patriotic League – the forerunner of the Muslim-led Bosnian Army which was founded secretly in March 1991. At the beginning of the conflict, the Patriotic League claimed specifically to be fighting for a Bosnia for all three nations, something which appealed to the pro-Yugoslav Vasiljević, especially if Bosnia could be persuaded to avoid war by accepting a 'historic agreement' and coming to a political arrangement with Serbia.

Vasiljević and Delimustafić were playing with fire, and ultimately they were burned. It was common currency at the time that there would not be a war in Bosnia because a 'balance of terror' existed. In fact war began because the scales tipped. The Bosnian Serb leadership, armed ultimately by the JNA, came into the possession of so much weaponry that it was convinced it would win a crushing victory within weeks. It also believed that the Croats would seize a share of the country and the Muslims would have to accept defeat.

To begin with, the Vasiljević–Delimustafić agreement ran smoothly. Occasionally things went wrong, though, and Bosnian policemen, who had not received orders to the contrary, halted trucks laden with arms. Where possible these incidents were hushed up, but embarrassingly for all concerned news sometimes leaked out. On the night of 9 April 1991, three lorries containing 1,119 Yugoslav-made Zastava rifles were discovered. According to Vukašin Filipović of Zastava, the weapons were destined for a JNA barracks, but the barracks professed complete ignorance of the shipment. Six weeks later, eighty assault rifles and 17,000 bullets in packaging which indicated that they came from Serbian or Montenegrin police stores were stopped in Bileća in eastern Hercegovina. The police tried to take the arrested men to Mostar, but were prevented by a group of local Serbs. An incident began to develop, defused by the arrival of Nikola Koljević, by now one of the two Serbian members of the Bosnian presidency (Biljana Plavšić was the other). 'Neighbours, Muslims, a neighbour can be dearer than a brother,' he said. Turning to the Serbs, he told them that the 'reflection of your honour and honesty will be the places where Muslims and Croats are in a minority'. The situation was defused. After the war began, almost all of Bileća's 2,000 Muslims, 14 per cent of its pre-war population, were cleansed.[3]

Despite these preparations, the SDS was not yet widely distributing arms but rather was storing them until the right time came. Once the war began in Croatia some guns began to be handed out, but the general arming of the Serbs was a slow process that took place over several months. At first only known and trusted men received weapons, and many had to pay for them too. Gradually more and more Serbs were armed, and finally, when war broke out, the remaining Serbs in what was becoming Serb-held territory were mobilised by their local TO unit. Before the outbreak of war a small number of men accepted guns from the SDS out of conviction and probably quite a few because it made them feel macho and powerful. A larger number took a weapon out of fear, not just of the Muslims and Croats but also of fellow Serbs who might cast aspersions on their loyalty to Serbdom. Increasingly the terms 'good Serbs' and 'Alija's Serbs' came to be heard. Mišo, who worked at TV Sarajevo, lived in Hadžići, a mostly Muslim-inhabited suburb of the city:

> I don't like to remember it. I'm a pacifist basically. I knew there was going to be a war but I didn't want to admit it to myself. Coming home from a café I was stopped by SDS people I knew from before. They said, 'We've all got to take up arms or we'll all disappear from here, it's 80 per cent Muslim.' I was the last to get a gun. I got it at the end of February 1992. Everyone knew. The 6 January was the Orthodox Christmas. There was a lot of shooting – testing – a signal to show how strong we were. On all religious days people were shooting. It was an important thing. We were much more afraid than they were.[4]

Mild-mannered Mišo was far from being a fanatic and had always lived happily with his Muslim and Croat friends. So if he was going to take a gun why had he not taken one from the Patriotic League, which claimed that it rejected ethnic separatism? 'No one asked me to defend a multi-ethnic Bosnia,' he said.

Boris, from Ilijaš, a town north of Sarajevo held by the Serbs during the war, was not a member of the SDS but willingly took a gun when it was offered to him. At work a Muslim colleague had been showing off his new pistol. When he went to visit an old girlfriend in an area that was to become Muslim-controlled some Muslims had jeered at him. 'You won't be able to come here much longer,' they said. Boris asked why. 'You know what is going to happen,' they said. It was in this atmosphere that Boris took a gun:

> In a café some people I knew who were involved with the SDS asked, 'What are you going to do? Do you realise how the situation is developing? Which side will you be on? It might come to war.' I said I didn't believe in war but that if there was a war what could I do? My father is from Serbia. We all said publicly that we wanted a mixed Bosnia and that we would defend it, but privately . . .

I said I would take a gun. I got an AK and 200 bullets. They came in the middle of the night. Later, when the conflict began, I volunteered but there was a larger group of people who had to be mobilised. They were waiting to see what was going to happen.

Slobodna Bosna, a new tabloid in Sarajevo, ran a story on 21 November 1991. 'Sarajevo in the Chetniks' Sights – Secret Plan to Attack Sarajevo,' it announced. The article claimed that the SDS was readying paramilitaries to surround the Bosnian capital and that these men were getting their guns from the JNA, which was also training them. Many of the details proved to be wrong, but in the main the story was extraordinarily accurate. It may well have been leaked from within the JNA itself in a bid to intimidate Bosnia's Muslim leadership.[5]

On the Highway to Hell

Although the Serbian leadership made preparations for the war in Bosnia, the fact that it broke out represents one of their greatest failures. After Milošević had been forced to drop his original idea of dominating all of the old Yugoslavia and had gone for the 'amputation' option, the idea had been to withdraw the JNA to the country's new frontiers. This had to be modified because of the Vance plan, and it was agreed that the JNA should pull out of what had become Krajina. Since Krajina's politicians and police-cum-army were beholden to Belgrade for everything anyway, Milošević considered the plan acceptable. Besides the JNA troops that had withdrawn from Slovenia and Croatia were concentrating heavy weaponry in Bosnia, and if there was trouble in Krajina they could return. The next part of the strategy revolved around Bosnia itself.

Because of the later bile and hatred poured out by Serbian politicians and the media against Bosnia's Muslims it has been forgotten that Serbia spent much of 1990 and 1991 attempting to woo the Muslims, even if contingency plans were at the same time being made for war. Milorad Ekmečić, the Bosnian Serb historian and *éminence grise* of the SDS until the war broke out, recalled the founding conference of the party in July 1990. The guest speakers were Jovan Rašković of the SDS from Knin and Alija Izetbegović, the leader of the SDA, which had been founded two months before. Also present was Muhamed Filipović, the father of Bosnian Muslim nationalism, the man who in 1967 had written of the Bosnian Spirit. The SDS gave Izetbegović a standing ovation. Ekmečić said:

Izetbegović was invited to extend a greeting and he said, 'We are glad to see our Serbian and Orthodox brothers creating a party, but I must chide you for being a bit late in doing so.' He also said that we had to co-operate. At the time he was for preserving the Yugoslav federation and his party's slogan was 'A Healthy Federation'. We believed that this was better than the Communist Party and we wanted to co-operate.

Although a Yugoslavia shorn of Croatia and Slovenia would inevitably be Serb-dominated, Serbian leaders thought that Bosnian Muslim leaders would opt to stay in this new Yugoslavia because, together with the Kosovo Albanians and Sandžak Muslims, they would make up some four million Muslims in the new state. To that end Mihailo Marković, the former dissident turned ideologue of the SPS, told the Belgrade daily *Politika* that, while the Bosnian Muslims 'should not dream' of trying to establish a Muslim state together with the Kosovo Albanians and Sandžak Muslims, 'the Serbs should not be deluded by the prejudice that the Muslims are Serbs of Muslim faith and that in any sense whatsoever Yugoslavia will become an alliance of Serbian states'.[6] This was a disingenuous argument because Kosovo Albanians had nothing in common with Yugoslavia's other Muslims. Ethnic Albanian leaders were not interested in political co-operation with them and if any new state was to be formed they wanted it to be an independent Kosovo or preferably a Greater Albania. In this sense, then, the Muslims would have been a minority in the Greater Serbian state.

Dobrica Ćosić also talked to *Politika* about the possibilities of a Yugoslavia without Croats and Slovenes, but he also made clear what he expected to happen if the Muslims rejected the proposal:

> Historical experience has imposed on the Serbian nation the necessity of definitively rejecting the idea of liberating and saving others, who consider such a role as oppression, enslavement and exploitation. I assume that the Serbian people are ready to live in a common democratic state with Muslims and Macedonians, if that is their free will too. A democratic federation of Serbia, Montenegro, Bosnia-Hercegovina and Macedonia would be rational and in line with the processes of European and world integration.
>
> If this does not happen, the Serbian people will create their own state in their ethnic areas . . . thus bringing to an end their struggle of liberation and unification, which has been going on for the past two centuries. In order to achieve that goal Serbs should not commit any injustice to neighbouring nations, just as Serbs would not like it if others did that to them.[7]

This was the contradiction, of course. It takes no more than a glance at the pre-war ethnic map of Bosnia to see that separation without injustice was impossible. Such language was regarded by many Muslims as a threat, which it was. It told them, 'Do as we say – or you're dead.'

Milošević was pursuing a dual-track strategy. While on the one hand trying whether by blandishments or threats to persuade the Muslims to stay in a new Yugoslavia, or Serboslavia as its detractors called it, he was also talking to Tudjman about partitioning the republic. In an interview in July 1991, President Tudjman said that he had agreed with Milošević that 'the major issue regarding a peaceful solution is demarcating the borders between Croatia and Serbia and solving the Muslim problem there'. Asked whether this somewhat awkward formulation of words meant the setting up of a Muslim state, that is a buffer state between a Greater Croatia and a Greater Serbia, he said, 'In some way, yes.' After all, he explained: 'If Serbian policy raises the question of creating a Greater Serbia we can raise the question of Croats living outside Croatia.'

Although Izetbegović had shown some initial interest in reaching an agreement with Belgrade, this became ever harder to realise because, with Tudjman making public statements like this, any agreement would begin to seem like a surrender without a fight. It also looked as though the price of peace, even on Belgrade's terms, would be partition anyway since only the most ideologically fanatical Serbs would want to keep politically hardline and ethnically almost purely Croat-populated western Hercegovina within the new federation. With the Serbs already beginning to arm, he dithered but finally opted for seeking 'sovereignty' – whatever the cost. Izetbegović also had an abiding faith in the JNA, which he could not bring himself to believe would actually attack Bosnia.

During the summer of 1991 Milošević did succeed in making a deal with a minor Muslim party called the Muslim Bošnjak Organisation. It was led by Adil Zulfikarpašić, a wealthy Bosnian émigré who lived in Switzerland, and Muhamed Filipović. The MBO had been supported by some intellectuals and middle-class Muslims who disdained the mass appeal of the SDA. Under the terms of the agreement Bosnia was to stay within a Yugoslav federation, and there was excited talk about making Sarajevo its capital. However, the MBO was a minority party and there was also bad blood between Izetbegović and Zulfikarpašić, who had earlier bankrolled the SDA. The so-called Belgrade Initiative came to nothing.

In the wake of its failure, the SDS began to make ever more intense preparations for option two, that is the creation of a Serbian state in Bosnia which would also serve as a landbridge to Serbs in Croatia. On the night of 14–15 October 1991, in a charged atmosphere and with war raging in neighbouring Croatia, the Bosnian parliament, dominated by its glowering bust of Tito, debated a motion to declare the republic 'sovereign', which would mean that republican laws would take precedence over Yugoslav ones. As the Serbian leadership contemplated the crumbling of its project of a Serb-dominated rump Yugoslavia, Radovan Karadžić thundered:

> You want to take Bosnia–Hercegovina down the same highway of hell and suffering that Slovenia and Croatia are travelling. Do not think that you will not lead Bosnia–Hercegovina into hell, and do not think that you will not perhaps lead the Muslim people into annihilation, because the Muslims cannot defend themselves if there is war – How will you prevent everyone from being killed in Bosnia–Hercegovina?[8]

In an attempt to forestall a vote, the SDS's Momčilo Krajišnik, who was the speaker of parliament, tried to adjourn the session. The SDS deputies walked out, but the SDA and HDZ voted for the motion. Three weeks later the SDS organised a referendum for Serbs, who predictably voted to stay in Yugoslavia. The Serbs were told that if Bosnia became independent they would once again be subjected to the laws of Muslim landlords, agas, begs and pashas, and that independence represented a rolling back of everything Serbs had died for since 1804, if not 1389. Nothing could better exemplify the threat faced by the Serbs, they were told, than the fact that for hundreds of years they had been Bosnia's largest single community but that in the last twenty-five years the Muslims had suddenly 'outbred' them. As in Croatia, the extreme stress of the situation left people feeling vulnerable. Many simply suspended their critical faculties and put their trust in their leaders. After all, they argued, they were well educated and well connected to Milošević, the man who had 'saved' the Serbs of Kosovo and now Croatia too.

From then on such Bosnian government authority as still remained in the Serbian Autonomous Regions, began to ebb away. It was the same in western Hercegovina, where the Croatian flag flew in every town and village, and sandbagged gun positions were being set up along the roads.

Among the preparations being made by the SDS were plans for the takeover of areas where the Serbs were not in control but which lay within the territory they wanted. Prijedor, for example, lay in the middle of the great arc of land coveted by the Serbs in western Bosnia; because Muslims and Croats were a majority, however, the local council had not joined the region's SAO. For this reason it would have to be eliminated. Preparations for the takeover there began in November 1991 and orders certainly went out at the same time to scores of other districts with Muslim and Croat majorities for the same clandestine work to commence. In April 1993 the local newspaper *Kozarski Vjesnik* discussed the role of Simo Drljača, Prijedor's police chief:

> The man whom the SDS of the Prijedor district put in charge of forming the Serbian police after half a year of illegal work, had done his job so well that in 13 police stations 1,775 well armed persons were waiting to undertake any difficult duty in the time which was coming. During the night of the 29–30 April 1992, he directed the takeover of power which was successfully achieved in only 30 minutes, without a single shot being fired.[9]

Internationally the situation was changing too. When the war broke out in Croatia, few if any western countries wanted to see Yugoslavia break up into its constituent republics, let alone into new countries based solely on the criteria of blood and the winner takes all. Lord Carrington, the former British foreign secretary, was asked by the European Community to chair a peace conference in The Hague. He proposed recognition for the Yugoslav republics that requested it after all outstanding issues had been resolved. In the face of German pressure, this point was ignored and the EC recognised Croatia and Slovenia on 15 January 1992. Bosnia was asked to have a referendum if it wanted recognition. Before the EC announced its policy, however, Lord Carrington wrote to Hans van den Broek, the Dutch foreign minister, on 2 December 1991. Van den Broek was co-ordinating EC foreign policy because Holland was the current EC president. Carrington told him that 'early recognition' would mean that none of the parties would be 'much interested' in continuing to talk. More particularly he warned of the consequences of the EC offer for Bosnia:

> There is . . . a real danger, perhaps even a probability, that Bosnia–Herzegovina would also ask for independence and recognition, which would be wholly unacceptable to the Serbs in that republic in which there are something like 100,000 JNA troops, some of whom have withdrawn there from Croatia. Milošević has hinted that military action would take place there if Croatia and Slovenia were recognised. This might well be the spark that sets Bosnia–Herzegovina alight.[10]

As Milošević had already embarked on a major programme to arm the SDS, his 'hint' appears to have been so genteel that it was not taken as the gangsterish threat that it was supposed to be. The other explanation is that Carrington's phrase is an extraordinarily refined example of British understatement. It also begs another question. Was Carrington not being kept up to date with events on the ground by western intelligence agencies and if not, why not? As far back as January 1991 the US State Department was reported to be getting 'good stuff' about the JNA's plans. According to one 'policy maker' this intelligence 'made it clear they were about to decapitate the republics'.[11]

In retrospect it seems extraordinary that the Bosnian war did not break out earlier than it did. It did not do so because no one was yet ready. The Muslims had few arms, the Croats were taking a beating in Croatia and the Serbs did not want to open a new front until they had secured a ceasefire in Croatia. They also had more preparations to make in Bosnia. There was another reason: the Croats and Serbs were still trying to reach an arrangement to divide Bosnia between them. In December, while Serbs and Croats were still locked in mortal combat in Croatia, Nikola Koljević went to Zagreb to meet Franjo Tudjman. 'It is my impression that the Croats want peace and they want a negotiated deal with Serbia over territory,' he said.

Koljević was speaking about his trip on 23 January 1992. He claimed that three days before this the leaders of the three Bosnian parties had struck a deal to 'cantonise' the republic on ethnic grounds, which would leave the Serbs free to associate with Serbia and the Croats with Croatia. He claimed that the Muslims pulled out at the last minute. Sitting in his cosy flat in a high-rise block on Sarajevo's Lenin Street, he also signalled the end of Milošević's hoped-for rump Yugoslav option: 'It's time to stop this absurd idea of a mini-Yugoslavia – this is just a game. If only Serbs and Montenegrins want it, what's the point of trying to force others to stay? We should start thinking in terms of a new federation of Serb lands.' This was to become the new Serbian political reference point. The idea was that, once a Bosnian Serb republic was formed, in due course a Greater Serbian state or union comprising Serbia, Montenegro, Krajina and the Bosnian Serbs could be fashioned. The problem was how to separate from Bosnia. Koljević said, 'Croats are increasingly demanding to join Croatia and Serbs to join Serbia. Our interests are identical. If we can't make a deal with the Muslims, we will have to think about separation and the Muslims will have their own state in the middle.'

Already by the end of December Haris Silajdžić, the urbane Bosnian foreign minister, had been calling for UN peacekeepers to prevent a war. President Izetbegović was uncertain what to do. He would have gladly accepted a loose federation or confederation if it included all of the old Yugoslav republics, but with Milošević and Tudjman sharpening their carving knives for Bosnia he knew that an association with Belgrade was no longer possible. It would mean, he said, 'a colonial feudal status within Greater Serbia. . . . we are not against Greater Serbia, only it cannot be achieved at our expense'.

On 9 January 1992 the SDS declared the foundation of the Serbian Republic of Bosnia–Hercegovina, later renamed the Republika Srpska (RS). It was a final threat, for Karadžić explained that the SDS would begin to build the institutions of its republic only if 'the Croats or Muslims try to separate from Yugoslavia or if they are recognised'. In February, in a last attempt to head off war, the EC chaired talks in Lisbon in which Izetbegović agreed (again?) to the ethnic cantonisation of the republic. Once he returned home, though, he changed his mind. It is by definition impossible to know what would have happened if Izetbegović had stuck to the agreement, but the Serbs often claim that there would have been no war if he had done so. It seems unlikely. Given the level of military preparations being made by the SDS, the distribution of arms and the plans being laid for the takeover of Prijedor and other towns, it seems that they may just have been playing for time. Besides, many subsequent agreements faltered over the question not of constitutional arrangements but of maps. On 26 February, Bosnian Serb and Croat leaders met again, this time in Graz in Austria, to discuss the territories that they disputed among themselves.

Over the weekend of 29 February–1 March, Bosnia voted in the referendum requested by the EC on independence. In areas controlled by the SDS, voting was virtually impossible. In Pale, for example, a mostly Serb ski-resort village sixteen kilometres from Sarajevo, Muslims were forced to hold the poll in private houses or shops. 'We've already had our poll,' said a group of Serb men, 'we've voted to stay in Yugoslavia.' Asked if they were scared of war, they just laughed. One man said, indicating his forehead, 'We're armed up to here.'

On the Sunday of the referendum, Sarajevo was quiet except for a shooting incident. A Serbian wedding party held downtown had been shot at and the father of the groom, one Nikola Gardović, was killed. Within hours the SDS had cut off the city. Barricades were thrown up by armed and masked men who were communicating with one another by walkie-talkie. This was no spontaneous insurrection, as the SDS claimed, but a highly stage-managed operation. 'We warned what would happen in the event of demands for an independent Bosnia–Hercegovina,' said Karadžić, 'Northern Ireland would be like a holiday camp compared to Bosnia.' Samir Djukić, a half-Serb, half-Muslim newspaper seller, said ruefully, 'I wish I could be put in a state of clinical death for two years, because that is how long it will take to solve this problem.' With the benefit of hindsight we can see that Djukić was an optimist.

On the night of 3 March, Izetbegović said that Serbs from Pale were marching on the city. 'I beg you to stay at home, do not attack,' he said, having assured Bosnia's Serbs that they could sleep peacefully because no one would attack *them*. Speaking on television he added that the Pale

Serbs 'want to attack Sarajevo and if Serbs are coming we are not going to sit with our arms folded'. In the event, war was postponed and the barricades came down. Croats and Muslims had voted massively for independence and most Serbs had abstained or been prevented from voting.

There is a widespread misconception that the war began in Sarajevo on 6 April, the day the EC recognised Bosnia. In fact, at the same time as the March barricades were erected in Sarajevo, clashes had already begun in Bosanski Brod, a northern town linked by a bridge over the River Sava to the Croatian town of Slavonski Brod. On 26 March, in the village of Sijekovac, outside Bosanski Brod, eleven Serbs were killed. The SDS said that they had been massacred by a Croat–Muslim militia, a claim which was denied. By this stage it hardly mattered. By 29 March the town was being besieged and shelled by the JNA and Serbian paramilitaries. An extraordinarily eerie feeling hung over the town. Few people were on the streets. A woman grabbed her laundry off the line as her husband and daughter packed their car with as many bags as they could cram in, the video and several large salamis. 'Almost everyone has left,' said the man. 'The JNA says it is going to make this the Bosnian Vukovar.'

Gunmen and militias from a multitude of groups prowled around town. A number of Muslims from Serbia's Sandžak region had 'Allah is Great' stitched to their arm flashes. They said they were in training for the struggle that they intended to take to Serbia itself. Croats from the Croatian Army were also in town, some sporting the 'U' symbol of the old Ustasha state.

Mate Blažević, a member of the local crisis committee, touched the wound on his face. He said, 'The civil war has begun, and it has begun right here in our town.'

11

IT WAS WAR . . .

'It was war,' said a Serbian soldier. For more than fifteen kilometres every single house along the Kozarac road had been devastated. Grimly cradling his AK-47 he said, 'Those that didn't resist are in the camps, those that did were killed. There will never be Muslims here again.'

In the little riverside town of Bosanska Kostajnica, the mosque had been dynamited and the Catholic church was a charred skeleton. In a backstreet a Muslim woman hissed from behind half-closed blinds, 'Help us please, help us to get out.'

In Prijedor a line of women and children queued silently in the blazing August sun in front of the town hall. They were waiting to sign their property over to the municipality in exchange for exit, or rather expulsion, permits. By doing so they hoped to have their menfolk released from the camps, into which thousands had been herded. In Čelinac the local 'War Presidency' promulgated a series of regulations by which non-Serbs could not swim or fish in the local rivers, could not gather in groups of more than three and could not dally in public places. In Sarajevo, where utilities had been cut off, people who ran to get water during a lull in the shelling were cut down by snipers or random mortar shells.

This was how the Republika Srpska was born. Its warplanes wheeled triumphantly over its northern capital of Banja Luka and its propagandists talked of a Serbian 'war of liberation'. It was no more a liberation, though, than the 'freedom' and war brought down on the Germans by Hitler, however enthusiastically some may have welcomed him. And the ethnic cleansing, the driving out of whole populations, made a mockery of claims that the Serbs were defending themselves from a 'genocidal' campaign being waged on them by their victims.

From a psychological point of view there is a comparison with the Nazi era, especially if one considers the effect of the intense propaganda from Belgrade, which inculcated in the Serbs a sense of grievance and victimhood. Whereas Hitler had told the Germans that it was 'Versailles' which had been their undoing, Serbian nationalists said that Tito's Yugoslavia had been a gigantic plot to keep the Serbs from their rightful place in the sun. Muslims who only months before had been courted as potential allies were now portrayed as raving fundamentalist fanatics and every Croat as a knife-wielding Ustasha.

In his seminal work *The Fear of Freedom* the psychologist Erich Fromm wrote about the Germans in the 1930s in terms which have a striking application to the Serbs and particularly the Bosnian Serbs in the early 1990s:

> One part bowed to the Nazi regime without any strong resistance, but also without becoming admirers of the Nazi ideology and political practice. Another part was deeply attracted to the new ideology and fanatically attached to those that proclaimed it.
>
> Psychologically, this readiness to submit to the Nazi regime seems to be due mainly to a state of inner tiredness and resignation. . . .
>
> For millions of people Hitler's government . . . became identical with 'Germany'. Once he held the power of government, fighting him implied shutting oneself out of the community of Germans. . . . It seems that nothing is more difficult for the average man to bear than the feeling of not being identified with a larger group. However much a German citizen may be opposed to the principles of Nazism, if he has to choose between being alone and feeling that he belongs to Germany, most persons will choose the latter. It can be observed in many instances that persons who are not Nazis nevertheless defend Nazism against criticism of foreigners because they feel an attack on Nazism is an attack on Germany. The fear of isolation and the relative weakness of moral principles help any party to win the loyalty of a large sector of the population once this party has captured the power of the state.[1]

One way the loyalty of ordinary Bosnian Serbs to the SDS could be ensured in circumstances of breakdown and extreme political tension was the pre-emptive tactic of making out that any attack would come from the other side. In this way the taking up of arms was justified in terms of self-defence. Biljana Plavšić, who became the vice-president of the Republika Srpska when it formalised itself after Bosnia's international recognition, declared just before the war, 'Serbs do not want to turn the wheel of history back to the nineteenth century. Independence would be violence without precedent against the Serbs. If the others want to live in a Muslim Bosnia then let them mark the borders out. Let us part peacefully but I will not live in such a state.' As she well knew, there could be no such thing as the peaceful marking out of borders without a Muslim capitulation. When this did not come 'violence without precedent' had to be used against the Muslims, and in some areas against the Croats, in order to draw the lines in blood. Those that looked for a justification, however, could say that they were fighting a just war because the Muslims had refused all entreaties to 'part peacefully'.

The Croatian Connection

During the first weeks of the war it seemed as though chaos reigned throughout Bosnia, and in many ways it did. This was not because the Serbian leadership did not know what to do. They did, but not in detail. Before the fighting began, Nikola Koljević confided that the problem with the Muslims was that they would not sit down, with maps, and tell the Serbs what they wanted. This was because they wanted to prevent the partitioning of the republic between the Serbs and Croats, but it also meant that because their leadership dared to risk war rather than surrender conflict became inevitable. Koljević said that, roughly speaking, Muslim territory would lie within a small central Bosnian triangle bounded by the three cities of Tuzla, Zenica and Sarajevo. Since there had been no demarcation, however, there remained a lot to fight over.

When the war began, the Serbian leadership had several objectives. The first was to secure the border towns with Serbia and Montenegro so as to keep the supply lines open. Secondly, they had to secure power in towns and regions within the area that they had earmarked for themselves but within which there were concentrations of Croats and Muslims. This was especially important in the north, because it was essential to carve out a land corridor from Serbia to Serb-held western Bosnia and Krajina beyond. Then there was the problem of Sarajevo, which, after Belgrade, had the second largest urban Serb population in Yugoslavia.

Although talks with the Croats had been going on for more than a year when fighting broke out, there had still been no final agreement on territories. In some places, though, there was either no dispute or local deals had been struck. In western Bosnia the ethnic demarcation was so marked that who got what was clear. The region of Bosansko Grahovo was 95 per cent Serb, while neighbouring Livno was 72 per cent Croat. Outside Sarajevo, however, Kiseljak was 52 per cent Croat and 41 per cent Muslim. It bordered the district of Ilidža, whose population was 43 per cent Muslim and 37 per cent Serb. Since neither the Croats nor the Serbs disputed either municipality, the Serbs took Ilidža and the Croats Kiseljak. At the end of April 1992 the local JNA command in Kiseljak actually clinked glasses with the officers of the new Bosnian Croat Army, called the Croatian Council of Defence (HVO), gave them their old barracks and the local TO arms and drove off with the heavy weaponry. The local Muslim men who had been mobilised to fight the Serbs were not allowed into the barracks and were certainly not given a share of the arms.

The implications of such deals, and especially this one, have never been fully understood. What the Ilidža–Kiseljak agreement amounted to was official Croatian complicity in the siege of Sarajevo. No one has ever doubted that the HVO was simply a branch of the regular Croatian Army, which for diplomatic reasons used a slightly different appellation. Kiseljak traders grew rich selling to their counterparts in Ilidža, who in turn fed like vultures on Sarajevo by selling to the mafias that controlled the city's black market. The level of Serbo-Croat co-operation was such that when, in mid-May 1992, Bosnian forces tried to lift the siege by attacking Serb lines from behind, through Ilidža, they found themselves coming into armed conflict not with Serbs but with their nominal allies, the HVO from Kiseljak.[2] So it was no surprise to anyone who had been in Kiseljak that spring that a full-scale Croat–Muslim war should be raging by the autumn of 1992 – a conflict fuelled wherever possible by the Serbs.

None of eastern Bosnia concerned the Croatian authorities, because there were virtually no Croats living there. The faultlines were the Neretva valley and the north. Serbian leaders often said that the western border of their new state would be the River Neretva, but as there was no agreement with the Croats about it, Croats and Muslims fought the Serbs there together. They cleansed the Serbian villages along the river and succeeded in preventing the JNA from taking Mostar, the historic capital of Hercegovina.

The campaign in the east began on 2 April when a unit of Arkan's troops seized power in the north-eastern border town of Bijeljina. He was acting as before, at the behest of Serbia's SDB. Few people died because the operation was so rapid that stunned Muslims barely had time to organise resistance. Arkan quickly moved south to Zvornik, a town on the River Drina, which commanded a crucial bridge to Serbia. After some desultory negotiations his men stormed the town on 9 April with back-up from JNA artillery across the river in Serbia. In the second line of attack came local Bosnian Serb TO forces and paramilitaries organised by Šešelj and a number of others who came under the wing of the JNA. On 16 April the JNA itself crushed any resistance to Serbian power in another border town, Višegrad. While these towns were being taken, the siege lines were being thrown up around Sarajevo, and Banja Luka was taken over by the SDS in a local *coup d'état*.

Corridor Life

Thanks to the Serbian–Croatian agreements about the various undisputed areas between them, the Bosnian frontlines came into existence very quickly. Over the next three years they were to move little. One of the few regions where there were real pitched battles, though, as opposed to violent seizures of power, was in the Posavina valley in the north. Here the regular Croatian Army crossed the River Sava border in a bid to bolster the local TOs made up of poorly armed Bosnian Croats and Muslims. For some time Serb lines across the north were cut. There were scenes of panic in Banja Luka as people tried to clamber on to the last flights out. But by the middle of July the Serbs had forced through a corridor, albeit at a tremendous cost. Derventa, Modriča and other towns and villages were devastated and their Muslim and Croat populations sent fleeing southwards to government-held territory and north to Croatia. The collapse came when the Croatian government pulled its troops out of the warzone. It did this both because it feared that international sanctions might be applied to Croatia as they had been to the Serbs, and also because the Serbs were preparing to attack in a massive pincer formation from east and west. The military situation was untenable. However, most ordinary mobilised Bosnian Croat and Muslim men were convinced that a deal had been made. They believed that the Croatian Army had abandoned them in fulfilment of a secret agreement to divide Bosnia between Serbia and Croatia.

'We fought as long as we had support from Croatian tanks,' said Suad Kurpejović, a twenty-five-year-old soldier who ended up on a train in a suburb of Zagreb with 4,000 other men and their families in late July. 'Last week they pulled them back saying they had to repair them. . . . They just sold us out.' It was a pathetic spectacle, but it was a portent of what was to come. Smart Croatian commuters on other platforms looked askance at this rag-tag army, the First Bosnian Volunteer Shock Brigade, whose symbol was a dragon. Mirela Mandić, a twenty-year-old Bosnian Croat girl who wore a silver Kennedy 'Liberty' dollar around her neck, had tears in her eyes as she said, 'Bosnia is Serbia now and Hercegovina is Croatia.' Even more miserable were the scenes in the remaining government-held Bosanski Brod enclave, where 2,000 refugees were stuck as the Croats refused to let them cross the Sava to safety in Croatia. The men said that they were ordered to retreat, and with few arms at their disposal they could not resist the overwhelming military might of the Serbs. Their rout had been total and there was no going back. So they took with them whatever they could. The firemen from Derventa drove into exile in their fire engines, the dustmen in their garbage trucks and from Odžak came the whole bus company. Spare tyres, piles of brake pads, oil filters, documents and computers, everything had been packed on to the sixteen-coach fleet. The drivers and entire staff of the company were having to guard their buses from the predatory fighters of

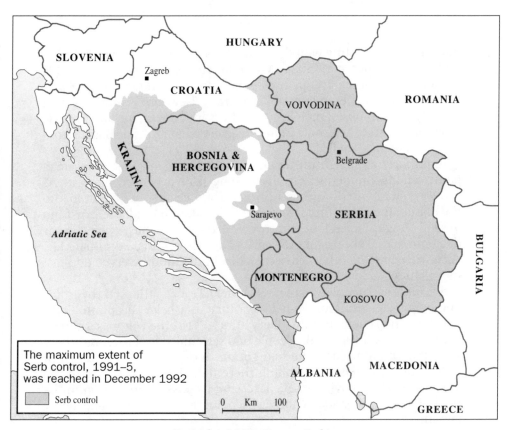

December 1992: Greater Serbia

Bosanski Brod. 'We left all our own belongings to save the company,' said Mišo Senković, its director. 'Our houses have been destroyed and our families scattered. Once we are out and safe, we'll fix something up and try and merge with another company.' It was an extraordinary leap of faith. When vehicles were allowed over the bridge into Croatia, they were often promptly stolen ('requisitioned') by the Croatian police.

Among the most tenacious Serbian fighters for the corridor were the men of Milan Martić's Krajina Militia. Once the fighting was over, the road sign from Odžak was taken as a trophy and installed in the office of Krajina's minister of defence. The Krajina Serbs and the Bosnian Serbs at the western end of the corridor called it the Corridor of Life, because if it was ever cut their supply line would have been severed. It was not just their only road to Serbia but, hemmed in on all sides by frontlines, it was their only road to the rest of the world.

Throughout the war the Serbs held on to the corridor, but at Brčko, at its narrowest, it was only two miles wide. For weeks all would be quiet and then fighting would flare up. For the Serbs who lived in Brčko and in the other corridor towns and villages it was a miserable existence. In winter, troops would walk for miles down its icy roads hitching lifts home to Banja Luka and elsewhere. Hundreds and probably thousands of men lost their lives in the corridor and in futile attempts to drive the Croats from Orašje, an enclave inside Bosnia from where it could be shelled.

In January 1993 fighting along the corridor led to a typical spasm of panic among the Serbs who lived along it or depended upon it. As artillery boomed in the distance Snežana bundled her two children into the back of the car in Brčko and said, 'It's followed us all the way from Teslić.' Dragan, aged four, threw up. A man wrenched open the car door and said, 'Take us, take us too, I'll pay!' He almost paid with his life. A car speeding the other way screeched in the mud, swerved and just missed him.

Snežana had set off at dawn. Serb-held Teslić, sitting on the front-line by a tongue of Muslim-held territory that licked deep into Serb-held land, had come under artillery attack. 'First the war was a game,' she said. 'Now it's for real.' People had scrambled for buses, but there were not enough seats. She had got on to one but it broke down in Doboj and the shells were falling there too. Her bus crept on to the outskirts of Brčko, where it died, tossing its passengers out on to the road. Here at the corridor's narrowest point they were left to flail at any passing car.

Brčko, on the River Sava, had been brutally cleansed during the spring of 1992 and was one of the oddest places in the whole of Bosnia. By the river there was a grain silo. From the top one could see the village of Gunja in Croatia and to the south, with binoculars, the minarets of mosques in Muslim villages on the other side of the corridor. Brčko was shattered and desolate, but children still played in the street. As the sound of artillery was constant in January 1993, why were they allowed out and why did Serbian policemen sit unperturbed in their office in the town centre sipping thick sweet Turkish coffee? 'We have an unspoken agreement with the Croats,' said the police chief. 'We only hit their military positions and they only hit ours. They don't target the town centre and we don't hit Gunja.'

This was typical of the hundreds of cosy local deals and tacit agreements which all sides made all the time during the war. To the south of Brčko lay the Mount Majevica front. Many of the Muslims chased out of Brčko were there. One of the policemen said, 'We know them all, we talk to them every day on the radio. On Majevica we have had two ceasefires and played football. It was unbelievable. We all promised just to hold the lines and not to launch any offensives. Not a single shell has fallen there since then.'

Sarajevo: Serbian Defeat

It may have been the longest siege in modern history, but it was also the strangest.

As Bosnia slipped into war, the headquarters of the SDS was the Holiday Inn hotel just opposite the Bosnian parliament building. This was not just because it was convenient for Serbian deputies but also because the SDS had taken advantage of recently passed privatisation laws to buy a controlling stake in the establishment. As the situation deteriorated, Radovan Karadžić and his family moved into a suite while SDS deputies used the conference rooms to declare the foundation of the Republika Srpska. In the last days of peace Karadžić and his entourage decamped to Pale, the ski-resort village just outside the Bosnian capital. As they did so, a very large young woman with a shock of black hair and an extraordinary line in fishnet stockings and similar clothing (as befitted an aspiring pop star) could be seen hauling suitcases across the hotel atrium. She was Sonja Karadžić, the daughter of the SDS leader and soon to become one of the most powerful figures in Pale.

On the morning of 6 April helmet-wearing, banner-waving miners arrived in Sarajevo to take part in a peace rally. Thousands gathered in the open space between the hotel and parliament. Up on a hill above the city, at the old Ottoman Višegrad Gate, Bosnian policemen were taking potshots at a new Serbian position on another hilltop. Back at the Holiday Inn, Cedric Thornberry, an important UN official, ran from the hotel saying that it was 'time to leave . . . I've just found a bullet hole in my bedroom'. He left with forty seconds to spare. With all guns blazing, a special unit of the Bosnian police stormed through the front door to hunt down a handful of SDS gunmen who had begun firing on the crowd below. Within minutes the operation was over. The SDS men were lying face down, but alive, on the atrium floor. Guests were ordered out. Those who ventured back a few hours later were to receive a salutary lesson in Balkan war-making. Every single room had been looted.

By dusk Muslim militia-cum-Bosnian-police barricades had been thrown up across the city, but they in turn were surrounded by Serbian barricades and JNA gun positions. The siege had begun. Long and thin and having been built in a valley surrounded by steep hills and mountains, Sarajevo could have been built for a siege. The JNA took full advantage of this as it dug into positions that had been prepared at least four months before.

When the war began there had been no Bosnian Army and the fighting force that was built over the next few years did well enough to defend what it could under the circumstances. It did not however, until 1995, inflict any major or lasting defeats on the Serbs. There was one exception to this, which came in the days before the army even really existed. It was a key battle which changed the course of the war. In the middle of May, just over a month into the siege, Serbian forces tried to cut the city in half. If they had succeeded the government would almost certainly have been defeated and have had to surrender. Serbian shells whistled over the city, houses exploded into dust. A factory burned, sending a thick pall of black smoke over the Bosnian capital. The Serbs had already taken Grbavica, a part of town which jutted into the centre, and from there they tried to cross the little Miljačka river which meanders through the town. After bitter fighting at the Brotherhood and Unity Bridge they were halted. It was the single greatest Serbian defeat of the war.

Throughout the siege, Serbian leaders came up with a variety of different justifications for their action. An oft repeated claim was that there was no siege at all but rather a circular line of defensive positions manned by men from Serbian villages outside Sarajevo who were fending off an attack from within the city. For good measure Karadžić would then add that his forces were not even firing on the city but that this was being done by government forces trying to make it seem as though Serbs were doing it. Another explanation was that a 'blockade' was necessary to pin down a large number of potential enemy soldiers who would otherwise be deployed against them elsewhere. Despite the mealy-mouthed explanation of Captain Aleksandar Petrović, a Serbian commander in Grbavica, there was some truth to this: 'We have encircled the city because the Muslims and Croats have more infantry. They are not imprisoned. It's a preventative measure.'

In truth the leadership in Pale made it up as they went along and as the situation changed. Until Christmas 1992 ordinary Serbian soldiers thought they were trying to take the city. 'We knew by then we would not do it,' said one soldier; 'there was no order but the realisation just filtered down from above.' After the defeat on the Brotherhood and Unity Bridge, Serbian leaders changed tack. If they could not defeat government forces militarily, they could try starving the city into submission. They were defeated again, but this time it was not due to the bravery of a small number of armed men within the city.

Outraged, or rather embarrassed at their impotence, western leaders felt the pressure to 'do something' but exactly what they did not know. They certainly did not want their young men to die fighting the Serbs, but at the same time an intense debate was taking place in Washington and between Washington and European capitals about whether to launch air strikes against Serbian positions. As the siege began, aerial photos clearly showed where these were, but the US military and the CIA were terrified of being sucked into a new Vietnam.[3] The psychiatrist in Radovan Karadžić knew this and fed the American paranoia: 'If there is armed intervention over Sarajevo, Bosnia will turn into a new Vietnam. This is not an ideological but a civil war. We shall fight to the death.'

Despite this rhetoric, Serbian leaders were unsure quite how far they could go before their actions pushed western leaders over the brink, so they consented to hand over Sarajevo airport to the UN. Because of its position, lying between two government-held areas, it was a vital link in the Serbian siege chain around the city. On Sunday 29 June, French President François Mitterrand slipped out of an EC heads of government meeting in Lisbon and without whispering a word to his colleagues left for Sarajevo. The seventy-five-year-old president donned a flak jacket and became the first person to land at the airport since the fighting had begun. Džeilana Pećanin, a young woman who had been cowering in the corridor of her apartment block because the walls were exposed to shellfire, saw Mitterrand's convoy racing down the street. She said: 'I thought it was a lie at first. This is a great gesture, it brings great hope. Now we know that this will soon be over.'

Mitterrand's visit was to prove the single greatest disappointment of the war. After that, no one dared to hope any more. Far from 'soon being over' the siege was only just beginning. Mitterrand took the credit for forcing the airport open – for showing it could be done. He never pretended it was anything else. While crowds shouted 'Vive la France!' he explained, 'I did not arrive in Sarajevo as a negotiator. I arrived to show the world the central point of the problem with humanitarian aid.'

But the 'problem' of the siege of Sarajevo was not humanitarian aid, just as that of Stalingrad or Troy for that matter had not been about food parcels. It was about winning and losing a war. The siege became the strangest in military history. After Mitterrand's visit, the UN and its refugee agency, the UN High Commissioner for Refugees (UNHCR), opened the city for emergency aid. Up to 4 January 1996 and despite many airport closures, the UNHCR was to fly 12,951 aid flights, which literally kept the city alive. In this way Sarajevo was saved from defeat and thus, in a hideous paradox, the war could go on for over three more years. And not only did the international community feed the defenders of the city but, with scrupulous fairness, they fed the besiegers too, because otherwise they would have closed the airport again. This is not to say that the UN should not have done what it did, because Sarajevo was the victim of aggression driven by the SDS and plotted by Serbia and the JNA's most senior officials. It is only to point out that the haphazard western response to the war helped to fuel it and prolong it. Opening the airport was a way of avoiding the more robust option of air strikes which western leaders were so frightened of but which, when they finally came in sufficient strength, were to prove doubters wrong.

As the situation in Sarajevo stabilised, the siege became even odder. Because the airport was no longer in Serbian hands, government forces could dig a tunnel underneath it in order to open a passage in and out of the city. At first it was top secret, only to be used by the military and politicians, and for the import of arms and ammunition, but soon the rules relaxed. Black-market and commercial goods began to enter the city this way. The Serbs knew perfectly well what was happening, but sought to profit from the situation. The leadership had blinked in the face of western threats and given up the airport. Now they had to use the new circumstances to their advantage. The first way to do this was by continuing the siege. They hoped that so many people would flee, via the tunnel or otherwise, that morale would sink and eventually break. The horror of the siege did indeed depress spirits but, by imposing strict rules on who could travel, the Bosnian authorities staunched the flow of people from Sarajevo. A critical population mass was kept up and a good part of the outflow began to be replaced by an influx of refugees whose presence began to make Sarajevo less of the cosmopolitan place it had been and more of a Muslim city.

At the height of the Muslim–Croat war, officials within the city and in Pale also confirmed that fighting around Sarajevo had diminished. This was because it served the Serbs' interests to relax pressure on the city, so that Bosnian troops could be released to travel through the tunnel to fight the Croats.

Many of those Muslims who crowded into government-held Sarajevo came from those parts around the city that the Serbs had managed to capture at the beginning of the war. Either people fled of their own volition or they were forcibly rounded up and expelled. Boris, a Serb from Ilijaš, just north of Sarajevo, explained how it had been taken just before the siege began:

> The police chief was a Serb and his deputy was a Croat. The Croat was on the Serb side because he did not want to leave. It was an ordinary day. They took their AKs and said, 'Who is going to stay or leave? Make up your minds now.' The Muslims all left. There were not very many Croats. With the police now under Serb control the municipal authorities were taken over. It was a police coup followed by a political one. The Muslims living in town couldn't do anything. They went to Misoća, part of Ilijaš, but the JNA barracks was there. Barricades were set up and the Muslims cut it off. The action lasted twenty-six days, but eventually the Muslims were pushed out.

The first people to be organised to fight were SDS members and volunteers like himself. The majority waited to see what would happen. Within three weeks of the beginning of the war they were mobilised by the now Serbian Ilijaš TO. For good measure Boris added his own reason for wanting to fight: 'It was for a final end of the Ottoman Empire. A fight not to allow them [the Muslims] to dominate once again. The time had come for revenge.'

Because Ilijaš lay between Sarajevo and government-controlled central Bosnia, it was given up in March 1996 along with Grbavica and three other suburbs of the city in accordance with the Dayton Accord of November 1995 which ended the fighting. Tens of thousands of Serbs left rather than live under Bosnian government control. This was another bitter paradox of the siege. The lines had never broken, yet the Serbs who manned the trenches for so long still lost the Battle of Sarajevo.

The Serbian leadership had expected to win the war and win it quickly. Thanks to the Serbian defeat on the Brotherhood and Unity Bridge and the opening of the airport to life-sustaining aid flights, the prospects of an all-out victory gradually began to slip through their fingers. This meant that the point of the siege of Sarajevo also began to change. Beginning as an aggressive military tactic designed to win the war for the Serbs, it slowly became, at least in part, defensive. This did not mean that Serbian forces ceased to fire on the city; far from it. It meant that a psychological change took place among the Serbian troops who looked down on it. With the UN firmly installed in the city and with a slow but sure increase in the amount of arms filtering into it, it became clear to the Serbs that they were no longer fighting to defeat the Muslims but rather to prevent them from bursting out of the city and killing them. The siege lines were far too strong for that, however, and occasional breakouts on to Mount Trebević to the south were easily repulsed. But every Serb knew what was awaiting him now. If, during combat, the besieged broke out there would be no quarter. This may seem obvious, but it had not looked like this to most Serbian fighters at the beginning of the war. Victory had seemed certain then. The SDS had also told them that they faced angry Muslims who wanted to slit Serbian throats, which was why they had to besiege Sarajevo. This had become a self-fulfilling prophecy. There was little point then in international peacekeeping officials appealing to Serbs to stay in what had been Serb-held parts during the spring of 1996. Even if most could have remained unharmed after the transfer of authority to the government, no man wanted to leave his family exposed to the risk of individual revenge attacks by people whom they had been trying to kill only months before.

In February 1994, a shell killed sixty-nine people in Sarajevo's Markale marketplace. Karadžić and the Bosnian Serb authorities said that it had been fired by the government side in order to provoke a western response. It was a frequent claim and according to Lord Owen, the EC peace negotiator, the UN told him that occasionally such things had happened.[4] In general, however, the Serbian argument was grotesque, since what they wanted the world to believe was that of the hundreds of thousands of shells they had fired none had ever hurt anyone. As Miroslav Toholj, the novelist who became the Republika Srpska's information minister, put it, 'We Serbs never kill civilians.' Unconvinced, the western powers decided that this time they had to act. The Bosnian Serb Army was given a deadline to pull out its heavy weaponry from around the city or have it bombed out by NATO. After much loud protestation that it would do no such thing, an eleventh-hour, face-saving deal was stitched together by the Russians. In return for Serbian compliance with the order, they offered to send in Russian UN troops who would be based in Serb-held Grbavica.

In the gathering gloom of the afternoon of 21 February, the cannons began to roll down the mountains. Tanks which had not moved for two years were levered out of their emplacements. They had been painted with women's names – Lenka, Biljana and even St Helena. The mood was almost one of elation because, very briefly, many believed that the war would soon be over. But it was a joy tinged with bitterness because it was the first time that many soldiers, especially those who had come from within the city, had had to confront the reality that they would now never go home. 'I would give a year's salary to walk through Sarajevo again,' said one soldier. When would that be possible? 'Maybe in ten or twenty years,' mused his friend, 'when the blood has passed and the wounds have healed.' Little did they realise the eventual extent of the Serbian disaster: the evacuation of the Serb-held suburbs when the siege came to its end more than two years later.

Tens of thousands of Serbs did not need to give a year's salary to walk the streets of Sarajevo. Since they had been so confident of a quick victory, the Serbian leadership had thought nothing of beginning the siege while Sarajevo remained full of Serbs. Even in July 1993, more than a year after the siege began, it was thought that some 50,000 people out of a besieged total of 250,000 were Serbs.[5] Because of their numbers and the international presence in the city, these people were afforded more protection than Serbs in smaller provincial cities who were vulnerable to attacks by extremists, criminals and angry neighbours. A few extremely courageous individuals like General Jovan Divjak, the deputy commander of the Bosnian Army, and Gordana Knežević, the deputy editor of the daily *Oslobodjenje*, were also willing to nail their colours to the mast of the multi-ethnic Bosnian ideal and to fight for it. Knežević divided the Serbs within the siege lines into three. There was a small 'anti-fascist' group, among which she counted herself, a small group that eagerly awaited 'liberation' by the gunners in the hills and a third undecided mass who approved neither of the

Bosnian government nor of Karadžić and his followers.

Dušan, an economist, was one of the small group who (secretly) supported Karadžić. Like many others, he said he had constantly been harassed and sent on trench-digging duty on the frontlines: 'Eighty per cent of us are Serbs. The Muslim soldiers get bored and so they fire at the Serbs across the frontline in order to provoke them into firing back. My brother is on the other side and as soon as I can escape I will join him.' An unknown number of Serbs died in incidents like this, but the situation improved after the first year. This was because a new government under Haris Silajdžić swept the city of mafia barons-cum-warlords who had played a vital role in defending it during the first days of the siege but had increasingly begun to terrorise it. It was they who had begun to pick people up off the streets, many of them non-Serbs, and despatch them on trench-digging duty.

Bojan was mobilised into the army but, like many Serbs, he was not given a gun but rather a job behind the lines. He worked at a military fuel depot.

At the beginning it was bad. There was chaos and because my father was a JNA officer people were convinced that I was a sniper. On 18 July 1992 they came with machine guns to get me. Seven hundred Serbs were taken to Zetra stadium, and they kept us there for about four or five hours. They were abusing us, saying we were a Fifth Column and saying we should go to Pale. There were many old people and they were provoking them. But still I decided not to go. I was not afraid. I said we were loyal to the government but some of them said, 'It's a war against Orthodoxy.'

Bojan retained his Muslim and Croat friends and, although it was harder for Serbs in Sarajevo than others, he also said, 'Some of our neighbours tried to prevent them taking us to Zetra. We didn't even know them before that. Because of such people I would like to stay.' Like so many Sarajevo Serbs, he was torn apart, mixed up and full of contradictions. He declared, for example, 'I think both sides are defending themselves.' He wanted to stay but he also wanted to go to New Zealand. Typically he feared that at the end of the war, once the state had been formally partitioned, there would be no future for Serbs in what would become a Muslim city.[6] Besides, he added, even if he did stay what would be the point? In another generation a new war would probably start and he did not want his children to go through what he had been through.

Throughout the war Serbs were murdered in Sarajevo by criminal gangs or individuals looking for loot or revenge or by angry refugees hunting for flats. The government did little about it. Under the circumstances, it had more pressing things to attend to and, in the prevailing situation of lawlessness, it was not just Serbs who were murdered. However, most Sarajevo Serbs had heard stories about these killings and even knew people who had been killed, but it was impossible to know how widespread a phenomenon it was. This ignorance helped feed their fear and meant that many Serbs were even more desperate to escape. Not only could they be killed by a Serbian shell, they could be murdered at home too. But the government was loath to let anyone out of the city, and this included Serbs. Karadžić accused the authorities of keeping ethnic hostages. The government knew, however, that if all the Serbs left then there would be nothing to prevent the complete and utter destruction of the city by the Bosnian Serb leadership. Philippe Lazzarini, the chief of mission of the International Committee of the Red Cross in the summer of 1993, said, 'There have been individual cases of harassment and revenge, but it is not as clear here as it has been in other parts of Bosnia.' He added, 'The city is besieged and the besieged are also holding people hostages – for political reasons and also as human shields. On this there is no discrimination.'

Although a number of Serbs remained vocal in support of a multi-ethnic Bosnia until the end of the war, others such as Gordana Knežević gave up the fight and eventually left. They saw that the republic was being partitioned by the SDS and the HDZ, and so Sarajevo and the rest of government-controlled Bosnia increasingly became an effective SDA one-party state. Many Muslims accepted the logic imposed on them by the Serbian and Croatian leaderships. The dream of a citizens' Bosnia, as opposed to a Bosnia of divided nations, was dying – or rather had been murdered. As a result, it was not just Serbs who wanted to leave the city. Zdravko Grebo, a prominent Sarajevo intellectual, said in 1995, 'We lost the war for a multicultural open society, and therefore many people have given up and left. That "multithing" is a special quality. But every day our number decreases. . . . There are still many people who share our views, but we would be lying if we insisted that we are in the majority.'[7]

Thanks to television coverage, the world became familiar with the barricades that blockaded Sarajevo streets and which shielded passers-by from Serbian snipers. They were less familiar with the strange world of Grbavica, that part of the city close to the centre which was held by the Serbs and from which almost all Muslims had been driven out. Makeshift walls had been built across the streets that ran down into the government-held part of the city and, because much of Grbavica was on a hill, sheets and blankets had been hung across intersections to hide passers-by from the view of snipers on the other side. Despite these so-called Chinese Walls, it was common to see old ladies panting after they had sprinted for their lives across exposed areas. In the spring of 1993 the local military command said that, on average, ten people a week were killed or wounded by Bosnian snipers or mortars. The middle of Grbavica was dominated by Lenin Street, once a busy city thoroughfare. As it now led nowhere, clouds of dust swirled up when the odd car drove down it.

In a yard flanked by blocks of flats with plastic sheeting for windows a line of elderly people queued beside a shiny red car with an aerial on its roof. 'Before the war I was a taxi driver,' said Radenko, its camouflage-jacketed driver. 'I call my Muslim taxi driver friend on the other side and people can talk to each other.' An old man, his eyes watering, grasped the microphone: 'It's Dad, I'm fine. Mummy is at home and she's okay too.' Sounding a thousand miles away, a daughter answered. The Muslim taxi driver had taken the daughter's telephone number, rung it up and held his microphone to the telephone.

Somewhere in Grbavica a couple of telephones, which had somehow not been severed from the main Sarajevo network, still functioned. People got to know of their existence and would take a day or so, hitching for miles around Sarajevo, to venture down into Grbavica to call family or friends inside the city.

Pale: Fiction Met Reality

Before the war, the population of Pale was 6,000. During the conflict it swelled to some 20,000. In the mountains above Sarajevo it was little more than an extended village with one main street. The wider area could house these people because many Sarajevans had ski chalets in the mountains which were taken by the refugees. Hotels which had been built for the 1984 Winter Olympics were also used to shelter them. When the war broke out, Pale was deemed a convenient spot from which to conduct operations. Before the war Karadžić had built a house here, which was handy. It was also only an hour's drive from Han Pijesak, where the Bosnian Serb Army under General Ratko Mladić had made its headquarters in an old JNA command centre designed for wartime operations.

Pale had historic resonances too. Members of the royal government had passed thtough the village after they had fled Belgrade in 1941. In 1914 some sixty Serbs had been murdered here by angry Croats and Muslims following the assassination of the Archduke Franz Ferdinand and his wife in Sarajevo. A memorial to those killed stands in Pale's churchyard.

As time wore on and the possibility of a quick victory faded in the war of 1992–5, it became necessary to build the institutions of the new

Bosnian Serb state in Pale. The government was housed in the old Famos engine factory, until a new building was erected for them. Karadžić and the other top Bosnian Serb leaders worked from an annexe building of the Hotel Panorama, which commanded a fine view of Pale and the mountains. Logically the leadership should have been based in Banja Luka, the only place approaching city status in the Republika Srpska, but Karadžić had always had problems with the authorities there and tried to steer clear of it. Indeed he had to base himself in Pale because his constituency was the Sarajevo Serbs, whose future became inextricably bound up with his. After most of the Serbs had left the wartime Serb-controlled suburbs in spring 1996, as a result of Bosnia's peace agreement, they were taken to be resettled in areas from which Muslims had been driven, such as Brčko and Srebrenica. Organised into associations of Sarajevo Serbs, they remained loyal to him, to the extent that they began to be described as his 'Falange'.

Despite being the 'provisional' capital of a newly self-proclaimed state, Pale remained a dismal place. It had a little market where women sold bags of coffee beans, chocolate and deodorant and another street where they sold cigarettes. There were few jobs and there was even less to do during one's free time. There was a pizzeria which closed at 7.00pm and a couple of cafés and bars. The VBC, the Video Billiard Club, was the café at which Pale's *jeunesse dorée* congregated. They included Saša Karadžić, son of Radovan. Despite his crewcut, pistol and sports car, few noticed him at first, but, as the war dragged on, he became an increasing irritation to ordinary people whose sons, unlike him, actually had to go to the front.

Pale also became the home of Kanal-S, the SDS's television mouthpiece. Known as TV-Pale, much of its basic equipment was stolen from the BBC, which had abandoned it at the beginning of the war when one of its crews had fled fighting in the suburb of Ilidža. It was soon discovered that, because of its exclusive access on the Serbian side, a tidy profit could be made by selling footage to television companies or agencies from around the world. This was done by holding auctions of 'hot' material. In May 1995, for example, after NATO planes had bombed a number of Serbian positions, some 375 UN personnel on Serbian territory were taken hostage. Within hours television viewers around the world saw film of UN troops chained up at strategic sites. Jovan Zametica, an adviser to Karadžić, said, 'It is not us who will carry out the executions but NATO.' In fact many of the prisoners had been chained up only during the filming. One was teased later as he drank beer with his guards who said that he had caught a suntan while being forced to pose. The propaganda value of such clips was obvious – its commercial value was even greater. Dragan Božanić, the political editor of TV-Pale, had sold the film in an auction to the international news agencies with offices in Pale.

Some days later, Božanić interviewed Karadžić live on television. Rumours were spreading that the first hostages were just about to be released. The programme was called 'Ask the President'. Viewers were invited to phone in their questions, but oddly none appeared to be interested in *the* question of the moment. Finally Karadžić mumbled something relevant: 'I don't expect we'll be holding them for decades.' After that he began to witter uncontrollably. It was clear that something was going wrong, because he had begun to talk about Christianity, philosophies of war and just about anything else that came into his head. There were then crash-bangs in the studio and a relieved Božanić said, 'Er, we have an announcement,' only to add, 'Er, sorry not yet.' So Karadžić had to keep talking. At last he could stop and a dramatic film report was shown of 126 hostages boarding buses and on their way to freedom. 'Well, thanks for appearing on the show,' said Božanić. 'Good night, Mr President.' Behind the scenes it had been a nerve-racking night. The film, made by TV-Pale's top reporter, who just happened to be General Mladić's nephew, had come in late. The problem was that it had to be sold and fed first to Belgrade and London because otherwise international broadcasters could pick it up for free when it was shown on TV-Pale. 'I almost had a heart attack,' said the local employee of the successful news-agency bidder. 'I was on the phone to the Belgrade office, who were on the phone to London, while my rival was screaming, "$10,000, $10,000!"'

Owing to her status as daughter of the president, Sonja Karadžić became head of the International Press Centre in Pale. This was a position of real power, as foreign journalists and later those from Serbia too could get into Bosnian Serb territory only with her express permission. At first the press centre had been the domain of Slavko Milanović, a pleasant former theatre director from Sarajevo, who appeared very lost among the warmongering nationalists of Pale. One day Sonja, one of his employees, wrote to him effectively informing him that he no longer had a job. Sonja Karadžić did almost as much to undermine the Serbian position in the world as her father himself. Movement was severely restricted. Whenever there was a story which could be used to explain the Serbian position or be exploited to win sympathy such as an influx of Serbian refugees, journalists were either banned or allowed to go too late or in insufficient numbers to make a significant international impact. Her press centre became deeply corrupt as a number of its employees sought out the highest bidders among certain news organisations. Those that refused to pay saw nothing or found it hard to gain permission to come back. Pale's answer to Marie Antoinette, Sonja would rise late, arrive at her press centre cuddling her poodle Mazoni, look at a list of requests for permission to come to Pale, grunt 'No, no, no,' as she crossed out most of the names, and then disappear for lunch.

Life in a political party is full of back-stabbing and intrigue at the best of times. Few places could have been worse than Pale, where the whole SDS party and the state hierarchy were compelled to live together in unhealthily close proximity. Sonja's throttling control over access to information and to interviews with her father led her into conflict with Jovan Zametica, the British-educated academic who had become Karadžić's adviser. Zametica had an unusual background, to say the least. He had been born Omer Zametica in Banja Luka to a Bosnian Muslim father and a mother who was half Serb and half of Yugoslav-Czech origin. They divorced when he was a baby and she remarried a Swiss. Now in his mid- to late thirties, Zametica had lived much of his life in England and had studied there as well as in Belgrade and Ljubljana. Declaring that he felt himself to be a Serb, he came to do what he could for the cause. Because he had lived abroad, he knew that it was important to cultivate the media and to talk to journalists. This led him into conflict with Sonja, who regarded Karadžić and other top politicians as her private property. During times of tension between the two of them, journalists who requested an interview with Zametica were told by the haughty Sonja, 'He is the president's spokesman. As the president has not spoken he cannot speak to you.' As a consequence of this typical Pale battle of wills, aspersions mysteriously began to be cast on Zametica's background and there were dark suggestions that he might be a Muslim spy. Supporters of Zametica said that Karadžić was well aware of Sonja's effective sabotage of the Republika Srpska's attempts to improve its image in the world, but that he had a real problem. He could lead his people into a bloody war, but he would not sack his daughter because, according to one insider, 'He has to go home every evening and face his wife.'

Ordinary people in Pale and in the rest of the Republika Srpska survived the best they could by scraping by on the minimum. Their problems of physical survival were never as hard as those in parts of government-held territory, but with industry working at 10 per cent, if that, of full capacity there was little non-agricultural work for those not at the front. Those with jobs were rarely paid and when they were it was often in the form of handouts of food or other necessities. Soldiers were sometimes paid with cigarettes or even chicks to take home to raise. Many had relatives abroad or in Serbia who sent money.

By far the hardest time in Serb-held Bosnia, or in Krajina for that matter, was endured by refugees or people who lived in the towns and had no access to land. The Bosnian and Krajina Serbs were able to fight for so long, with little support apart from handouts from Serbia and the international aid agencies, because many, if not most of them, were peasants. This meant that they had land and livestock and so were virtually self-sufficient. With their men often at the front, the women worked the land even harder than usual and the late summer was spent pickling peppers and cabbage and other winter staples. Cheeses were smoked and hams were cured. Houses were kept warm with wood stoves, which were also used for cooking on, and extra income was procured by selling wood, fruit and vegetables in town. Almost every aspect of ordinary life was eased by bribery and corruption. Also, local deals across the front lines included exchanges of prisoners and hostages for foodstuffs or fuel.

Corrupt as they were, deputies to the Bosnian Serb parliament did not forget the rural roots of most of their constituents. On one occasion, when called together to discuss one of the many peace plans to be put before them, they saw nothing odd in discussing the question of goats first. Although many people had goats, they were technically illegal, having been outlawed long ago by the communist authorities because they had been causing havoc by stripping bark from trees, especially in Hercegovina. However, as one deputy explained, this had been a deeply anti-Serbian act because 'most people who owned goats were Serbs'. Goats passed muster, the peace plan did not.

Although the Bosnian and Krajina Serb leaderships often said that every single man aged between sixteen and sixty would somehow be mobilised 'for the defence of the fatherland', there was one class who could escape the draft. These were the considerable numbers of gastarbeiters who worked in Germany, Austria, Slovenia and elsewhere. Coaches full of them and their families could often be seen crossing the Serbian border with Hungary on their way back to Germany, or glimpses could be caught of their mud-spattered Mercedes making high-speed dashes through the 'corridor'. The Serbs were always short of manpower, compared to the Croats or Muslims, but these people were far too valuable to mobilise. They were a source of hard cash, as they had to pay a considerable sum to be able to come and go. The penalty for non-payment by someone abroad could be the loss of property. The gastarbeiter community provided not only money but refuges for those who had fled the warzones. More discreetly, and where it was possible to secure visas, they also provided a haven for those young men whose families had no intention of seeing them slaughtered on the frontline for a cause some at least did not believe in.

In one of the few lighter interludes of life in the Republika Srpska, Slavko Milanović, the sacked head of the Pale press centre, returned to public life with *Naked Life*. This was the title of TV-Pale's first six-episode soap opera. While Serbian soldiers manned the trenches around Sarajevo, half an hour's drive away the *Naked Life* team were out on a bitterly cold February night filming. With Milanović crying 'Cut! Cut!' and with a clapperboard being clapped, Pale's answer to *EastEnders* or *Dallas* proceeded apace. This was an episode called 'Operation Parachute', in which some peasants were trying their luck in a get-rich-quick scheme. They had heard that, if they lit a night-time bonfire, humanitarian aid, at that time indeed being dropped over Muslim enclaves, would come tumbling down to them because the pilots would think they were over Muslim territory. The ploy worked – up to a point. Instead of food the peasants got Turkish *mujahedin* (freedom fighters). The peasants tried to sell them to the government but got only congratulatory certificates instead.

Although there was a clear patriotic backdrop to *Naked Life*, Milanović insisted that it would not cross the line into becoming a tub-thumping morale raiser. This would be pointless, he said. 'What I keep trying to say is that the audience is not stupid, to say that we are Serbs and at war is self-evident.' Milan Šećerović, a screenwriter from Belgrade, took a rather harder line: 'This is a time when you need to take a stand.' This did not mean taking a stand on the most fundamental issues, though, such as the rights and wrongs of the war itself, because these were either seen as givens or not the topics you addressed on TV-Pale. Real issues had to be looked at rather more obliquely. Slaviša, one of *Naked Life*'s central characters, is a sophisticated economist from Sarajevo who has escaped to come and live with his conservative parents in Pale. When his girlfriend also escapes from the city his parents refuse to let her move in because they are not married. Slaviša, who does not want to fight, is tormented by his all-action war hero brother. 'Many of us wanted to stay, but did not want to go to the frontline . . . on any side,' said Milanović, himself a sophisticated former Sarajevan who lived with his parents in Pale. Any resemblance to real life was not coincidental.

Before leaving Sarajevo, Milanović had been the manager of its Chamber Theatre 55. 'We produced the last anti-nationalist play before the war,' he said. *Division* by Bosnian Muslim writer Skender Kulenović was written in 1946 and had been banned by the communists. All Bosnia's nationalist leaders were invited to the opening night. As Serbs, Muslims and Croats squabbled on stage, television cameras managed to catch the faces of the politicians in the audience, framed behind the actors. 'Fiction met reality,' sighed Milanović.

12

The Madmen Take Over the Asylum

Bosnia was shattered, madness reigned and in the asylum the doctors envied the patients. This was how it was at the height of the war. In one of the cruellest but least noticed episodes of ethnic cleansing, Serbian forces closed in on Sarajevo's City Psychiatric Hospital, shelled it and then told the patients to get out or die. Despite the shooting, the patients left and wandered the few miles into town. No one knew what happened to those who were left behind. The only place that could be found to house the patients who had escaped was a kindergarten.

It was a world turned upside down. They sat on tiny chairs, the walls were adorned with giant murals of dancing bunnies and musical grasshoppers, and the bathrooms were equipped with miniature toilets. The patients had no beds, so they slept on mattresses on the floor. In a corner one of them had built a shrine. It comprised a box adorned with seashells, a medal of Lenin, a portrait of Tito and a book of Islamic teachings. 'Why not?' shrugged psychiatrist Dr Ferhid Mujanović, 'it's all strange here, nothing is normal.' The location of Serbian positions, on the top of nearby green and pleasant hills, could be seen from the windows.

'I am your mother,' said a toothless old woman from Foča, an eastern Bosnian town brutally cleansed in 1992. 'They only want to go home,' said Mujanović. 'One of them tried to go to [Serb-held] Ilijaš. He passed through our lines and theirs. No one knows how. They could see he was mad. He kicked a Chetnik [Serbian soldier] in the arse and they sent him back. Most of them know what is going on but there is not the emotional effect. Sometimes I think it's better for them than it is for us.' Mujanović had a much more profound observation, however. He had discovered that far from aggravating their condition the war had made his patients better: 'I think they have had some improvement. Symptoms seen before the war have gone down. By contrast normal people have got worse. It's bizarre, a paradox, but that's the effect.'

In a few years' time psychiatrists will be churning out books on the effects of the war in Bosnia. While the most numerous will be on worthy subjects such as post-traumatic stress syndrome in children, the more interesting will be the ones that follow up Mujanović's line of enquiry, especially the extreme cases. The most important question will be how apparently normal people suddenly became mass murderers, subjecting their former neighbours to incredible tortures before killing them. If they choose not to pass over the topic, it will also be interesting to read their thoughts on how a working psychiatrist, Radovan Karadžić, came to preside over the Serbian side.

Bosanski Novi and the Spare Ribs

At the beginning of the war in Bosnia, the world media concentrated on Sarajevo, with the result that extraordinary and dreadful things took place in the rest of the country, especially in the areas that the SDS was seizing for itself. Slowly rumours began to circulate about camps and killings on all sides, but with no way of confirming these stories they were given neither particular credence nor priority. Gradually the truth began to emerge.

In the early hours of 24 July 1992, some 7,000 people expelled from the northern town of Bosanski Novi and packed on to UN trucks streamed into the Croatian town of Karlovac. For the first time it became possible to build up a picture of what was happening in zones that had been either impossible or too dangerous to reach. Mostly Muslims, they had fled from a reign of terror, murder and madness. Their tales confirmed the most chilling of rumours seeping out of inaccessible parts of Bosnia.

While the town of Bosanski Novi had a slight Serbian majority, power was firmly in the hands of the SDS because Serbs constituted 60 per cent of the whole district's population. As the republic slipped into war the local authorities secured military power by mobilising the TO, a call which Muslims boycotted. The police force was purged after Muslim policemen refused to wear the new Serbian insignia. Because most people with guns and hunting rifles had permits, the authorities were able to collect these weapons, thus disarming any potential Muslim resistance.

The ethnic purification of Bosanski Novi took place in two waves. In May, as the war started in earnest, the people of eleven Muslim villages near the town were rounded up at gunpoint and herded into one village. There, crammed thirty to a house, they were kept for eighteen days. They were then forced onto freight trains, men in the back wagons, women and children in the front ones. 'As this was happening they fired on the crowds,' said Emsuda Krilić, aged thirty-seven. 'We saw thirty or forty dead.' There were up to 300 in each wagon. There was no food or water for four days. 'You crouch, you faint, you come to, you faint,' said Namka Ekić, aged thirty-one, whose baby was fifteen days old at the time. Her sister Arifa Ekić said that they knew the men who had forced them on to the trains: 'They were our school friends and Serbian neighbours. They said they had been threatened with death if they did not drive us out. I don't believe them, they are all the same.' According to the Ekić sisters, at one point some girls of about eighteen and nineteen years of age had been taken off the trains, ostensibly to fetch water. They were not seen again. After five days travelling the men were sent back and imprisoned in Bosanski Novi's sports stadium. The women and children were then expelled to Croatia.

At the same time as people were being driven from the villages, a slow but steady reign of terror began in the town itself. 'At first we just sensed things,' said Samir, a young musician, '. . . then people were arrested and accused of wanting to blow up the bridge. Then they switched our television reception from Sarajevo to Belgrade.'

On 2 June anti-tank weapons were used to destroy the town's two mosques. A well-known local Serbian mafia called the Spare Ribs donned uniforms and quickly gained a reputation as the most brutal of five Serbian armed groups now roaming town. At an increasing tempo Muslim-owned cafés, shops and restaurants were blown up during the night and houses were sprayed with bullets. An outlying suburb was shelled and houses burned down by men in camouflage uniforms. 'There was not so much killing,' said Samir, 'it was just that no one knew what was happening a hundred metres away.' The town was festooned with Serbian flags. Serbian property was not touched. The police began to make sweeps, raiding homes and arresting able-bodied Muslim men. Almost all of the men who arrived in Karlovac that night said that they had spent up to five days imprisoned in the sports stadium. Numbers there ranged up to 1,000 at any one time. Abdelhaid Dautović, aged twenty-three, said:

> There were sixty rounded up in my group. They fired into the air as they pushed us onto the bus. When we got there we were made to kneel with our hands behind our necks. They beat the older ones who could not do this with their rifles butts. We got tea and salami once a day and we slept in the shower and locker rooms by night. Everyone went to the toilet, one by one, once a day. After a couple of days the guards asked for volunteers for their army. About 150 went. They did it to protect their families.

The pattern was that after five days most people were released. Meanwhile Muslims were sacked from their jobs and, with armed Serbs patrolling the streets, people hid indoors. There was a curfew, there was no electricity and all normal life collapsed. While ordinary men passed through the stadium, local dignitaries, politicians and businessmen were taken to the Hotel Una, the headquarters of the military police. 'I was kept for five days with a group of nine in the basement,' said a trade union leader. 'I was blindfolded when they took me to the third floor for interrogation.' Prisoners were beaten. A few days before the men were expelled to Croatia, a group was seen being marched into the hotel carrying broken oars. 'They were ordered to bash the person in front if he looked around,' said an eyewitness. In one two-week period corpses floated down the River Sana. 'First there was one, then fifteen minutes later a couple more,' said Dautović.

In a bid to survive, people began to sell their possessions at knock-down prices. The going rate for a video recorder was £30. Asked if he thought local Serbs were ashamed to buy in such circumstances, Samir said, 'They couldn't wait to get their hands on the stuff, they set the prices.' Armed gangs robbed houses and businesses. One group forced a man to sell his successful café at a nominal price or die. Everyone who came out that night could name people who had 'disappeared' or worse. A biologist and former Muslim mayor, Hamdia Ekić, was gunned down in the street 'as he went to get an asthma spray for his child', said one man.

On 15 July notices were posted on the town hall announcing that buses would be leaving for Croatia. Having been suitably softened up, non-Serbs queued for up to fourteen hours to get their permissions to leave. The municipality extended working hours to process this cleansing operation. Many were granted permission to leave only after signing their property over to the local authorities. Others scoffed, saying they had not had to do this as it had already been seized. Then, the final indignity, those in flight for their lives had to pay for their bus tickets. The buses took them to a rendezvous point where the cleansed were decanted into UN trucks.

The UNHCR had briefly agonised about doing this sort of job. Some argued that, by agreeing to help Muslims and Croats leave, the UN would become an accomplice to Serbian ethnic cleansing. Bosanski Novi was a relatively civilised affair, however. By this time it was becoming clear that far worse things were happening, that psychopaths as opposed to brutal political extremists were on the loose. In these circumstances, saving lives was the priority. Debates on the ethics of the matter faded into the background.

The Banality of Evil?

What happened in Bosanski Novi was happening all over territory claimed by the SDS. There were killings, people were rounded up, non-Serbs were sacked and there was fighting where Muslims and Croats managed to raise some resistance. The pattern was that soon after the seizure of power in any given region camps were opened and, again after a certain period, the inmates were expelled to government-controlled territory, or to Croatia or to Serbia. In the latter case the authorities obliged during the early days of the war by laying on trains to take the non-Serb deportees to the Hungarian border. Within Serb-held Bosnia there were massacres, scores of Serbian groups were out of control and rape was widespread. The effect was that within weeks of the outbreak of fighting the Serbs had consolidated control over wide areas of the republic, except for various enclaves where their power had been resisted. The most important of these lay in the east, in hilltop Srebrenica and riverside Goražde.

The camps had two purposes. First, they were used to intern men of fighting age, and local leaderships, to prevent any resistance from forming. Secondly, they were designed to intimidate non-Serbs into leaving Bosnia. That there was a rough plan which was being followed is clear from the fact that across Serb-held territory the organisation of round-ups and camps was much the same. According to a pains-takingly detailed UN study:

> Reports suggest a common method of initial apprehension and identifi-
> cation of those non-Serbs detained for ultimate disposition (either
> long-term detention, deportation, or execution). A common plan is also
> suggested by the implementation of a system whereby prisoners were
> detained, classified, and subjected to similar types of abuse (e.g., it was
> often regularly reported that intellectuals, politicians, police, and the
> wealthy were regularly tortured and killed in certain camps). There is
> also a similarity in the command and control of the camps, whereby
> there was a mix of civilian, political, JNA, paramilitary, and local Serb
> reservists and civilians involved in camp operations. With regard to
> practical aspects of camp operation, large suitable facilities appear to
> have been selected and prepared, to some extent, in advance. Whether a
> plan was established by the military, police, or politicians, is something
> that could not be ascertained.[1]

The authors could have written that who participated in what meetings to make what plans had not *yet* been ascertained. Such information is bound to seep out sooner or later. In the meantime there is enough evidence, sometimes provided by Serbian boasts, that, chaotic and brutal though the initial cleansing campaign was, there was a good measure of organisation. Simo Drljača, the Prijedor police chief who was one of those responsible for cleansing the Kozarac area and for organising the most infamous of the camps, Keraterm and Omarska, told the local newspaper:

They [the police force, including the secret services] carried out my orders and the orders of the CSB [the Public Security Centre] Banja Luka and the Minister of Interior.

The cooperation was excellent with the Army of the Republika Srpska and with the officers of that army. The cooperation was manifested in the joint cleansing of the terrain of traitors, joint work at the check-points, a joint intervention group against disturbances of public order and in fighting terrorist groups.[2]

The question of if and when the JNA ever ceased to be involved in the Bosnian conflict is a vexed one. A programme had been instituted to transfer Bosnian Serb JNA officers and men who were not actually serving in Bosnia back to their home republic. Thus by the spring of 1992 the vast majority of JNA troops in Bosnia were Serbs. This was because other nationalities were leaving the army or were no longer responding to call-ups. Although as the war broke out there were some tensions between Bosnian Serb militias and the JNA, because it was seen to be transporting to Serbia a lot of heavy military and military–industrial equipment, what was to become the Bosnian Serb Army was simply that part of the JNA which remained in the republic. Only some time after the fighting had begun, however, was its creation publicly mooted. This came as the JNA announced that it would leave Bosnia by mid-May. Just before this happened Ratko Mladić, the commander of the JNA's Knin garrison, was transferred to Sarajevo. Shortly afterwards he became the first head of the new Bosnian Serb Army.

Although Mladić became a hero to his men, his war was a coward's war. He fought few pitched battles but managed to drive hundreds of thousands of unarmed people out of their homes. How autonomous his military were seems to have depended on the political climate between Pale and Belgrade, but there is little doubt that, especially at first, his army was simply an adjunct of the JNA. Indeed, while ordinary men fought unpaid, the Yugoslav Ministry of Defence continued to pay the salaries of its former officers if they had transferred to the Bosnian Serb Army. As General Kadijević wrote, 'The command and units of the JNA were the spine of the army of the RS complete with arms and equipment. That army, fully leaning on the Serbian people . . . protected the Serbian people and created military suppositions for a political solution which will be adequate for the national interests and aims if . . . of course the international situation allows this.'[3]

Mladić is often described in caricature terms as a ruddy-cheeked soldier's soldier. In fact he was certainly much more than that. Miloš Vasić, a military commentator for the Belgrade magazine *Vreme*, was fond of saying 'He was a fine officer and great organiser . . . he went mad in the meantime.' There seems to be a good deal of truth to this. While Serbian politicians were fond of ranting about the Islamic fundamentalist–Vatican–Austro-Hungarian–German plot to destroy Serbdom, there is nothing to suggest that they truly believed much of this nonsense. Mladić was different: 'Regardless of what we decide, the west will continue to implement its infernal plan. What is at stake is an attempt to disunite the Orthodox world, and even annihilate it.'[4] From the way he talked, fixing his interlocutor with his piercing eyes, it was clear that Mladić not only believed this sort of thing but also believed that the survival of the Serbs depended on a fight to the death in which no quarter should be given. For him everything was black and white and, without a trace of cynicism, he was a true crusader for the cause. In this, perhaps, he could feel that he was following in the footsteps of his Partisan father, who had died during the last war while raiding the birthplace of Ante Pavelić. Compromise was not a word in Mladić's vocabulary. If mass killing and the burning of villages was good enough for Karadjordje, it was good enough for his men.

Mladić revelled in his power over life and death. In 1993 convoys of women, children and elderly were permitted to leave besieged Srebrenica, cross Serb-held territory and go to Muslim-held Tuzla. As they checked the UNHCR trucks which were transporting the people, Mladić's soldiers found a man who was trying to smuggle his way through. He was brought before Mladić and the senior UNHCR official present. Mladić asked him some questions and then told the man he could go free. Smiling, he told the representative of UNHCR, 'I want you to see that I have given this man back his life.' In 1995 he was to order, or at least condone, the massacre of thousands of men who had remained trapped inside Srebrenica. It never seemed to occur to him that 1992 was not 1804 or even 1941 and that what was deemed acceptable practice in war had changed, if only because such behaviour did your cause more harm than good in a world of satellites and television news.

The question of the mental stability of the Bosnian Serb civilian leadership is also of vital importance. Brutal as it may have been to round up hundreds of thousands of people and expel them from their homes, it does not necessarily make the instigators active organisers of the deaths of thousands in camps or in mass executions – though of course it may indicate an evil side to their characters. But as political leaders they were liable, because they must very soon have known what was happening. Thus their guilt lies in letting events repeat themselves, worst of all in the Srebrenica massacre of 1995. However, it is just possible that in the first weeks after the camps had been set up they were ignorant of the full extent of what was taking place in some of them. This is, of course, a charitable view, but it is hard to square people who may be individually charming one moment with men or women ordering mass murders the next. On the other hand, we know that the commandant of Auschwitz went home to his wife and children after a day at work. So, until such time as they come to trial or the details of their involvement are revealed in some other fashion, the question must remain unanswered.

What is possible is that Karadžić and the other top Serbian leaders simply closed their eyes to the horrors that were happening after they had given orders for such and such an area to be 'pacified'. In this way they could perhaps excuse mass murder as the excesses of groups out of their direct control. They could also sleep easily, deluding themselves that the orders they had given sanctioned nothing more or less than could be expected in wartime and in a region with vivid, reawakened and inflamed memories of the last war. If this is the case then one is forced to recall the words of Draža Mihailović at his trial in 1946. When asked about the massacres in Sandžak and eastern Bosnia he said that he knew that the commander in question wanted to 'settle accounts' there 'but I never thought he would clear it up in this way'.[5]

The massacres, both inside the camps and outside, were obviously a disaster for the victims but in a more abstract sense they were a catastrophe for the Serbs too. From the moment of their discovery, all lingering doubts in the international community about whether all sides in the war were guilty or not were driven into the background. The Serbs were branded as the aggressors and as the Balkan successors to the Nazis. Of course, on a far smaller and less dramatic scale Serbian villages which fell behind enemy lines were cleansed too, although the government side was at least publicly pledged to support a multi-ethnic Bosnia. Likewise Serbs were tortured by Croats and Muslims but it was never possible, after the enormity of the crimes committed by Serbian groups, to get this message across. On the international stage, the fact that children suffered and may have died in Belgrade because there were no more medicines for leukaemia made little impression when hundreds of children were dying as a result of Serbian shells in Sarajevo. The Serbian authorities also made little or no attempt, unlike their enemies, to find Serbian victims from Muslim or Croatian camps to bear witness to their experiences. This was arrogance, which cost them dearly in the battle for international public opinion being waged in the world press.

In August 1992 Karadžić was firmly denying that there were Bosnian Serb concentration camps rather than internment or POW camps. In a bid to quash the rumours of killings and mass murder, he authorised a small number of journalists to visit Omarska near Prijedor. Simo Drljača, the Prijedor police chief, was furious. The conditions there were appalling and he knew what the journalists would see. The implication is that Karadžić himself did not know what had happened there, otherwise why would he let journalists in? Whatever Karadžić knew or had hoped, it was a public relations disaster and within days a massive clean-up operation began. Most of the camps were closed down and their inmates shipped out of Bosnian Serb territory, where they could talk freely of the hell they had endured.

In the interview quoted above, Simo Drljača made clear that everything that happened in his region was organised by the police, which came under the Ministry of Interior in Pale and General Mladić's newly formed army. Although in Bosanski Novi and many other places there had not been large-scale killing, it was now revealed that in a number of other places such as Prijedor, Brčko and Bratunac not only had there been an orgy of murder but real psychopaths were rampaging across the countryside indulging in cruel, bizarre and sadistic killings. It is inconceivable that General Mladić did not know what was going on.

Several years after the event, the accounts of the survivors of the cleansing of Kozarac and the tortures of Omarska, Keraterm and Brčko, (where bodies were disposed of in an animal-feed plant) make grim reading.[6] Kozarac was a town of some 20,000 people, mostly Muslims, which lay on the road between Banja Luka and Prijedor. To permit Serbian freedom of movement along this vital road, it had to be subjugated. At the end of May 1992 police, Serbian army units, militias and TO forces surrounded it, pounded it with artillery and then interned most of the population. It was one of the largest single cleansing operations until Srebrenica fell in July 1995. There is little point in going into extensive detail about what happened in all of these places in 1992, because this would simply be a catalogue of hundreds and thousands of gruesome and insane acts of barbarism which have been well collated elsewhere. A few examples will suffice. The UN-appointed Commission of Experts compiled thousands of pages of documents on all the atrocities that took place during the wars in Croatia and Bosnia and has archives of individual testimonies of survivors of some of the worst places and incidents. Typical of its dry prose is the following from a survivor of Omarska:

One subject reported that each night the guards at the camp would select 10–20 prisoners, beat them up, and then shoot them with pistols. He said that on the following morning, the [surviving] prisoners would have to get up early to load the bodies on a 'Combi' truck. The subject was not sure where the bodies were taken. Another subject estimated that on many occasions, 20–40 prisoners were killed at night by 'knife, hammer and burning'. He stated that he had witnessed the killing of one prisoner by seven guards who poured petrol on him, set him on fire and struck him upon the head with a hammer. The subject reported that there were about 100 such killings at the camp. He stated that the intelligentsia of the camp were selected first for killing.[7]

During the Second World War a dreadful massacre of Serbs had taken place at Omarska, which was a Serbian village. Today the area is part of an iron-ore mining complex and as such has several large hangars. In 1992 hundreds of prisoners were crammed into them, sardine style, and were then called out for questioning, beating, torture and execution. Hundreds were certainly killed there, if not thousands. If this was revenge for 1941, it was done on a grand scale. The name of Omarska has become synonymous with the evil committed during the summer of 1992 because it was one of the largest camps. However, people also died in small and anonymous places. Asim Behrem, a labourer who had been held in the small town of Ripač, described, soon after he had been exchanged for Serbian prisoners in Bihać, how he had been held for fifteen days with his hands tied with wire:

> They did not let us sleep and they beat us. They kept asking whether there were weapons in our village and where they were. . . . One day a crazed guard tried to throw a hand grenade at us but he was restrained by the others. Then he was drunk and he started calling for someone he was at school with because he wanted to kill him. Then he just shot the man who was eating next to me in the back of the neck.

As other refugees from the same village wept silently, Behrem slumped over the table to demonstrate how the man next to him had died. 'Then he keeled over on to the floor. The guard was arrested, but he came back a few days later.'

A woman from another part of north-west Bosnia who had been kept in a primary school and had been exchanged for a Serbian army officer trembled as she described how she had been hit in the face by guards and how they had stamped on her feet: 'My husband was next to me, he shook like a reed as they did this to me. We thought they would execute us. You just cannot imagine the fear. He was a teacher and many of the guards had been his pupils. Some of them got very bad marks so they made him wear a woman's wig. They beat him every day.'

The woman was desperate because her husband had not been exchanged with her and remained behind. The terror and the insanity that spread across Serb-held parts of Bosnia was palpable. This was not a well-organised Nazi sweep or a Stalinesque deportation of whole nations but a ham-fisted Balkan attempt at the same thing. Through the summer of 1992 there was both method in the madness which ruled in Bosnian Serb territories and also utter chaos and lawlessness. Whole towns such as Kozarac or little Pudin Han were simply wiped from the map. Other communities were just told to hang out white flags and wait.

Ališići, just outside Prijedor, was one such Muslim village. Its residents had hung out pillow cases, vests, rags and sheets to signify that they were ready to go without a fight. 'They said if we did this then everything would be okay,' said Hamdija. His family's bags were packed. The whole village was waiting to leave. On 25 July Serbian troops had raidedAlišići. Cars, tractors, jewellery and money were stolen. Fifteen men, chosen at random, had been hauled off to the camps. MedihaAlišić, a thirty-two-year-old woman with two children had been shot dead in her home. 'We found her here,' said her brother Ahmet, pointing at the bloodstain on the sitting-room carpet. The house was dusty because nobody lived in it any longer. Mrs Ališić's big doll still sat on the sofa. Spent bullet cartridges were produced. No one really knew how she died. 'They were drunk,' said Ahmet. 'There was a lot of firing in the air. How can we know? She was alone in the house and dead lips don't speak.'

Because the village cemetery was beside the road, the villagers had not dared bury Mediha there in case they were shot at by Serbs in passing cars. They buried her behind the mosque, which had failed to burn when a Molotov cocktail had been tossed inside. On the village notice board the Serbian authorities had pinned a little typed-up announcement which read, 'The citizens ofAlišići are ordered . . . not to leave their village. Three people can go for supplies to Oštra Luka once a day between 7.00–10.00. They should go to the checkpoint by the school.' Oštra Luka was the Serbian village next door. Before the war the people of the two villages did everything together – weddings, funerals and football matches. WhileAlišići lived in terror in August 1992 it was clear that at least some of the people of Oštra Luka passed that summer in the grip of some form of collective insanity. Perhaps they had to believe the most bizarre of tales in order to justify to themselves what they were doing to their neighbours. Darko, a young policeman from Oštra Luka, claimed, 'We captured documents and lists that prove what the Muslims were going to do to the Serbs here. We found hermetically sealed boxes that they were going to put our kidneys and hearts in which they were going to send to Germany and France in exchange for tanks.'

Kozarac and the Prijedor region had seen some of the worst massacres and deportations of Serbs during the Second World War. This certainly explains some of the Serbian passion for 'never again' which they manifested that summer, but it does not explain how they simply suspended all critical faculties. Needless to say, Darko had never seen the purported documents and hermetically sealed boxes, but such beliefs were widespread and broadcast widely by the Bosnian Serb media. After these areas had been more or less cleansed, the war turned into a far more classical affair of trenches and frontlines. This part of the conflict did not require much thought or justification. Soldiers were in the army, they fired at an enemy they could not see and who was firing back and so emotions were no longer intimately involved.

One of those who had organised the cleansing of the Prijedor region and the setting up and running of Omarska was Dr Milan Kovačević. In 1996 he was director of Prijedor hospital. Like many of those who came to power in 1992 he had had some form of personal experience of the last war; he had been born in Jasenovac. In an extraordinary interview he said:

> We knew very well what happened at Auschwitz and Dachau, and we knew very well how it started and how it was done. What we did was not the same as Auschwitz or Dachau, but it was a mistake. It was planned to have a camp for people, but not a concentration camp. Omarska was planned as a reception centre. . . . But then it turned into something else. I cannot explain the loss of control. I don't think even the historians will find an explanation in the next 50 years. You could call it collective madness.

He added that he had left politics because 'I saw many bad things. This is my personal secret. Things did not turn out the way I planned. If you have to do things by killing people, well . . . Now my hair is white. I don't sleep so well.'[8]

While the ethnic cleansing of the non-Serbs was part planned and part madness, it also had elements of 'the banality of evil'. This was the subtitle of Hannah Arendt's famous book on the trial of Adolf Eichmann, the consummate civil servant who organised a large part of the Nazi holocaust against the Jews. In Prijedor the civil servant who executed the bureaucratic part of the cleansing plan was Slavko Budimir, the 'Secretary of People's Defence'. Women and children would queue outside his office and he would sign the papers which they hoped would enable them to get their menfolk out of the camps. Their forms also requested permission to leave the district after they had signed over their property to the municipality. Despite the terror and the reality of the situation the bureaucrat Budimir was prepared to indulge in a little fantasy for the sake of well-kept files. He said that 3,000 people, mostly Muslims, had applied to leave the region in the last few days of July and the first ten days of August 1992. With a bulging folder before him he said, 'We have no right to stop anyone who wants to go. All these forms say they want to go for "material" reasons. After all there is not much work to do around here.'

After being pressed a little he admitted that 'insecurity and psychosis' might also have something to do with it. Clearly confused in front of foreigners, he also tried to claim that nobody was being detained. At the time, as the world reeled from the revelations about Omarska and the camps that had been set up by the Bosnian Serb authorities, a UN War Crimes Tribunal was now being mooted. Rather alarmed, Budimir said, 'Look, all this has to do with forces over my head. There is no reason for anyone to leave, nor do I support this.'

Of all the women queuing outside Budimir's office only one was brave enough to take visitors to meet Muslim men released from the camps and living in fear before their expulsion from Prijedor. She was a Serb called Mira. Through all the documents and testimonies of all of the crimes committed in Bosnia there is a constant refrain that a small group of Serbs were willing to help their Muslim and Croat neighbours. Tens of thousands of Serbs, especially the educated and better off, fled from towns like Banja Luka because they did not want to take part in the war. The insanity then was not total. Others who also did not believe in the cause did not or could not flee. If they actually chose to help Muslims or Croats, though, their lives were as much at risk as those of the persecuted. Mira, aged twenty, was married to a Muslim, which was why she too was in the line to get papers to have him released from a camp and leave. She said her brother in Banja Luka had been shot, 'because he refused to put on a Serbian uniform'. Her brother-in-law, Esad, who had survived Omarska, said that a small number of Serbs had also been detained in the camp: 'One was a friend of mine. The story was that he had been smuggling arms to Muslims. I saw him once and after that I did not see him again. His [Serb] girlfriend was also there and she said, "Igor has been killed." I think he was beaten to death.'

In the reports of the UN Commission of Experts there are also brief mentions of Serbs who were murdered by their fellows for refusing to participate in orgies of killing or similar outrages. Gradually, over the next few years, their stories will begin to be told as will those of Serbs who sheltered Muslims or Croats and helped them to escape without taking financial advantage of their situation – which was common enough.

It may be asked why in the Bosnian Serb-held territories more individuals did not take a stand to prevent massacres, rapes or executions. It is a legitimate question, but one which fails to grasp the sheer terror of those times and the fact that many of the most sadistic killings were done by dangerous men who, according to many testimonies, had been on extended drinking binges. There is no more eloquent answer to the question than testimony cited by Hannah Arendt of one Peter Bamm, a German Army doctor who gave his account of the murder of Jews in Sebastopol during the Second World War. They were killed in mobile gas vans by SS units and the corpses were then dumped into ditches. He said:

> We knew this. We did nothing. Anyone who had seriously protested or
> done anything against the killing unit would have been arrested within
> twenty-four hours and would have disappeared. It belongs among the
> refinements of totalitarian governments in our century that they don't
> permit their opponents to die a great, dramatic martyr's death for their
> convictions. A good deal of us might have accepted such a death. The
> totalitarian state lets its opponents disappear in silent anonymity. It is
> certain that anyone who had dared to suffer death rather than silently
> tolerate the crime would have sacrificed his life in vain. This is not to say
> that such a sacrifice would have been morally meaningless. It would
> only have been practically useless. None of us had a conviction so deeply
> rooted that we could have taken upon ourselves a practically useless sac-
> rifice for the sake of a higher moral meaning.[9]

Why so little was said or done in Serbia itself, however, remains
another question. Not only were people disoriented but, brought up
with an heroic image of themselves as the people who had opposed
fascism, unlike the Croats, they simply refused to believe the most
appalling camp stories. Naturally they were not reported on Serbian
television, but anyone who wanted to could listen to foreign radio
stations, read the small independent press and follow, at least in
Belgrade, independent television and radio and thereby gain a fair idea
of what was going on. But the fact that Serbs were in flight from Croatia
and government-held parts of Bosnia and that some of them had been
in their camps too confused people. If they did not deny stories, then an
equivalence was made. A courageous band of individuals at *Vreme*
magazine, in the human rights group the Humanitarian Law Fund, in
the intellectual Belgrade Circle and among the protesting Women in
Black did what they could. In the end, however, they failed to rouse the
righteous indignation of people who increasingly came to be concerned
with how to feed their family rather than with the latest horror story
from Bosnia. Precisely because they were singularly ineffectual,
Milošević allowed these groups to continue their work. If they had had
any influence outside middle-class Belgrade they would have been
swiftly outlawed. As it was they unwittingly served the regime because
it could use their existence as a figleaf enabling it to claim that Serbia
was not an authoritarian state but a true democracy. Asked whether he
thought that after the war there would be a great soul-searching in
Serbia just as there had been after the war in Germany, Belgrade
University psychology professor Žarko Korać said, 'No, it will be like
Austria. Either people will say "we did not know" or they will justify
everything by saying "we only did to them what they did to us".'

26 The Chetnik leader General Draža Mihailović (*right*), a Montenegrin Chetnik (*centre*) and Colonel Bill Hudson, the British liaison officer attached to Mihailović's forces (*left*), 1942.

27 Partisans in Belgrade. Off to the front, 1945.

28 Tito holds it together, 1954.

29 Serbian police beating an Albanian, Kosovo, 1989.

30 1988: rising agitation. Kosovo Serbs march
on Belgrade to protest against the 'unbearable
condition of the Serb nation in Kosovo'.

31 Dobrica Ćosić, novelist and nationalist, arrives by taxi for his inauguration as President of the new Yugoslavia of just Serbia and Montenegro, 15 June 1992. He is greeted by Mihalj Kertes, one of Milošević's right-hand men.

32 Serbs gathered for the Kosovo anniversary celebrations, with a priest and a banner of Lazar, 28 June 1989.

33 Bosnian Serb leader Radovan Karadžić, Muslim Alija Izetbegović and Croat Stjepan Kljuić meeting after the first multi-party elections in Bosnia in 1990. From the wall Tito looks down on them.

34 Elderly civilians cower with soldiers under a JNA tank during early battles of the war in eastern Slavonia, 1991.

35 Dubrovnik in the JNA's sights, 1991.

36 A JNA unit deserting the front in eastern Slavonia, 1991.

37 1994: Fikret Abdić, Bosnian Muslim businessman and rebel, with Krajina President Milan Martić.

38 Serbian soldier looking down on Sarajevo from Mount Trebević, summer 1993.

39 Radovan Karadžić and General Ratko Mladić, January 1993.

40 Idol to a generation of young gangsters:
Aleksandar Knežević or 'Knele' who died in
Room 331 of Belgrade's Hyatt Hotel in
March 1992.

41 Gangster, politician, secret service agent 'Arkan' marries 'turbofolk' star, singer Ceca, Belgrade, February, 1995.

42 March 1993: Dafina Milanović invited the press into the vaults of her bank in an attempt to prove it was not collapsing. It was.

43 Warning to a generation: detail from the Niš tower of skulls built with Serbian heads by the Turks in 1809.

44 A photo of Serbian heads found by their comrades when they raided a Mujahedin base in northern Bosnia in 1993.

45 Best of friends? Serbian President Slobodan Milošević and Croatian President Franjo
Tudjman shake hands, 1991.

46 Serbs leaving the former Serb-held suburbs of Sarajevo for Pale and other parts of Bosnia, March 1996.

47 Serbian refugee from the Krajina in theČačak collective
centre, Serbia, October 1995.

48 Making way: Croats, expelled from Banja Luka by Serbs in flight from Krajina, arriving in Croatia after crossing the Sava river, August 1995.

No One Will Harm You!

By the end of 1992 the Republika Srpska covered some 70 per cent of Bosnia. From then until the summer of 1995, despite constant skirmishing and fighting, the frontlines moved very little. Within Bosnian Serb territory, ethnic cleansing of the remaining Muslims and Croats continued, but it was desultory – a couple of hundred expelled here or exchanged there or individuals murdered by the drunken friends of those who had just lost comrades at the front. Serb refugees would also commandeer houses of Muslims or Croats. Almost all mosques, including the historic ones, were dynamited and sometimes grassed over as if to pretend that they had never been there. There were many dramatic periods but nothing quite as convulsive as the summer of 1992. That is, until the fall of Srebrenica.

What had happened in 1992 was already so bad that it triggered the great powers into setting up the International Criminal Tribunal for the Former Yugoslavia. Based in The Hague, it was the first international war crimes court since the ones which had tried top Nazis and Japanese leaders after the Second World War. Its existence was well known throughout the former Yugoslavia, and it was frequently discussed in the media. That most of those indicted were Serbs, however, did not lead the Serbs to the conclusion that their side had committed more crimes but rather reinforced their prejudice that the whole world was against them. Nobody knows whether the existence of the court had any effect in changing or moderating behaviour on any side, but it was not enough to prevent the greatest single massacre and manhunt of the war. This was the execution of several thousand Muslims – the precise figure is as yet unknown – following the fall of Srebrenica. Judge Fouad Riad, who reviewed the indictments of Karadžić and Mladić issued from The Hague as a result of the killings, said, 'These are truly scenes from hell, written on the darkest pages of human history.'[10]

Despite the fact that Srebrenica had been declared a UN 'safe area', Bosnian Serb forces began an all-out drive to capture it on 6 July 1995. As a result as many as 12,000 people, mostly men, formed a twelve-kilometre-long column to try and march the seventy kilometres to government-held territory. Survivors claimed that no more than half of those who attempted to flee made it to safety. One of them recalled a particularly harrowing moment:

> We arrived close to a road. The Serbs were waiting for us. They had gathered some buses full of civilians from Srebrenica. They passed them the loud hailers so that they could beg us to surrender. Soldiers heard their wives imploring them. We were 500 metres away and there was nothing we could do. Some cried, others threw down their rifles and

surrendered. One of my friends committed suicide.[11]

Summary executions followed, often after the Muslims had been ordered to dig their own graves. It has also been alleged that at one point the fleeing men were attacked with shells containing hallucinogenic gases which led some to kill each other believing that they were Serbs.[12] The accounts of the survivors are among the worst of the war. Some who lived to tell the tale survived under piles of bodies and managed to flee as night fell – a tale reminiscent of the darkest days of the Second World War.

Thousands who did not try to flee across country gathered at a Dutch UN base hoping for protection. Bosnian Serb soldiers surrounded it and at first seemed friendly enough. As cameras were present they gave out sweets to the children, and General Mladić himself is recorded telling the people, 'No one will harm you!' Mladić wanted the people out of the base. Sixty buses arrived which were to take the women, children and elderly to Tuzla. Men from the ages of seventeen to sixty, however, were separated from their families and executed. While there have been a number of testimonies of survivors from some of the Srebrenica massacres, they have also produced one other extraordinary testament. That is the confession of one of the soldiers who claimed to have participated in the shooting of some 1,200 men picked up by the Serbs from the UN base.

Dražen Erdemović was, unusually, a Croat from Tuzla who had come to the Serb side after being arrested in the city in 1993 for helping Serbs flee. Once in the Republika Srpska he had been drafted into the army and later became a member of a commando unit which was one of those sent in to execute men from Srebrenica. After this he had quarrelled, apparently for quite unrelated reasons, with his commander, who had tried to have him killed and then had him expelled from his home. Seemingly driven by vengeance and by the need to escape his former boss, Erdemović claimed that he had contacted the court in The Hague and come to a deal. He would testify in exchange for immunity from prosecution and for the guarantee that he and his family could settle in a western country. Erdemović eventually got to The Hague where he was sentenced to ten years', but only after his arrest by the Serbian police and strong international pressure on President Milošević to send him there. Hours before his arrest, though, he recounted his tale to Renaud Girard of the French newspaper *Le Figaro*.[13] He said that the Muslims were brought by bus to their execution site and then led out in groups of ten. After the first group had been shot, the second realised what was going to happen to them:

> They began to beg us: 'Don't kill us! Our families in Austria will send you money!'

At one moment I whispered to one of my comrades, a Croat like me, 'God knows how this is going to come back on us one day!' He said: 'Shut up and shoot! Otherwise you know very well it will be our turn to be killed. We're only Croats.'

Brano [the unit commander] and his mates were guzzling down more and more cognac. They had become mad. They hit the Muslims with iron bars. When they knocked one out, they got the others to carry him to the execution place. To speed things up Brano decided to use the machine gun. But it was not very professional: the bursts of fire wounded rather than killing straight off. The wounded begged us to finish them off. So, Stanko Sovanović, a friend of Brano, came and fired a bullet in their heads with his revolver. Afterwards he boasted that he used up 700 bullets.

According to Erdemović's account, the massacre was well organised, and all those who participated were regular soldiers of the Bosnian Serb Army. The Serbian bus drivers were terrified, but Erdemović claimed that in a bid to make sure that none of them would ever be tempted to bear witness they were each made to shoot at least one Muslim. 'A Muslim of about fifty came up to me to explain that he had helped about twenty Serbs escape from Srebrenica. So that I could check, he gave me a list with names and numbers in Serbia. Like me he had helped people escape! We chatted for half an hour.' Erdemović tried to see if he could save the man. Finally a soldier arrived with the answer: 'Sorry! The boss doesn't want to leave a single living witness behind us!'

So history came full circle. Unwittingly perhaps, the boss had come to mimic Vojvoda Batrić from Njegoš' *The Mountain Wreath* when he said:

> No single seeing eye, no tongue of Turk,
> Escap'd to tell his tale another day!
> We put them all unto the sword. . . .[14]

13

THE WAR FOR MORE

Serbian leaders conducted the wars in Croatia and Bosnia with such cynicism that it is hardly surprising that, for many, 'defending Serbdom' was indistinguishable from making money. The vast arsenal bequeathed to the Bosnian and Krajina Serbs by the JNA meant not only that they could seize large tracts of land but that there were also plenty of guns left over to sell to the enemy. Although some trade was pure corruption and war profiteering, other transactions also had a strategic aspect, for example 'rent-a-tank' services rendered to the Bosnian Croats.

When the war began, there was little if any evidence that the JNA or its officers were trading with their Croatian counterparts. The old mechanisms of control were still in place and the JNA itself was directly involved in the war. As the focus shifted to Bosnia, however, discipline collapsed. The JNA was tasked with distributing weapons to the SDS and Serbian TOs, but a certain amount of weaponry was almost certainly also sold to the Muslims. During the war years, hundreds of millions of Deutschemarks' worth of weaponry, ammunition, fuel and goods were traded across the frontlines and even more was looted by Serbs, not just from their enemies but from their own people too.

The Bihać Bazaar and the Human Hens

From the outset of fighting, the Bihać area was one of Bosnia's busiest markets. It was a place which brought together Muslims, Croats and Serbs, all with one thought in mind: profit. A glance at the wartime map makes it clear why this was so. An overwhelmingly Muslim area, known properly as Cazin Krajina, it found itself completely surrounded when the Bosnian war began. On two sides this former Ottoman frontier region was bounded by the Krajina Serbs, while along the Una river a frontline with the Bosnian Serbs was rapidly established. Tens of thousands of Muslims fleeing ethnic cleansing in the Prijedor and Sanski Most regions ran for the safety of this large Muslim enclave, while Serbs abandoned it for Serb-held areas.

For some three months after the war began, there was little news from Bihać. By August 1992, though, it became clear that the area had survived the initial Serbian onslaught in northern Bosnia and that with its population of 300,000 it was not about to fall either. In part this was because the region was simply too large and populous for the Serbs to take without high losses, but it was also because too many people were making too much money out of it to want it snuffed out. There were political considerations as well. The region was the personal fief of Fikret Abdić, the popular Muslim politician, who, as we have seen, enjoyed close relations with the JNA and military counter-intelligence.[1]

On the small-time, individual level, the easiest way to make money around Bihać – or indeed anywhere else in the warzone – was to sell arms or fuel to the enemy. Tomislav Dretar was a sociologist and poet before the war, but the conflict found him the commander of Bihać's small Croat HVO detachment. A bearded, Falstaffian character, Dretar enjoyed nothing more than giving visitors copies of *Gypsy Rhapsody*, his last anthology, which had been translated into Romany. But, whimsies aside, Dretar was a hard-nosed businessman when it came to procuring weaponry for his men:

> Our arms come from various sources. We make some, we steal some and buy some from the Serbs themselves. I myself bought an anti-aircraft gun from a Serbian officer that he had stolen from the JNA. I told him that we would use it against Serbs and he said that he couldn't care less. It cost DM5,000. It was dismantled and we brought it in here over a five-day period. I asked him why he was selling it and he replied sarcastically, 'I'm helping a just cause.' People who have something to offer know each other. Serbian officers send their emissaries here. After all, we know them, they were our neighbours before the war.

Later the struggle along the Bihać front became far more bitter and much of the hitherto quiet border with Krajina became a frontline. Bosnian forces nevertheless managed to fly some arms and ammunition in to an airstrip they had carved out at Coralići in the centre of the pocket. In October 1994 the Bosnian Army's 5th Corps finally broke out of the enclave, briefly taking large swathes of Bosnian Serb-held territory. The Bosnian Serb leadership furiously blamed the UN, saying that the Bosnians could do this because they were operating out of what was supposed to be a UN 'safe area'. Then they boasted that they had retaken the lost territory because their Krajina Serb brothers had come to their aid. What they did not say, though, was far more interesting. In fact it was the Bosnian Serbs themselves who had sold the 5th Corps a good part of its weaponry – and had then been taken by surprise when it was used against them.

Along the Una river the 5th Corps faced the Bosnian Serb Army's 2nd Krajina Corps. It was senior officers of this Bosnian Serb regiment who sold the 5th Corps arms and ammunition. This was confirmed by Lieutenant-Colonel Milovan Milutinović, the Bosnian Serb Army's spokesman, when he later admitted that there had been a major problem here. 'We have dealt with it,' he said sternly. The story of the deal was that ever since the beginning of the war Bihać Muslims working in Germany and elsewhere had contributed generously to the local war chests. However, after three years the frontlines had not moved an inch. The Muslims began to clamour for action. According to some sources as many as forty or even sixty truckloads of weaponry were then purchased from the Serbs. So confident were those Serbs, however, of their good relations with their business partners in the 5th Corps that when it launched its attack only 20 per cent of Serbian troops who should have been at their positions along the Bihać front were actually there.

The other element to the Bihać story is the failed attempt to buy off Cazin Krajina's Muslims. Initially the Serbian leadership was divided about what to do with Bihać and its people. Some argued that this Muslim enclave had to go because otherwise it would remain like a stone stuck in the gullet of Greater Serbia. In the long run they were proved right, as the extended lines around the enclave tied up large numbers of men who could have been deployed elsewhere. Others argued that since its people were overwhelmingly Muslim it was not Serbian land and so an accommodation would have to be found with its leaders. Because it would have been far too costly to try and capture the whole area, rather than just the strategic railway line that skirted the Una and connected Banja Luka to Knin, Serbian leaders decided in favour of the second option. They were also fascinated by the possibilities of what they could do if they succeeded in splitting the Bosnian Muslim leadership by recruiting Fikret Abdić.

After his return home in 1993 Abdić dominated what had become the 'Bihać pocket' from Velika Kladuša. To begin with, Abdić kept his peace with the Krajina Serbs, but he soon began to negotiate with the Bosnian Serbs and the Croats too. Inevitably he fell out with the leadership in Sarajevo and began parroting Serbian and Croatian claims that Izetbegović had embarked on an Islamic fundamentalist path. By this time, the Bosnian Serbs and Bosnian Croats had made peace and were co-operating against the Muslims. On 26 September 1993 Abdić proclaimed the foundation of the 'Autonomous Province of Western Bosnia' and so literally became a pocket 'president'.

At first all went well. A current joke asked what would be left of former Yugoslavia after the war. The answer was Velika Srbija, Velika Hrvatska and Velika Kladuša – Greater Serbia, Greater Croatia and Greater Kladuša.

As a result of the agreements Abdić signed with the Serbs and Croats, commercial traffic again began to flow from Velika Kladuša. Convoys went to Croatia across Krajina Serb territory and a bus line was also established. As the Croats were at that time waging war against the Bosnian government, they shared the Serbian aim of splitting the Muslim leadership. For their part of the deal Abdić's Agrokomerc republic was granted a duty-free area in the Croatian port of Rijeka. In Zagreb, Pale and Belgrade, Abdić was fêted as a man of peace and the kind of Muslim that both Serb and Croat could do business with. In Sarajevo, not surprisingly, he was stripped of his official post of member of the republic's presidency and denounced as a traitor.

For the year that the Abdić pipeline was in operation almost everyone concerned reaped the benefits. The Krajina Serbs sent food to be processed by Agrokomerc, ordinary life began to revive in the part of the Cazin Krajina still under his control and above all millions were made through sanctions-busting. The key part of the Abdić deal was that the Croats made money by selling him fuel and other goods which, in theory, were only for his Autonomous Province. In fact UN officials noted that Abdić convoys that made their way across Krajina carried far more fuel than the area could possibly use. The extra petrol was not just for the Krajina and Bosnian Serbs but for Serbia itself. By August 1994, however, the greatest scam yet devised to make money out of the war came to an end. The government in Sarajevo proved itself powerful enough to initiate and carry through a successful revolt led by the 5th Corps. Abdić was driven out, but as he departed from Velika Kladuša he led with him some 30,000 refugees, whose devotion to their 'Daddy' verged on the cultish.

Once inside Krajina, Abdić's followers ended up stranded because the Croats would not let them cross into government-held territory. Also, since the halcyon days of war profits for all, the Bosnian political kaleidoscope had turned and Croatia was no longer a friend of Abdić but had switched sides again to support the government in Sarajevo. Some 20,000 Abdić followers now found themselves housed in the Batnoga camp, less than three kilometres from their homes in Velika Kladuša but firmly inside Krajina. It was here that the sheer madness and the utter cynicism of the war reached new heights. Batnoga was not just any old camp – it was one of Agrokomerc's chicken farms. So, courtesy of the Serbs, Abdić's people were settled in the long hen-coops where they waited patiently until they could be put to good use again. This came to pass in October 1994 when, having partly armed themselves from their shopping spree with the ever helpful Serbs, the 5th Corps launched their attack.

Batnoga was the epitome of the Bosnian nightmare. There was neither electricity nor running water. In each of the twenty-four hen-coops families staked out tiny squares of floor space on which to live. The huts were not just gloomy but smoky too, as the women cooked on stoves next to their family mattresses. Outside children played in the mud while other families lived inside their cars, lorries or makeshift tents. Bizarrely, considering that the Serbs were locked in mortal combat with the Muslims, the 20,000 people living in the hen-coops constituted, after Knin, Krajina's 'second city' in terms of population.

It is unlikely that the Serbs originally intended to keep Abdić's people as their own Bosnian Zouaves or first Muslim infantry regiment, but the changing circumstances meant that this is what they became. As soon as the 5th Corps led by General Atif Dudaković thrust out southwards from the pocket, the Krajina Serbs began arming Abdić's men. Officers from Serbia's SDB also began to arrive to help sort out this delicate situation. With the support of artillery and manpower from Krajina, Abdić's men were sent in to hit the 5th Corps from behind, so forcing it to fight on two fronts. It was a successful strategy. Velika Kladuša was recaptured, but the 5th Corps retained control over the rest of the pocket. If the Serbs could no longer make money in Bihać they could still profit from the situation. A mini-Muslim civil war fuelled by themselves obviously sapped manpower that would otherwise be employed fighting them.

The Battle of Velika Kladuša bore witness to some of the strangest scenes since the beginning of the war. Some of Abdić's men went to war wearing badges with his picture on and others fought under a hand-made flag bearing the slogan 'Long Live Daddy!' The Serbs also gave Abdić some tanks, which were of the same 1942 Soviet vintage as ones that had fought in Stalingrad. Much of the Serbian-directed Muslim-versus-Muslim fight was centred around Velika Kladuša's 900-year-old castle, which dominates the town. Just before the war, Abdić had been converting the fortress, complete with turrets and pointed roofs, into a luxury abode fit for a local seigneur such as himself. From here in November 1994 Abdić's snipers peered down on their home town and shot at men on the other side who could have been their brothers. One man said that he could see his mother come out of their house every morning to get water, as she had chosen to remain behind when the rest of Velika Kladuša's population had left town.

The Serbs had originally hoped that Abdić would be able to conquer the whole area, which he could then rule for them, but this proved impossible. The Serbs were unwilling to risk large numbers of their own troops to try and take it, something which would in any case have been virtually impossible unless the 5th Corps collapsed. This it stubbornly refused to do, and in the end it was Serbian military power which was to collapse. When in August 1995 Croatian forces launched Operation Storm, which swiftly retook Krajina, Abdić's Serbian-backed army collapsed in a matter of hours. Once again his people took the road into exile, fearing the wrath of fellow Muslims angry at what they saw as their treachery. Abdić sought refuge in Croatia.

As elsewhere in Bosnia the ghosts of the past are an ever lowering presence and so the story of Abdić would be incomplete without mention of the spirit that lurks in Velika Kladuša. During the Second World War, Cazin Krajina also mapped out an autonomous path for itself. Nominally part of the NDH, in reality much of the area, especially Velika Kladuša, fell under the control of one Huska Miljković, a man who like Abdić sprang from humble origins in a nearby village. Miljković became the leader of his own 'Muslim Militia', which at various times lent its support either to the Ustashas or to the Partisans. Now he lies buried in the mosque of Velika Kladuša.

An Abdić supporter said at the time that they were fighting to return to Velika Kladuša: 'The two men are different, but their aim, to keep the region safe, is the same.' Huska Miljković did not live to see the end of the war, because he was murdered by fellow Muslims working for the Serbs or the Croats or the Partisans or the Ustashas, depending which version you choose to believe.

Bosnia: Open for Business

In many other areas in wartime Bosnia there were always places which were open for business. Generally the point of contact was a region where Serb and Croat lines met but which they did not contest and which was therefore peaceful. This was the case close to Sarajevo, where the Serb-held suburb of Ilidža bordered Croat-held Kiseljak. Across this 'frontier' much trade was conducted, especially in petrol. Among the greatest petrol barons of Bosnia was the brother of Momčilo Krajišnik, the speaker of the Bosnian Serb assembly, who used his protected position to make millions buying Croatian fuel to sell to the Bosnian Serb Army.

Vareš, forty kilometres north of Sarajevo, became a notorious turntable town for cross-frontline business. In the summer of 1993 the northern government-controlled town of Tuzla had been cut off for several months because fighting with the Croats had closed the roads to the south. So it was something of a mystery how cigarettes from Macedonia were on sale in the market. Life was undoubtedly very tough, but there was no widespread hunger. This was not just thanks to the best efforts of the UN and local farmers. Serbs and Croats were both cashing in on Tuzla's plight and they were able to do this due to the strategic location of the Croatian enclave of Vareš.

Vareš lay on the main wartime road from Tuzla to the south, and after the conflict began it found itself bordered by the Serbs to the east. Vareš and the nearby Serb-held town of Ilijaš had no territorial disputes between them, so amicable relations were quickly established. At first, while the Croats and Muslims fought side by side, these contacts were private and there was little if any major commerce across this inactive front. A nearby Muslim village, which lay sandwiched between Croatian and Serbian territory and was clearly visible from Serb-held land, also passed the first few years of the war entirely peaceably. This was thanks to the mercantile spirit of the area, which was soon to flourish. A senior Serbian commander from Ilijaš had sold the Muslim village some heavy artillery before retiring with his family to a peaceful life in Serbia.

The Vareš connection came into its own when the Croat–Muslim alliance broke down. Vareš was small and vulnerable, and although it professed loyalty to Herceg–Bosna, the breakaway Bosnian Croat statelet based in Hercegovina, it was not in a position to fight for it. It could, however, provide both it and Tuzla with valuable services. The key man in this operation was Boro Jakić, the director of a local firm called Veleprodaja. His opposite number was Brane Damjanović, a Serb from Ilijaš. When visitors came looking for them in the summer of 1993 they found them together in a Vareš house. Damjanović introduced himself and his partner with the words, 'I'm a Chetnik and he's an Ustasha.' At this point their whole party dissolved in fits of laughter.

Zdravko Barkić, the commercial director of Veleprodaja, explained that every week they received four deliveries of produce from the Serbs including those Macedonian cigarettes, sugar, oil and flour. Indeed they were buying so much that UNHCR officials were stunned when Vareš local council actually turned down an offer of aid on the ground that they already had enough supplies.

Vareš council officials were, however, somewhat embarrassed by their Serbian business connection. Kruno Ridjić, the council's commercial director, said that any cross-frontline trade was 'irregular, illegal and black-marketeering'. If this was so, it was interesting that Veleprodaja was actually sub-contracted by the council itself to do the business. In the same way Damjanović's company was working with Ilijaš council. The whole deal was sanctioned right the way to the top as Jakić would drive with a police escort to Pale to meet Velibor Ostojić, then a Bosnian Serb minister and always a top SDS official, to discuss the terms of trade. Zdravko Barkić suggested that business across the frontlines was perfectly legitimate despite its ramifications: 'We are business people. We are not interested in politics. Economics has brought the French and Germans close together, so why not Croats, Serbs and Muslims? When the lines have been drawn, everything will be fine. People will live together as before.'

Meanwhile they were dying, and it is worth examining the implications of such trade. Vareš bought food and other goods which it intended to sell on. Because the HVO in Vareš was not engaged in fighting the Muslims, it had good relations with the HVO in Tuzla, which not only was not fighting the Muslims but was still fighting alongside them against the Serbs. It was through this HVO connection that the goods sold by the Serbs ended up with the Muslims in Tuzla. In other words, via Vareš the Serbs were selling food which soon ended up in the mess halls of the troops in Tuzla who then went out to try and kill them. The story grows even more grotesque. While Croats were selling Serbian goods which ended up with the Muslims in Tuzla, Muslims to the south of Vareš were locked in combat with other Croats. So thousands of these Croats fled before them, some 20,000 ending up crammed into Vareš.

Because of the fighting in the south, these refugees could not get out, so a new deal was struck with the Serbs. They were allowed to go to Herceg–Bosna in convoys that snaked their way for 1,000 kilometres through Serb-held territory. But the cars and buses did not travel alone. They were accompanied by empty trucks which returned with Croatian humanitarian aid and commercial goods. Officially it was denied that they also transported arms, but given the warm relations at the time between Herceg–Bosna and the Republika Srpska it was quite possible that they did. Bosnian Serb officials said openly that they preferred a weak Croatian enclave on their 'borders' to the consolidation of Muslim territory. But if they did permit arms to travel to Vareš it is also highly probable that they eventually ended up in Tuzla, where they would then have been used against them.

'Business', as Jakić and his partners liked to point out, 'is business.' Unfortunately for them, it was no more than that. While the Vareš connection was open, there was a lot of money to be made, and Serbs escaping from central Bosnia could get to Serb-held territory via Vareš by bus every Wednesday. But all good things come to an end. Vareš officials said that the Serbs had told them that if the Muslims ever moved to attack they would come to their defence. Slaviša Raković, a senior Serbian official in Pale, confirmed this. When the attack finally came, however, the Serbs did not lift a finger. Vareš' Croats were evacuated through the Republika Srpska and the Serbs did not fire a single shot to save their business partners.

A similar arrangement to Vareš also existed in the Croatian enclave of Žepče, but here strategic concerns were involved. When fighting broke out between Croats and Muslims, the town entered a local military alliance with the Serbs. Sandwiched between Muslim-held territory to the north and to the south, but with access to Serb-held land, it received all of its supplies from the Serbs and in return helped besiege a pocket of land within which were the towns of Maglaj and Tešanj. Cut off for almost a year, the area was helped to survive by NATO airdrops of food. The siege of the pocket pitted a combined Serbo-Croat force not just against the Muslims but rather against a combined Muslim–Croat force. This was because in Tešanj there was a Croat HVO detachment which did not break its own local alliance with the Muslims. Eventually the enclave was rejoined to the body of central Bosnia after Croatia and the Muslims made peace under American pressure in 1994. Serbian forces then simply pulled out and the Žepče Croats switched sides again.

While Žepče was allied to the Serbs it was possible to see Serbian tanks in town. Less visible were the tank-renting facilities, stories of which were frequently reported, especially from Hercegovina. Here it was said that the Croats could rent tanks from the Serbs for DM1,000 a day. Croat troops could also cross through Serb-held territory, but it is not clear whether they had to pay for this. Close to Mostar, the Serbs occupied the heights behind the town. The Bosnians held the eastern part of the town and the Croats the west. A sliver of Bosnian-held territory also ran north from Mostar, connecting it to the main body of government-held territory in central Bosnia. In east Mostar, during the worst days of the Croatian siege, the Serbs could be persuaded for a fee to shell the Croats. However, it has also been claimed that the Serbs would take the money and duly fire the number of shells the Muslims had ordered but, so as not to jeopardise their relations with the Croats, they warned them first to get out of the way.

In June 1993 in Bijela near Konjic, Serbs and Croats celebrated their Bosnian partnership when Serbian representatives were invited to a thanksgiving mass celebrated by the local Franciscans. Drago Simunović, the leader of local Croatian forces, thanked the Serbs for their help and said, 'The Croatian population and army would simply have been destroyed if the Serbs had not proffered the hand of salvation.' He said that the Serbs had looked after Croatian refugees and helped with food and medical supplies, and 'we even got artillery help'.[2] Around this period the Serbian media even began to refer to 'Christian forces', when they meant Serbs and Croats fighting together, but it was a phrase that never caught on.

Economic links also continued to bind the Croatian town of Dubrovnik and Serb-held Trebinje just over the border in eastern Hercegovina. Dubrovnik's water came from Serb-held territory and so, after the end of the JNA siege of the city, its inhabitants had to pay for it.

According to Božidar Vučurević, the mayor of Trebinje, the Croats at first delivered fuel in exchange, but later they paid in cash, which was handed over at monthly meetings. Such co-operation did not extend much further, though. The Trebinje Serbs did their best to make sure that Dubrovnik's tourist trade did not revive by lobbing the occasional shell on to Dubrovnik airport.

Throughout the war there were frequent unconfirmed reports that power cuts in Serbia itself were a result of the authorities selling electricity to Croatia in exchange for fuel. These stories were certainly believed in diplomatic circles in Belgrade, where one diplomat charged with keeping an ear out for such things reported 'gurgling in the pipeline'. He claimed that his sources had heard strange noises in the oil pipeline which ran from Croatia's oil terminal at the port of Rijeka right through to Serbia's main refinery at Pančevo, just outside Belgrade.

Around Sarajevo all sorts of money-making combinations arose. After the first few hellish months of war, Serbian cigarettes and fresh produce such as tomatoes began to appear in the city's markets. These arrived courtesy of the mafia connections of some of the men who were organising the frontlines. A Croatian connection also evolved, as an HVO unit controlled one of the entrances into the city at Stup. For several months this was one of the main ways in which Serbian goods could enter the city. The Croatian connection also enabled Serbs, for a price, to escape the city.

As the siege ground on, the Bosnians dug their tunnel under the airport, so connecting Sarajevo to the outside world. At some points, too, roads were actually opened under agreements negotiated with the Serbs. However, before that, in the first year or so of the siege, there were some other, rare ways to get goods into the city – fighting permitting. All you needed were the right connections and lots of money.

Djordje Radović was the director of the Serbian humanitarian aid group Dobrotvor, which operated within the city. Because of his status he was able to travel between Sarajevo, Pale and Belgrade. A lawyer and businessman, he used his contacts to keep trading after the siege began. As he explained it, though, such trade hardly seemed worth the effort:

You have to hand over 8 per cent of the goods to the HVO in Kiseljak, 33 per cent to the Serbs in Ilidža, 20 per cent to the Bosnian state reserve, 20 per cent to the Bosnian Army and then you still have to pay taxes. You can do it but there's no profit. Out of every 13 tonnes you are left with four. Something which should cost half a Mark ends up costing DM15 and people can't pay these prices.

His conclusion was: 'It is a war of criminals . . . you cannot find logic in this war.'

One of Dobrotvor's jobs was to bring in parcels for people in Sarajevo who had family in Serbia or Serb-held territories. It also took parcels out of the city, for example winter clothes for those who had fled. However, many Serbs in Sarajevo were not happy with the job Dobrotvor was doing, complaining that the parcels they received often arrived half empty. Eventually the authorities in Pale became fed up too, suspecting that much of the operation was being used by people in Dobrotvor to smuggle in goods for the black market.

As the war continued, corruption began to take its toll on the morale of ordinary Serbs, who were expected to fight and die for Krajina and in the name of the Republika Srpska. Hardly anyone was paid during the war and if they were it was a pittance. Those that had cars could rarely use them because the price of petrol was so high. And when they needed them they no longer worked, because mice had gnawed through the cables. However, the opportunities for a few to make large amounts of money meant that while the roads were generally deserted the few cars that did drive on them were, more often than not, new luxury models. The longer the war went on, the more Mercedes were parked in front of the presidency building in Pale and outside favourite watering holes such as the Hotel Bosna in Banja Luka.

On 10 September 1993 soldiers in the Banja Luka region staged a mutiny, so angry were they that so many were getting rich while they got poorer. They brought tanks and armoured cars on to the streets and demanded the arrests of local 'war profiteers'. There was much speculation at the time that the whole affair had been staged for someone's political interest but, if it was, it was never clear whose. The statement put out by the rebels over Radio Banja Luka declared, 'We, who with patriotism and chivalry entered the history of our people, have become beggars and strangers among our people in our own land.' It also noted that many of those who had evaded the draft had become rich while they had been at the front. 'They spit on the graves of our dead comrades and are preparing Golgotha for us . . . but no one cares.' These same people, they claimed, had become rich 'with the blessing of the current political powers'. The rebellion was rapidly suppressed.

Part of the problem was that it was extremely difficult for ordinary soldiers, who lacked political protection, to make much money trading with the enemy even if his trench was a bare fifty metres away. This was because, to avoid arrest, the whole unit would have to be both involved and utterly trustworthy. Secondly, it was dangerous because of mines and the risk of snipers, even if the area was quiet. There were, however, occasional tales of contacts being made and small-time smuggling carried out. In Croatia the UN organised meetings between Serb and Croat soldiers as part of confidence-building measures. This provided a safe opportunity for deals to be struck. In the village of Novo Selo, close to Sisak, there were periods when Croatian soldiers sold fuel, beer and fertiliser to the Serbs on the other side. According to Ivan Lovac, a Croat engaged in the business, things soured when the Serbs kidnapped some Croats and demanded ransoms.

At the beginning of May 1995 Croatian forces launched their massive operation in western Slavonia which drove out Serbian troops within forty hours. Over the next few days and weeks there was much debate about 'who lost western Slavonia'. Dušan Ećimović, a former Krajina information minister, told the Belgrade daily *Naša Borba* that the real reason why the region had not been properly defended was because corruption had undermined its defences. As more than 10,000 Serbs had had to flee it was a blistering attack.

> It happened that, during the Croatian Army attack, [Krajina] army corps commander Lazo Babić was smuggling oil with 'Aran' – Aca Dragićević, mayor of Okućani and the owner of a gas station. The oil goes somewhere to Bosnia, the documents are stamped with army stamps (as if it were for the corps), and the ring includes [Krajina army commander] Milan Čeleketić and [Krajina president] Milan Martić.
>
> The oil is bought from the Croats for DM1 and sold to Fikret Abdić, Atif Dudaković even, for DM5 or even up to DM17 a litre. Also during the attack some officers were here in Belgrade with their families, leaving territorial defence commander Rajko Narančić in charge and a few other officers from the 1991 war. Jasenovac was not even defended. There were only a few of Mladić's men there who pay Čeleketić DM100 a day to certify that they are at war, so they won't have to fight in Bosnia.[3]

Serbian politicians are adepts at backbiting and flaunting their divisions, especially when the times call for unity, so there is no reason to believe everything Ećimović says. However, his allegations came at the same time as so many others that a good proportion of them were certainly true. The next month, for example, the Bosnian Serb parliament meeting in Pale accused Vladan Lukić, the former Republika Srpska prime minister, of involvement in a scandal concerning the disappearance of DM3.5m which had been set aside for the sanctions-busting import of oil from Bulgaria. Branko Ostojić, a former deputy prime minister, was named for allegedly being involved in a similar scandal involving the loss of DM5.5m which had been intended for oil imports from Romania. At an earlier parliamentary session in Sanski Most, deputies had blamed the generals for losing territory. Angrily the generals retorted that if the deputies had not stolen so much petrol their men would have been better able to deal with enemy offensives.

One scandal that lingered for a long time over the Republika Srpska was the mystery of what had happened to thousands of Volkswagen Golf cars that were stolen from Bosnia's Volkswagen factory during the first weeks of the war. According to some sources, the brand-new vehicles which were at the plant in the Sarajevo suburb of Vogošća were divided between the Serbian and Sarajevo mafias. Other reports imply that Bosnian Serb officials, working in collusion with the Belgrade mafia, managed to steal most of them, perhaps 5,000 cars in all. This haul was reputed to be worth DM90m. Either way the pillage of Vogošća must rank as the largest car theft in history. One report says that many of the Golfs which were sold in Serbia were subsequently stolen from their new owners and then sold in Bulgaria and Belarus.[4] As too many people close to power among the Bosnian Serbs were connected with this, the Bosnian Serb parliament shied away from naming those responsible. In the summer of 1995 senior officials tried to bury the embarrassing business by urging the government to issue a statement saying that the vehicles were 'looted by the people in the chaotic situation at the beginning of the war'.[5]

The war also provided ample opportunities for local Serb officials to enrich themselves with the possessions and property of the Muslims and Croats they had ethnically cleansed. They could do this without actually getting their hands dirty like common or garden looters. According to Bogdan Delić, the chief of police in Prijedor, the assets of 50,000 Muslims and Croats expelled from the region had amounted to 'several billion' Deutschemarks. Although many houses had been destroyed, other assets, including thousands of cars, lorry-cab units and agricultural vehicles, had been stored in local warehouses, 'although only for a short period of time'.

> By various machinations, the whims of individual members of the local police, army and civilian authorities, and the governing political party – the largest part of the . . . 'preserved assets' disappeared. . . . It may be stated with certainty that . . . the greater part of the resources have either been transferred to Serbia through private agents, or have been expropriated by private individuals.[6]

It was not just expelled Muslims and Croats that were robbed. Local industrial and agricultural assets that would have helped sustain Serb-held areas both during and after the war were simply stripped and sold off. Again in Prijedor the local newspaper was forced to turn to a discussion of how 'war profiteers' had sacked the region 'on the model of the Sicilian mafia'. One source told the paper that 'tens of electric motors, assembly lines and other valuable objects have disappeared from the workshops of the Ljubija mine and other Prijedor enterprises. ... We must ask ourselves how these enterprises are to continue their work once the situation settles down. Six thousand head of cattle have been stolen and transferred to Sremska Mitrovica and Šid [both in Serbia].[7]

It is impossible to underestimate the debilitating effects of such corruption on the Serbs. When in August 1995 Krajina and later much of Serb-held western Bosnia collapsed, ordinary soldiers said they had been betrayed and saw no more reason to fight. It was not only that they believed that they had been sold out politically, but that for four years they had manned the trenches while many of their officers and political chieftains had made millions for themselves. It was well known that many if not all of their superiors had acquired flats and houses in Serbia in readiness for the moment when they would make off with the loot. It was hardly the stuff of legend – the struggle against the Turks, the heroic march across Albania or the Salonika front. As a consequence, it goes a long way to explaining how the Serbian martial spirit was sapped of its strength until it finally snapped like a reed.

Belgrade–Chicago

According to the authors of a book on crime in Serbia: 'Belgrade epitomised the Chicago of the twenties, the economic crisis of the Berlin of the thirties, the intelligence intrigues of the Casablanca of the forties and the cataclysmic hedonism of the Vietnam of the sixties.'[8] They were absolutely right.

On a sunny day at the beginning of March 1995 a hand grenade exploded 150 metres from the door of Slobodan Milošević's presidency building in the middle of Belgrade. Behind the building there is a small park with a play area for children. The young man who died next to the sandpit was a policeman who had been chasing another young man, a suspected criminal, who promptly tried to shoot himself in the head – but failed. A few weeks earlier, just on the other side of the park, a four-wheel-drive car of the type favoured by Belgrade's gangster classes exploded outside the door of a casino. The 'businessman' driver died in hospital a few days later. On 21 March 1992 Aleksandar Knežević 'Knele', aged twenty-one, the icon of a younger generation of the Belgrade underworld, was murdered in Room 331 of the city's luxurious Hyatt Hotel.

The end of Yugoslavia turned Serbia and the Serb-held lands in Croatia and Bosnia into a patchwork of mafia fiefs. The unprecedented breakdown of law and order and the fantastic business opportunities provided by sanctions-busting meant that many Yugoslav gangsters who had hitherto operated in the richer pastures of Germany and Switzerland returned to reap the profits of war. Some became involved with Serbian paramilitaries, which under the cover of patriotism became rapacious looting machines. After they had stolen all the cars and other goods from the frontline towns, they turned their attention to the home front.

Among the more prominent gangsters-cum-militia leaders were Branislav Matić 'Beli' and Djordje Božović 'Giška'. They led the Serbian Guard of opposition politician Vuk Drašković before he decided that he was against the war. Giška's record included racketeering and escaping from prisons in Switzerland and Italy. In 1983 in Germany he murdered Stjepan Djureković, a former commercial director of the Croatian oil company INA. This was a contract killing commissioned by Yugoslav secret services, with whom many top gangsters, notably Željko Ražnatović, known as Arkan, maintained cordial and mutually profitable relations. Giška's view of his new role was that 'All over the world in liberation and resistance movements, patriotic "criminals" have taken to the frontlines and made a great contribution such as only they, in such conditions, could make.'[9]

Beli was murdered and Giška died in Lika in Krajina in 1991, probably as a result of a bullet fired by a fellow Serb. Drašković, embarrassed by their looting, was anxious to distance himself from his militia, which the authorities were also keen to break up as they did not approve of any armed groups not directly or indirectly under their control.

The king of the gangsters was undoubtedly Arkan, whose role as an agent of the SDB has been described earlier. His men combined military operations at the front with 'business' at home, while Arkan himself rapidly turned into a media star. He built himself an extraordinary Gothic-style mini-castle opposite Belgrade's Red Star football stadium and paraded for the cameras in a First World War-style uniform. The high point of Arkan adulation came in 1994 when he married Ceca, Serbia's most popular young singer and star of the raucous 'turbo-folk' scene.

The gangster presence in Belgrade was inescapable. Many cafés and restaurants asked their clientele to check their weapons in with their coats, and while murders in the city were common the vast majority were mafia related. Even small children could not escape their effects, as the deaths in the park showed. 'I could not drag Isidora away from the window,' complained one woman, whose six-year-old daughter had insisted on watching while the remains of a neighbour were zipped into a bodybag and carted off after his murder in an affair related to the petrol business. It was not only classic gangsters who died. In the autumn of 1995 the director of Coca Cola in Serbia was gunned down in his office.

In a brilliant television documentary made by B-92, an independent Belgrade radio station which was branching into television, Serbia's gangsters spoke openly about their lives and work. The older generation complained bitterly about the youngsters, saying that the business was not what it used to be. They moaned that the young guns just wanted 'to shoot straight away', and regretted that Belgrade had become a 'little pond with many crocodiles'.[10] In a gruesome triumph for the film-makers, three of the gangsters interviewed died before the documentary was finished. After showing them talking, the film cut to their funerals. Fittingly it was called *See You in the Obituaries*.

Željko Rutović, one of the more enterprising mafiosi starring in the B-92 film, despaired of the situation at home, comparing it to the well-organised rackets being run in the Black Sea coastal resort of Sochi, where he had invested in casinos. In Belgrade, he said, no one had any respect for anyone else, while in Sochi everyone, the Armenian mafia, the Georgian mafia, the mayor's office and the police, all worked together. He identified the problem as short-termism. He lamented that the Serbian criminal philosophy was not to make DM5m in five years but to make DM10,000 today.

Among the most prominent interviewees was Goran Vuković, legendary in underworld circles as the man who had killed a former lord of the underworld known as Zemunac. Vuković had survived five attempts on his life including an attempt to kill him by firing an anti-tank missile at his car. He complained that the police had a shoot to kill policy and warned that if 'they hit our families we'll hit theirs'. He met his demise in December 1994, gunned down as he came out of a restaurant and riddled with twenty-five bullets. Now he lies under a conspicuous white marble tomb in Belgrade's Topčider cemetery, flanked by his young sidekicks, Roki (aged twenty-four) and Boki (aged nineteen). In death as in life.

In 1993 Jugoslav Pantić, the director of the Belgrade casualty centre, complained that the victims that he saw had in the past generally been hit with only one or two bullets, 'in the legs usually'. Now, however, 'they have normally been hit by a full clip load aimed at the head or chest'.

Belgrade's mafias dealt in all the usual businesses, including drugs and arms, but the UN sanctions against Serbia introduced in 1992 gave them their greatest boost. This was because the embargo offered them the opportunity to seize control of important sections of the economy, especially imports, which were normally the preserve of ordinary businessmen. Car theft was also widespread, as was its international dimension. This meant the organised traffic of stolen cars from Germany and other places to Serbia itself, either for sale there or for distribution further eastwards in an arc that spread from Russia to Syria. With contacts in the right places, new papers could easily be obtained and many corrupt policemen are reputed to have grown rich on this trade.[11]

At a lower level the gangsters operated widespread protection rackets and ruled the roosts in the high-rise housing complexes of New Belgrade. So pervasive was their influence that many young men, not necessarily sucked into the underworld itself, began to imitate their fashions and haircuts. They became known as Dizelaši, or Diesel Boys, after their favourite make of jeans.

Despite sanctions and the general impoverishment of the population, many people were puzzled by the fact that there was no let-up in the opening of small boutiques, many of them selling the most expensive western fashions available. It might be surprising that there were some people who could afford to shop in them, but it was still more surprising that there were obviously not enough wealthy clients to keep so many exclusive shops going. The answer was simple. They were opened, as were many cafés, as fronts for laundering gangster cash. In many cases leading gangsters made little attempt to conceal their wealth. Every day car cleaners polished the world's most expensive cars, which they brought to the Hotel Metropol garage to wash. Many had number plates showing that they came from Serb-held Bosnia or Vukovar. There were a large number of plates from that shattered city only because many shell businesses were opened there to avoid taxes. In this way Vukovar, Croatia's symbol of suffering, became the Serbian mafia's own private Liechtenstein.

Another favourite haunt for the gangster aristocracy was the pool and fitness club of the Hotel Hyatt. Here the paunchy elders of the trade, their necks almost buckled by the weight of the gold chains they wore, would frolic with some of the most nubile girls to be seen in the city. The girls were, one assumed, 'resting' with the boss, between jobs.

Among the gangster classes were those who sent their children to Belgrade's French- and English-speaking International Schools. In the heyday of Tito's non-alignment, these were the sedate preserves of diplomatic families. During the Bosnian war the father of one such child incurred the wrath of several families when, in the gardens of Belgrade's exclusive Diplomatic Club, he gave a demonstration to his son's seven-year-old friends of how to kill someone with a pistol. As the man would boast that he was related to Dobrica Ćosić, who in 1992 and 1993 had enjoyed a brief spell as president of the rump Yugoslavia, he epitomised a process that had been predicted by Žikica Simić, a Belgrade court psychiatrist. She said that she believed that once the wars in former Yugoslavia were over the prevalent gangsterism in Serbia would fade away: 'The violent redistribution of wealth and power will have ended and today's criminals will become a new elite. They will need a state and legal order to protect them.'

14

363 QUADRILLION PER CENT

'I would like to inform you that our economy has collapsed.' So said Ljubomir Madžar, a distinguished economist and former government minister speaking before a gathering of his colleagues in July 1993. Whatever the suffering caused to ordinary people by the destruction of Yugoslavia and the general impoverishment that accompanied it, the one group that cannot complain of not living through 'interesting times' are Serbia's economists. Rarely has the profession had the luck – or misfortune – actually to experience such economic turmoil. At one point hyperinflation meant that a bunch of carrots cost a year's salary while a thirty-six-hour international telephone call cost £3. At the same time middle-class pensioners were reduced to scavenging in dustbins as Belgrade's young gangsters took to flaunting themselves and their molls in ever more exotic sports cars.

There is an irony in all this: Professor Madžar was wrong. Serbia's economy did not collapse. It contracted massively, but it adapted. Millions, perhaps billions, of Deutschemarks were robbed from ordinary people with the blessing of the state, but at the same there was no widespread hunger. When hyperinflation reached an annualised rate measured in numbers too large to have meaning to anybody but astrophysicists, Professor Madžar made a far more acute assessment. He said, 'This situation has never been experienced before. It is not described in the books. My guess is that this cannot go on for ever and that a breakdown will take place. But this is like a thick fog in which no one can see anything. We can only guess and later analyse why we were wrong.'

The Price We Must Pay . . .

For the last two years before the war, reforming the economy of Yugoslavia was the priority of the government of Ante Marković.

Fighting against the odds, he managed to bring the country close to signing an association agreement with the European Community. He instituted a stable and convertible currency and began the task of economic transition from communism or rather socialist self-management. The shops were full and entrepreneurs began to open private businesses. Advanced compared to other parts of eastern Europe, the Yugoslav economy would have been far easier to reform if the country had not been divided into feuding and antagonistic republics. However, Yugoslavia's peculiar brand of communism, while not leaving the economy in good shape, certainly left it far healthier than any of its socialist neighbours. The way Yugoslavia had been decentralised since 1974 also meant that, when war came, strong republican governments existed. So, as the centre fell away, they were not simply cut adrift. Another consequence was that, except in the war-zones themselves, there was no power vacuum to fill when the federal government stopped functioning, because it had long since ceased to be a source of real power in itself.

The federal government's ever diminishing power was best demonstrated by two seminal events. In 1989 it was Milošević who ironically instituted the first sanctions regime in the region by ordering a Serbian boycott of Slovene goods. And in December 1990 his government excelled itself by instigating one of the greatest bank frauds in modern financial history. Despite republican autonomy, the dinar was the preserve of the federal Yugoslav authorities. All of a sudden, however, the balance sheets of Serbian banks swelled to the tune of some DM2.6bn (US$1.5bn). This was then promptly distributed as credits to large companies, which used them to buy hard currency. Mladjan Dinkić, an economist who wrote about the financial wonder-land that was to develop in Serbia, noted, 'It appears that only certain companies received "grey dinars". All of them were reliable financial supporters and recruiting grounds for the ruling party.'[1] The Serbian authorities were able to issue the phantom dinars that they had printed because, although they did not (yet) control the National Bank of Yugoslavia, they did control the National Bank of Serbia and its counterpart in Vojvodina. Other republics had done this before, but the sheer scale of the Serbian swindle has often been cited as one of the key events which made the death of Yugoslavia inevitable.

At the time, however, the fact that Milošević had succeeded in literally plucking vast amounts of money out of thin air was of great encouragement to him. It meant that from then on until January 1994 he could implement a policy of economic improvisation, though it was little more than a series of conjuring tricks. However, in the place of the conjurer shouting to disbelieving children 'Oh yes there is!', the Serbian media was loud in calling for patriotic forbearance. When UN sanctions were imposed at the end of May 1992, Milošević said simply, 'This is the price we must pay for supporting the Serbs outside Serbia.' In this way the population could be persuaded to suffer almost any hardship and con trick. Until January 1994 there was simply no economic policy that would be recognised as such anywhere else and certainly not in the middle of Europe. Instead there was the state-sponsored theft from millions of hard-working citizens who had been fooled into believing that somehow their sufferings were worth it and that the cause of the Serbian people was worth their sacrifices.

The initial shock to Serbia when the war began was inflicted by the loss of former domestic markets and suppliers. Croatia and Slovenia were more industrialised than Serbia, but Serbia was the breadbasket of Yugoslavia. The collapse of the federation and the division of the country by frontlines meant that Serbian producers lost their buyers, while many industries practically ground to a halt because of the loss of imported inputs for their products. Most Serbian industrial goods had a relatively high proportion, at some 30–40 per cent, of inputs from other republics. Cars were assembled by Zastava in Kragujevac in central Serbia, but parts came from producers all over the country. Agricultural goods from Serbia were often processed in Slovenia or Croatia, while Serbia was a major market for Slovene washing machines and telephones. On average 70 per cent of everything produced in Serbia was 'exported' either to other Yugoslav republics or abroad. However, of that 70 per cent some 50 per cent went to the other republics; in other words, foreign exports were only 20 per cent of production.

The war not only brought about the collapse of the domestic market. It also caused most incomes to be slashed so drastically that demand all but collapsed. Most economies would be hard put to absorb these shocks without then having to cope with the *coup de grâce* of a total economic blockade ordered by the UN Security Council. On 30 May 1992, one day after sixteen people had been killed in a bread queue in Vase Miškina Street in Sarajevo, the UN Security Council passed Resolution 757. It banned all imports from Serbia and Montenegro and forbade all exports to them, including oil, with the exception of 'supplies intended for medical purposes' and foodstuffs which had the permission of the UN Sanctions Committee. Financial transactions were prohibited and commercial air and sea traffic to the rump Yugoslavia were suspended. This resolution, as it would soon become clear, left gaping loopholes. Serbia lies on one of the main European traffic arteries, which flows from western, northern and central Europe south to Greece and east via Bulgaria to Turkey and beyond. Imports could therefore still enter the country, or rather pass through the customs of a neighbouring state, so long as they had papers stating a false destination. This could either be a third country or Serb-held parts of Croatia or Bosnia. These gaps were filled by Resolution 787 of 16 November 1992 and Resolution 820 of 17 April 1993.

Despite the blockade, sanctions-busting was never stopped and Belgrade often gave the impression that there were no sanctions. It was a misleading picture, however. Sanctions coupled with the disintegration of the former Yugoslav market and the cost of financing the war wreaked devastation on the economy, but did not destroy it. Serbia's resilience lay in the fact that, having previously been a food exporter, it could never be starved into submission. Indeed, not being able to export large quantities of grain often presented storage problems. Secondly, its private businessmen proved adaptable and energetic and were able to plug many of the new gaps in the market. The irony is that when the economy really did seem close to collapse the blame lay chiefly with the authorities rather than with the situation into which they had led the country.

Banks, What Banks?

One of the early signs that something was seriously amiss with the management of Serbia's finances was the emergence of so-called banks, which were in fact get-rich-quick pyramid schemes. They were designed to suck in as much foreign currency as possible before their inevitable and inglorious end. Two of them, Jugoskandik and Dafiment, came to dominate the scene in one of the most bizarre episodes of the whole wartime period.

Jezdimir Vasiljević was known to all and sundry as Gazda Jezda. Literally Jezda the Boss. He had clearly led a colourful life before opening his bank, claiming among other things to have laboured on rubber plantations in Australia. He also told people that he had lived in almost every country from Monaco to Thailand. He spoke good English with an Australian twang and had no banking experience. Scruffy and jowly, he said that he was not a Serb but a Vlach. His rise to fortune and fame began during the liberalising days of the Ante Marković government, when he imported televisions from Hong Kong and sold them for a 50 per cent profit. In 1991 he moved into banking.

Mladjan Dinkić, the economist and writer, believes that Gazda Jezda promoted his 'bank' with a policy of judicious bribes and investments in a Montenegrin cigarette factory that was believed to manufacture fake Marlboro cigarettes from local tobacco. He also briefly shot to international prominence when he sponsored what was billed as the 'Revenge Match of the Century'. In autumn 1992 Gazda Jezda brought together two chess players from the 1970s, Boris Spassky, a former

Soviet champion, and an American called Bobby Fischer. For a prize of $1m they were to meet once more in a match in Iceland and Spassky would try to avenge his 1972 defeat. Gazda Jezda garnered credit for this spectacular sanctions-bust and, even better, was photographed shaking hands with Milošević. Ordinary investors could scarcely fail to be impressed. Jugoskandik was paying them fantastic sums of interest on their savings and many reasoned that if Gazda Jezda was a crook then the President of Serbia would hardly be seen hobnobbing with him. On hard-currency accounts Jugoskandik was paying out 15 per cent *per month* in hard currency. The Boss explained how he could afford to do this: 'Don't you ever wonder why western bankers have the best buildings and drive the best cars? It's because they are robbing depositors' money. They could easily afford to pay out much larger rates.'

Later, presumably when he realised that time was running out, the flamboyant banker opted for another high-profile ruse. He ran in the presidential elections of December 1992. Either he hoped he would be elected and so be able to use his position to prevent his bank collapsing, or he saw yet another opportunity for the publicity needed to keep the cash flowing in. During his electoral television spots he dutifully intoned his views, while a message flashed on screen giving the latest Jugoskandik interest rates.

So many people wanted to deposit their money in Jugoskandik and in Dafiment, which was soon to outgrow it, that permanent queues built up outside their branches. Pensioners especially would camp there, keeping warm by bringing thermos flasks and singing the night away.

Both banks operated as classic pyramid operations – that is, they could afford to pay out large sums of interest so long as the number of depositors was constantly growing. Sooner or later this had to come to an end, but the trick was to stay afloat as long as possible. During the same period similar banks were in operation in other parts of the former communist world where regulations were weak and officials corrupt. The best known were Caritas, which rose and fell in Cluj in Romanian Transylvania, and the Russian MMM bank. Inevitably the heads of both Serbian banks were widely believed to be involved in all sorts of other businesses, such as the sanctions-busting petrol and possibly arms dealing. When Gazda Jezda fled the country in March 1993, he stopped in Israel on his way to Ecuador. From Israel, Yugoslav newspapers reported that he was known there as an arms dealer. Dinkić has another theory and argues that a significant slice of Jugoskandik's income came from money laundering – not the classic laundering of mafia money linked to drugs and such like but rather legal profits laundered to evade tax. 'Politically unrecognised, surrounded by war, ridden by monetary chaos and isolated by an international blockade, Yugoslavia was obviously a money launderer's paradise. It also seems that the main intermediary in all these operations was in reality the state, while para-state banks or "savings funds" were no more than a front.'[2]

It is a compelling theory, but to go as far as to claim, as Dinkić does, that western companies financed the survival of Serbia and Montenegro by virtue of the massive scale of their money laundering seems far-fetched. His problem is that, though he describes in minute detail how such operations could work, he does not tell us the names of any foreign companies that indulged in such practices. This may be less an indication that he does not know than a prudent decision, in a country where gangsterism is rife and life is cheap, to stay alive. When Jugoskandik finally collapsed, DM100m were missing. Some believe that members of the 'political establishment' pocketed this as the price for letting Gazda Jezda escape, but again, unsurprisingly, there is no proof.

Dafina Milanović was another person from nowhere, who for a few months was the toast of Serbia. Known simply as Dafina, the founder of Dafiment Bank was a large and imposing woman with a penchant for fur coats and fraud. Her rise and fall was even more extraordinary than that of Gazda Jezda. A former cashier, she had been sentenced several times for embezzlement and forging official documents. She had often escaped jail by pleading for clemency on the ground that she had only done what she had done as a poor woman desperate to feed her children or help her sick brother. Over the years she cultivated a network of strong connections, including a link with Slobodan Stanojević, who, when she started her bank in October 1991, was a retired vice-governor of the National Bank of Yugoslavia and still a key adviser. Says Dinkić, 'It is clear that from the very beginning the state more or less directly pulled all the strings in Dafiment bank.'[3]

Like Jugoskandik, Dafiment offered phenomenal rates of interest. So famous did Dafina become that she was soon dubbed a *Srpska Majka*, literally a 'Serbian mother', though perhaps more akin in sentiment to a Serbian Queen of Hearts. She contributed, or was forced to contribute, to the national pension fund at critical moments, but like Gazda Jezda her use to the country was in supplying a short-lived parallel social security system. For middle-class families whose incomes had dwindled to nothing the interest on their accounts meant the difference between the poverty line and relative comfort. For many pensioners, though, it meant the difference between the poverty line and teetering on the brink of hunger. The bank was also a fantastic cash facility for those with the power to raid it. Dinkić explains how some of the pensioners' money was invested:

[Dafina] was asked to make a huge investment in the construction of Belgrade's new underground system and high speed rail links in the rest of Serbia. The decision was made at the end of July 1992 at a meeting with the director of Belgrade's railway service, Milomir Minić, soon afterwards promoted to general secretary of the ruling Socialist Party of Serbia, and Milutin Mrkonjić, director of the CIP planning institute, in the intimate atmosphere of a villa in Užiča Street in Belgrade's most exclusive residential suburb, Dedinje. Only two days later, several employees of the National Bank of Serbia and a dozen policemen visited Dafiment Bank and took DM40m from its vaults in sacks, put them in an armoured vehicle and drove off in an unknown direction.[4]

It was hardly surprising that later there were claims that none of this cash was ever actually invested in the underground.

Throughout the war various attempts were made to drum up support by using Jews, both Yugoslav and foreign ones. Dafina was no exception, and her particular ploy may well have impressed some of the more gullible. To an outsider, however, the use of one Israel Kelman was one of the crudest forms of subliminal advertising to be applied in Europe in many a year. At one point Dafina gave a press conference flanked by the wizened figure of Kelman, who sported a *kippa* or skullcap. The message was obvious: 'Don't worry – your money is safe with me. The Jewish bankers are here.'

What Kelman really thought he was up to remains a mystery. He said that he was born in Canada, raised in Britain and was now an Israeli citizen. Away from the press conference he wittered on about a Belgrade parking scheme in which he was thinking of investing or had even already put some money into. Living up to his caricature image, he then went on to explain how his wife bought his shirts in Marks & Spencer. Some claimed that he had already poured large amounts of money into the bank (and was taking large amounts out), but he said that because of sanctions he was only making a prospector's trip to Serbia. Whatever the truth of the matter Kelman was never to grace the screens of Serbian television again. Within weeks not only had Jugoskandik collapsed, but Dafiment bank was in ruins too.

The collapse of the two banks brought more people on to the streets of Belgrade than virtually any other single event during the war years. They came not to protest, though, but to queue in mostly vain attempts to retrieve their money. It is an interesting gloss that a thousand times more people came out to try and get their money than protested the fall of Krajina and the flight of its entire population in August 1995. It proves that once the war had started the vast majority of people in

Serbia itself were too preoccupied with keeping body and soul together to worry about the great national goals for which they had been impoverished.

The Boss fled Serbia at the beginning of March 1993, claiming that senior officials, especially in Montenegro, were attempting to extort money from him. His flight immediately provoked a run on the bank as thousands jostled to grab the forms they needed to pull their money out. The collapse was not without its farcical aspects. Stevan Protić, the acting head of Jugoskandik, said gloomily that he did not know whether there was any gold bullion in the vaults because bank officials could not find the key.

Dafina reacted to the fall of Jugoskandik by leading television cameras into her vault, which appeared to be a veritable Aladdin's cave full of bundles of money. It did not help, though. By the beginning of April crowds were beginning to besiege her bank's branches too. Of course those with friends or relations who worked in the bank all got their money out in time – as, one suspects, did depositors in high positions of authority. But for everyone else it was a frantic and ultimately fruitless quest. And, as always, there was profit to be made in misery. In Belgrade's lush ultra-modern Genex Apartments building one man died in a till-front shootout. A group of security guards who had been sacked for taking bribes from customers desperate to jump the queue had launched an attack on their replacements.

As the crowds besieging Dafina's branches grew ever larger and angrier, the authorities in Belgrade asked the bank to transfer much of its business to the city's Partizan football stadium. Here thousands began camping overnight. When the tellers closed their hatches for a coffee break, or in the evening, hundreds of people who were nearing the front of the various queues and who were mostly elderly surged forward booing and screaming abuse. This inevitably led to injuries. The old folk who had been crushed were then pulled out as teams of paramedics leaped from ambulances yelling, 'Where's the one they said was close to death?'

The final loss following Dafina's collapse, in so far as these things can be estimated with any reliability, was believed to be some DM500–600m. She was caught trying to flee the country but was not arrested, and continued to live in Belgrade's exclusive Dedinje area. At the same time as the bank collapsed her two children and husband were killed in a car crash in Hungary, a tragedy which inevitably sent the imaginations of Serbia's conspiracy theorists into overdrive.

With inflation now sky-rocketing, many of Belgrade's clever commentators predicted that the fall of the banks would lead to social unrest. This was because so many people had lived off the interest the banks had paid them. As is so often the case in the Balkans, such a logical deduction proved utterly false. Once the crowds had dispersed after generally failing to retrieve their money, nothing happened. There were two reasons for this. First, many of the depositors were not half as stupid as the clever people thought they were. They had gambled, always knowing that there was a good chance that they would lose their money. Inevitably there were stories of people who had lost everything, but they were not common. The second reason was that following the collapse of the banks a new phenomenon came to dominate everyday life. Hyperinflation of such drastic proportions now set in that all normal everyday accounting was simply suspended. The state and people, especially the middle classes and the elderly who had relied on their interest payments, adapted their survival mechanisms to suit the new situation.

The Inflationary Tsunami

A look at some of the raw data is the best place to start a survey of what happened to the economy up to January 1994. Instead of GDP the equivalent Yugoslav statistic is the Gross Material Product (GMP) concept. GDP is then estimated at between 15–20 per cent greater than GMP. In 1989 the GMP of Serbia and Montenegro was $24.6 billion, but by 1993 it had plummeted to $9.5 billion.[5] Annual growth rates were -8.2 per cent in 1991, -26.1 per cent in 1992 and -27.7 per cent in 1993.[6] At the beginning of 1994 industrial production was 30 per cent of its 1990 level.[7] All the statistics show similar drops and indicate that, by the time the government saw fit to introduce its emergency stabilisation measures in January 1994, the economy was operating at approximately one-third of its pre-war level. When sanctions were introduced, legislation was passed making it illegal to lay off redundant workers. This meant that at any one time at least one-third of the workforce was kept on 'paid holidays' at 60 per cent salary, which were mostly worked out on a rotation basis.

Although all of these figures sound dramatic, they were nothing compared to the real drama of the period leading up to January 1994, which was hyperinflation. While the monthly rate remained relatively 'low' until the beginning of 1993 it began to edge over the 200 per cent per month level in February of that year. By July it was creeping over 400 per cent, in August it reached 1,880 per cent. At an annualised rate that is 363,000,000,000,000,000 per cent, or in plain English 363 quadrillion per cent. This was but a fraction of what it was to become. Closely linked to the inflation rate was the black-market exchange rate for hard currency. Ever more dealers appeared on the streets waving wads of dinars and whispering 'devize, devize' ('hard currency'), until the streets where they congregated appeared to drone constantly with what sounded like a low-level buzzing noise.

From August 1993 until the next January, Serbia lived through times recalling Germany's ill-fated Weimar Republic. When the November inflationary rate hit 20,190 per cent *Vreme* spoke of an 'inflationary Tsunami', recalling giant Japanese tidal waves. There were no words then for the final figure some six weeks later, which was a monthly rate of 313,563,558 per cent. At an annualised rate this is 851,000,000,000,000,000,000,000,000,000,000,000,000, 000,000,000,000,000,000,000,000,000,000,000,000,000,000,000 per cent.[8] Amazingly, this was not the highest figure in recorded economic history. In October 1923 the German monthly inflation rate hit a measly 32,400 per cent, but in November 1944 Greece peaked at a monthly 855,000,000 per cent. The highest ever recorded monthly inflation figure was that of Hungary in April 1946 which was 4.19 trillion per cent. Serbia's place in the economic history books is secure, though, because its two-year period of hyperinflation was the longest ever recorded.[9] During this time the National Bank of Yugoslavia produced thirty-three new bank notes, twenty-four in 1993 alone. In September 1993 six zeros were knocked off the currency in a bid to keep figures manageable, but three months later new notes, this time shorn of nine zeros, had to be introduced. Twenty-four days later the 'new dinar' was introduced, bringing to a close the era of monetary chaos. The largest bank note issued during the period of hyperinflation had a face value of 500,000 million dinars and was virtually worthless two weeks after its introduction.

The pace of hyperinflation made coinage redundant, which led in turn to an extraordinary curiosity. As the lack of coins meant that Belgradians and their children could no longer toss their metal small change into the city's fountains, they threw in bank notes instead. This meant that billions upon billions of dinars floated about until gypsy children or hungry pensioners waded in to fish out their soggy loot.

Dinkić claims that much of the money raised via Dafiment and Jugoskandik and through street black-market dealing was taken abroad, where the 'political establishment' set up a network of companies in which to park it. He says that cash was taken out via the diplomatic bag and flown in special planes from Timişoara in Romania to Cyprus, where much of it ended up.[10] There may be some truth to this, but there will be no evidence until a future administration decides to publish all. For whatever reason, the government created hyperinflation by printing billions of worthless dinars in a bid to suck in hard currency. Every bank and state-connected company had its own network of dealers who worked overtime but, by January 1994, hyperinflation had simply worked itself out. The dinar simply expired as a currency and was replaced by the Deutschemark. Boris Begović, an economist at Belgrade's CES-Mecon institute, says that this had nothing to do with criminality at the top but everything to do with poor economic management:

> I don't agree that there was a massive conspiracy to rob people of their money for personal gain. These people are simply not intelligent enough to plan such things. They have a mental time frame of twenty-four hours. Between 1992 and 1993 there was a significant budget deficit. They printed the money to cover the deficit but the result was that the real value of money went down. You can print Din10,000 and say that it's worth DM10,000, but if you print more and more of the stuff then its value is quickly reduced to DM100. If you still continue to print money on such a massive scale then eventually everything is reduced to zero. They did manage to reduce the budget deficit and originally the banks and the government got money, but in the long run hyperinflation is counterproductive. They were like poker players and they were still playing even though they were on a losing streak.

Because inflation could be measured per hour, most wages or pensions were worthless by the time they were paid out. Immediately wages were paid, workers had to rush out to convert them to Deutschemarks, thus fuelling the spiral, or they had to spend them before their value melted away entirely. Businesses began to abandon the national currency in favour of the Deutschemark or barter, and some simply closed, battened down the hatches and waited until the chaos had come to an end. Some private shops would take only Deutschemarks, while others, tired of having to write out new prices every few hours, resorted to pricing in 'bods', literally points. If a customer wanted to buy, the shop assistant would check the up-to-the-minute exchange rate of the Deutschemark, which was usually pegged at the rate of one to one with the bod, and then accept payment in dinars.

For the vast majority of Serbs in Serbia, the winter of 1993 will be remembered as the hardest of days. 'I am waiting to die,' said a pensioner in a soup kitchen who could not afford to pay for his heart medicines. In all probability, these could not be found in state chemists anyway but only in private ones which, despite the war, still imported Slovene and even Croatian medicines trucked through Hungary. Monthly pensions, if converted quickly enough, were worth £3 but a litre of milk, if it could be found, cost £1. The saving grace for the vast majority of the population was that hyperinflation rendered utilities such as gas, electricity and the telephone as good as free. Between the day companies sent out their bill and the day it had to be paid hyperinflation had reduced the sum owed to nothing *vis-à-vis* the Deutschemark. So, while an impoverished pensioner might not be able to afford to eat, he could at least talk with his family in Australia for several hours for next to nothing.

Although life was of course extremely tough, especially for pensioners, few starved. There was a spate of well-publicised suicides of old folk who could not afford to eat or who could not bear the humiliation of asking for help, but in the main they were cared for by their families. In the countryside the problems faced by most people were far less severe than those experienced in the cities because peasants simply grew their own food. The effects of hyperinflation were also far less drastic than they would have been in the west. One of the main reasons for this was that the bulk of the industrial working class moved to work in factories only after the Second World War and so retained close links with the home village. So, even if people no longer owned land of their own, though many did, they still had family who could send them food.

The government also made judicious use of the state reserves, so workers often received a substantial part of their pay not in cash but in kind, be it in flour, oil, sugar or detergents. Many people also had family living abroad, people who had left after 1945 to escape communism or had settled in Germany or Austria or elsewhere as gastarbeiters. They were a constant source of income for the folks back home, and relatively modest sums were enough to keep the wolf from the door.

The other survival mechanism was the humble cheque, which evolved into a sort of *de facto* social security system. The trick was not to use cash but to pay by cheque, so that by the time it had cleared the original amount that you had paid was by then a fraction of the cost. At the height of hyperinflation, something which cost DM100 would in reality cost only DM20 by the time the money was taken from your account. This of course also fuelled hyperinflation because, if they still accepted cheques, shops would try and beat the system by inflating their prices to compensate for the depreciation that would take place while the cheque wound its way through the clearing system. In a bid to keep this going as long as possible the government tried to oblige private shops to keep taking cheques, but eventually many closed down or opened with empty shelves rather than lose money. At this point the newspapers delighted in exposing entrepreneurs who had rented nuclear bunkers and bomb shelters as warehouses in which they stashed all the goods no longer available in the shops while they waited for better times.

Surfing the Tsunami

If there was a Nobel Prize for business, there is little doubt that Serbia's private businessmen would have carted off a collective award. The hurdles they had to face included the UN embargo, an economy operating at one-third of its pre-war level and the loss of markets and suppliers in half of the old Yugoslavia. Fuel prices were up to five times the European average and hyperinflation made the national currency worthless.

The situation affected different firms in different ways. The hardest hit were the large quasi-state industries which were too large and reliant on too many non-Serbian inputs and export markets to be able to adapt. They were also crippled by the law, which prevented the laying off any workers while sanctions were in force. The vast electronics conglomerate Elektronska Industrija (Ei) of Niš was a prime example. It employed some 25,000 people and produced goods such as televisions. The collapse of Yugoslavia caused the loss of half of its domestic markets, but with real incomes reduced to 10 per cent of what they had been output dropped to 20 per cent of pre-war levels. Officials explained that just before the war they had struck a deal to sell one million televisions to the former Soviet Union. While small-timers could sanctions-bust their products out of Serbia, one million televisions was clearly a bit much for anyone. Besides requiring such a volume of imported parts, under embargo conditions it would have been impossible to make so many sets. Similarly Zastava, pre-war Yugoslavia's car maker, produced 220,000 cars in 1989 and a mere 7,000 in 1994. By contrast Zastava's arms-production wing suffered no such decline in its fortunes, until after the war in Bosnia.

The heroes of Serbian industry, then, were not the captains of the becalmed and sinking battleships like Ei but the buccaneering private entrepreneurs and the managers of some extremely well-connected 'socially owned' companies.

Lab-Ajk, a glue manufacturer, was typical of small companies which managed to survive hyperinflation. Before the war it just made glue and sold it. With hyperinflation out of control, it had to adapt to survive. It did this through barter. Typically it traded glue for tins of meat with a producer who needed the glue to stick its labels on to its cans. Lab-Ajk then part-paid its workers with meat. It bartered glue with a brewery which also needed to stick on its labels and then sold beer in a Lab-Ajk shop set up specially to sell goods that it received as payment.

Mihajlo Stojkov was the director of a graphic printing firm in Novi Sad. Even during the darkest days of hyperinflation he managed to break even, but he said that the art of the deal was timing things to the minute. In the autumn of 1993, with inflation running at 20 per cent a day, he accepted no job that was not fully paid in advance. 'I write the invoice early in the morning and they must pay the same day,' he said. With the dinar depreciating by the minute, ink and paper suppliers had to be waiting on standby. Once a payment was made to him, Stojkov rushed through payment to suppliers and any cash left over was rapidly converted into Deutschemarks. 'In this race you always lose,' he said. 'Hyperinflation is too big.'

The small private companies that could make the most out of the situation were those which found that they could fill the gaps left by the departure from the market not just of foreign suppliers but also of former Yugoslav ones. Feman, a small outfit making electric cables and machine tools, expanded as it began to produce a large range of products which Serbian companies had previously had to 'import' from Croatia and Slovenia. Based in Jagodina, 120 kilometres south-east of Belgrade, Feman worked flat out while the town's main employer, a 'socially owned' cable maker, languished with output at barely 30 per cent.

Dragan Nikolić, Feman's owner, had previously run a factory in Germany, and his Serbian company was run on German lines, permitting no intrusion of any lax Balkan habits. Pinned on the notice board were announcements about workers whose pay had been docked for being late or for other such sins. The 156-strong workforce were paid way over what they would have earned anywhere else in Jagodina, and besides theirs was an expanding company.

While big firms could not possibly sanctions-bust the large amount of raw materials they needed to keep going, nor export to any great degree, small firms like Feman soon learned how to break the embargo. At first Nikolić erased the 'Made in Yugoslavia' stamp on his products but complained that exports did not pay because 'We are blackmailed, foreign buyers demand too low a price.' Later Feman bought a company in Bulgaria. This enabled it to import raw materials and export products as 'Made in Bulgaria'. Customs officials and even international Sanctions Assistance Monitors were taken care of in the traditional manner, which is to say DM10,000 a truck.

Thousands of entrepreneurs evaded sanctions in a similar manner through Skopje, the capital of Macedonia, which was the favoured location for front companies. Indeed, such was the level of sanctions-busting via Macedonia that this 'invisible' certainly became one of the country's main foreign-currency earners. Officials would say that they were being blackmailed by the Serbs who, as they controlled a large part of Macedonia's electric power supply, would threaten to cut it off if the Macedonians tried to clamp down on sanctions-busting. With an embargo imposed by Greece on Macedonia itself, there was little the authorities in Skopje could do but obey.

Among those to benefit from the Macedonian connection was the franchise holder of one of Belgrade's Benetton clothes boutiques. He explained that he imported everything via his company registered in Skopje. Likewise Radoje Djukić, the owner of Serbia's eponymous and most luxurious knitwear firm, exported all his produce to Germany via his Munich-registered firm, which imported everything legally from his Skopje firm. Indeed his exports proved absolutely vital as the general collapse in domestic demand meant that few ordinary Serbs could afford his garments any more. By 1994 exports took 80 per cent of production. During the same period his company moved from modest premises to a brand-new state-of-the art factory which included marble fountains on the shop floor. At the same time Djukić became the Serbian minister in charge of small businesses. In this position it was his duty to advise and help companies to circumvent sanctions in exactly the same way as ministries of trade the world over have import and export advice departments.

Not all the companies that managed to keep going and even profit under sanctions were private. The best known of the 'socially owned' was the furniture manufacturers Simpo. Its managing director was, like Djukić, a minister, but that alone did not explain its success. Strolling through its plush showrooms, company executive Slobodan Stojanović pointed out not just imports from as far afield as Italy, Iran and Vietnam, but also items such as sofas made domestically with capital from Cyprus and elsewhere. Simpo adapted to the challenge of economic turmoil by spinning off many of its production facilities into private hands. Managers or workers were encouraged to set up small firms in which Simpo took a large stake and which would then supply the mother firm with various inputs. It also helped that Simpo, headquartered in Vranje, was not too far from the Macedonian and Bulgarian borders, so that some products could be exported.

The sanctions imposed by the UN were suspended (but not officially lifted) in November 1995 following the Dayton peace accords. However, even before this, some small businesses which had thrived in the hothouse atmosphere of the embargo were becoming nervous of the coming chill wind of foreign competition. Radovan Ajkalo, the founder of Lab-Ajk, complained in early 1995 that an ever laxer policing of the embargo had already had a negative impact on his firm. He was increasingly having to compete with cheap sanctions-busting imports from Bulgaria, Romania and Poland.

The biggest but riskiest money was always to be made in sanctions-busting oil. This operated on two levels. At the bottom end there was what was called the 'ant trade'. This consisted of individuals driving back and forth across the border, filling up their cars with petrol and siphoning it out and selling it once they got back to Serbia. At the top end official connections were necessary and the business staked out the twilight zone where paramilitaries, mafia gangs and ministers met. Although it would have done no good to enquire too closely, it is probably a safe bet to say that a high proportion of the mafia-related murders which plagued Serbia during the sanctions years were connected with the petrol trade. Before the war Serbia produced 20 per cent of its domestic oil needs, a proportion which grew as consumption plummeted. There were also modest oilfields in Serb-held eastern Slavonia, which passed under the control of Željko Ražnatović 'Arkan', politician, militia leader, SDB employee and so on . . .

Although they complained about the adverse effects of sanctions on their economies, some in the neighbouring countries profited handsomely. Groups of the poorest villages in Romania, close to the border, hit the boomtime selling petrol to the Serbs which was despatched by boat across the Danube. There were also times when fuel in Albania or Bulgaria was scarce because so much had been exported. Greek businessmen also probably played a major role in keeping Serbia supplied not just with oil but with many other sanctions-busting products.

Meanwhile there was another small group of prospering private businessmen. They might operate from Belgrade but their companies were registered in Switzerland or Cyprus. General wheeler-dealers, they cut their business teeth in the days when Yugoslavia perched happily between east and west. Making use of their contacts they now traded between east and west and raised western capital to finance their own investments in the former Soviet republics. To what extent this legal business shaded into sanctions-busting no one knew. Many of these wheeler-dealers also took over the running of the foreign branch offices of major Serbian companies, for example those involved in trade or construction. The branches were re-registered as wholly foreign owned so that they could avoid being closed down during the embargo.

Others, like advertising man Ivan Stanković, kept their Belgrade businesses going but also spent time propagating their companies abroad that may or may not have existed before the war. Stanković divided his time between Serbia, Macedonia, Slovenia and Bulgaria. None of this was sanctions-busting because the companies were locally registered and the non-Serbian ones did not work for Serbian firms.

Supergrandpa to the Rescue

After hyperinflation there was only one thing more remarkable to behold. Out of the blue the Serbian authorities produced Dragoslav Avramović, a seventy-two-year-old economist and former World Bank official. He had presided over teams of economists who had spent the last part of 1993 working out how to end the hyperinflationary spiral. His trademarks were trainers and cardigans. When he announced that as of 24 January 1994 hyperinflation would cease it was hard to take him seriously. He explained that on this day the old dinar would be abolished and replaced by the new dinar, fully backed, he claimed, by gold and foreign currency reserves. One dinar would henceforth be worth one Deutschemark, and there would be no more uncontrolled printing of money. This was a pledge, he said, that he would be able to honour because he was going to be the governor of the central bank.

The results were little short of spectacular. For the next eight months there was not only no inflation but the dinar kept parity with the Deutschemark. Shops filled up again, production picked up and the economy began to recover.

'Sanctions,' chortled Avramović, 'we wriggled out.' Without doubt the end of the unrestricted printing of money was the main cause of the success of Supergrandpa, as he was dubbed, but Avramović's reforms could only do so much. In 1994 the economy grew by 6.5 per cent and in 1995 by 6.0 per cent, but to put this in a broader perspective it meant that GMP was still worth only $11 billion compared to $24.6 billion in 1989. During 1995 the dinar began to slip again and in February 1996 it was devalued from the official 1:1 rate to the Deutschemark to 1:3.3 to keep up with the black market. The annual inflation rate for 1995 was a comparatively modest 119 per cent.[11]

The Avramović effect was above all psychological. Although life remained difficult, there was no longer the feeling of general and complete economic collapse. Avramović stabilised the economy at a sustainable level and kept it there until the UN suspended – but did not formally lift – sanctions on 21 November 1995. The effect was not only domestic. Western businessmen came to Serbia in increasing numbers not just to sanctions-bust but also to inspect the post-sanctions opportunities. Many of them said they wanted to stake a claim in order not to lose out once the embargo was properly lifted. Projects that they looked at included the completion of the motorway which crossed Serbia, the electrification of the main international railway line and several other major capital projects. Fiat and French car makers also came to examine the Zastava car plant and other industrial facilities. These visits led to much excited talk about Serbia's bright economic future.

Sanctions were formally lifted by the UN Security Council on 1 October 1996 but it was already clear by then that Serbia's economy was not going to bloom overnight as many had hoped. Indeed in the period since sanctions had been suspended standards of living actually declined. Prices remained high and salaries low. There were some positive indicators though. For example industrial output in July 1996 was 15 per cent higher than a year before. By contrast it remained a full 41 per cent below that of July 1991.

One of the main problems was the so-called 'outer wall' of sanctions. This referred to the fact that Serbia remained barred from the International Monetary Fund and the World Bank because the US had linked return to these institutions to progress on human rights in Kosovo and to co-operation with the International War Crimes Tribunal. Without fresh foreign capital there was no hope of an economic upturn and credit was so restricted in Serbia itself that a semi-legal grey market was in operation on which money cost some 60 per cent.

As for new foreign partners in Zastava and other corporations early excitement proved premature. Their ownership structures were complex and unreformed. There was virtually no progress towards privatisation or the break-up of the large industrial complexes, and foreign partners could generally find better investments elsewhere. Serbia's legal protection for foreign investments was found to be lacking and, with massive demonstrations against Milošević in November 1996, the country was seen to be unstable. The number of visiting western businessmen declined sharply after the first flurry of interest.

Serbia's Loss, Canada's Gain

The hardest hit by the impoverishing effects of the war and economic collapse were Serbia's professional and urban middle classes. Unlike most ordinary workers, they were far less likely to have family in the villages or living abroad as gastarbeiters. But this was to change, as the situation provoked a massive emigration of the young and educated in a disastrous brain drain which will have a long-term and debilitating effect on Serbia's post-war economy. No one knows how many young people left the country, either as young men to escape the draft or as professionals emigrating to a new life, but the figure could be as high as 200,000 for the war years. The lack of an effective political opposition also prompted many to leave, because they felt that Serbia's future was hopeless for as long as Milošević remained in power.

Examples of the intellectual impoverishment of Serbia abounded. The best place to witness it was outside the Canadian Embassy. Every morning during the war a large queue formed outside. While most western countries fought to keep out refugees and migrants from the ex-Yugoslavia, the Canadians operated a shameless and highly profitable policy of creaming off the best of Serbia's up-and-coming scientists, engineers and others. 'The quality of the migrants is excellent,' enthused Michel Dupuis, an embassy official; 'they are highly skilled and they have little problem settling down.'

The migrants were not just from Serbia and Montenegro. They included the remnants of the educated middle classes from Krajina, Serbs who had left government-controlled Croatia and Bosnian Serbs too.

In 1992 there were ten to fifteen immigration applications lodged daily with the Canadian Embassy. In 1993 there were 150 a day. By 1995, however, the figure had mushroomed to between 300 and 500 a day or 100,000 a year. By then the chance of getting in was 7 per cent, since in the 1994–5 period the Canadians were giving 7,000 visas a year, of which about half were to refugees. At least one-third of those getting immigration papers, including the refugees, were highly skilled and highly educated. Nervous that they would be refused if they applied to emigrate straight out, many of these Serbs asked instead for visitors' visas. Michel Dupuis recounted that he often refused to grant qualified people visitors' visas if he suspected that their real intention was to leave Serbia for good. 'Then I tell them to apply at the next counter for information on emigrating to Canada.'

Canada's gain was obviously Serbia's loss. It was at places like Belgrade's prestigious Mihajlo Pupin research institute that the brain drain was most keenly felt. According to Miomir Vukobratović, a world-renowned robotics specialist at the institute, 1,000 of Serbia's top young scientists and engineers out of a pool of between 6,000 and 7,000 left the country in 1992 alone. He predicted that at such a rate of emigration 80 per cent of the cream of the Serbian scientific, mechanical and electrical engineering elite aged between twenty-eight and thirty-eight would be gone within the next few years. By 1993 out of a previous total of 350 researchers at the institute 70 had already left, mostly for Canada.

The more who left, the more could leave. Those already established abroad could reassure their colleagues and if necessary write guarantee letters for them. Indeed so many Mihajlo Pupin people had emigrated that every week, it was said, two teams of ex-Pupin scientists and engineers met to play football with each other in Toronto.

Just before the war the average scientist could expect to take home a monthly salary of DM1,300. During the war he would be paid DM100 if he was lucky. But pay was not the only problem. Serbia was bankrupt and could not afford to pay for research. Sanctions meant that the country's scientific and engineering institutes were cut off from international projects and funding. And there was worse. Like the rest of the country, institutes and university libraries were placed in isolation, because even their subscriptions to scientific journals were suspended. An outraged Professor Vukobratović pushed forward a sheaf of terse letters from foreign symposium organisers and journals.

'In view of the sanctions imposed by the United Nations . . . we are unable to consider your paper for publication,' was their standard line. 'We have been placed in a ghetto,' said Professor Vukobratović, who was bitter that none of his old colleagues abroad had protested against the isolation of Serbia's scientists. The fact that the Pupin institute had long conducted research for the military appeared to have no bearing on his attitude.

15

SKULL TOWERS

Travelling through the Ottoman lands in the early 1830s, Alphonse de Lamartine, the French Romantic poet, came to Niš. It was then the last Turkish town before the border of the Serbian principality:

> the sun was scorching. When I was about a league from the town, I saw a large tower rising in the midst of the plain, as white as Parian marble. I took the path which led to it, and having approached it . . . I sat down under the shade of the tower to enjoy a few moments' repose. No sooner was I seated than, raising my eyes to the monument, I discovered that the walls, which I supposed to be built of marble or white stone, were composed of regular rows of human skulls; these skulls bleached by the rain and the sun, and cemented by a little sand and lime, formed entirely the triumphal arch which now sheltered me from the heat of the sun. . . . In some places portions of hair were still hanging and waved, like lichen or moss, with every breath of wind. The mountain breeze, which was then blowing fresh, penetrated the innumerable cavities of the skulls, and sounded like mournful and plaintive sighs.[1]

In 1809 during Karadjordje's uprising against the Turks a battle was fought at Čegar, close to Niš. The larger Ottoman force lost thousands of troops but eventually overwhelmed the Serbs. As the Turks swarmed into the Serbian trenches, Stevan Sindjelić, the Serbian commander, fired his pistol into the powder magazine. The resulting carnage was terrible. But the Serbs had the satisfaction of knowing that, although they lost the battle, Sindjelić's last act had saved his men from death by impalement or some other gruesome method. He had also made the Turks pay dearly for their victory. It was not the end of the story, however. Hursid Pasha, the Ottoman leader, had the heads of Sindjelić's dead Serbs skinned, stuffed and sent to the sultan. And then, as a terrible warning to future generations, he built the Skull Tower. It consisted of 952 skulls on four sides in fourteen rows.

Over the years the tower lost its skulls, some fell out, some were taken by souvenir hunters and others were carried away for burial by families who thought they could identify their own. But it was not completely denuded, and even today some fifty-three skulls remain, plus one other in a glass case which is reputed to be that of Sindjelić himself. After Niš was liberated in 1878 the tower was roofed over and in 1892 a chapel was built around it. 'To the First Serbian Liberators after Kosovo' reads a plaque dated 1904. Another quotes from Lamartine's writing: 'This monument must remain! It will teach their children the value of independence to a people, showing them what price their fathers paid for it.'

And duly the skull tower did become a place of pilgrimage. In the years before the dissolution of Yugoslavia tens of thousands of school children from all over the country were brought to goggle at the skulls. When the war began, the spirit of Sindjelić returned to haunt the Serbs. Just as they had lost the Battle of Čegar and made the Turks pay for their victory, so it was with Yugoslavia. The Serbs lost the battle for Yugoslavia and paid dearly for it, but they made their enemies pay in blood too. The result of the wars in Croatia and Bosnia was not just death and destruction and the ethnic cleansing of non-Serbs by Serbs, but new waves of Serbian migration too, which were to alter centuries-old patterns of settlement.

Days in Hell

Even before the conflict started, *Vox*, an extremist Muslim magazine from Sarajevo, helped the cause of Serbian propagandists by publishing suggestions for a new board game: 'the best game of all time: The Skull Tower': 'Use your talent, imagination and architectural skills to show to the world what sort of builders the Turks were. You can play the game yourself or with your Croatian friends. The idea is to place twenty (or more) Serbian heads in the tower, in alphabetical order and as soon as possible.'[2]

As the war began and the Serbs did not win the quick victory that they had hoped for, the skull became a new/old icon of suffering. Lodged in the Serbian collective historical memory were the tales of Karadjordje's men stealing back the heads of executed revolutionaries from the Turks, or the stories of Ivo Andrić, Yugoslavia's most famous modern novelist, who had often made reference to Serbian staked heads and impaled bodies.

One photograph that became well known to Serbs during the war showed a grief-stricken Bosnian Serb woman clutching the exhumed skull of her son. In eastern Bosnia, where battles were the most vicious of all, mourners in the cemetery of Bratunac claimed that among the victims that lay there were some who had died after being impaled and roasted in the oldest of cruel Turkish punishments. Photographs showed horribly blackened corpses, but what exactly had happened to them was impossible to say. When the Serbs captured the nearby Muslim village of Kamenica in February 1993, they began to exhume the mass graves which they found in a wood on a hill above the village. Because it was a sunny winter's day and the earth was frozen, the corpses began to steam as they were peeled out of the ground. By the time the workmen had finished, there were eighteen putrid bodies. One corpse had no head, the feet of another were tied with wire.

A day in Kamenica was a day in hell. For ten months the hamlet had withstood the full force of a Serbian siege. But in the days after it was taken it was looted and burned. Washing machines, clothes and anything worth stealing were collected and neatly stashed at the gates of the houses, which were then set on fire. The gardens of the houses and Kamenica's fields were still crisscrossed with the ghostly footprints of those who had lived here until a few days before. Washing still hung on lines. Now they were gone and the Serbs had come to look for their dead. Pointing at a half-empty skull one soldier said, 'Rade Pavlović, my cousin.'

Some of the men in the Kamenica pit may have died in combat, but the presence of the headless corpse and the body whose feet had been tied with wire suggested that at least some of them had died horrible deaths after being captured. Kamenica was close to Hranča, where the Serbs had killed seven-year-old Selma Hodžić. Near by was Kravice, where Muslims had killed more than sixty. Kamenica was on the road to Srebrenica, where in 1995 this particular cycle of vengeance was to reach its bloody conclusion.[3]

In Banja Luka, the Bosnian Serb military press centre produced photographs, negatives and documents, which they claimed had been captured from *mujahedin*. These were groups of foreign Muslims, mostly Arabs, Afghans or veterans of the Afghan war, who had come to fight on the Bosnian Muslim side. The photographs were widely distributed and used in political posters to bolster the local fighting spirit. One showed a box with three severed heads and a man's foot on one of them. Another showed a grinning, bearded man, said to be a Saudi Arabian, holding up the severed head of a man by his hair. The names of the dead Serbs were published. The pictures and their negatives did not appear to be fakes, but there is little evidence to suggest that beheading or impalement or any other such wartime deaths were commonplace, as opposed to the ordinary summary executions of POWs. But Kamenica, the heads and the *Vox* game could all be put to good use by the Serbian media. The message was simple: 'We are at war with the Turks again, expect no mercy, fight to the death.'

In the Banja Luka press centre, the girl who had translated the captured Arabic documents was Suzana Vranjković, a twenty-six-year-old former student of Arabic and Persian at Sarajevo University. Her father was a car mechanic, her mother a pharmacist. Her grandparents had been Partisans in the last war. After finishing her degree she had worked in a Persian rug shop in Baščaršija, the old Muslim centre of Sarajevo. 'Because no one suspected that I was a Serb I heard all the things they were preparing. One woman said to me, "The Serbs will kill us all, we must slaughter them first." Another man told me that an Islamic republic would soon be proclaimed.' Suzana pushed forward a tatty, oft folded letter written in Arabic. She said it had been found on the body of a dead *mujahedin* and was his will. She translated: 'My parents, I beg Allah to inform you of my death and that you be joyful because I am not going to die either for freedom or patriotism or any other false aim. I will die . . . so that Islam can spread and take root in the world.'

It was the ultimate Serbian nightmare. At first the Serbs had been told that the Ustashas were back – now they were told they were fighting militant world Islam. In the first weeks of the war everything had gone well, but the longer it went on the more Serbs died and the more refugees there were. In Banja Luka there was a rock band called Honeymoon who, on one of their video clips, sat atop tanks singing, 'We gotta show the world that this is a hard nut to crack.' Slowly but surely, though, the nut was beginning to crack.

In August 1992 Serbian forces around the besieged enclave of Goražde were routed. Fleeing civilians were killed. By September it was clear that there was a serious military problem in the region. The road to Višegrad was plagued with snipers. Serbian villages were burning and the trees along forest roads had to be cleared because ambushes had become so frequent. In September Sladjen Simić, aged twenty-four, lay in a hospital bed in Užice in Serbia:

> We were guarding a tunnel between Goražde and Višegrad. They attacked us and surrounded us. We were taken by surprise. There were eleven of us. Four died. We were in the tunnel for eight days. They fired rockets in and threw in hand grenades. They threw in tear gas and burned tyres to try and smoke us out. We had no water. We had to drink our own urine. After eight days the Muslims had dropped their guard. Many had gone on to fight elsewhere. The ones that were left went to have dinner and we ran for it. One of our friends could not run so he said goodbye and shot himself.

By October the authorities in Serbia were reporting that they had 421,000 registered refugees from Croatia and Bosnia and estimated that there were another 110,000 who were unregistered. There were of course many more inside Krajina and the Republika Srpska. The longer the war went on the more refugees there were going to be. In the hospital where Simić lay the doctors said that recently there had been an increase in the numbers of dead and injured, many of them, they believed, thanks to newly imported Iranian- and Arab-made mines.

It was not supposed to be like this. A few months into the war Serbian leaders had begun to say that the war was won so why did the Croats and Muslims not understand this and sue for peace? The answer was that, now they were arming themselves, they had time on their side and the Serbs did not. Milošević and Karadžić had offered the Croats a deal. It was the division of Bosnia. Croatia could compensate itself for the loss of Krajina with territory in Bosnia. But Tudjman would have none of this. He argued that the Serbs could compensate *themselves* for their future loss of Krajina with land in Bosnia, especially eastern Bosnia where there were no Croats. The failure to win the war quickly and decisively, especially after the west intervened in Sarajevo, meant that the longer the war continued the more the Serbs were going to have to pay for the sins of their leaders.

The Idea Is on the Table

In July 1991 Mario Nobilo was a key adviser to President Tudjman. He later became Croatia's ambassador to the UN, where he was loud in his defence of human rights and, above all, of the borders of his country. Such things were not always sacrosanct. The war was just beginning, but it was still far from clear that a catastrophe of such tragic proportions was looming. In the elegant Banski Dvori, the Croatian presidential palace high on the hill overlooking Zagreb, Mr Nobilo whipped out a piece of paper and began to describe how Croatia and Serbia would divide up Bosnia between them. 'The idea is on the table,' he said. 'Maybe this is now the best option for a lasting solution.' With his pencil Mr Nobilo carved up Bosnia, labelling regions as belonging to the 'Cs', the 'Ss' and the 'Ms'. He said, 'If the Muslims believe they can turn the whole of Bosnia–Hercegovina into an Islamic state they are wrong. There should be some deal. If they want a sovereign state we would respect it. It would be the size of Slovenia – they should seriously consider this.'

Apart from the fact that Serbian and Croatian leaders could never agree on exactly where to draw the dividing lines between them, there was another glaring problem with Nobilo's little proposal. This was the inconvenience of several million people not living within their neatly designated areas. But this was no problem for Nobilo. He explained that there was after all the perfect Balkan precedent for solving such things. Greece and Turkey had exchanged several hundred thousand people as a consequence of the 1923 Treaty of Lausanne, and the same principle could be applied in Yugoslavia, albeit 'voluntarily'. At the time such ideas seemed not just evil but, in the Europe of the 1990s, simply insane. What is not yet clear, though, is how much of the massive population exchange that was to take place was actually tacitly agreed upon and how much was simply the fortunes of war. After the Serbo-Croat meeting in Graz on 26 February 1992 Karadžić said that Josip Manolić, the top Croatian negotiator, a former head of the secret police in Croatia and a confidant of Tudjman, had 'proposed that the Croats living in Serbia go to Croatia, and that the Serbs from Krajina, Zagreb and Rijeka go to Serbia. He suggested that pressure could be exerted to make them leave.'[4]

The strange thing was that almost as Nobilo was speaking a chaotic form of forced population exchange had already begun. It was not, however, quite the exchange the Croats had in mind. On 9 July 1991 the tiny eastern Croatian village of Ćelije was set on fire. It sat amid rich farmland close to the regional capital of Osijek. It was difficult to get to, surrounded by Serbian villages which had set up barricades both to carve out their territory and to defend themselves against any Croatian police action. In neighbouring Croatian villages terrified farmers stood by the roadside holding stones with which, pathetically, they were preparing to defend themselves. In the distance Ćelije lit up the night sky. After threats it had been evacuated, and now Serbian militiamen had gone in, looted it, tossed grenades into houses and finally torched it. Days before, an armed clash in nearby Tenja had resulted in the first wave of refugees, but Ćelije was the first village of the war to burn. It was the first of thousands of hamlets, settlements and even towns that would eventually light up the night sky. It was also a microcosm of the ethnic cleansing that was to come. It had to go for two reasons. First because, by its location, it represented an unacceptable enemy or 'minority' population surrounded by a larger grouping of the other nationality. Secondly, Ćelije was a village born with the mark of Cain. Because the area had a majority Serbian population Ćelije had been implanted there by the Ustashas during their brief rule in a bid to 'Croatise' the region.

Ćelije set the dismal precedent. Raking over their collective memories, every village in Croatia and Bosnia was now beginning to remember what the neighbours had done fifty years before. If they were not actually plotting revenge, they began to prepare, as best they could, against the possibility that the neighbours might be doing so. With the razing of Ćelije a threshold had been crossed. From now it would not just be a remote war of the politicians or the theatrics that had characterised the struggle in Slovenia, but a war of the villages too.

Imbued with or rather brainwashed by months and years of television propaganda about the 'return' of the Ustashas and endless documentaries about the Ustasha camps and Pavelić and Hitler, it was the Serbs who struck first and struck hardest. But the result could not simply be the expulsion of Croats and later of Muslims from territories that Serbian leaders claimed. The logic of war dictated that this had to be answered by the flight of Serbs too. Thus the half-baked idea of an exchange of populations rapidly became a self-fulfilling prophecy.

As the war began, Croats fled in the face of Serbian militias and in many cases angry Croats took individual revenge on Serbs in Croatian government-controlled territory. The phenomenon was not widespread at first, but it was enough to prompt the gradual flight of the Croatian Serbs, two-thirds of whom lived not in what was to become Krajina but in the big cities. Serbs, seeing they had no future in an angry and nationally radicalised Croatia, began to pack up and leave. Thousands lost their jobs, there were murders, thousands of Serbian houses were blown up in villages and angry people demanded to know when their neighbours, to whom they had lived next door all their lives, were going to go. This is how the exchange began.

House Hunters

Within months of the torching of Ćelije, hundreds of thousands had already fled. Most of the quarter of a million Croatian refugees who were not put up by friends and family were taken to empty tourist hotels along the Adriatic coast.[5] For the Croats there were no empty lands to repopulate yet, and besides, in Croatia itself, as opposed to Bosnia, there could be no question of a straight exchange of populations since Croatian leaders did not intend to lose any land to the Serbs. For the Serbs, of course, things were very different. Not only did they have large numbers of refugees to house but very soon they had whole towns and regions empty of people. To consolidate their gains, then, the Serbs had to repopulate them.

In the first major disaster for the Serbs, tens of thousands of them were told to flee their villages nestling in the lush hills of western Slavonia and the Papuk Mountains. The area where Serbs had lived licked up deep into central Croatia, but the further north you went the less dense the area of Serbian settlement became. Nevertheless the JNA had distributed weapons to these people and encouraged them to rise in rebellion. Despite the weakness of the fledgling Croatian Army, by the end of 1991 the JNA realised that in the north of the area it simply could not hold the territory. There were too many Croats, Serbian villages were too scattered and the area was indefensible. They did not wait for the Croats to come. Orders were issued for the Serbs to flee because, as the villagers were told, 'The Croats are coming and we cannot defend you.' Panic set in and who would risk staying behind if everyone else had gone? Columns formed and thousands began the trek into exile.

In the winter of 1991 Banja Luka was still a major JNA tank garrison. However, that December there were pitiful scenes on the great ground where in peacetime the tanks would have been parked. Their place was taken by serried ranks of tractors, at times up to 500 of them. Mostly peasant farmers, the Serbs had fled on their tractors, pulling their families and bundles of belongings behind them in trailers. Thousands of the refugees slept in sports halls and schools. Those with families elsewhere set off on their tractors or in their laden cars while the authorities deliberated about what to do with the rest of them. Then they hit upon a bright idea – or possibly this had been the intention all along – of shifting them, *en masse*, to land recently taken in eastern Croatia from which tens of thousands of Croats had just fled. Some of the refugees were convinced that they were the victims of a secret deal by which the Serbs of western Slavonia were being exchanged for the Croats of eastern Slavonia.

Within weeks of their flight, many of the western Slavonian Serbs found themselves in the Bačka Palanka sports hall in Vojvodina. Just over the Danube lay Ilok, a picturesque town with the misfortune not just to be the easternmost extremity of Croatia but also to lie at the end of a narrow thirty-kilometre-long spit of land surrounded by Serbia. Given its location and the fate of nearby Vukovar, which was being pummelled into submission, the Croatian authorities in Ilok made a wise decision. They gave up without a fight. On 17 October they signed a deal with the JNA under the terms of which the army would occupy the town. Before that, the Croatian population would leave. The authorities feared that Šešelj's or Arkan's murderous militiamen would follow the JNA, so it was deemed better for the Croats to leave and, hopefully, return at a later date. Or so they thought. When the Croats left, most took little or nothing with them because they really believed they would be back at the weekend.

In the otherwise empty Ilok museum a curator began her tour. She began with a print of Ilok during a previous incarnation – Ottoman Turkish Ilok. First the settlement had been a Catholic or Croatian one. In 1526 the Turks had conquered it and the Franciscan friars who had made their home here retreated, not just with their people but carrying the mortal remains of their own St John of Capistran. By 1688 the Turks had been driven back over the Sava into Bosnia, so Ilok's by then Muslim population fled with them. The Franciscans and Catholics returned. On the eve of the Second World War, Ilok was a typical post-

Austro-Hungarian cocktail. It was a town of Croats, Serbs, Germans, Jews and Slovaks. The Slovaks were the descendants of agricultural labourers brought to work in the vineyards in the nineteenth century. After 1941 the Jews were deported and most certainly perished. In 1945 the Germans fled or were expelled. In 1991 then, of Ilok's 7,500 people, about 4,000 were Croats. The Slovaks amounted to some 1,900, the Serbs to 500 and assorted others and 'Yugoslavs' made up the rest.

The babbling, manic curator seemed close to nervous breakdown. History had always been confined to the museum – now the museum itself, full of what had only recently seemed to be quaint folk costumes representing Ilok's various peoples, had become history itself.

The museum needed updating because Ilok's baleful tradition of shifting populations was proving very much a living one. Some 3,500 Croats had left, but according to Vladislav Stepančev, the JNA's local information officer, 3,000 mostly western Slavonian Serbs had already arrived by February 1992. 'We made a list of empty houses and gave it to the [new Serbian] civilian authorities.' Since many of the western Slavonian refugees who now found themselves unwilling material in this haphazard game of population exchanges were still sleeping in Bačka Palanka five kilometres away and the army had made lists of empty houses, surely a neat transfer of people could now be effected? It seemed not. Ilok was not just to be a perfect example of how populations were to be shoved around in half-planned ethnic cleansing-cum-ethnic consolidation exercises but also, even worse, of how they were supposed to pay for it too.

The Serbs who had fled their homes and who knew that there were empty houses waiting for them in Ilok could not figure out why they seemed to be spending weeks camped on the floor of Bačka Palanka's sports hall. As it was only the beginning of the war everyone was still a little naive. People learned quickly though. Sava Bjelobrk and his family, who only four days before had moved into an Ilok house, explained, 'We thought, "If they are settling Ilok we want to be on the list.' But, of course, it's all a dirty business. The ones with the Deutschemarks got all the best houses and we were pushed right out of the game.'

So Bjelobrk took matters into his own hands. He marched over the Danube bridge, found a house and moved in. 'We just came over and got the keys off the neighbour.' And indeed Bjelobrk was neither the first nor the last. Desultory couples wandered the streets rattling gates and peering into windows. If there was no key they just broke in. Meanwhile the handful of Croats who remained lived in terror. They received midnight telephone calls demanding to know when they were leaving. The telephones to anywhere outside the town did not work, but the Croats were not allowed out of Ilok to call their families. Nor were they allowed to leave – unless they were departing for good. Later, once the UN arrived in the area, they would frequently complain of murders committed by uniformed Serbs which, even if not planned, were not discouraged because they spurred the remaining non-Serbs to leave.

That Ilok soon filled up with western Slavonians did not mean that its new population was a happy one. Typically the settlers felt demeaned and embarrassed. 'Doing this feels absolutely horrible,' said Sava Bjlobrk's wife Mira. In many ways Ilok was untypical because it had been abandoned as a kind of *Marie Celeste* town. So much so that literally everything had been left behind in the Bjelobrks' new house. Becoming emotional, Sava Bjelobrk suddenly began waving the driving licence that the owner of the house, one Anto Musa, had left on the sideboard: 'When he gets back he's going to find this right where he left it – we're not staying.' Impassively Anto Musa and his family gazed down on the Bjelobrks, from their family photos, still hanging on the walls. The Bjelobrks came from Daruvar, which remained under Croatian government control, and said that they wanted to go home.

On 1 May 1995 the Croatian Army launched a successful operation to recapture that part of western Slavonia around Okučani which the Serbs had managed to keep hold of in 1991. More than 12,000 Serbs again took to their tractors. And, yet again, more than half of them found themselves being directed to Serb-held eastern Croatia.

Every refugee's story was different, but the net result was the same. Serbs were being consolidated either in areas somehow designated for Greater Serbia or simply in those territories that the Serbs had managed to capture and hang on to. That is, until Operation Storm of August 1995, which finally cleared the Serbs out of Krajina; in its wake came an agreement that Ilok and eastern Slavonia would be returned to the Croats, which they were in January 1998.

While some like the Bjelobrk family were 'lucky' to find themselves a choice property ready to move into, others either had to make do with gutted houses and render them habitable again or, in some cases, personally eject the occupants. While the most brutal and direct way of doing this was simply to evict the owner from his house at gunpoint, others – who after all were refugees themselves – found themselves moving in while the original owners were still at home. Such was the fate of people in the Croatian village of Potkonje. In January 1993 the Croatian Army launched an attack to recapture the Maslenica Bridge and other strategic points held by the Krajina Serbs. Several thousand Serbs fled before the Croatian advance. Standing on a ridge high above the sparkling Adriatic Sea they could see the smoke of their flaming homes twisting high into the crisp winter sky. Either they were being torched by the victorious Croats or they had been hit during the fighting.

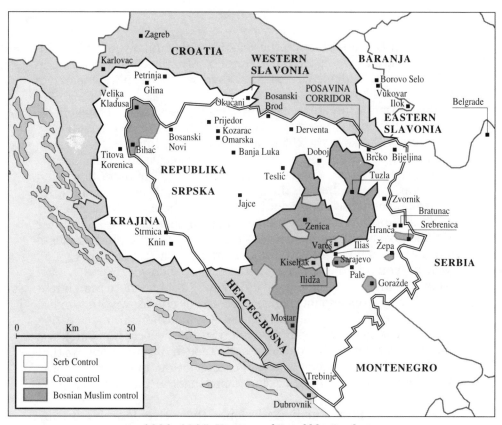

1992–1995: Krajina and Republika Srpska

As usual the refugees were housed in sports halls and schools. Within days though the question arose of where they should go. Some found the answer in Potkonje, a small Croatian settlement which had somehow survived just outside Knin. Its population consisted of sixty-five mainly elderly people, the younger generation having fled at the beginning of the war. What enraged the new Serbian refugees was the thought that here were family-sized houses with only a few old Croats in them. Worse was the thought that the children of these people might well have been the very ones who had just burned down their own houses. 'Well, he was a bit surprised,' admitted Mladen, the Serbian soldier who threw Slavko Maričić and his wife out of his house, 'but then I was a bit surprised when the shells started falling on Smoković.'

Smoković was one of the first Serb-held villages to fall when the Croats launched their offensive. The women and children fled immediately but the men resisted as long as they could. Once the village fell Mladen said that its people had nowhere to go. 'Then we heard that Croats were living in total security here. It wasn't right.' Mladen's children curled up asleep on the sofa. His Kalashnikov and that of his friend Željko were propped up on the end. 'My stable was cleaner than this village,' said Mladen. 'Yeah, Smoković was California compared to here,' said Željko.

Slavko Maričić and his wife spent a day and a night with Mladen, his family and friends when they moved into their house. Along with most of the other Croats in the village and another one hundred others from the area, they then went by bus to a UN-protected shelter before the 'blue helmets' drove them to safety across the frontline. It was an embarrassing operation for the UN since their job was to help refugees return home rather than help them flee, but there was little else they could do under the circumstances. Mladen said that he had let Mr Maričić take whatever he wanted. 'It was a bit difficult but he realised that there was no other way. I gave him my address in Smokovic and said "It's yours," but the house has been burned down. He took a lot of salamis with him. He left a goat and a cow, but I had more than him. I had three tractors and lots of pigs. He took his chainsaw with him but when he got to the bus he said, "Fuck it, you take it."'

In August 1995, following Operation Storm, the people of Smoković found themselves on the road again, this time in the great convoys that went to Serbia. Soon the Croats of Potkonje began to return, not only happy to have their homes back but happy that the 'Chetniks' had gone for ever.

Especially in Bosnia many Serbs found themselves forced to occupy more or less derelict houses that had belonged to the Muslims and Croats who had been forced from them when the war began. After the owners had gone, the looting began. First the televisions went, then the washing machines, the stoves, the furniture, the bathtubs and the toilets. Once the movables had been stripped, the doors were prised off, the window frames unscrewed and then the roof tiles taken off. So later, when the newcomers arrived, it was hard to find a habitable house.

Ratko Bajagić and his wife Mirjana were typical late arrivals. They had spent their whole working lives in Zenica, which fell under Muslim control at the beginning of the Bosnian war. Bajagić said he had never believed that war was coming and, once it started, he had hoped it would soon be over. He spent eighteen months hunting for food and trying to keep warm like everyone else. Finally he applied to leave. Some of the neighbours had been demanding to know when the 'Chetniks' were going. Worse, he added, the people upstairs happened to be Albanians who had told Bajagić straight to his face that he had better get out because their own flat was too small.

The Bajagićs put their name on the list at Zenica's Red Cross office. On 6 January 1994 they were exchanged along with 204 other people, almost all Serbs, for sacks of food from Banja Luka. They came to eastern Bosnia because Bajagić had been born there and had family there. They immediately began to house-hunt. Unlike Ilok, the scores of cleansed Muslim villages near the border town of Zvornik had not just been looted but burned too. In Kalesia, close to the frontline, they found a house. Also unlike Ilok, the procedure for moving in had, by this stage, become rather more orderly.

Once he had found his house, Bajagić went to the town hall where he applied for permission to move in. No money had to change hands, so all that the Bajagićs needed was an authorisation, which was obtained immediately. Unlike Bajagić, the Muslims of Kalesia had not had the time to ponder whether they wanted to leave or not. At the beginning of the war they had been herded on to lorries and driven away. So this made Bajagić's permission all the more extraordinary. For the 'temporary resolution' of his housing problem the town hall had authorised him to reside in the house which it clearly stated was the property of one Šefkija Smajlović. In all probability Šefkija Smajlović and his family had been trucked out of Kalesia in 1992 by the very same authorities who were now inexplicably acknowledging his ownership of his house. It was also possible that he had been executed in a camp such as the one at nearby Vlasenica.

If Smajlović survived he probably went to Tuzla, the destination of most Muslims expelled from eastern Bosnia. The UNHCR has published rough figures which demonstrate just how dramatic have been the population shifts within Bosnia. Before the war there were 301,641 Muslims and Croats in the eastern Bosnian and southern Hercegovina region excluding Goražde. This number had shrunk to an estimated 4,000 by the end of 1995. Likewise the pre-war Muslim population of Tuzla of some 316,000 more than doubled to 659,000. By contrast the pre-war Serbian population of Zenica, which had been 79,355, tumbled to 16,000 and the Serb population of Tuzla dropped from 82,235 to an estimated 15,000.[6]

Early in 1995 the Croatian government and the Krajina authorities agreed on the opening of the motorway across Croatia which had been closed by the war because it cut through what remained of Serb-held western Slavonia. Immediately, divided families began to meet. In petrol stations on either side of the lines hundreds of cars brought thousands of families back together again for tearful reunions. 'It does not need to rain here, the soil is already soaked with tears,' said one man from Serb-held territory who had come to meet that part of his family from government-held Croatia on the Orthodox Easter Sunday. Many of the families were mixed, because many of the Serbs who had remained in government-held territories had non-Serb spouses.

For a moment it seemed as though something had really changed. The idea behind the agreement negotiated by the team of EC peace envoy Lord Owen and the UN was that once people began to meet again the poison would be sucked out of the conflict and the will to return to war would be sapped. Peter Galbraith, the American ambassador to Croatia, was less sanguine. He said that the meetings reminded him of Christmas truces between German and British troops during the First World War, when the soldiers would play football with one another before returning to the trenches to try and kill each other. A day after the Orthodox Easter, Krajina leader Milan Martić closed the highway for twenty-four hours. When it reopened a Croat waiting in one of the petrol stations murdered a Serb who had earlier killed his brother. That Serb's brother then shot at motorists on the road. A day or so later, on 1 May, the Croatian Army launched Operation Blitz. Within forty hours all of western Slavonia had been recaptured.

The results of this first lightning Croatian operation deserve mention. Due to the economic agreement that had opened the motorway, the Serbian guard in western Slavonia had been lowered. Of the 12,000 to 15,000 Serbs who lived there before the Croatian assault, only a few hundred remained afterwards.

The logic of an exchange of populations or rather of ethnic-territorial consolidation was that the Croats who had fled during the Serbian capture of the area in 1991 could now return. The Croatian government announced that there were some 14,000 Croats who could now come home. Some of them could be found weeping at the side of the road by the often gutted remains of their houses, which they were now able to see again for the first time. Others discovered that Serb refugees from Croat-held areas had since 1991 been living in their houses, which they had abandoned as Croatian forces closed in.

As the Serbs fled, soldiers and their families mixed in together, one of their columns came under fire and an unknown number of people died. A few days later their cars remained in the ditches where they had crashed. Just as everywhere else where such scenes took place in the former Yugoslavia, it was the presence of thousands of scattered family photos which brought home the tragedy. Grabbed in haste and later abandoned in panic, trampled in the mud or flying in the wind, these were mute witness to the end of centuries of history. This second outflow of Serbs from western Slavonia meant that there were now hardly any Serbs remaining in an area which for hundreds of years had had a considerable Orthodox population. One of the lost photos showed a little boy and his grandfather standing together with a giant pumpkin. In western Slavonia, for Serbs, such simple scenes would never be seen again.

Of course, the dismal story of the Serbs from western Slavonia did not just end with their flight. As noted above, many of these refugees were directed to Serb-held eastern Croatia, but in the region around Banja

Luka their arrival provoked a new round of attacks against its remaining Croats. The UNHCR wrote in its monthly report:

> One of the most brutal attacks took place on 12 May, when the church and parish building in Presnace were blown up. The parish priest and a nun disappeared. When the villagers asked the Serb authorities for their whereabouts, they were reportedly told that they were 'where they should be'. Subsequently, their burnt bodies were found in the ruins of the parish building. Five days later the church in Trn was also destroyed and the priest's house was burnt down. Similar incidents have continued. . . .
>
> There have also been several attacks against Croat homes with hand grenades and other explosives. On 15 May an elderly Croat couple was reportedly killed in a village north of Banja Luka.
>
> Evictions of Croats from their homes have also continued. On 27 May, armed men in uniform arrived in buses at the village of Šargovac. They dragged all Croats (about 50 of them) out of their homes and put them in the buses. Some elderly people who tried to resist were beaten. Most of the houses were then immediately occupied by Serb refugees from western Slavonia.[7]

Exactly the same was to happen again when the tens of thousands of Serbs flooded out of Knin Krajina in August.

In the early weeks of the Bosnian war the UNHCR announced that some 10,000 people a week were being ethnically cleansed or were in flight. The majority of them were Muslims, but Croats and Serbs also shared this misery. By the end of 1992 more than two million people had left their homes, or roughly half the pre-war population of Bosnia. That so many left so quickly, in the first two months of the war, bears testament to the brutal organisation of the initial cleansing operation. Soon, though, those Serbs whose villages ended up on the 'wrong' side of the lines found that they would pay the price for the crimes that had been committed in the name of their nation and freedom.

Serbian villages, for example those near Kalesija in eastern Bosnia but on the government side of the lines, were quickly cleared in operations that actually helped establish the lines. While the Muslims on the Serbian side were evicted at gunpoint, the Serbs left mostly under different circumstances. In the first weeks of the war individuals or whole groups just got in their cars and fled. Bosnian government forces also descended on villages which had been armed by the SDS and gave them an ultimatum to disarm. This usually produced panic which prompted the villagers to flee. Sometimes they did not travel very far. The Serbian population of Jeginov Lug fled *en masse* in April 1992 having been told to disarm. They left in a convoy during the night while the JNA gave them cover. Twenty miles later they came to the majority Serbian village of Osmaci, from where, within weeks, the local Muslims were expelled. The Jeginov Lug refugees then began to paint the name of their old village on the walls of their new, formerly Muslim-owned houses. Asked why Jeginov Lug's people had been ready to abandon their houses so quickly one man said, 'During the Second World War, 178 Serbs were killed there, so people were afraid it would happen again.'

In other areas, such as along the Neretva valley or in the warzones in the north, Croatian and Muslim forces moved quickly to seize control of Serbian villages. Men were interned in camps and often the women and children too. Conditions were appalling and beatings were common, as were rapes and murders. Some camps such as Čelebići were far worse than others, but it does not seem that at any of these places mass murder on the scale of Omarska was committed.

For the Serbs the situation was always worse the further away their settlements were from the big towns, especially Sarajevo. Even in those cases where Serbs did not feel any personal pressure to leave, many wanted to go because they found themselves separated from the rest of their families who had ended up on the other side of the lines. Discreet channels of escape were also open far more often than is generally realised. For example the Croatian HVO helped Serbs escape from Zenica and other parts of central Bosnia. Likewise the Bosnian Serbs frequently helped Croats to escape from Muslim-held territory. Money was generally a factor here, but mutual interest was of equal importance.

16

ARSENIJE'S CHILDREN

There is a theory which holds that history is accelerating. While the great empires of the past, the Chinese, the Roman or the Ottoman for example, lasted for centuries, 'modern' empires are increasingly short-lived affairs. Take the British or French colonial empires: at their maximum extents they lasted for only a matter of decades, as did Soviet *de facto* rule in eastern Europe.

Serbian history provides its own modest parallel. The new Serbian Empire founded by Slobodan Milošević reached its territorial peak in the autumn and winter of 1992. Apart from 'inner Serbia' and Vojvodina it covered Kosovo, 70 per cent of Bosnia and more than one-quarter of Croatia. In January 1993 the Croats launched their successful military operation to take back certain strategic points in Krajina. From then on, with a few exceptions such as Srebrenica, the Serbs were in retreat. In this way they seem to conform to the theory. Tsar Dušan's empire, which reached its height in 1355, lasted barely twenty years. But the second empire lasted just three months at its maximum extent, and by the end of 1995 was drastically reduced in size. As the matter of Kosovo remains unresolved, the possibility that the 'Serbian Lands' will continue to shrink cannot be ruled out.

Serbs to Sacrifice

Embittered and in exile, Svetozar Pribićević, the Croatian Serb politician who had played such a key role in the foundation and first years of the Kingdom of Yugoslavia, wrote that 'Belgrade power holders always called upon the Serbs of Croatia for help when it was feignedly necessary to defend imperiled state unity or to fight against "Croat separatism". But as soon as official Belgrade felt it could compromise with the Croats, it would sacrifice the Serbs of Croatia without hesitation and with merry heart, making them a red rag to Croat eyes.'[1]

These words were as true in the 1990s as they had been in 1933 when Pribićević wrote them.

After four years of war and diplomatic stalemate, 1995 was the year that everything changed. It was not just that Croatia was now well armed. It was the realisation among the Serbs outside Serbia that they had been betrayed, that Milošević really would sacrifice them 'without hesitation and with merry heart', which undermined morale. This was coupled with the bitterness felt towards so many of their leaders, who they now realised had only been after money or power. This mood of defeatism was fatally to weaken the Serbs outside Serbia and to lead tens of thousands to vote with their feet.

Before the Croats took back Knin Krajina, large parts of the area were already almost empty of people because, apart from the Croats who had been cleansed, so many Serbs were leaving of their own accord. The same was true in vast areas of Serb-held Bosnia, which were also almost without people. Derventa and Modriča in the north were virtual ghost towns. Their Muslims and Croats had fled and there was little work for the Serbs left to eke out an existence in their ruins. Kozarac, near Prijedor, which had been completely cleansed of its original Muslim inhabitants, was a ruin that stretched for fifteen kilometres along the road. Pudin Han and hundreds of other small settlements were left completely uninhabited. The problem that the Serbian authorities found was that, especially as the war dragged on, fewer and fewer wished to fight, let alone stay in the Republika Srpska or in Krajina. Reports frequently stated that hundreds, if not thousands, of people, especially those with a good education and qualifications, were leaving every month.

By the early summer of 1995 the problem of emigration had become so great that police were forced to trawl the restaurants of Belgrade looking for young Serb men from Bosnia and Croatia, whom they were packing on to buses and off home to fight. It was no coincidence that Mirjana Marković, Milošević's wife, chose to write in her magazine column in June:

Some of the fighters for the Serb cause in Bosnia and the Serbian Krajina live in Belgrade, without having spent a single day on the battlefield and without any intention of doing so. Most of them came from the battle zones on time, before the war broke out or at its very beginning. They came to Belgrade, and other cities in Serbia, with their children, their money and their ambitions – to take up business, political and social positions in general that would make them first class citizens.

As regards the Serb people in Bosnia and Serbian Krajina, only the poor are left there to wage war. The patriots from Bosnia and Krajina living in Belgrade are not satisfied with the results of the war, and they express their dissatisfaction aggressively. They are angry with the poor in Bosnia's and Krajina's rugged hills for not being more efficient. . . . It simply does not occur to them that they must take part themselves in the war which they have launched with so much propaganda. If they are so bitter about what is happening to Serb homes, why didn't they stay in Bosnia to defend them? Why did they come here in the first place?! Did they expect someone else to defend their homes? Their poor neighbours in Bosnia and Krajina, for instance, who do not have anywhere to go, or do not want to go anywhere? Or the youths from Serbia's towns and villages who are supposed to prove their patriotism by getting killed for the homes of those who left them and came to Belgrade to run their restaurants and firms.[2]

It had all been so different at the beginning. Most men who found themselves on the Serbian side of the frontlines were mobilised whether they liked it or not, but there was also enthusiasm. Not only did most genuinely believe they were waging a defensive war to prevent a 'new genocide' of the Serbian people but they were borne aloft by their early victories, intoxicated with the joy of the military triumphs which they believed were their generation's contribution to Serbian martial history. These were illusions that only gradually began to fade. Early Serbian victories did not mean defeat for their enemies. And indeed the longer the conflict continued the more the prospect of actually winning the war began to recede. As peace plans came and went it seemed as though this was a war without end, and the longer the situation went on the better armed the enemy became. Meanwhile the rich had either long since left or were getting richer and everyone else was simply left to survive as best they could. Many Bosnian Serbs also came to resent the fact that Karadžić, a notorious gambler, not only spent much time at the tables of the Hotel Metropol in Belgrade but was gambling with their lives too. By 1995 it was common for Bosnian Serbs privately to whisper things such as 'Karadžić and the others are all crooks. Everyone I know wants to get out. But if I go the authorities will take revenge on my parents, they could be kicked out of their flat. So what can I do?'

The operation in May 1995 which had crushed the Serbs in western Slavonia proved not just that the Croats were no longer the puny military force they had once been but that the morale of ordinary Serbs had been shattered. Following the withering comments from Mrs Marković, those attuned to such signals understood that the Krajina and Bosnian Serbs were now on their own.

Mrs Marković's piece was proof positive of the enduring truth of Pribićević's observation. The Krajina Serbs and those of Bosnia too had been willing tools of Milošević when he believed he could have his way in carving out a new Serbian state from the old Yugoslavia. Now they were a burden to be shuffled off so that Serbia could have sanctions lifted and Milošević, who had already transformed himself from communist to nationalist, could now evolve into a peacemaker. He was shameless in his cynicism. In November 1995 Bosnian, Serbian and Croatian leaders all found themselves negotiating for peace at an American air force base in Dayton, Ohio. Afterwards Haris Silajdžić, then the Bosnian prime minister, recalled that Milošević had said to him, 'You deserve Sarajevo because you fought for it and those cowards killed you from the hills. . . .'[3]

Simplifying Matters

The decision by Milošević to abandon the Krajina Serbs in particular was not one that was made overnight. It came about as part of a gradual realisation that there was little that could be done to help them without involving Serbia itself in a full-scale war. The involvement of ordinary troops from Serbia had proved deeply unpopular at home, so after the Vukovar campaign, which ended in November 1991, they were rarely used again. Of course professional commando and police units as well as paramilitaries from Serbia were still used in Croatia and Bosnia, but the increasing reluctance of ordinary Serbs to die for their brothers affected morale. It also affected the way Milošević looked at the problem. The quintessential opportunist, he decided that the best solution was to try and put Serbian gains 'on hold'. To this end, the UN had already been invited to safeguard the winnings in Croatia and he felt that in Bosnia the Serbs should profit from the various diplomatic initiatives to win time and to find a formula to preserve Serbian gains there too.

What went wrong for Krajina was that its politics became inextricably bound up with those of the Bosnian Serbs. In its dying months it was paralysed by the dispute between hardliners who rejected a compromise with Croatia and those who, in tune with Milošević, wanted to settle for some form of autonomy within Croatia which left open the possibility of secession at a later date. The hardliners, who were in the ascendant, were linked to the Bosnian Serbs and the problem was that their leadership had outgrown Milošević's tutelage and were capable of independent political action.

This came into sharp focus with the Bosnian Serb rejection of the Vance–Owen peace plan in May 1993.[4] Lord Owen, the special peace envoy of the EC, working together with Cyrus Vance, the UN envoy, came up with a plan to divide Bosnia into ten provinces. The effect of this, if it had ever been implemented, would have been to reverse ethnic cleansing and remake some form of Bosnian state. At a tense meeting of all the parties in Athens on 2–3 May 1993 Milošević prevailed upon Karadžić to sign the plan. Days later, at the prompting of General Mladić and despite the pleading of Milošević, the Bosnian Serb parliament rejected it. The Vance–Owen plan was infinitely preferable to the Dayton Accord which halted the war in 1995. However, it is a mistake to believe that, had the Bosnian Serb parliament sitting in the Paradise Valley Hotel in the mountains above Sarajevo accepted it, it would ever have been implemented. Milošević urged the Bosnian Serbs to accept the plan on the premise that they had won the war and the Vance–Owen plan was the best guarantee that they could keep most of the land they now controlled. There was no intention of actually fulfilling its terms, just as the Serbian leadership had never intended to fulfil the terms of the Vance plan for Croatia. And they never hid this. Dragoslav Rančić was an aide to Dobrica Ćosić, then in the more or less nominal post of Yugoslav president. Both were in the delegation to Athens. As Lord Owen celebrated his short-lived success by talking of 'a happy day in the Balkans', Rančić crowed that while the plan was a 'basis to stop the bloodshed' it was 'just a first stage'. Of the proposed Vance–Owen Bosnia he said, 'This new state is just a monster, it is not going to last long. Not even Lord Owen believes it.'

Rančić said that the view of the delegation from Belgrade was that acceptance was an 'interim solution' until such time as Bosnia collapsed and a formal union of the new Federal Yugoslavia of Serbia and Montenegro with the Republika Srpska and Krajina could be accomplished.[5] When that happened Bosnia's Muslims would be left with a 'Balkan Lesotho'. Radovan Karadžić may rue the day the Bosnian Serb parliament rejected the Vance–Owen plan. On the same day, in New York, Boutros Boutros Ghali, the UN secretary general, urged the Security Council to set up an international tribunal in The Hague, to try those accused of war crimes in the former Yugoslavia. If the war had stopped then, this idea might have died. As it was the tribunal was created and was to indict both Karadžić and Mladić.

The death of the Vance–Owen plan was not the end of diplomatic efforts to end the war. For the next two years various plans were canvassed which, despite being rejected either by the Bosnian Serbs or by the Muslims, were to provide the basis for the eventual plan accepted at Dayton in November 1995. The first post-Vance–Owen plan envisaged a Bosnian 'Union of Three Republics'. In this way the international community accepted the ethnic partition of the country. In December 1993 the European Union Action Plan came up with the formula of dividing Bosnia by giving 51 per cent to the Muslims and Croats and 49 per cent to the Serbs. Diplomatically 1994 was dominated by the activities of the Contact Group, which was made up of diplomats from the United States, Russia, Britain, France and Germany. Frustrated by the lack of progress, the Americans, originally wary of involvement, came to take the lead.

In February 1994 following the deaths of sixty-nine people killed by a shell in Sarajevo's Markale market, NATO at the request of the UN demanded that the Serbs withdraw their heavy guns from around the city.[6] Threatened with bombing, the Serbs eventually complied. Over the year however the UN asked NATO to hit various Serbian positions in retaliation for numerous hostile acts, but General Mladić quickly came to understand that his forces could well absorb these relative 'pinprick' raids. This bolstered the Bosnian Serb leadership's spirit of rejectionism. In May 1995 Mladić's troops took some 375 UN soldiers hostage after NATO had flown its most serious raids to date, hitting two Bosnian Serb ammunition dumps close to Pale. By 18 June the hostages were released, but these events were to set in train a sequence of events which was to lead to a Serbian disaster.

The hostages affair had two immediate consequences. First, from then on there were very few UN personnel, or potential hostages, left on Bosnian Serb territory, which meant that an obstacle to further air raids had been removed. Secondly, an Anglo-French-led Rapid Reaction Force was set up to react more vigorously to attacks on the UN or to perform other tasks set for it. Nervous about its potential, General Mladić decided that now was the time for action, before it was up and running. It was also clear from the diplomatic messages being sent that Srebrenica was a major obstacle to any agreement, and American diplomats were discreetly suggesting that it should be exchanged for territory elsewhere. Srebrenica had tremendous symbolic importance for the Muslims but strategic importance for the Serbs because of its location on the border with Serbia. However, one month before the Serbs attacked, Nasir Orić, Srebrenica's commander, and his HQ staff were called to Tuzla for consultations and, despite their pleadings, never allowed back. Later he let it be known that he believed that Srebrenica had been sacrificed by the government in Sarajevo.[7] After the town's fall there were reports which suggested that US intelligence had known about Serb preparations to attack but had done nothing to prevent it.[8] This seems highly likely if one takes into account the US suggestions that Srebrenica should be exchanged, which effectively meant that far from reversing ethnic cleansing a decision had been made that more was needed. The removal of Nasir Orić suggests that the government in Sarajevo had come to the same conclusion, otherwise why else would Srebrenica have been left to its fate without its highly capable commanders? Anthony Lake, President Clinton's national security adviser, said later that a decision was made that, 'rather than draw the lines [in Bosnia] in a kind of higgledy-piggledy way that might make sense' in terms of where the current populations were, they should 'do what we could to have a territory that was as simplified as possible'.[9]

Thinking like this was the green light for the conquest not only of Srebrenica but of Krajina too. Even if there were no formal meetings in which such forms of brutal population exchanges were mooted, the messages were clearly understood by all concerned. The disaster was that, while it was possible, if not highly likely, that the Croatian offensive on Krajina would drive out its population, no one had foreseen that Mladić would oversee the wholesale slaughter of thousands of Srebrenica's men after it duly fell in July. This horrible event could not be ignored, but it could nonetheless be used thanks to a little 'news management'. Immediately after the massacres took place, the Americans had satellite pictures showing the location of mass graves but these were released in the UN Security Council only on 9 August, at such a time as to distract attention from the exodus of Krajina's entire population which was then taking place. There can be no underestimating the cynicism of politicians, especially when they have a precise aim in mind. As Warren Christopher, the US secretary of state, admitted later about the Croatian offensive on Krajina, 'We did not think that kind of an attack could do anything other than create a lot of refugees and cause a humanitarian problem. On the other hand, it always had the prospect of simplifying matters.'[10]

Unlike in 1991 Croatia was now a well-armed power and waiting for the right time to strike. The west had turned a blind eye to the arming of Croatia and actively encouraged the clandestine arming of Bosnia, both in contravention of the UN arms embargo on former Yugoslavia. Retired American officers, with official US backing, had also been training the Croatian Army. By itself, however, compared to the combined might of Serbia, Montenegro, the Bosnian Serbs and the Krajina Serbs, Croatia was still weak. With a large arsenal of rockets at their disposal the Serbs could have devastated Croatian cities, but when Milan Martić, the Krajina leader, had fired a rocket at Zagreb city centre in May, during the Croatian offensive on western Slavonia, Milošević had been furious. He then pulled out many of the remaining rockets. Just before the Croats attacked Krajina the Americans delivered a mild warning which President Tudjman interpreted as a signal that he could attack. And, of course, he knew that Serbia would not help the Krajina Serbs because Milošević had as good as told him. After all, as Mrs Marković had written in the wake of the Serbian flight from western Slavonia, 'Did they expect someone else to defend their homes?'

While the fall of Srebrenica to the Serbs in mid-July and the fall of Krajina to the Croats two week later ironed out these particular cartographic and demographic problems, they did not have the desired effect of bringing the Bosnian Serb leadership to heel. This meant getting them to endorse the proposed 51–49 per cent split in Bosnia. There was also another problem: because Bosnia was an internationally recognised country, the Serbs had to be made to agree, at least on paper, that Bosnia was *de jure* one country, even if in reality it was not. In the wake of the traumatic events of the past few weeks American diplomats decided that now was the right time to finish the job. On 28 August a shell deemed by the UN to come from a Serbian position killed thirty-seven people in Sarajevo. The Serbs had not realised to what an extent things had changed. As Richard Holbrooke, the American under secretary of state for European affairs, who was leading the diplomatic offensive, said, 'Finally the decks were cleared for a real military response, not some piece of garbage.'[11]

Wave after wave of NATO air raids began which were designed to cripple the Bosnian Serb Army. Arms and fuel dumps were hit and, even more importantly, so was the military's communications network. Taking advantage of this, Croatian and Bosnian Army forces surged forward in western Bosnia. Serbian lines collapsed and the region's population fled. Much of this area was sparsely populated, but for hundreds of years it had been an indisputably Serbian area. The region of Bosansko Grahovo had been home to only 8,303 souls before the war, but 95 per cent of them had been Serbs. Similarly neighbouring Titov Drvar had been home to 17,079 people, 97 per cent of whom had been Serbs.[12] Before the fall of Krajina these areas were in the middle of a belt of Serb-held territory, so no defences had ever been prepared. To what extent western Bosnia was abandoned by the Serbs because morale had collapsed or because military officers acting on orders from Belgrade did not defend it or because of a tacit deal to exchange territory remains an open question. However, it is an extraordinary fact that by the time the Serbs started to put up an active defence the proportion of land held by the Serbs in Bosnia had dropped from 70 per cent to almost exactly the 49 per cent deemed to be their share by the diplomats. Bosnian Muslim generals wanted to continue the offensive on to Banja Luka, but the Croats having taken as much as they wanted – a wide defensive swathe along their border – were no longer prepared to help the Muslims carry on. As they had the heavy artillery and Alija Izetbegović was now under strong American pressure to stop fighting, the campaign which had changed the map in Bosnia and Croatia ground to a halt. A ceasefire in Bosnia came into effect on 5 October.

The ebullient Holbrooke struck while the iron was hot. The various Balkan leaders were corralled into going to Wright-Patterson airbase in Dayton, Ohio, where for twenty-one days in November they negotiated a final settlement. The Bosnian Serb leadership, in the face of events,

1996: Former Yugoslavia after the Fall of Krajina, August 1995, and the Implementation of the Dayton Accord, Signed November 1995

had reluctantly agreed to hand over all their decision-making rights to Milošević. Although the proportion of land held by the various parties in Bosnia now roughly conformed to the desired 49–51 per cent split, much of the hard bargaining that followed was about territorial adjustments to 'correct' the map. Milošević gave up the Serb-held areas of Sarajevo, while some of the former Serb-held lands in western Bosnia were returned to him. The deal was struck on 21 November 1995. On paper, Bosnia was to remain one state, but it was divided into two entities: the Federation, which included Croatian and Muslim parts, and the Republika Srpska. In theory it was to have a loose form of central government and all refugees were supposed to return home. The plan was to be guaranteed by 60,000 mostly NATO troops, one-third of whom were American and who, initially, were to stay in Bosnia for a year.

The disengagement of forces foreseen by the NATO-led Imple-mentation Force, IFOR, proved a great success. Soldiers went home. But refugees did not. Although lip-service was paid to articles in the Dayton Accord that called for their return, it was apparently accepted, by the international community at least, that returning Bosnia to its pre-war mixed population would not 'simplify matters' in the future. By contrast it was believed in Serbia that sooner or later the bulk of the Bosnian Serb refugees who had taken shelter there would be returned to the Republika Srpska, whether they came from the parts under its control or not. It was thought that this was necessary to bolster its depleted population.

Throughout the spring of 1996 pressure mounted for something to be done about Radovan Karadžić, indicted by The Hague War Crimes Tribunal. IFOR troops were reluctant to arrest the man, fearing reprisals if they did. On 19 July though Richard Holbrooke secured his withdrawal from public life. Perhaps awaiting eventual arrest Karadžić remained holed up in his house in Pale. His official functions were taken over by Biljana Plavšić.

On 14 September 1996 Bosnians voted in their first post-war elections. The Republika Srpska voted for its institutions and for a common three-man presidency and parliament. On the hustings Karadžić was hailed as 'our Karadjordje'. Biljana Plavšić was elected president of the Republika Srpska and Momčilo Krajišnik as the first Serbian representative on the common presidency.

In the short term, with IFOR in Bosnia and with scaled-down successor forces foreseen for several years to come, a return to war did not look likely. At first, though, Serb intransigence in refusing to let refugees come home appeared to be laying the ground for the excuse Muslims and Croats might need to start the war again at a later date. However, in 1997 the unexpected happened. Mrs Plavšić fell out with Karadžić, and Krajišnik accused them both of corruption on a massive scale. Supported now by the Western powers she declared that the future survival of the Republika Srpska depended on its support for Dayton and pledged to cooperate to make it work.

The Land of the Living Past

When the war began in Croatia, many believed that it was only a matter of time before Kosovo exploded in violence too. Afer all, the cancer of discontent which ended up killing Yugoslavia had begun in Kosovo. The first lesson of the Balkans, however, is to expect the unexpected. While war raged across the rest of the former Yugoslavia Kosovo remained quiet.

Despite Milošević's ending of the province's autonomy, the process of Serbian emigration was not halted and Serbia kept Kosovo under tight police control. Ymer Muhaxheri, president in Peć of the main Albanian political party in Kosovo, summed up what forms this took:

> The pressure is continuous. Police expeditions, raids on villages, armed civilians parading around. They always use weapon searches as excuses. They harass families and beat parents in front of their children. Very rarely are there no incidents. Here, in town, the repression takes an uglier form. They use fiscal controls . . . to break the Albanian shop owners. They surround one part of the town and search everyone to collect hard currency. No one dares react. There is no contact between the citizens and the government.[13]

Another man explained:

> The police charge into the marketplace whenever they want and search everyone. Last Saturday, they blocked seven streets and searched everyone who was there. They took everything that people were selling. I was in a little bar near the market at the time. Policemen entered the place and said, 'Put everything you have on the table!' They were wearing police uniforms and they had machine-guns. I had twenty Deutsche-marks on me, and they took it.[14]

Albanians in Kosovo say they live under occupation, and for them Serbian rule is an occupation. Armoured cars prowl through towns, war-planes swoop overhead and since 1989 most Albanians have either been sacked from their jobs or have left them in protest. Just as many Serbs have abandoned the area in search of work, scores or maybe hundreds of thousands of Albanians have left for Germany, Switzerland and other countries to look for jobs. Repressed though it is, Kosovo is also one of the oddest places in Europe.

In a curious mirror-image to Milošević's SPS, for so long the dominating power in Serbian politics, Kosovo Albanian politics are dominated by the Democratic League of Kosova (LDK). (Kosova is the Albanian for Kosovo.) The party is led by Ibrahim Rugova whose father was executed by the communists when they restored the region to Yugoslav control. His trademark is a scarf worn at all times. The LDK brooks little dissent and those that challenge it are howled down in LDK publications and can even be ostracised in the tight-knit Albanian community. Kosovo is odd because, despite constant police repression, Albanian politicians have held semi-underground polls, have declared Kosovo 'independent', have set up a parallel educational and health system, and have hailed Rugova as president of the Republic of Kosova.[15] Woe betide any Albanian family or shop or businessman who will not pay his dues to Kosova's tax collectors. In his capacity as president, Rugova sweeps out of his headquarters, a ramshackle wooden building, hops into a limousine surrounded by aides and bodyguards and drives about Priština just like a real Balkan president. A government-in-exile complete with ministers commutes between Tirana, Germany and Skopje. Rugova travels abroad to lobby for international recognition for his phantom state, but despite the odd hassle over his passport he has not been arrested since challenging Serbian power in such a blatant fashion. Presumably the Serbian authorities believe that as long as he keeps his militants in check it would only serve to aggravate the situation if they decided to do anything about him.

Edith Durham, a redoubtable Englishwoman who travelled through this part of the Balkans in the years before the First World War, wrote in 1908 that in the then still Turkish province of Kosovo life had been 'an elemental struggle for existence and survival of the strongest, carried out in relentless obedience to Nature's law, which says, "There is not place for you both. You must kill – or be killed."'[16]

Serbs argue that Kosovo is kept under such a tight regime because the LDK is a separatist party. The LDK indeed proclaims this loud and clear. It has already declared its notional independence, and opinion polls show that the vast majority of Kosovo Albanians support this.[17]

Many westerners in search of simplicity like to portray the Kosovo problem as merely a question of human rights. Inevitably it is far more complex than that. During the wars in Croatia and Bosnia, the Kosovo Albanian leadership in no way stuck up for the Croats or the Bosnian Muslims. This was because, although in their hearts they wanted to see the Serbs defeated and humiliated, their heads told them that a Serbian victory was in their political interests. At first this seems contradictory. Why would they want their enemies to defeat potential friends? The answer is that Kosovo Albanian leaders declared that they only wanted the same as the Serbs. They said that if the Serbs, at 12 per cent of the population of Croatia or 31 per cent of the population of Bosnia, were entitled to their own states, by the same logic Kosovo's Albanians, at some 16 per cent of rump Yugoslavia's population and more than 90 per cent of Kosovo's, were more than entitled to the same thing. If Krajina and the Republika Srpska could join Serbia, as they had so desired, they argued that Kosovo equally had the right to join Albania if its people wished.

Like the Serbs, they did not want the international community to uphold the principle that Yugoslavia's old republican borders could turn into new inviolable international ones, because that left Kosovo, as a mere province rather than a republic, trapped inside Serbia. If the Serbian leaders succeeded in their aims and managed to have internationally recognised borders changed, the precedent would be set by which it would be very hard for the international community to refuse to Kosovo Albanians what it had granted to Serbs in Bosnia and Croatia. As it is, the Croatian Serbs have lost their homes, but maybe the autonomy of the Republika Srpska will mean that one day its territory will accrue *de jure* to Serbia. The Serbian fear is that, if Kosovo returns to full autonomy, this too will just be a stepping stone to the real aim.

While he was president of Yugoslavia in 1992 and 1993, Dobrica Ćosić made discreet contact with Kosovo Albanian leaders. He wanted to discuss the territorial division of the province, with the Albanian part, except for a number of Serbian enclaves, leaving Serbia. This was rejected by Albanian leaders.

After the Dayton Accord for Bosnia, Serbs in Kosovo were downcast. They believed that sooner or later the international community would apply pressure on Serbia to restore Kosovo's autonomy. As far as they were concerned the harsh reality of this would mean restoring police and economic powers to Albanians. And just as in the past, this would mean that the whip would change hands and pass to the 'enemy' community. Of all the leaders of former Yugoslavia, Rugova has perhaps played the shrewdest game. By preventing an Albanian *intifada*, he has avoided giving the Serbs an excuse to use force to try to ethnically cleanse Kosovo. His policy is one of waiting until there are simply no more Serbs left in Kosovo or their numbers become so insignificant that somehow the province falls to his people like a ripe fruit. It is a long-term policy and, despite discontent aroused by the belief that so far it has achieved nothing, in fact it has achieved much. It has saved lives and, unlike the Krajina Serbs for example, kept Kosovo's Albanian population of perhaps 1.7 million in their homes.[18]

During the early 1990s, Rugova came under intense international diplomatic pressure not to open some form of hostilities. Just as the international community has on paper, if not in reality, insisted that Bosnia is one country, the borders of Serbia too are sacrosanct.

There is another element in the Kosovo equation which is rarely considered. While the Bosnian and Croatian Serbs had a powerful backer in Serbia, Kosovo does not have such a godfather in Albania. Albanian history has been very different from Serbian history and, except under the Ottoman Empire, which is not comparable, Albanians have never lived in one state together. In Albania itself, many look on their brothers in Kosovo as potential troublemakers who, if they start a war, will bring disaster upon Albania too. Most Albanians in Albania are desperate that their country should never again be isolated from the rest of Europe as it was under Enver Hoxha, and they fear that trouble in Kosovo will suck them into a war and swamp them with refugees. After the fall of communism, an enormous residue of ill will was left behind in Albania by a number of sharp-suited Kosovo businessmen who embezzled large amounts of money having promised much in terms of investment. Another factor is that Kosovo Albanians tend to look down on their brothers in Albania as country cousins. They point out that modern Albanian nationalism was born in Kosovo, in Prizren in 1878, and they assume that in a future Greater Albania Priština will be its capital, not little Tirana.

In 1908 Edith Durham wrote that 'it seemed folly' to her to maintain a 'large and costly' Serbian Orthodox theological college in Prizren, a 'Moslem Albanian town' in which 'around us in the daylight was the Albanian population, waiting, under arms, to defend the land that had been theirs in the beginning of time'. Whether or not Kosovo had in fact been Albanian 'in the beginning of time' was of course questionable, but, as we have seen, it is what people believe rather than what is true that matters. Invited by the director of the college, she 'accepted his hospitality unhappily, for I felt that, so far as Prizren and its neighbourhood were concerned, the cause was lost, dead and gone – as lost as is Calais to England, and the English claim to Normandy. . . . Yet I could not but admire the imaginative nature of the Serb, who will lead a forlorn hope and face death for an idea.'[19]

Serbs say that Kosovo is their Jerusalem, the heart of the Serbian nation. Kosovo Albanians retort that, if this is the case, the Serbian heart beats in a foreign body. Even if Kosovo remains quiet today, that is little guarantee of its future. Durham believed that so overburdened with history and emotion was Kosovo that it was the 'land of the Living Past'.[20] She said of one town: 'Mitrovitza, though it looked so peaceful, is tinder waiting for a spark.'[21] That is the case in Kosovo today.

In 1995 a guerrilla cum terrorist organisation called the Kosovo Liberation Army (KLA) began to emerge in the province. It rejected Rugova's pacifist policies and called for war on the Serbs. Beginning at the end of February 1998 the Serbian police took action against it, after it had begun to claim that it had 'liberated' territory in the central Drenica region. This was an area famed for its resistance to the Serbs after both world wars. The Serbian action claimed the lives of many women and children, and predictably therefore, the opprobrium of the world.

The emergence of the KLA signalled that the uneasy status quo would not last forever. It also seemed to indicate that, if and when it came to war, the conflict in Kosovo would, at least to begin with, resemble the West Bank rather than Bosnia. Aleksa Djilas, the Belgrade historian and commentator, noted sadly that he was pessimistic that talks on a compromise solution would succeed. He predicted that his government would be 'obstinate to the end and then lose everything like in Croatia'. He added that the province looked set to become the 'Serbian Algeria, except that Kosovo means more to us than Algeria did to the French'.

Even if all-out war does not break out, the future is bleak. Ironically, in the wreckage of post-Tito Yugoslavia, it is the two peoples who loathed each other most of all who are still condemned to live together within the same state.[22]

Heavenly People

Serbian leaders have said that they went to war to safeguard the Serbian populations outside Serbia. The result was that hardly any Serbs remained in Croatia, while hundreds of thousands lost their homes in Bosnia too. Hundreds of thousands of Muslims were driven from their homes, as were Bosnian Croats. The destruction of Krajina and the centuries-old Serbian communities in Croatia meant that, with the removal of Serbian power, most Croatian refugees within the republic could go home. Croatian officials also talked excitedly about repopulating former Serbian areas in Croatia with Bosnian Croats from Serbian- or Muslim-held areas. From Serbia itself, as many as 200,000 Serbs may have left to escape the war and the draft, while 300,000 is the oft quoted number of Kosovo Albanians who left the province because of poverty and repression. At least 30,000 Muslims (some say 70,000) left Sandžak and 25,000 Croats and 25,000 Hungarians left Vojvodina. In Bosnia the three ethnic groups were winnowed out by war. Ironically, of Serbia, Croatia and the three post-war bits of Bosnia, the least ethnically pure remained Serbia itself, its Albanian, Hungarian and other minorities ensuring that only two-thirds of its ten million people were actually Serbs.

Before the war began, a frustrated President Tudjman exclaimed, 'What can we do with these Serbs? We can't send them to the moon or stick them on our hats!' The Serbo-Croat idea of exchanging populations was not really about exchanging populations at all. It was all about driving out as many of the other nation as possible. Days after Croatia's victory over the Krajina Serbs in August 1995, Tudjman remarked that the Serbs had 'disappeared ignominiously, as if they had never populated this land. We urged them to stay, but they didn't listen to us and, well, bon voyage.'[23]

Was the war about 'ancient hatreds' or was it simply the manipulation of whole populations whipped up into a frenzy of nationalism by evil politicians for whom standing your ground was more important than the fate of millions? The answer is that the politicians could not have succeeded if there had been no embers to fan. With the exception of Kosovo, most people had lived peacefully together since 1945 and intermarriage, especially in towns, was common. By raking over the coals of history and by using the media to deliver ethnocentric messages, everything that could possibly be done to reawaken all the old demons of the past was done. But everyone must answer for their own actions and, despite the manipulation of the media, far too many people simply abdicated their responsibility.

Exact figures are hard to calculate, but of at least 3.5 million people who fled or left their homes in the former Yugoslavia between 1990 and 1995 at least one million of them were Serbs.[24] Milošević had spun the Serbs dreams of the Empire of Heaven and clothed himself in the glory of the Kosovo myth. Unlike Lazar, however, he chose a kingdom on earth, which is not the kingdom of Lazar's truth and justice. The Serbs like to think of themselves as a 'heavenly people', a strange expression but one which somehow encapsulates the spirit in which they have so often set out to war. This time they were misled and justice was mislaid. Serbian history was misused to do harm to others and give power to the few. When they realised that there would be no quick victory, many soldiers from Serbia gave up on their brother Serbs and deserted. As the conflict dragged on, too many Serbs in Serbia no longer wanted to know. They looked the other way: they stopped watching the news on television and said that there was nothing that they could do. There were small anti-war groups in Belgrade, but few showed their support. Tens of thousands emigrated instead.

For a year after Dayton, Serbia itself remained in a state of stunned post-war shock. In November 1996, though, following the success of opposition parties in local elections, the SPS tried to falsify the results. Hundreds of thousands came out onto the streets and after weeks of daily demonstrations Milošević gave in.

Goran, a thirty-four-year-old film technician, put it this way: 'I was never sure about Milošević but now it is clear to me. These people are just bastards and thieves . . . and they lost the war.' The mainly middle-class protestors felt they were reclaiming Serbia's soul. Inadvertently, they were also beginning the process of redeeming the Serbs in the eyes of the world.

In the end their cause was lost. The opposition coalition which led the rallies fell apart. On 15 July 1997 Milošević traded in his old job as Serbian president and became president of Yugoslavia. There were mutterings of discontent from Montenegro and what looked like the beginnings of a guerrilla war in Kosovo. The future remained bleak.

It is still too early to know how many people died in the war of 1991–5. What seems likely though is that because of the different nature of the war from that of 1941–5 the final death tolls, for Serbs and Croats at least, will be far lower than those of half a century ago.[25] By contrast the destruction of ancient settlements has meant the radical 'simplification' of the maps of Croatia and Bosnia. For the Serbs who lost their homes there was no Empire of Heaven, just flight and humiliation. These people were Arsenije's children. The Serbs, caught up with Lazar's myth, believe that they always stand and fight. When defeat looms, though, they are as prudent as any other people. They run.

Appendix 1: National Structure of Yugoslavia, 1918

	No.	%
Serbs	4,665,851	38.83
Croats	2,856,551	23.77
Slovenes	1,024,761	8.53
Bosnian Muslims[a]	727,650	6.05
Macedonians or Bulgars	585,558	4.87
Other Slav	174,466	1.45
Germans	513,472	4.27
Hungarians	472,409	3.93
Albanians	441,740	3.68
Romanians, Cincars, Vlachs	229,398	1.91
Turks	168,404	1.40
Jews	64,159	0.53
Italians	12,825	0.11
Others	80,079	0.67
Total	12,017,323	100.00

Source: Ivo Banac, *The National Question in Yugoslavia: Origins, History, Politics* (Cornell, Ithaca and London, 1984), p. 58.

Banac has extrapolated these figures from the Yugoslav 1921 census, which was not broken down in this fashion. He says, 'These findings agree generally with similar reconstructions based on various censuses conducted a decade before and a decade after the 1921 census. Still they are greatly flawed.' He believes that the number of Croats is too small and that 'there are reasons for accepting the often repeated charges that the census takers deliberately falsified the figures on the size of minority nationalities, notably the Hungarians and Albanians' (Banac, *National Question*, p. 58).

[a]The term Bosnian Muslim excludes non-Slav Muslims, that is Albanians and Turks, and includes other Slav Muslims such as those of Sandžak. The Muslims in Bosnia were reckoned to be 588,247 strong. The Sandžak Muslim population was calculated to stand at 90,302 people (Banac, *National Question*, p. 50).

APPENDIX 2: YUGOSLAV CENSUS OF 1961

	No.	%
Serbs	7,806,152	42.08
Croats	4,293,809	23.15
Slovenes	1,589,211	8.56
Macedonians	1,045,516	5.66
Montenegrins	513,832	2.77
Muslims	972,960	5.25
Albanians	914,733	4.93
'Yugoslavs'	317,124	1.70
Hungarians	504,369	2.72
Others	591,585	3.18
Total	18,549,291	100.00

Source: Prvoslav Ralić, *Minority Rights in Serbia* (Belgrade, 1992), p. 21.

APPENDIX 3: YUGOSLAV CENSUS OF 1981

	No.	%
Serbs	8,140,000	36.3
Croats	4,428,000	19.8
Muslims[a]	2,000,000	8.9
Slovenes	1,754,000	7.8
Albanians	1,730,000	7.7
Macedonians	1,340,000	6.0
'Yugoslavs'	1,219,000	5.4
Montenegrins	579,000	2.6
Hungarians	427,000	1.9
Others[b]	811,000	3.6
Total	22,428,000	100

Source: Bogdan Denitch, *Ethnic Nationalism: The Tragic Death of Yugoslavia* (Minneapolis and London, 1994), p.29.
[a]'Muslims as an ethnic group', that is mostly Bosnian and Sandžak Muslims.
[b]Including Turks, Romanians, Slovaks, Gypsies, etc.

Population of Serbia and Serbs outside Serbia

Serbia

Population, 1988

Central Serbia	5,850,000
Vojvodina	2,050,000
Kosovo	1,850,000
Total	9,750,000

Population breakdown, 1981 Census

Central Serbia

Serbs	4,865,000
Muslims	152,000
Montenegrins	77,000
Albanians	72,000
Croats	31,000
Bulgarians	31,000
Macedonians	29,000
'Yugoslavs'	272,000

Vojvodina

Serbs	1,107,000
Hungarians	385,000
Croats	109,000
Slovaks	70,000
Romanians	47,000
Montenegrins	43,000
'Yugoslavs'	167,000

Kosovo

Albanians	1,227,000
Serbs	209,000
Muslims	59,000
Montenegrins	27,000

Serbs outside Serbia

Bosnia–Hercegovina	1,321,000
Croatia	532,000
Macedonia	44,000
Slovenia	42,000
Montenegro	19,000

Population of Bosnia–Hercegovina and Slav Muslims outside Bosnia–Hercegovina

Bosnia–Hercegovina

Total population, 1988

4,440,000

Population breakdown, 1981 Census

Muslims	1,630,000
Serbs	1,321,000
Croats	758,000
'Yugoslavs'	326,000

Slav Muslim Population outside Bosnia–Hercegovina

Central Serbia	152,000
Montenegro	78,000
Kosovo	59,000
Macedonia	40,000
Croatia	24,000

Population of Croatia and Croats outside Croatia

Croatia

Total population, 1988

4,680,000

Population breakdown, 1981 Census

Croats	3,455,000
Serbs	532,000
Hungarians	25,000
Slovenes	25,000
'Yugoslavs'	379,000

Croats outside Croatia

Bosnia-Hercegovina	758,000
Vojvodina	109,000
Slovenia	56,000
Central Serbia	31,000

Source: André Sellier and Jean Sellier, *Atlas des peuples d'Europe centrale* (Paris, 1991), pp.143–66.

Appendix 4: Yugoslav Census of 1991

Serbia and Montenegro

Population

Montenegro	616,327
Serbia	9,721,177
Total	10,337,504

Serbia's Population as Broken Down between Central or 'Inner' Serbia and the Two Provinces

Central Serbia	5,753,825
Kosovo and Metohija	1,954,744
Vojvodina	2,012,605

Ethnic Breakdown for Serbia and Montenegro Combined (%)

Serbs	62.3
Montenegrins	5.0
'Yugoslavs'	3.3
Albanians	16.6
Hungarians	3.3
Muslims	3.2
Croats	1.1
Romanies	1.3
Others	3.9

Source: Statistical Pocket Book: Federal Republic of Yugoslavia (Belgrade, 1993).

Croatia

Total population

4,760,344

Ethnic breakdown (%)

Croats	77.9
Serbs	12.2
'Yugoslavs'	2.2
Muslims	1.0
Others	6.8

Source: Milovan Baletić (ed.), *Croatia 1994* (Zagreb, 1994).

Bosnia–Hercegovina

Total population

4,354,911

Ethnic breakdown (%)

Muslims	43.7
Serbs	31.3
Croats	17.3
'Yugoslavs' and others	7.0

Source: Prof. Dr Ante Markotić, Ejub Sijerčić and Asim Abdurahmanović, 'Ethnic Map of Bosnia–Herzegovina', *Why* (Sarajevo), February 1992.

NOTES

Preface

1. Oddone Talpo, *Dalmazia: Una cronaca per la storia (1941)* (Rome, 1985).

Chapter One: Death Does Not Exist

1. Miloš Crnjanski (Tsernianski in French transliteration), *Migrations* (Paris, 1992), p. 1163. Crnjanski (1893–1977) was one of the most illustrious Serbian novelists of the century. *Migrations* follows the fortunes of the Serbs in eighteenth-century (Austrian) Vojvodina and their migrations to 'Holy Russia' – in fact mostly to Kiev and lands now in the Ukraine.
2. Slobodan Mileusnić, *The Monastery of Krka* (Belgrade, 1994), p. 11.
3. *Vreme/Dossier: From the Memorandum to War* (Belgrade, n.d.). For a full English text see Kosta Mihailović and Vasilije Krestić, *Memorandum of the Serbian Academy of Sciences and Arts: Answers to Criticisms* (Belgrade, 1995).
4. *Ibid.*
5. *Politika*, 30–31 August 1991.
6. John V. A. Fine, *The Early Medieval Balkans: A Critical Survey from the Sixth to the Late Twelfth Century* (Ann Arbor, 1983), p. 57. An indispensable study for this period.
7. *Ibid.*, pp. 52–53. See also Henrik Birnbaum, 'Was There a Slavic Landtaking of the Balkans and, If So, Along What Routes Did It Proceed?', in Dimitrije Djordjević, and Radovan Samardžić, *Migrations in Balkan History* (Belgrade, 1989).
8. Some sources date the conversion of the Serbs, or at least the first Serbian grand *župan*, to the 870s, during the reign of Mutimir, who died in 890 or 891. He is not to be confused with the Croatian Mutimir who began ruling the Croats in 892. On the conversion of the Serbs see Stephen Clissold (ed.), *A Short History of Yugoslavia: From Early Times to 1966* (Cambridge, 1966), p. 89. See also Fine, *Early Medieval Balkans*, pp. 141–142.
9. Dragoslav Antonijević, 'Cattle-breeders' Migrations in the Balkans through the Centuries', in Djordjević and Samardžić, *Migrations*, p. 152. I am indebted to this piece for many of the details about the Vlachs contained here.
10. Alberto Fortis, *Travels into Dalmatia* (London, 1778), p. 63.
11. Oddone Talpo, *Dalmazia: Una cronica per la storia (1941)* (Rome, 1985), pp. 281 and 182.
12. Fortis, *Travels*, p. 53.
13. Dragoljub Dragojlović, 'Migrations of the Serbs in the Middle Ages', in Djordjević and Samardžić, *Migrations*, p. 65. Although Martić is a common name, we may indulge an interesting if idle speculation: was Milan Martić, the Knin police chief who became Krajina's second and last president and hence a modern Duke of Knin, a descendant of the fourteenth-century duke?

14. See Noel Malcolm, *Bosnia: A Short History* (London, 1994), p. 72.
15. Slavko Gavrilović, 'Serbs in Hungary, Slavonia and Croatia in Struggles against the Turks, (15th–18th Centuries)', in Radovan Samardžić and Milan Duškov (eds), *Serbs in European Civilization* (Belgrade, 1993), p. 47.
16. *Ibid.*, pp. 41–54, for a summary of this period.
17. Gunther E. Rothenberg, *The Military Border in Croatia, 1740–1881: A Study of an Imperial Institution* (Chicago, 1966), p. 9.
18. *Ibid.*, p. 20.
19. *Ibid.*, p. 103.

Chapter Two: An Empire on Earth

1. Jovan Nešković and Radomir Nikolić, *L'Eglise Saint-Pierre près de Novi Pazar* (Belgrade, 1987), p. 10.
2. Dragoljub Dragojlović, 'Serbian Spirituality in the 13th and 14th Centuries and Western Scholasticism', in Radovan Samardžić and Milan Duškov (eds), *Serbs in European Civilization* (Belgrade, 1993), p. 35.
3. Miloš Blagojević, 'On the National Identity of the Serbs in the Middle Ages', in *ibid.*, p. 29.
4. *Ibid.*
5. Desanka Milošević, *Gračanica Monastery* (Belgrade, 1989) p. 19. The loros was a kind of bejewelled scarf-cum-sash-cum-necklace and part of the Byzantine repertoire of royal adornment.
6. Rebecca West, *Black Lamb & Grey Falcon: The Record of a Journey through Yugoslavia in 1937*, 2 vols (London, 1943), vol. 2, p. 226.
7. Djurica Krstić, *Dushan's Code: The Bistritza Transcript* (Belgrade, 1989).
8. Rade Mihaljčić, *The Battle of Kosovo in History and in Popular Tradition* (Belgrade, 1989), p. 16.

9. *Ibid.*, pp. 21–31, on the decline of central power.
10. Anne Pennington and Peter Levi, *Marko the Prince: Serbo-Croat Heroic Songs* (London, 1984), p. 30.
11. *Ibid.*, p. 36.
12. George Tomashevich, 'The Battle of Kosovo and the Serbian Church', in Wayne S. Vucinich and Thomas A. Emmert (eds), *Kosovo: The Legacy of a Medieval Battle* (Minneapolis, 1991), p. 212.
13. Field of Blackbirds is the most common translation of the name Kosovo Polje. Just as good a translation, however, is Blackbird's Field, which also conveys some of the ambiguity about the battlefield's name. Although the origin is not known, it may well be that the name does not refer to blackbirds as such but to a man, the land's owner perhaps, called or nicknamed 'Blackbird'. Many old Serbian names are derived from the names of animals or plants and Kos, blackbird, is one of them. Although the name Kos still exists the derivation, Kosović, is more common.

Chapter Three: It Is Better to Die in Battle Than to Live in Shame

1. Slavoljub Djukić, *Izmedju slave i anateme: Politička biografija Slobodana Miloševića* (Belgrade, 1994), p. 49.
2. Thomas Emmert, 'The Battle of Kosovo: Early Reports of Victory and Defeat', in Wayne S. Vucinich and Thomas A. Emmert (eds), *Kosovo: The Legacy of a Medieval Battle* (Minneapolis, 1991), p. 24.
3. Rade Mihaljčić, *The Battle of Kosovo in History and in Popular Tradition* (Belgrade, 1989), p. 47.
4. *Ibid.*
5. Anne Pennington and Peter Levi, *Marko the Prince: Serbo-Croat Heroic*

Songs (London, 1984), p. 17.

6. *Ibid.*, pp. 14–15.
7. Mihaljčić, *Kosovo*, pp. 117–18.
8. *Ibid.*, p. 118.
9. Rebecca West, *Black Lamb & Grey Falcon: The Record of a Journey through Yugoslavia in 1937*, 2 vols (London, 1943), vol. 2, pp. 285–6.
10. Patriarch Danilo quoted by Mihaljčić, *Kosovo*, p. 70.
11. The shroud and Lazar's original embroidered coat can still be seen. They are housed in the Museum of the Serbian Orthodox Church, which is in the Patriarchate Building in Belgrade.
12. Pennington and Levi, *Marko the Prince*, p. 9.
13. While Jug Bogdan may not have existed, it is not impossible that this part of the epic, like the rest, conflates historical events and real people with pure myth.
14. Pennington and Levi, *Marko the Prince*, p. xiv, introduction by Svetozar Koljević.
15. Leopold von Ranke, *The History of Servia and the Servian Revolution* (New York, 1973), p. 80.
16. *Ibid.*, p. 76.
17. Arthur J. Evans, *Through Bosnia and the Herzegovina on Foot during the Insurrection, August and September, 1875* (London, 1877), pp. 138–9.
18. Pennington and Levi, *Marko the Prince*, pp. 152–3, notes by Svetozar Koljević.
19. John Reed, *War in Eastern Europe: Travels through the Balkans in 1915* (London, 1994), p. 12.
20. *Bookmark*, BBC2, 'Serbian Epics', 16 December 1992.
21. George Vid Tomashevich, 'The Battle of Kosovo and the Serbian Church', in Vucinich and Emmert, *Kosovo*, p. 214.
22. *Ibid.*, p. 215.
23. Tomashevich and others go so far as to identify Makarije as Sokollu's younger brother or nephew. See *ibid.* In Bosnia today there are both Orthodox and Muslim Sokolovićs.
24. Edward Brown, *A Brief Account of*

Some Travels in Divers Parts of Europe (London, 1685), p. 49.

25. Radmila Radić, 'Crkva i "srpsko pitanje"', *Ogledi, Republika*, 1–31 August 1995, p. ix.

Chapter Four:
Resurrection and Beyond

1. *The History of the Turkish Wars in Hungary, Transylvania, Austria, Silesia and other Provinces of the German Empire* (London, 1664), p. 23.
2. Denis Diderot and Jean Le Rond d'Alembert, *Encyclopédie . . .* (1765), vol. 15, p. 122.
3. Edward Brown, *A Brief Account of Some Travels in Divers Parts of Europe* (London, 1685), pp. 26–7.
4. *Ibid.*, p. 27.
5. *The War in Turkey*, supplement to the *Illustrated London News*, 29 July 1876, p. 113.
6. Michael Boro Petrovich, *A History of Modern Serbia, 1804–1918* (New York and London, 1976), vol. 1, p. 23. An indispensable book for the serious study of this period.
7. *Ibid.*, p. 37.
8. *Ibid.*, p. 60.
9. *Ibid.*, p. 81.
10. Rebecca West, *Black Lamb & Grey Falcon: The Record of a Journey through Yugoslavia in 1937*, 2 vols (London, 1943), vol. 2, p. 581. Although the Obrenovićs certainly died a horrible death, it is possible that some of the finer details of it, like this one, may have been slightly embellished in the telling.
11. Although some Turks and Muslims who had fled during the time of Karadjordje returned to Serbia after Obrenović came to power the majority of those not connected to the garrisons were extremely poor. In 1834 there were reckoned to be 15,000 Turks and Muslims in the principality. For details, including

the various Ottoman proclamations concerning their fate, see Alexandre Popovic, *L'Islam balkanique: les musulmans du sud-est européen dans la période post-ottomane* (Berlin, 1986), pp. 260–7.

12. See Ivo Banac, *The National Question in Yugoslavia: Origins, History, Politics* (Cornell, Ithaca and London, 1992) pp. 74–5.

13. Little is known about the Tribalians. They are believed to have lived and moved through areas now in modern Serbia as contemporaries of Philip of Macedon (382–336 BC) and Alexander the Great, (356–323 BC). They may have been of Thracian origin. They did not survive the subsequent migrations to the region. During the Middle Ages and later, at the same time as the name Illyria was being revived in Dalmatia, the name Tribalia was sometimes used to describe the Serbian lands.

Karadjordje's flags can be seen in the Museum of the 1804 Revolution in Topčider, Belgrade.

14. Exhibited in the Museum of the 1804 Revolution, Topčider, Belgrade.

15. Petrovich, *Modern Serbia*, p. 233.

16. Mirko Grmek, Marc Gjidara and Neven Simac, *Le Nettoyage ethnique: Documents historiques sur une idéologie serbe* (Paris, 1993), p. 76.

17. *Ibid.*, p. 74.

18. David MacKenzie, *Ilija Garašanin: Balkan Bismarck* (Boulder, 1985), p. 99.

19. *Ibid.*, p. 106.

20. *The Mountain Wreath of P. P. Nyegosh, Prince–Bishop of Montenegro, 1830–1851* trans. James W. Wiles (London, 1930), p. 83.

21. Vladimir Dedijer, *The Road to Sarajevo* (London, 1967), p. 320.

22. *Ibid.*, p. 255.

23. John Reed, *War in Eastern Europe: Travels through the Balkans in 1915* (London, 1994), p. 26.

24. Olga Žirojević, 'Kosovo u istorijskom pamćenju – (mit, legende, čin-

jenice)', *Ogledi, Republika*, 1–15 March 1995, p. 15. Also see Milovan Djilas, *Njegoš* (New York, 1966), pp. 135 and 158–9.

25. Dimitrije Djordjević, 'The Tradition of Kosovo in the Formation of Modern Serbian Statehood in the Nineteenth Century', in Wayne S. Vucinich and Thomas A. Emmert (eds), *Kosovo: Legacy of a Medieval Battle* (Minneapolis, 1991), p. 314.

26. Banac, *National Question*, p. 274.

27. Jovan Cvijić, *La Péninsule balkanique: Géographie humaine* (Paris, 1918), pp. 282 and 290.

28. Djordjević, 'Tradition of Kosovo', p. 317.

29. Dedijer, *Road to Sarajevo*, p. 83.

30. Thomas Emmert, *Serbian Golgotha: Kosovo, 1389* (New York, 1990), p. 129.

31. See *ibid.*, pp. 126–30, and Djordjević, 'Tradition of Kosovo', pp. 318–19.

32. See R. W. Seton-Watson's introduction to the catalogue for the *Exhibition of Serbo-Croatian Artists: Meštrović-Rački-Rosandić* (Grafton Gallery, London, 1917), p. 1.

33. *Ibid.*

34. *Ibid.*, p. 2.

35. After the Second World War, Meštrović lived in exile in the US. He died in 1962 but was buried in Drniš in a mausoleum which he had erected for his family in 1926. Between 1992 and 1995 Drnis fell under the control of the Krajina Serbs, during which time it was badly damaged.

36. Emmert, *Serbian Golgotha*, p. 133.

37. West, *Black Lamb*, vol. 1, p. 604.

Chapter Five: Cutting the Turks into Pieces

1. Carnegie Endowment for International Peace, *Report of the International Commission to Inquire into the Causes and Conduct of the*

Balkan Wars (Washington, DC, 1914), p. 73. (Republished in 1993 under the title *The Other Balkan Wars*.)

2. Mirko Grmek, Marc Gjidara and Neven Simac, *Le Nettoyage ethnique: Documents historiques sur une idéologie serbe* (Paris, 1993), p. 24.

3. Anne Pennington and Peter Levi, *Marko the Prince: Serbo-Croat Heroic Songs* (London, 1984), p. 166. From: 'The Beginning of the Revolt against the Dahijas'.

4. *The Mountain Wreath of P. P. Nyegosh, Prince–Bishop of Montenegro 1830–1851*, trans. James W. Wiles (London, 1930), p. 117.

5. *Ibid.*, p. 209.

6. *Ibid.*, p. 22.

7. Rebecca West, *Black Lamb & Grey Falcon: The Record of a Journey through Yugoslavia in 1937*, 2 vols (London, 1943), vol. 2, p. 398.

8. Aleksa Djilas, 'The Yugoslav Tragedy', *Prospect*, October 1995, p. 36.

9. Vuk Drašković, *Le Couteau* (Paris, 1993), p. 263.

10. The slogan 'This is Serbia' was sprayed the length and breadth of Serb-held lands in Bosnia and Croatia. It was matched by Croats in Bosnia with 'This is Croatia' and of course by Muslims with 'This is Bosnia'. In Velika Kladuša in the former Bihać pocket, the occasional Muslim hardline-cum-humorist sprayed 'This is Turkey'.

11. By far the best work on this subject is J. R. Fine's *The Bosnian Church: A New Interpretation. A Study of the Bosnian Church and its Place in State and Society from the Thirteenth to the Fifteenth Centuries* (Boulder, 1975). Noel Malcolm outlines both the discredited theories of Bosnian Bogomilism and modern thought on the question in his *Bosnia: A Short History* (London, 1994).

12. Arthur J. Evans, *Through Bosnia and the Herzegovina on Foot during the Insurrection, August and September, 1875* (London, 1877), Introduction,

p. XCVII.

13. *Ibid.*, p. 263.

14. *Ibid.*, p. 284.

15. Carnegie Endowment, *Report*, p. 95.

16. *Ibid.*, p. 51.

17. West, *Black Lamb*, vol. 2, p. 394.

18. Carnegie Endowment, *Report*, p. 272.

19. Milan St. Protić, 'Migrations Resulting from Peasant Upheavals in Serbia during the XIXth Century', paper in Dimitrije Djordjević and Radovan Samardžić (eds), *Migrations in Balkan History* (Belgrade, 1989), p. 94.

20. Barbara Jelavich, *History of the Balkans*, 2 vols (Cambridge, 1989–93), vol. 1, p. 81.

21. Dimitrije Djordjević, 'Migrations during the 1912–1913 Balkan Wars and World War One', in Djordjević and Samardžić *Migrations*, p. 124.

22. Figures from the Turkish Embassy, Belgrade.

23. For a copy of the text of the convention see Ibrahim Berisha *et al.* (eds), *Serbian Colonization and Ethnic Cleansing of Kosova: Documents and Evidence*, (Priština, 1993), pp. 43–55.

24. Information supplied by the Turkish Embassy, Belgrade.

25. Djordjević, 'Migrations', p. 124.

Chapter Six: Union or Death

1. S. C. H. Goetze, 'Mural Decorations at the Foreign Office: Descriptive Account by the Artist, October 1921', p. 5. From the archives of the Foreign & Commonwealth Office, Library and Records Department, Historical Branch.

2. From the catalogue prepared for the *Exhibition of Serbo-Croatian Artists: Meštrović–Rački–Rosandić* (Grafton Gallery, London, 1917), p. 16.

3. Edward Crankshaw, *The Fall of the*

House of Habsburg (London, 1963), p. 377.

4. *Ibid.*, p. 378.
5. Barbara Jelavich, *History of the Balkans*, 2 vols (Cambridge, 1989–93), vol. 2, p. 66.
6. *The Annual Register*, 1878, cited in Vladimir Dedijer, *The Road to Sarajevo* (London, 1967), p. 67.
7. Jelavich, *Balkans*, pp. 66 and 77.
8. See Ivo Banac, *The National Question in Yugoslavia. Origins, History, Politics* (Cornell, Ithaca and London, 1992), p. 98. For a highly detailed account of the politics of the empire up to 1911 see R. W. Seton-Watson, *The Southern Slav Question and the Habsburg Monarchy* (New York, 1969).
9. Seton-Watson, *Southern Slav Question*, pp. 181–2.
10. For an account of the trial see *ibid.*, pp. 209–87.
11. Jelena Milojković-Djurić, *Tradition and Avant-Garde: Literature and Art in Serbian Culture, 1900–1918* (Boulder, 1988), pp. 23–5. Paja Jovanović, the painter of the Migration of the Serbs (see p. 1 above) was said to dominate the Serbian section. For the teachers' conference, see Michael Boro Petrovich, *A History of Modern Serbia, 1804–1918*, 2 vols (New York and London, 1976), vol. 2, p. 606.
12. Petrovich, *Modern Serbia*, p. 607.
13. The statement was made by the Serbian minister in Vienna on 31 March 1909. See Dedijer, *Sarajevo*, p. 309.
14. *Ibid.*, p. 375.
15. *Neues Wiener Tageblatt*, 28 June 1924. See Dedijer, *Sarajevo*, p. 507, n. 103, and p. 395.
16. Dedijer, *Sarajevo*, p. 418.
17. *Ibid.*
18. *Ibid.*, p. 419.
19. *Ibid.*, p. 341.
20. *Ibid.*, p. 348.
21. See *ibid.*; Petrovich, *Modern Serbia*, p. 625; and Banac, *National Question*, p. 316, including n. 18, in which he

cites a Muslim leader asserting that some Serbs too were involved with the *Schutzkorps*.

22. Jelavich, *Balkans*, p. 116, citing Vladimir Dedijer *et al.*, *History of Yugoslavia* (New York, 1974), p. 480. Some of the regiments were also up to 50 per cent Croat. Josip Broz Tito was sent to fight Serbia in one of these units at the beginning of the war, but Dedijer was obliged to omit this in his biography of the Marshal.
23. Petrovich, *Modern Serbia*, p. 626.
24. Nicolas-Jiv Petrovitch, *Agonie et résurrection: Récits de la prise de Belgrade de la retraite en Albanie et d'un séjour au lazaret de Corfou* (Courbevoie, 1920), p. 74. (In the text, but not in these notes, I have transliterated his name back to 'Petrović'.)
25. *Ibid.*
26. *Ibid.*, p. 99.
27. *Ibid.*, p. 128.
28. Petrovich, *Modern Serbia*, p. 624.
29. Petrovitch, *Agonie*, p. 152.
30. *Ibid.*, p. 155.
31. Petrovich, *Modern Serbia*, p. 622; and Banac, *National Question*, p. 222.
32. Banac, *National Question*, p. 120.
33. *Ibid.*, p. 121.
34. Petrovich, *Modern Serbia*, p. 634.
35. Banac, *National Question*, p. 132.
36. See Petrovich, *Modern Serbia*, p. 644.
37. *Ibid.*, p. 661.
38. Milovan Djilas, *Land without Justice* (New York, 1958), p. 89.
39. Until 1925 it was called the Croatian Republican Peasant Party.
40. Cited in Banac, *National Question*, p. 226.
41. See Appendix One.
42. Banac, *National Question*, p. 218.
43. See Vladko Maček, *In the Struggle for Freedom*, trans. Elizabeth and Stjepan Gazi (University Park and London, 1957), p. 90.
44. See Banac, *National Question*, p. 298.
45. *Ibid.*, p. 367.
46. See specifically Banac's chapter on the Muslims of Bosnia in *ibid.*, pp.

359–78.

47. Maček, *Struggle*, p. 94.
48. Banac, *National Question*, p. 410.
49. *Ibid.*, p. 405.
50. Maček, *Struggle*, p. 91.
51. *Ibid.*, p. 109.
52. Svetozar Pribitchevitch, (Pribićević), *La Dictature du Roi Alexandre* (Paris, 1933), p.74.
53. *Ibid.*, p. 81.
54. *Ibid.*, pp. 81–2.
55. See p. 169 below.
56. See Alex N. Dragnich, *The First Yugoslavia: Search for a Viable Political System* (Stanford, 1983), pp. 52–6.
57. Maček, *Struggle*, p. 111.
58. *Ibid.*, p. 154.
59. Dragnich, *First Yugoslavia*, p. 109.
60. See Fred Singleton, *A Short History of the Yugoslav Peoples* (Cambridge, 1989), p. 169.
61. Maček, *Struggle*, p. 190.
62. *The Ciano Diaries, 1939–1943. The Complete, Unabridged Diaries of Count Galeazzo Ciano, Italian Minister for Foreign Affairs, 1936–1943*, ed. Hugh Gibson (Garden City, NY, 1947), p.84.
63. See Dragnich, *First Yugoslavia*, p. 130; and Jozo Tomasevich, *The Chetniks: War and Revolution in Yugoslavia, 1941–1945* (Stanford, 1975), p. 24.

Chapter Seven: We Chose the Heavenly Kingdom

1. Winston S. Churchill, *The Second World War*, vol. 3: *The Grand Alliance* (London, 1950), p. 148.
2. See Thomas Emmert, *Serbian Golgotha: Kosovo, 1389* (New York, 1990), p. 140.
3. Casualty figures for the 6 April bombing range up to 20,000. However, see Jozo Tomasevich, *The Chetniks: War and Revolution in Yugoslavia, 1941–1945* (Stanford, 1975). On page 74 he says that while the first estimate for losses was 10,000 this figure 'has been much reduced after careful post-war investigations'. He gives a figure of between 3,000 and 4,000 for 6 April. He also notes that during the whole invasion German deaths were a mere 151, with 392 wounded and 15 missing.
4. Churchill, *Second World War*, vol. 3, p. 155.
5. Tomasevich, *Chetniks*, p. 41.
6. *Ibid.*, p. 54.
7. Vladko Maček, *In the Struggle for Freedom*, trans. Elizabeth and Stjepan Gazi (University Park and London, 1957), p. 230.
8. See Tomasevich, *Chetniks*, pp. 73–74 for a summary of the question of numbers of POWs. Soon after their capture most non-Serbs and Montenegrins were released. The Montenegrins were released because it was hoped to win their loyalty to the Italian quisling state that was being set up. Montenegrin Serbs from the NDH were also released 'if they desired'. Tomasevich cites one source which states that after the releases there remained some 200,000 POWs in Germany and 10,000 in Italy, 'of whom 90 per cent were Serbs'.
9. *The Trial of Dragoljub-Draža Mihailović: Stenographic Record and Documents from the Trial of Dragoljub-Draža Mihailović* (Belgrade, 1946), p. 499.
10. Post-war biographies of Tito in English tend to be afflicted either by gushing admiration for the man or by an overriding ambition to puncture the myth. Luckily, as far as Tito biographies are concerned, we are now in the post-post-war period. An excellent short summary is Stevan Pavlowitch's *Tito, Yugoslavia's Great Dictator: A Reassessment* (London, 1992). Another good one is Jasper Ridley, *Tito: A Biography* (London, 1994).
11. Tomasevich, *Chetniks*, p. 146. In note 92 on the same page he writes:

'German sources indicate the shooting of 1,736 male inhabitants and 19 women in the town of Kraljevo . . . and 2,300 inhabitants in the town of Kragujevac. Some estimates of the number executed on that occasion at Kragujevac alone go as high as 7,000, but the foremost authority on German terror in Serbia puts this figure for Kragujevac at about 3,000.'

12. *Ibid.*, p. 152.

13. General Fabijan Trgo, *The National Liberation War and Revolution in Yugoslavia (1941–1945): Selected Documents* (Belgrade, 1982), p. 556. The document in question (pp. 552–6) is the Resolution of the Anti-Fascist Council of National Liberation of Bosnia and Hercegovina. The Council of 247 delegates met in Mrkonjić Grad on 25–26 November 1943.

14. *Trial*, p. 131.

15. Tomasevich, *Chetniks*, p. 194.

16. Tomasevich cites the document at *ibid.*, p. 170 without questioning its authenticity. Noel Malcolm, however, in his *Bosnia: A Short History* (London, 1994) raises doubts on p. 179 and specifically on p. 287, n. 17.

17. See *Trial*, pp. 361 and 93.

18. *Ibid.*, p. 361.

19. *Ibid.*, p. 358.

20. *Ibid.*, p. 359.

21. See Tomasevich, *Chetniks*, pp. 167–8.

22. Malcolm, *Bosnia*, p. 188.

23. Author's interview, 1995.

24. Fitzroy Maclean, *Eastern Approaches* (London, 1991), p. 281.

25. *Ibid.*, p. 402.

26. I am grateful to Nenad Petrović, the president of the Serbian Writers Society in London, for the information about the Eboli camp, and the numbers involved. Mr Petrović believes that the different treatment meted out to Chetniks in Italy and Austria was related to antagonistic views about their fate inherent in a conflict between the Foreign Office and the British Army. The former inclined to cultivate good relations with Tito, while the army, at least its command in Italy, was very friendly to these men.

I am also grateful to Professor Stevan Pavlowitch of Southampton University for his information that among these Serbs were a number of Nedić's former State Guards who had defected to Mihailović and some of Ljotić's volunteers.

27. Author's interview, 1995.

28. See p. 11 above.

29. Stella Alexander, *Church and State in Yugoslavia since 1945* (Cambridge, 1979), p. 22. Alexander cites Budak's quotation in *Hrvatski Narod*, the official NDH newspaper, dated 26 July 1941. I use the word 'allege', however, because some Croats believe that Budak in fact never made this remark.

30. Oddone Talpo, *Dalmazia: Una cronaca per la storia (1941)* (Rome, 1985), p. 617. An indispensable book, especially because of the large number of Italian military and other documents from the archives that it reproduces.

31. Alexander, *Church and State*, p. 23.

32. Maček, *Struggle*, p. 235.

33. See Talpo, *Dalmazia*, p. 995.

34. See Alexander, *Church and State*, p. 32.

35. Author's interview, 1995.

36. See Alexander, *Church and State*, p. 23.

37. Smilja Avramov, *Genocide in Yugoslavia* (Belgrade, 1995), p. 380.

38. See Talpo, *Dalmazia*, pp. 474–6.

39. *Ibid.*, p. 979.

40. Avramov, *Genocide*, p. 380.

41. *Ibid.*, p. 384.

42. Curzio Malaparte, *Kaputt*, trans. from Italian by Cesare Foligno (Evanston, 1995), p. 266. On the semi-fictional style of Malaparte see Gianni Granna, *Curzio Malaparte* (Milan, 1961), esp. pp. 78–9, in which the eyes scene is discussed. Granna notes Malaparte's full use of the 'legends of war', his tendency

towards exaggeration and even his 'degeneration into an aesthetic of horror and the macabre, a type of Shelleyesque thrilling . . .'.

43. Ivo Banac, *The National Question in Yugoslavia: Origins, History, Politics* (Cornell, Ithaca and London, 1992), p. 298. On 17 April 1941 Mussolini approved a document giving details about the delimitation of borders within occupied Yugoslavia. It noted that the Albanian population of Yugoslavia was between 700,000 and one million. See Talpo, *Dalmazia*, p. 365.

44. *Perparimi*, (Priština), January–February 1974, p. 127, cited by Peter Prifti, *Socialist Albania since 1944: Domestic and Foreign Developments* (Cambridge and London, 1978), p. 227.

45. Veselin Djuretić, 'The Exodus of the Serbs from Kosovo in the Twentieth Century and its Political Background', in Dimitrije Djordjević and Radovan Samardžić (eds), *Migrations in Balkan History* (Belgrade, 1989), p. 134.

46. Rebecca West, *Black Lamb & Grey Falcon: The Record of a Journey through Yugoslavia in 1937*, 2 vols (London, 1943), vol. 2, p. 390.

47. See Alex N. Dragnich and Slavko Todorovich, *The Saga of Kosovo: Focus on Serbian–Albanian Relations* (Boulder and New York, 1984), p. 120. See also Dušan Bataković, *The Kosovo Chronicles* (Belgrade, 1992), p. 13, and Avramov, *Genocide*, p. 192.

48. See Avramov, *Genocide*, p. 186.

49. Author's interview, 1995.

50. Dragnich and Todorovich, *Saga*, p. 138.

51. Miranda Vickers, *The Albanians: A Modern History* (London and New York, 1995), p. 161.

52. *Ibid.*, p. 165, citing *Zeri-i-Popullit*, 17 May 1981.

53. The two were Bogoljub Kočović and Vladimir Žerjavić. The former, a Serb, published his work in London in *Žrtve Drugog svetskog rata u*

Jugoslaviji (1985). The latter, a Croat, published his in Zagreb in *Gubici stanovništva Jugoslavije u Drugom svetskom ratu* (1989). For a useful summary see Srdjan Bogosavljević's paper in *Ogledi*, published by *Republika*, 1–15 June 1995 in Belgrade: 'Drugi svetski rat – žrtve u Jugoslaviji'.

Chapter Eight: You Used to Warm Us Like the Sun

1. General Fabijan Trgo, *The National Liberation War and Revolution in Yugoslavia (1941–1945): Selected Documents* (Belgrade, 1982), p. 585.
2. *Ibid.*, p. 661.
3. *Ibid.*, p. 696.
4. *Ibid.*, p. 727.
5. *Ibid.*
6. *Ibid.*, p. 725.
7. Sabrina P. Ramet, *Nationalism and Federalism in Yugoslavia, 1962–1991*, 2nd edn (Bloomington and Indianapolis, 1992), p. 106.
8. See *ibid.*, p. 103. For Croatian population statistics (1780–1991) see Milovan Baletić (ed.), *Croatia 1994* (Zagreb, 1994), p. 34.
9. See Ramet, *Nationalism*, p. 110.
10. See *ibid.*, p. 115.
11. See *ibid.*, p. 117. For the 1920s see Ivo Banac, *The National Question in Yugoslavia: Origins, History, Politics* (Cornell, Ithaca and London, 1992), p. 184.
12. See *ibid.*, p. 125.
13. Jasper Ridley, *Tito: A Biography* (London, 1994), p. 395.
14. Ibrahim Berisha *et al.* (eds), *Serbian Colonization and Ethnic Cleansing of Kosovo: Documents and Evidence* (Priština, 1993), p. 23.
15. *Ibid.*, p. 25.
16. See p. 88 above.
17. See Ramet, *Nationalism*, p. 190.
18. See *ibid.*, p. 18.
19. Anton Logoreci, 'A Clash between Two Nationalisms in Kosova', in

Arshi Pipa and Sami Repishti (eds), *Studies on Kosova* (Boulder, 1984), p. 190.

20. Fred Singleton, *A Short History of the Yugoslav Peoples* (Cambridge, 1989), p. 213.

21. Noel Malcolm, *Bosnia: A Short History* (London, 1994), p. 202.

22. See Table 1, Wartime Casualties by Republic, 1941–1945, on p. 134 above.

23. See Malcolm, *Bosnia*, p. 198.

24. Smilja Avramov, *Genocide in Yugoslavia* (Belgrade, 1995).

25. Ramet, *Nationalism*, p. 189.

26. *Ibid.*, p. 25.

27. Laura Silber and Allan Little, *The Death of Yugoslavia* (London, 1995), p. 33.

28. Branka Magaš, *The Destruction of Yugoslavia: Tracking the Break-up, 1980–92* (London and New York, 1993), p. 49.

29. See Stevan K. Pavlowitch, *The Improbable Survivor. Yugoslavia and its Problems, 1918–1988* (London, 1988), p. 139.

30. For a detailed examination of the role played in this period by the Academy and Academicians see Olivera Milosavljević, 'Upotreba autoriteta nauke. Javna politička delatnost Srpske akademije nauka i umetnosti (1986–1992)', *Ogledi, Republika*, 1–31 July 1995.

31. Kosta Mihailović and Vasilije Krestić, *Memorandum of the Serbian Academy of Sciences and Arts: Answers to Criticisms* (Belgrade, 1995), p. 129.

32. *Ibid.*, p. 128.

33. *Ibid.*, p. 133.

34. *Ibid.*, p. 127.

35. *Ibid.*, p. 140.

36. *Vreme/Dossier: From the Memorandum to War* (Belgrade, n.d.).

37. Slavoljub Djukić, *Izmedju slave i anateme: Politička biografija Slobodana Miloševića* (Belgrade, 1944), p. 14–15.

38. Djukić, *ibid.*, repeats the widely believed claim that Davorjanka Paunović was Mirjana Marković's aunt. However, as the words brother or sister are often used loosely in Serbian to mean cousin too it may well be that Paunović and Mirjana Markosvić's mother were in fact just that. N.B. After she married Milošević Marković kept her surname.

39. Silber and Little, *Death*, p. 37.

40. See *ibid.*, p. 38.

41. Ramet, *Nationalism*, p. 229.

42. Silber and Little, *Death*, p. 77.

43. See Tom Gjelten, *Sarajevo Daily: A City and its Newspaper under Siege* (New York, 1995), p. 64.

44. Trgo, *National Liberation War*, p. 727.

Chapter Nine: Frankie and Badger Go to War

1. Borisav Jović's diaries, *The Last Days of the SFRJ*, extracts published in *VIP Daily News Report* (Belgrade), 614, 16 November 1995, p. 4.

2. Sabrina P. Ramet, *Nationalism and Federalism in Yugoslavia, 1962–1991*, 2nd edn (Bloomington and Indianapolis, 1992), p. 237.

3. Mark Thompson, *Forging War: The Media in Serbia, Croatia and Bosnia–Hercegovina* (London, 1994), p. 157.

4. Jović, *Last Days*, VIP, p. 4.

5. Veljko Kadijević, *Moje vidjenje raspada: Vojska bez države* (Belgrade, 1993), p. 110.

6. Mirko Grmek, Marko Gjidara and Neven Simac, *Le Nettoyage ethnique: Documents historiques sur une idéologie serbe* (Paris, 1993), p. 272. See also Laura Silber and Allan Little, *The Death of Yugoslavia* (London, 1995), p. 141.

7. Silber and Little, *Death*, p. 122.

8. Cited in the *Final Report of the United Nations Commission of Experts Established Pursuant to Security Council Resolution 780 (1992)* S/1994/674/Annex V, p. 20.

9. One of the best accounts of the meeting and its consequences is the film 'A Greater Croatia' made for *Dispatches*, Channel Four, by Soul Purpose, which was shown on 13 January 1994.
10. *UN Commission of Experts*, Annex V, p. 21.
11. Silber and Little, *Death*, p. 139.
12. Kadijević, *Moje vidjenje*, p. 113.
13. *Ibid.*, p. 134.
14. Author's interview with General Kadijević, 1995.
15. Silber and Little, *Death*, p. 153.
16. Kadijević, *Moje vidjenje*, p. 119.
17. Author's interview with General Kadijević, 1995.
18. Luigi Villari, *The Republic of Ragusa* (London, 1914), p. 395.
19. *Duga*, 1 February 1993, Dada Vujasinović, Biographic Data on Serbian Fighter Arkan. Cited in *UN Commission of Experts*, Annex III.A, p. 207, n. 259.
20. *UN Commission of Experts*, Annex III.A, p. 11.
21. Arkan interviewed in *Srpsko Jedinstvo*, November 1994, cited in Ivan Čolović, 'Fudbal, huligani i rat', *Ogledi*, *Republika*, 1–15 June 1995, p. 8.
22. Silver and Little, *Death*, p. 142.
23. *Vreme News Digest Agency*, 115, 6 December 1993, p. 12. Also *Vreme*, No. 163.
24. For a full version of the Vance plan, see Document S/23280 issued by the UN.
25. Kadijević, *Moje vidjenje*, p. 143.
26. *Ibid.*, pp. 142–4.

Chapter Ten: We Are the Strongest

1. *Vreme*, No. 48, 23 September 1991.
2. *Vreme*, No. 49, 30 September 1991.
3. *Vreme News Digest Agency*, 151, 13 September 1993, p. 10. Also *Vreme*, No. 151.
4. The actual ethnic breakdown of Hadžići according to the 1991 census was Muslims 64 per cent, Serbs 26 per cent, Yugoslavs and others 7 per cent, Croats 3 per cent. Source: Prof. Dr Ante Markotić, Ejub Sijerčić and Asim Abdurahmanović, 'Ethnic Map of Bosnia–Herzegovina', *Why* (Sarajevo), February 1992.
5. See Mark Thompson, *Forging War: The Media in Serbia, Croatia and Bosnia–Hercegovina* (London, 1994), p. 247.
6. Marković's interview was reprinted in a collection by Milorad Vučelić, *Conversations with the Epoch* (Belgrade, 1991), p. 96.
7. Ćosić interview in *ibid.*, p. 48.
8. See Laura Silber and Allan Little, *The Death of Yugoslavia* (London, 1995), p. 237.
9. *Kozarski Vjesnik* (Prijedor), 9 April 1993. Cited in the *Final Report of the United Nations Commission of Experts Established Pursuant to Security Council Resolution 780 (1992)* S/1994/674/Annex V, p. 8.
10. Copy of letter in author's possession.
11. Ed Vulliamy, 'America's Big Strategic Lie', *Guardian*, 20 May 1996.

Chapter Eleven: It Was War . . .

1. Erich Fromm, *The Fear of Freedom* (London and Henley, 1980), pp. 180–2.
2. Author's interview with General Jovan Divjak, 15 May 1992.
3. See Ed Vulliamy, 'America's Big Strategic Lie', *Guardian*, 20 May 1996.
4. David Owen, *Balkan Odyssey* (London, 1995). See pp. 106, 244, 260–1. On p. 261 he wrote about the Markale marketplace massacre: 'the fact that the Muslims might have fired on their own people to provoke NATO to come in and fight on their side, one of their long-stand-

ing objectives, did not alter the need for preventive action'. See also Laure Adler, *L'Année des adieux* (Paris, 1995). Written in close co-operation with François Mitterrand, it covers the president's last year in office. On p. 175 she quotes him on 18 May 1994 as telling ministers that 'A few days ago, Mr Boutros-Ghali told me that he was sure that the shell which fell on the Sarajevo marketplace was a Bosnian provocation.'

5. For political reasons the Bosnian government claimed that there were some 380,000 people besieged in Sarajevo. The UNHCR went along with this because it needed a high figure to present to donors when looking for funds and aid. Privately, though, UNHCR officials admitted that they believed there were no more than 250,000 in the city in 1993, but later that number probably went up as more refugees came into the city.

6. In 1991 the census returns showed that Sarajevo's population was 50 per cent Muslim, 28 per cent Serb, 7 per cent Croat and 15 per cent 'Yugoslavs', mixed or 'others'. By early 1996 Muslims were believed to make up 75 per cent of the population of government-held Sarajevo. The daily *Oslobodjenje* claimed in September 1994 that, of the 380,000 people in the city at that time, only 100,000 had lived there before the war. The numbers are absurd (see note 5 above), but they do provide an interesting insight into the demographic turnover experienced by Sarajevo. See Daria Sito Sučić, 'Sarajevo's Intellectual and Cultural Elite – and the City's Unique Spirit – May Never Return', *Transition* (Prague), vol. 2, No. 5, 8 March 1996.

7. Grebo cited in *ibid*.

Chapter Twelve: The Madmen Take Over the Asylum

1. *Final Report of the United Nations Commission of Experts Established Pursuant to Security Council Resolution 780 (1992)* S/1994/674/Annexes pp. 48–49.

2. Interview in *Kozarski Vjesnik* (Prijedor), 9 April 1993. Cited in *UN Commission of Experts*, Annex V, p. 12.

3. Veljko Kadijević, *Moje vidjenje raspada: Vojska bez države* (Belgrade, 1993), p. 148.

4. Interview in *Večernje Novosti* (Belgrade), 7 May 1993.

5. *The Trial of Dragoljub-Draža Mihailović: Stenographic Record and Documents from the Trial of Dragoljub-Draža Milhailović* (Belgrade, 1946), p. 361.

6. The *UN Commission of Experts* reports, e.g. S/1994/674/Annex VIII, which gives a detailed breakdown of camps and torture facilities belonging to all sides in Bosnia, are the best resources so far available on the subject.

7. *UN Commission of Experts*, Annex VIII, p. 221.

8. Ed Vulliamy, 'Horror Hidden beneath Ice and Lies', *Guardian*, 19 February 1996.

9. Hannah Arendt, *Eichmann in Jerusalem: A Report on the Banality of Evil* (London, 1979), p. 232. Arendt cites Bamm, who had originally written this in *Die Unsichtbare Flagge*, published in 1952.

10. International Criminal Tribunal for the Former Yugoslavia, press release CC/PIO/026-E, The Hague, 16 November 1995. In the months following the fall of Srebrenica the numbers of missing, presumed dead, ranged all the way up to 8,000. This figure is almost certainly false because it does not take into account the fact that many of the missing, who did turn up, did not register

with the authorities or with the Red Cross. Nevertheless, in August 1996 the Red Cross had processed tracing requests for 6,546 people from Srebrenica, almost all of them men. Many of those missing may have been killed in combat before the enclave fell or have died in fights as they tried to cross Serbian territory. The final figure cannot be established until the forensic experts, who were working at the mass grave sights throughout 1996, come up with their conclusions.

11. Patrick de Saint-Exupéry, 'Bosnie: "Et les Serbes nous ont hachés à la mitrailleuse . . .'", *Le Figaro*, 8 March 1996.
12. *Ibid.*
13. Renaud Girard, 'Bosnie: la confession de Drazen, criminel de guerre', *Le Figaro*, 8 March 1996.
14. *The Mountain Wreath of P. P. Nyegosh, Prince–Bishop of Montenegro, 1830–1851*, trans. James W. Wiles (London, 1930), p. 117. See also pp. 75–8 above.

Chapter Thirteen: The War for More

1. See Chapter 10 above.
2. *The Times*, 28 June 1993.
3. *Naša Borba* (Belgrade), cited in *VIP* (Belgrade), 10 May 1995.
4. Aleksandar Knežević and Vojislav Tufegdžić, *Kriminal koji je izmenio Srbiju* (Belgrade, 1995), p. 115.
5. 'RS Parliament Accuses Former Prime Minister', *VIP* (Belgrade), 16 June 1995.
6. *Kozarski Vjesnik* (Prijedor), 2 July 1993. Cited in the *Final Report of the UN Commission of Experts Established Pursuant to Security Council Resolution 780 (1992)* S/1994/674/Annex V, p. 104. Bogdan Delić succeeded Simo Drljača as police chief of Prijedor, but in 1996 Drljača was back in his

old job.
7. *Kozarski Vjesnik* (Prijedor), 16 July 1993. Cited in *UN Commission of Experts*, Annex V, p. 104.
8. Knežević and Tufegdžić, *Kriminal*, p. 3. N.B. the author of the book and the gangster of the same name were not the same person.
9. *Ibid.*, p. 13.
10. *Kriminal* is the book of the B92 film from which these quotes are taken.
11. Knežević and Tufegdžić, *Kriminal*, p. 112.

Chapter Fourteen: 363 Quadrillion Per Cent

1. Mladjan Dinkić, *Ekonomija destrukcije: velika pljacka naroda* (Belgrade, 1995), p. 63. I am indebted to Philip Hepburn, whose English translations from Dinkić's book I have used. They come from a publicity leaflet about the book called *The Economics of Destruction: The Great Robbery of the Yugoslav People: Could It Happen to You?*
2. *Ibid.*, p. 182.
3. *Ibid.*, p. 198.
4. *Ibid.*, p. 221.
5. *Economic Developments in FR Yugoslavia: A Country Report prepared for the UN Economic Commission for Europe*, CES-Mecon report, September 1994 (Belgrade), p. 27. The CES-Mecon reports are an invaluable source of data and charts published in English.
6. CES-Mecon report, February 1995, No. 4, p. 4.
7. CES-Mecon report, September 1994, No. 3, p. 5.
8. I am grateful to *The Economist* for this calculation.
9. See Dinkić, *Ekonomija*, p. 239.
10. *Ibid.*, p. 146.
11. CES-Mecon report, March 1996, No. 6, pp. 2–9.

Chapter Fifteen: Skull Towers

1. Alphonse de Lamartine, *A Pilgrimage to the Holy Land: Comprising Recollections, Sketches, and Reflections, Made during a Tour in the East in 1832–1833* (London, 1835), vol. 3, pp. 105–6.
2. *Vox* reproduced in Vesna Hadživuković, *et al.*, *Bosnia–Herzegovina: Chronicle of an Announced Death* (Belgrade, 1993), p. 16.
3. See pp. 73–5 and 239–41 above.
4. Laura Silber and Allan Little, *The Death of Yugoslavia* (London, 1995), p. 242.
5. For Croatia refugee figures see Milovan Baletić, *Croatia 1994* (Zagreb, 1994), pp. 294–5.
6. UNHCR, *Information Notes on Former Yugoslavia*, No. 12/95, December 1995, p. 8.
7. UNHCR, *Information Notes on Former Yugoslavia*, No. 6/95, June 1995, p. IV.

Chapter Sixteen: Arsenije's Children

1. Svetozar Pribitchevitch (Pribićević), *La Dictature du Roi Alexandre* (Paris, 1933), p. 192. I have used Ivo Banac's version taken from the Serbo-Croatian original text because it would be difficult to better the elegance of his translation. See his *The National Question in Yugoslavia: Origins, History, Politics* (Cornell, Ithaca and London, 1992), p. 189.
2. Mirjana Marković's column for the fortnightly *Duga* reproduced in *VIP* (Belgrade), No. 509, 23 June 1995, p. 4.
3. *The Death of Yugoslavia*, BBC2, 6 June 1996.
4. For a day-by-day account of the diplomacy, at least from Lord Owen's point of view, see his *Balkan Odyssey* (London, 1995).

5. The Federal Republic of Yugoslavia (FRY), comprising Serbia and Montenegro, was founded on 27 April 1992. Its constitution declared it to be the successor state of the old Yugoslavia, but this was challenged by the four other former Yugoslav republics. According to Article 2 of the constitution, the FRY could be joined by other 'republics', presumably the Republika Srpska and Krajina. See *Constitution of the Federal Republic of Yugoslavia* (Belgrade, 1992).
6. See p. 215 above.
7. Patrick de Saint-Exupéry, 'La Double Ambiguïté de Belgrade et Sarajevo', *Le Figaro*, 8 March 1996.
8. See for example Charles Lane and Thom Shanker, 'How the CIA Failed in Bosnia', *New York Review of Books*, 9 May 1996.
9. *Death of Yugoslavia*, BBC2.
10. *Ibid.*
11. *Ibid.*
12. Prof. Dr Ante Markotić, Ejub Sijerčić and Asim Abdurahmanović, 'Ethnic Map of Bosnia–Herzegovina', *Why* (Sarajevo), February 1992.
13. *Open Wounds: Human Rights Abuses in Kosovo*, Human Rights Watch/Helsinki (New York, 1993), p. 35.
14. *Ibid.*
15. Pinpointing exactly when Kosovo Albanian deputies declared the province independent is complicated by the fact that, rather like the Krajina and Bosnian Serbs, the did it several times. And, like them, they used a slightly different formulation of words each time around. On 2 July 1990 they declared Kosova's independence within Yugoslavia. The Kacanik declaration of sovereignty on 7 September 1990 was similar. On 22 September 1991 the 'Republic of Kosova' was declared a 'sovereign and independent state' by its assembly. This was followed by a semi-underground referendum in which 99.87 per cent of voters reportedly declared themselves in favour of independence. Elections for

Kosova's 'parliament' were held on 24 May 1992. The LDK won ninety-six seats and twenty-nine went to other parties. See *Albanian Democratic Movement in Former Yugoslavia: Documents, 1990–1993* (Priština, 1993).

16. Edith Durham, *High Albania* (London, 1985), p. 294.

17. See for example Julie Mertus, 'A Wall of Silence Divides Serbian and Albanian Opinion on Kosovo', *Transition* (Prague), vol. 2, No. 6, 22 March 1996.

18. Exactly how many Albanians there are in Kosovo and indeed in the whole of Serbia and Montenegro is uncertain. In 1991 Albanians boycotted the last Yugoslav census, so the official figures are extrapolations from previous ones. According to the official figures in 1981, there were 1,340,000 Albanians in Serbia and Montenegro, or 13.6 per cent of the population. This was calculated to have risen to 1,728,000 in 1991, representing 16.6 per cent. By contrast Kosovo Albanian demographers claimed that by 1993 there were more than two million Albanians in the FRY. The vast majority live in Kosovo, with smaller numbers in 'inner Serbia' and Montenegro. The matter is further complicated by the lack of data about how many Albanians, who may or may not show up in statistics, are actually living and working abroad. Albanian sources claim that this is up to 400,000 people, but this seems too high a figure. See *Statistical Pocket Book: Federal Republic of Yugoslavia* (Belgrade, 1993), and Dr Hizvi Islami, *Demographic Reality in Kosova*, Kosova Information Centre. (Priština?, 1993).

19. Durham, *High Albania*, p. 275.

20. *Ibid.*, p. 296.

21. *Ibid.*, p. 294.

22. Given the effective tripartite partition of Bosnia, to say that its Serbs, Croats and Muslim all lived in the same state would be a pedantic resort to legalism rather than a statement of reality.

23. *Agence France Presse*, 26 August 1995.

24. The figures in this section have been compiled mostly from UNHCR sources, including their monthly bulletin, *Information Notes on Former Yugoslavia*. According to a UNHCR *Information Fact Sheet* of May 1996, produced by their office in Belgrade, the FRY had granted asylum to 650,000 refugees, including 480,000 from Bosnia and 170,000 from the former Krajina. The total figure of wartime refugees would be far higher, because many men did not register for fear of being sent back to fight and because, after settling down, many refugees were no longer counted as such. The Belgrade figure also does not include Serbian refugees within the Republika Srpska and Serb-held eastern Slavonia.

    UNHCR noted that 30,000 Krajina Serbs had 'approached the Office of the Croatian government in Belgrade to express their desire to repatriate. Authorisations to return have been given to over 3,600 individuals. However, there are indications that a large number of refugees may opt ... to settle locally.'

25. For figures of casualties during the Second World War, see Table 1 on p. 134 above. For 1991–5, for Bosnia only, see Emma Daly, 'Arithmetic of Death That Does Not Add Up', *Independent*, 1 May 1996. Estimates of an unnamed foreign official are given as 60,000 dead on the government side and 15,000–20,000 dead on the Bosnian Serb side. The latter figure is in tune with numbers I have heard quoted in the Republika Srpksa.

SELECT BIBLIOGRAPHY

Books

Alexander, Stella. *Church and State in Yugoslavia since 1945* (Cambridge, 1979)

Avramov, Smilja. *Genocide in Yugoslavia* (Belgrade, 1995)

Banac, Ivo. *The National Question in Yugoslavia: Origins, History, Politics* (Cornell, Ithaca and London, 1992)

Biserko, Sonja (ed.). *Yugoslavia: Collapse, War, Crimes* (Belgrade, 1993)

Brown, Edward. *A Brief Account of Some Travels in Divers Parts of Europe* (London, 1685)

Clissold, Stephen (ed.). *A Short History of Yugoslavia: From Early Times to 1966* (Cambridge, 1966)

Crankshaw, Edward. *The Fall of the House of Habsburg* (London, 1963)

Crnobrnja, Mihailo. *The Yugoslav Drama* (London and New York, 1994)

Cvijić, Jovan. *La Péninsule balkanique: Géographie humaine* (Paris, 1918)

Dedijer, Vladimir. *The Road to Sarajevo* (London, 1967)

Denitch, Bogdan. *Ethnic Nationalism: The Tragic Death of Yugoslavia* (Minneapolis and London, 1994)

Deroc, Milan. *British Special Operations Explored: Yugoslavia in Turmoil 1941–1943 and the British Response* (Boulder, 1988)

Dinkić, Mladjan. *Ekonomija destruk-cije: velika pljačka naroda* (Belgrade, 1995)

Djilas, Milovan. *Land without Justice* (New York, 1958)

—— *Njegoš* (New York, 1966)

Djordjević, Dimitrije and Samardžić, Radovan (eds). *Migrations in Balkan History* (Belgrade, 1989)

Djukić, Slavoljub. *Izmedju slave i anateme: Politička biografija Slobodana Miloševića* (Belgrade, 1994)

Dragnich, Alex N. *The First Yugoslavia: Search for a Viable Political System* (Stanford, 1983)

——. *Serbia's Historical Heritage* (Boulder, 1994)

Dragnich, Alex N. and Todorovich, Slavko. *The Saga of Kosovo: Focus on Serbian–Albanian Relations* (Boulder and New York, 1984)

Drašković, Vuk. (Draskovitch in French transliteration). *Le Couteau* (Paris, 1993) (first published in Yugoslavia in 1982 under the title *Nož*)

Durham, Edith. *High Albania* (London, 1985) (first published in 1909)

Emmert, Thomas. *Serbian Golgotha: Kosovo, 1389* (New York, 1990)

Evans, Arthur J. *Through Bosnia and the Herzegovina on Foot during the Insurrection, August and September, 1875* (London, 1877)

Fine, J. V. A. *The Bosnian Church: A New Interpretation. A Study of the*

Bosnian Church and its Place in State and Society from the Thirteenth to the Fifteenth Centuries (Boulder, 1975)

——. *The Early Medieval Balkans: A Critical Survey from the Sixth to the Late Twelfth Century* (Ann Arbor, 1983)

——. *The Late Medieval Balkans: A Critical Survey from the Late Twelfth Century to the Ottoman Conquest* (Ann Arbor, 1987)

Fortis, Alberto. *Travels into Dalmatia* (London, 1778)

Gjelten, Tom. *Sarajevo Daily: A City and its Newspaper under Siege* (New York, 1995)

Glenny, Misha. *The Fall of Yugoslavia: The Third Balkan War* (London, 1992)

Grmek, Mirko, Marc Gjidara and Neven Simac *Le Nettoyage ethnique: Documents historiques sur une idéologie serbe* (Paris, 1993)

Jelavich, Barbara. *History of the Balkans*, 2 vols (Cambridge, 1989–93)

Jukić, Ilija. *The Fall of Yugoslavia* (New York and London, 1974)

Kadijević, Veljko. *Moje vidjenje raspada: Vojska bez države* (Belgrade, 1993)

Kandić, Nataša, (ed.). *Spotlight on Human Rights: Violations in Times of Armed Conflict* (Belgrade, 1995)

Karchmar, Lucien. *Draža Mihailović and the Rise of the Četnik Movement, 1941–1942* (New York and London, 1987)

Knežević, Aleksandar and Tufegdžić, Vojislav. *Kriminal koji je izmenio Srbiju* (Belgrade, 1995)

Koljević, Svetozar. *The Epic in the Making* (Oxford, 1980)

Krstić, Djurica. *Dushan's Code: The Bistritza Transcript* (Belgrade, 1989)

Lees, Michael. *The Rape of Serbia: The British Role in Tito's Grab for Power,* *1943–1944.* (San Diego, London and New York, 1990)

Maček, Vladko. *In the Struggle for Freedom,* trans. Elizabeth and Stjepan Gazi (University Park and London, 1957)

MacKenzie, David. *Ilija Garašanin: Balkan Bismarck* (Boulder, 1985)

Maclean, Fitzroy. *Eastern Approaches* (London, 1991) (first published 1949)

Magaš, Branka. *The Destruction of Yugoslavia: Tracking the Break-up, 1980–92* (London and New York, 1993)

Malaparte, Curzio. *Kaputt,* trans. from Italian by Cesare Foligno (Evanston, 1995) (first published 1945)

Malcolm, Noel. *Bosnia: A Short History* (London, 1994)

Mihailović, Kosta and Krestić, Vasilije. *Memorandum of the Serbian Academy of Sciences and Arts: Answers to Criticisms* (Belgrade, 1995)

Mihaljčić, Rade. *The Battle of Kosovo in History and in Popular Tradition* (Belgrade, 1989)

Milojković-Djurić, Jelena. *Tradition and Avant-Garde: Literature and Art in Serbian Culture, 1900–1918* (Boulder, 1988)

Njegoš, Petar. *The Mountain Wreath of P. P. Nyegosh, Prince–Bishop of Montenegro, 1830–1851,* trans. James W. Wiles (London, 1930)

Open Wounds: Human Rights Abuses in Kosovo, Human Rights Watch/Helsinki (New York, 1993)

Owen, David. *Balkan Odyssey* (London, 1995)

Pavlowitch, Stevan K. *Yugoslavia* (London, 1971)

——. *The Improbable Survivor: Yugoslavia and its Problems, 1918–1988* (London, 1988)

——. *Tito, Yugoslavia's Great Dictator:*

A Reassessment (London, 1992)

Pennington, Anne and Levi, Peter. *Marko the Prince: Serbo-Croat Heroic Songs*, with introductory notes by Svetozar Koljević (London, 1984)

Petrovich, Michael Boro. *A History of Modern Serbia, 1804–1918*, 2 vols (New York and London, 1976)

Petrovitch, Nicolas-Jiv. *Agonie et résurrection: Récits de la prise de Belgrade de la retraite en Albanie et d'un séjour au lazaret de Corfou* (Courbevoie, 1920)

Popovic, Alexandre. *L'Islam balkanique: les musulmans du sud-est européen dans la période post-ottomane* (Berlin, 1986)

Pribićević, Svetozar (Pribitchevitch in French transliteration) *La Dictature du Roi Alexandre* (Paris, 1933)

Ramet, Sabrina P. *Nationalism and Federalism in Yugoslavia, 1962–1991*, 2nd edn (Bloomington and Indianapolis, 1992)

Ranke, Leopold von. *The History of Servia and the Servian Revolution* (New York, 1973) (first published 1848)

Reed, John. *War in Eastern Europe: Travels through the Balkans in 1915* (London, 1994) (first published 1916)

Ridley, Jasper. *Tito: A Biography* (London, 1994)

Rothenberg, Gunther E. *The Military Border in Croatia, 1740–1881: A Study of an Imperial Institution* (Chicago, 1966)

Samardžić, Radovan and Duškov, Milan. *Serbs in European Civilization* (Belgrade, 1993)

Seton-Watson, R. W. *The Southern Slav Question and the Hapsburg Monarchy* (New York, 1969) (first published 1911)

Silber, Laura and Little, Allan. *The Death of Yugoslavia* (London, 1995)

Singleton, Fred. *A Short History of the Yugoslav Peoples* (Cambridge, 1985; repr. 1989)

Talpo, Oddone. *Dalmazia: Una cronaca per la storia (1941)* (Rome, 1985)

Thompson, Mark. *Forging War: The Media in Serbia, Croatia and Bosnia–Hercegovina* (London, 1994)

Tomasevich, Jozo. *The Chetniks: War and Revolution in Yugoslavia, 1941–1945* (Stanford, 1975)

Trgo, General Fabijan. *The National Liberation War and Revolution in Yugoslavia (1941–1945): Selected Documents* (Belgrade, 1982)

The Trial of Dragoljub-Draža Mihailović: Stenographic Record and Documents from the Trial of Dragoljub-Draža Mihailović (Belgrade, 1946)

Vučelić, Milorad. *Conversations with the Epoch* (Belgrade, 1991)

Vucinich, Wayne S. *The First Serbian Uprising, 1804–1813* (Boulder, 1982)

Vucinich, Wayne S. and Emmert, Thomas A. (eds). *Kosovo: Legacy of a Medieval Battle* (Minneapolis, 1991)

Vulliamy, Ed. *Seasons in Hell: Understanding Bosnia's War* (London, 1994)

West, Rebecca. *Black Lamb & Grey Falcon: The Record of a Journey through Yugoslavia in 1937*, 2 vols (London, 1943)

Other Materials

Ever since June 1993, Bratislav Grubačić in Belgrade has produced the *VIP Daily News Report*. This has provided, in English, a round-up of the news including the most important extracts from the Serbian newspapers. It is now an invaluable historical resource. Regarding economics, CES-Mecon, a private research and consulting firm in Belgrade, provided throughout the war years a regular and excellent English survey of economic trends for the UN Economic Commission for Europe. For basic statistics see booklets produced by the Federal Statistical Office in Belgrade. Regarding refugees, the monthly UNHCR *Information Notes on Former Yugoslavia* are a prime source. For highly detailed reports on several aspects of the war including camps and paramilitaries consult the annexes of work of the UN Commission of Experts, *Established Pursuant to Security Council Resolution 780 (1992)*. See also work by Human Rights Watch/Helsinki based in New York. From Belgrade, reports produced in English by the Humanitarian Law Fund (later Humanitarian Law Centre) are excellent. Of a consistently high standard on a wide-ranging field of topics are the Serbian-language papers produced by the Belgrade journal *Republika* under the imprint *Ogledi*.

INDEX

Index

Index

Index

Index

Index